# FOUNDATION PRESS

## EVIDENCE STORIES

*Edited By*

RICHARD LEMPERT

Eric Stein Distinguished University Professor of Law and Sociology
University of Michigan

FOUNDATION PRESS
2006

THOMSON

WEST

© 2006 By FOUNDATION PRESS
        395 Hudson Street
        New York, NY 10014
        Phone Toll Free 1–877–888–1330
        Fax (212) 367–6799
        foundation–press.com
Printed in the United States of America

**ISBN–13:** 978–1–59941–006–7
**ISBN–10:** 1–59941–006–0

TEXT IS PRINTED ON 10% POST
CONSUMER RECYCLED PAPER

To Lisa, my love, and to the best beloveds of the authors of these essays.

\*

# TABLE OF CONTENTS

## OPINIONS AND EXPERT TESTIMONY

## HEARSAY

# Contents

*

# FOUNDATION PRESS

## EVIDENCE STORIES

*

# Introduction

## Richard Lempert

I have found that the more deeply I am engaged in a scholarly project, the more the details of my life become relevant to what I am working on. Thus, it was that sitting in a dentist's chair for reconstructive work following a root canal, I saw a metaphor for what had been troubling me about some of the evidence stories essays I was in the midst of editing. The dentist had covered my mouth and part of my face with a rubber dam, pierced so that only the tooth she was working on was visible. It was as if the rest of the mouth, in which the tooth was set, did not exist or, since it did exist, was irrelevant to the task at hand. The dentist knew what she was doing, the rest of the mouth *was* irrelevant. So it often is with great evidence cases. Evidence is procedure. There need be no special story—no great dispute or fight for justice—behind a great evidence case. Nor will deeper knowledge of case facts necessarily reveal reasons for a rule or suggest the concerns that motivated a court's decision. All that a great evidence case requires is a dispute over whether a single item of evidence—as little as a single sentence or a few questions in a 500 page transcript—should be admitted. The court's focus will be on that sentence or question. Other case facts may be cited to give the issue some context, but their importance to how the court resolves the admissibility issue varies immensely. Sometimes they are essential to the outcome if not determinative, but in other instances they do not matter at all. Moreover, even when case context is integral to the resolution of an evidentiary issue, the case need not be especially interesting or noteworthy; the case story may be one that is hardly worth the telling.

This does not mean that there are no evidence stories worth recounting. The essays in this volume show how interesting evidence stories can be. Rather it means that evidence stories are not only highly varied, but also that the central actors in an evidence story may have played no role in the dispute giving rise to the case. Thus, the most interesting actor in George Fisher's story of *People v. Collins*, the classic case involving probability evidence, is neither Janet nor Malcolm Collins, the defendants in the case, about whom little is known, nor the prosecutor who sought to bolster a weak but probably winnable case with statistical evidence, nor the professor who, answering a phone message, found himself that afternoon in court giving expert testimony. Rather it is the renowned Harvard Law School professor, leading Supreme Court advocate and undergraduate math whiz Laurence Tribe, who as a law clerk to Justice Tobriner of the California Supreme Court drafted much of the opinion for which the case is celebrated, and then, in his first major article as a law professor wrote, without mentioning his role in *Collins*, the magisterial article, *Trial by Mathematics*. This article, written in response to an article by Michael Finkelstein and William Fairley that advocated more sophisticated modes of presenting probabilistic evidence, placed the issue of probabilistic proof and the application of Bayes' Theorem in litigation on the agendas of evidence scholars for generations to come. Similarly, in Christopher Mueller's discussion of *Michelson v. United States*, which is the Supreme Court's most definitive statement on the inquiries that may be made of a defendant's good character witnesses, the story of the defendant Michelson is less interesting and less integral to the law the case gave rise to than the story of Mr. Justice Jackson, who wrote the opinion for which the case is known. In another story, Richard Friedman's account of *Crawford v United States*, the author, more than anyone else, is the story's protagonist, for Professor Friedman developed the confrontation clause theory that the Supreme Court would later adopt in the case, and he consulted with Crawford's appellate counsel throughout the litigation and on the Supreme Court brief.

Most of this volume's essayists do more than tell a story. They go on to discuss how their case shaped the law of evidence and, often not content to stop there, they critique the doctrine the case shaped. Indeed in a few essays, most notably Paul Giannelli's treatment of the so-called *Daubert* trilogy, the development of doctrine—in *Daubert*, rules regarding the admissibility of scientific evidence—is the heart of the story line.

Despite the special nature of some evidence stories, this volume does not depart substantially from the spirit of the "Stories" series. Having as one's protagonist a law professor or judge does not, as the reader will see, preclude a good story, and even when actors like these are the main protagonists, we learn about the characters and incidents that figured most prominently in the litigation, often with the benefit of story facts that have not heretofore been known. Moreover, not every evidence story is special in the way I have just described. Indeed, most of the essays in this volume did not bring the dentist's dam to mind, for in most the case story is front and center, and key to other analysis. Thus, Peter Tillers uses *State v. Radziwell*, perhaps the least well-known case in this volume, to explore the boundary between character and habit by reconstructing the fatal accident that led to this prosecution and probing deeply into the sad life of the defendant. Eleanor Swift elucidates the admissions "exception" to the hearsay rule, as she skillfully tells the tale of Sophie the wolf and the bites Sophie may or may not have inflicted on the child plaintiff in *Mahlandt v. Wild Canid Survival & Research Center, Inc.*. And Marianne Wesson takes one of evidence law's classic stories—the story of *Mutual Life Insurance Co. v. Hillmon*—and turns it on its head, arguing that the Supreme Court was most likely mistaken when, speaking through Mr. Justice Gray, it constructed a narrative that seemingly compelled the conclusion that a man had been murdered to perpetrate an insurance fraud, thereby motivating a broad exception to the hearsay rule for statements of intent.

When an author writes a book or article or compiles and edits a volume, somewhere, even if not articulated, there is a vision of the intended audience. When law professors are authors that intended audience is usually either other law professors, who are to be impressed by the depth, care and subtlety of the writer's analysis, or judges or policy makers, who, if they are fair-minded readers, will leave the article persuaded that the author has outlined the best interpretation of received doctrine or the optimum path for doctrinal or other legal development. The essays in this volume, however, have a different intended audience. I see most readers as students, primarily students in evidence courses, especially problem-oriented courses.

Readers who know me as a co-author of *A Modern Approach to Evidence*, will know that there are few more enthusiastic proponents of the problem-oriented approach to teaching evidence than I. Nevertheless, something is lost when evidence instruction is focused on the meaning of the Federal Rules and their application across a range of abstracted if not artificial problem situations. Students do not get the same sense of the history of evidence rules, or of the factual settings in which they are applied and out of which they developed, when they read text rather than cases. Indeed, they often don't get a rich sense of context even when the case method is used, for so many rules have to be taught in the typical evidence course that casebook authors tend to extract most of the juice from most of the cases they reproduce. What is left, and what once drove me to write a problem-oriented course book, is in most cases a dry statement of facts with a judge expounding—much as a problem-oriented writer does—on a rule and the reason for it. Thus I see this book as a companion to the main text used in evidence courses. It contains a collection of essays that allows students to appreciate the rich contexts out of which evidence rules and interpretations of the Federal Rules arise and in which they are applied. In doing so the essays highlight the special roles that parties, case facts, judges, lawyers, social critics and law professors can play in shaping the law of evidence, for these features and actors are all important parts of at least some of the essays in this volume.

My conception of the intended audience for this volume explains some characteristics of the essays that appear. First, they are short as legal writing goes, usually between 25 and 30 pages or less. Stories intended as adjunct reading can't be too lengthy. Some original submissions were shortened by as much as 50% to achieve this goal. Often eliminated were detailed explanations of the evidence rules involved, for these essays are not meant to teach students what the law provides. That will be done by the teacher working from a problem text or casebook. The stories in this volume are intended to add to basic instruction, not to substitute for it.

Second, the reader will have noted that I refer to these stories as essays and not as articles. I do this to emphasize that these works should not be confused with most law review scholarship. The difference between then and the typical law review article is most evident in the footnoting conventions I have used and to some degree imposed on some authors. Although the reader will find exceptions, footnotes are largely confined to substantive information that would be awkwardly placed in the text, cites to specific cases and articles the first time they are mentioned, block quotes or other particularly important quotations, and information that my conventions might have eliminated but which I thought would be useful for readers to have. I assumed students would properly regard the authors of these essays as experts and not feel a need to have the authors justify their expertise by referencing work expressing views similar to the views they present in the text or laying out facts that the author asserts. Also eliminated are most cites of quotations to pages, so long as the source for the quotation is clear or the quote is so short that its source is insignificant. In addition, I cut side excursions, the little essays expanding on text that law professors, myself among them, love to write but that, although interesting, are not integral to the story line. I also eliminated from footnotes citing cases and articles most parenthetical descriptions of what the cited material was about. Most such elaboration was unnecessary because the text almost always made it clear why the materials were referenced. The idea, in short, was to minimize the need of readers to glance down for additional information unless a note added something of interest to the text or was a cite to an important sources or a case or article specifically referenced.

Applying these conventions led to the elimination of as many as three quarters of the footnotes in some of the essays as originally submitted. Not all authors, it is fair to say, were completely pleased. Not all readers, particularly professorial readers, will be completely pleased either. Some may think a point firmly asserted is not as widely accepted as the author indicates and will want to know more about the assertion's justification. Some may want to check the context of a particular quotation and will be disturbed if a page number, or worse yet a source, is not indicated. Some may think that law review citation standards should apply to all serious scholarship that law professors publish (and the essays in this volume are serious scholarship). Some readers may be particularly upset, indeed they may feel there has been a breach of scholarly norms, when their own pioneering or directly on point research is not mentioned. Thus, the kindest thing that some readers may have to say about the conventions I adopted is that they are misguided. Readers who have any of these complaints should not blame the essayists for omitted citations, but should blame me. It was I who insisted the footnotes be kept to a minimum. This included, I should note, cutting references to my own work in a number of places, although in one instance an author was adamant about retaining a reference to my work along with that of others, and after twice eliminating the citation, I let the author have his way.[1]

It would be foolish to pretend that I like all the essays in this volume equally, and it would be even more foolish for me to list my favorites. While I have referenced some specific essays as illustrations of points I wish to make or as examples of what will be found in these pages, I did not choose which pieces to mention based on what I saw as the essays' relative merits. The reader will discover a number of excellent essays without any alert in this introduction. I will say, however, I am extraordinarily pleased by the submissions I received. I do not think there is a weak essay in this collection, and there are a large numbers of essays that I think are not just good, but extraordinarily so. I am very grateful to the authors who agreed to write for this volume, who put up with my editorial nitpicking, or who submitted such polished first drafts that there were no nits to pick. Their intelligence and scholarship add fundamentally to our knowledge of the cases and rules we teach and learn. I feel lucky that I was asked to edit a volume whose introduction I can conclude with a single word—ENJOY.

---

[1] There is one exception to the application of these conventions. This is the article by Marianne Wesson on the *Hillmon* case. Professor Wesson has contributed an original and important work of historical scholarship that goes beyond the historical excavations that most of the volume's authors engaged in. Hence I thought it important that her original sources be fully documented.

*

# 1

# Green Felt Jungle: The Story of *People v. Collins*

## George Fisher[*]

Janet and Malcolm Collins are fugitives from history. Even as the case that bears their name took its place among legal landmarks, its title players slipped into time. Within weeks of the California Supreme Court's 1968 ruling that the "sorcerer" mathematics had fatally infected their trial, Janet and Malcolm Collins left prison—and vanished. There appears no further trace of Janet. Malcolm's name surfaces in the public record once more, in August 2000, when the County of Los Angeles filed notice of his death at age 64.

And so the Collinses melt into history bearing only the identity this case gave them: They are the mixed-race couple in the partly yellow car, charged with snatching Juanita Brooks's handbag from her shopping caddy as she walked home from the grocery store. So they will remain.

Surviving sources add few facets to their existence. She was nineteen, he twenty-eight, when they married on June 2, 1964, only sixteen days before the crime that gave them fame. On their wedding day they had twelve dollars between them with little prospect of bettering their fortunes. Malcolm had no job, and Janet's once- or twice-weekly housekeeping earned them at most twelve dollars a week. Their yellow Lincoln with its eggshell white top, so at odds with this image of penury, was a

---

* Judge John Crown Professor of Law, Stanford University. I want to thank Matt Buckley for his extraordinary help in discovering the lost actors in this case and Katie TafollaYoung for her sharp-eyed editorial guidance and research support. Thanks as well to Sonia Moss and Kate Wilko of the Crown Law Library (and again to Matt Buckley) for gathering the widely scattered *Collins* documents and other sources. Rick Lempert, this collection's editor, suggested valuable revisions. And I owe a great debt to several participants who generously responded to my inquiries—prosecutor Ray Sinetar, trial defender Don Ellertson, witness Dan Martinez, law clerk (now Professor) Laurence Tribe, and a trial juror who prefers to be unnamed. Finally I'm grateful to Ed Reid and Ovid Demaris, who—as I explain below at note 26—crafted my title.

wreck—they abandoned it even before their trial when it died on a mountain pass. A police photo taken soon after the crime shows Janet Collins with her famous ponytail in profile, suppressing a teenage grin. A press photo taken later shows Malcolm Collins without his famous beard, chopping trees on a prison labor project. Both appear handsome, young, hopeful even in the worst of times. Still later, long after their case was concluded, one of their lawyers would hint that they were never married at all.[1] Today there is no ready way to know.

These suggestive details of the Collinses' lives have faded in the forty years since their trial, leaving only the mixed-race couple in the partly yellow car. They survive as a classroom hypothetical—an evidence-law cliché. They are not the Collinses but the *Collins*es. Eponym to epitaph.

Yet the lawyers live on. Whatever misfortune this case may have brought upon the Collinses and whatever lessons they may have lived all the other days of their lives, their role in this case was as stock players in a lawyers' contest. The couple at the heart of *Collins* were not Janet and Malcolm, but the two lawyers who battled over their fate. This was not the classic courtroom battle, for the dueling lawyers in this case never faced each other in court or anywhere else. Instead they shadow-boxed across a divide of time, space, and intellectual milieu.

* * *

In one corner was Ray Sinetar. The son of Jewish émigré parents who fled Hungary in the 1920s, Sinetar had taken the long road to law. After his father sold his share in a Long Island laundry and moved the family to Southern California, Sinetar studied speech at UCLA, then dropped out of Stanford Law School after an apathetic start. He was pulling shifts at his father's liquor store when a draft notice sent him north to Fort Ord and east to Fort Lee. Later, with feet more firmly planted, he earned a fourth-place finish at UCLA Law School and promptly made himself a trial lawyer. In November 1964, when the Collinses faced trial, Sinetar was a Los Angeles deputy district attorney billeted in the Long Beach Courthouse, a Bauhaus glass box with a

---

[1] On the Collinses' age, see Bob Schmidt, *Justice by Computer*, [Long Beach] INDEPENDENT-PRESS-TELEGRAM, Nov. 29, 1964, at A–1. On their finances and wedding day, see Brief for Respondent at 11–12, *People v. Collins* (Calif. Ct. App., Crim. No. 10819). The California Supreme Court described their car's colors. *See People v. Collins*, 68 Cal. 2d 319, 322 n.2 (1968). Trial counsel Don Ellertson told me of the car's fate in a phone interview on July 19, 2005. The two photographs appear in *Decisions: Trial by Mathematics*, TIME, Apr. 26, 1968, at 41. Malcolm Collins's appellate counsel, Rex DeGeorge, told Professor David McCord "that he remembers finding out that . . . [the Collinses'] marriage had been void for some reason that he cannot now recall." David McCord, *A Primer for the Nonmathematically Inclined on Mathematical Evidence in Criminal Cases:* People v. Collins *and Beyond*, 47 WASH. & L. L. REV. 741, 766 n.93 (1990).

surfside view. The view, since blocked, was a point of indifference to Sinetar, huddled over case files in his remote, windowless office. By then, at age thirty, he was two years out of law school and had tried a hundred cases, large and small, before a jury.[2]

So it was no big deal when the calendar deputy phoned one morning in mid-November and assigned Sinetar a second-degree robbery case just sent out for trial. A purse-snatching with two eyewitnesses seemed straightforward enough. Nor did Sinetar lack confidence in front of a jury. At 6'2" and 190 pounds, long-armed and lean, he had a boxer's torque in a close-cut suit. But with a James Dean pout and horn-rimmed blue eyes, he was an arresting mix of diesel and honey.[3] And he had plenty of time to prepare—at least by the standards of a Los Angeles deputy prosecutor—since jury selection would take at least half a day.

So on Wednesday, November 18, 1964—five months to the day after a ponytailed blond woman fled with old Mrs. Brooks's purse in the partly yellow car of a bearded African–American man—the *Collins* trial began. Jury selection absorbed the whole first afternoon. By Thursday morning Sinetar had mastered the facts and assembled his witnesses. He assessed his case warily. On the one hand, he had Mrs. Brooks. Rarely does a prosecutor find a more sympathetic victim. Here was a seventy-one–year-old woman lugging her groceries home, her cane in one hand, her purse resting on her shopping caddy, a precious $35 or $40 inside. Robbed in broad daylight, she was knocked to the ground and left with a dislocated shoulder and twice-fractured arm. Screaming in pain and fright, she had the presence of mind to look at her attacker and remember the fleeing woman's blond hair. Meanwhile, sixty-six–year-old John Sheridan Bass stood watering his lawn nearby. Mrs. Brooks's screams turned his attention to the bearded African–American man in the yellow car who passed within six feet of Bass as he snatched up the fleeing woman with the blond ponytail and sped off. Even in the hands of a less talented prosecutor—and Sinetar had talent—this case would play well to the gut.[4]

---

[2] Ray Sinetar kindly supplied these and other details of his life and his work on the *Collins* case in a telephone interview on June 30, 2005, and in later, follow-up interviews.

[3] Sinetar told me how he was assigned the case and his height and weight. The balance of the physical description is based on my viewing a 1968 film featuring Sinetar. *See* "Bill of Rights in Action: Freedom of Speech" (BFA Educational Media 1968).

[4] Many details of the trial come from the minutes of the Los Angeles Superior Court. *See People v. Janet L. Collins & Malcom* [sic] *R. Collins* (Los Angeles Superior Court, Cr. 291449 (1964)). I am grateful to Renée Dennard of the Criminal Archives Division for her help in obtaining these documents. On Mrs. Brooks's age, see Schmidt, *supra* n.1. Bass's age is supplied in Petition for Hearing (Calif. Sup. Ct., 2d Cr. No. 10819 (Apr. 24, 1967)), at 3. For the nature of the attack on Mrs. Brooks, the amount of the theft, and Bass's testimony, see *Collins*, 68 Cal. 2d at 321; Brief for Respondent, *supra* n.1, at 5–8 (quoting

Still, Sinetar knew there were flaws. And as he built his case on the first day of testimony, they began to show. Mrs. Brooks could say only that her robber was blond, appeared young, weighed about 145 pounds, and wore "something dark"—maybe a sweater, maybe a jacket, maybe a dress. She never identified Janet Collins and never saw the yellow car or its driver. As for Mr. Bass, he eagerly pointed out Malcolm Collins at counsel table as the getaway driver. But Bass had seen the driver only fleetingly as the yellow car rolled by—and Bass had been wearing his reading glasses. At a police lineup only days after the crime, he was "not certain" of his selection of Malcolm Collins. As Collins's lawyer wrote on appeal, this was "one of those instances where the identifying witness becomes surer and surer as he sees the defendant at the defense table."[5]

True, Sinetar scored a few points that first day. There was Janet Collins's claim about when she left work the day of the crime. When first interviewed by police detectives, she said she was cleaning Mary Conner's home until 1:00 P.M. and therefore could not possibly have robbed Mrs. Brooks between 11:30 and noon, as Brooks and Bass claimed. But Sinetar had brought Conner to court, and she testified that Malcolm Collins picked up his wife in his yellow car at about 11:30—in plenty of time to drive the short distance to where Mrs. Brooks was ambling with her shopping caddy. Sinetar knew he could argue that Janet Collins's lie showed her consciousness of guilt. The same was true of her changed appearance. A detective testified that shortly after police told the Collinses that eyewitnesses had described a blond, ponytailed robber, Janet Collins cut and darkened her hair. Detectives noticed too that Malcolm Collins shaved his beard. Even better (from Sinetar's perspective) was what detectives said about Malcolm Collins's behavior when police returned to the couple's home to arrest them. As officers approached the front of the house, another waited at the rear and watched as Malcolm Collins fled through the yard and hid behind a tree. Police ultimately found him hiding in a neighbor's clothes closet.[6]

Sinetar therefore did not end the day empty-handed. Still, as he lay in bed that night, he had the nagging sense he was not connecting with the jury. In his mind, the strongest evidence of the Collinses' guilt was

from trial transcript). Sinetar recorded the nature of Mrs. Brooks's injuries in his trial journal. I have on file a photocopy of the relevant journal entry, which Sinetar sent me. Trial counsel Don Ellertson generously described Sinetar as "a very fine lawyer—excellent."

[5] On Brooks's and Bass's testimony, see *Collins*, 68 Cal. 2d at 324–25; Brief for Respondent, *supra* n.1, at 6; Petition for Hearing, *supra* n.4, at 29–30; Gene Blake, *State Supreme Court to Rule: Can Courts Apply Theory of Probability to Cases?*, Los Angeles Times, Oct. 20, 1967, at A6.

[6] All these facts are gleaned from *Collins*, 68 Cal. 2d at 322–23 & nn.3, 5, and from Brief for Respondent, *supra* n.1, at 5–6, 8–10 & n.2, 12–13.

not their suspicious behavior as police began circling. He knew even innocent people sometimes act guiltily under the glare of police spotlights. For him, what clinched the Collinses' guilt was the sheer unlikelihood that any other couple in the area could match Brooks's and Bass's descriptions of the robbers and their car. After all, that's how the Collinses were caught. Shortly after the crime, Mrs. Brooks's son canvassed neighborhood gas stations asking attendants if they knew a matching couple. According to a local news report, one replied, "Sure, they come in here for gas all the time." Police then followed the attendant's lead. Sinetar lay in bed wondering how he could get the jury to see what he and Mrs. Brooks's son saw so readily—that the Collinses, even if not one of a kind, were one of an exceedingly rare kind.[7]

Then Sinetar fixed on a strategy. There was a mathematician in his family—his brother-in-law Edward Thorp, whose popular book, *Beat the Dealer*, had taught would-be blackjack sharps how to use the laws of probability to beat the house. Though "a zero aptitude math major in high school," Sinetar realized he could bring the principles of probability to bear on the Brooks robbery.[8] But he would need a mathematician—and he would need some data.

The obvious place to find a mathematician was Cal State Long Beach, just across town from the courthouse. First thing next morning, Sinetar called the math department. It was still early, and faculty offices were empty, so he left a message with the person who answered the phone. He was mid-trial, he told her, and he needed a witness—a mathematician who specialized in probability. Then Sinetar set about collecting some figures to plug into the mathematician's theory. He strode down the hall to the secretaries' office and sought out their de facto dean, Vivian Max, her graying hair in a rigid bun, and asked her estimates: What were the odds that a randomly chosen car would be partly yellow? that a randomly chosen woman would be blond? that a randomly chosen couple would be mixed race? Other secretaries offered

---

[7] The role of Mrs. Brooks's son, who did not testify at trial, appears in Jerry Cohen, *Justice Invokes Science: Law of Probability Helps Convict Couple*, LOS ANGELES TIMES, Dec. 11, 1964, at 1. Sinetar related his musings to me in our phone interview on June 30, 2005. David McCord previously reported Sinetar's nighttime deliberations based on a similar interview. *See* McCord, *supra* n.1, at 766–77.

[8] *See* EDWARD O. THORP, BEAT THE DEALER: A WINNING STRATEGY FOR THE GAME OF TWENTY-ONE (1962). On the connection between Sinetar and Thorp, see Schmidt, *supra* n.1. According to Schmidt's report of the case, written within days of trial, "Sinetar explained later that he is probably more aware of the laws of probability than most people" because of his connection to Thorp. But Sinetar says today that Professor Ward Edwards was mistaken in reporting that Thorp "suggested [Sinetar's] probabilistic line of argument to him." *See* Ward Edwards, *Influence Diagrams, Bayesian Imperialism, and the* Collins *Case: An Appeal to Reason*, 13 CARDOZO L. REV. 1025, 1029 (1991). Sinetar says he did not discuss the case with Thorp until long after the trial.

their views as Sinetar jotted notes. His survey complete, he made up a chart and headed to court.

Not long after testimony resumed that morning, a young, casually dressed man walked into court and stood, uncertainly, waiting to be acknowledged. "Mr. Sinetar?" he called out loudly. "Mr. Sinetar?" Sinetar realized that the bookish man making the commotion was his math expert from Cal State Long Beach. At twenty-six, Assistant Professor Daniel Martinez was only two months into what proved to be a forty-one–year teaching career. That morning he had arrived at work to learn that a local prosecutor had phoned for an expert in probability—a subject Martinez was teaching. "I had a chance to perform a civic duty," he recalled decades later. "So I went right to court." But when he saw the crowded courtroom, he took pause. "I had an inkling that I was stepping into something I really shouldn't."[9]

The testimony that followed, together with Sinetar's argument on that testimony, supplied the tinder for the California Supreme Court's condemnation of the Collinses' trial four years later. Sadly, no transcript of the trial or of Martinez's testimony survives. And while various sources help reconstruct his examination, critical gaps remain. It is certain Martinez first established the basics of the "product rule": If the probability of rolling a die and coming up two is one in six, he said, the probability of rolling two dice and coming up two on both is one in thirty-six. That is, one multiplies together the probability of each event to arrive at the probability that both occur together. It is certain, too, that Martinez then qualified the operation of the product rule: It works only if the two events occur independently of each other. The rule would not work if one die's coming up two made it more or less likely that the other die would do so. It is also certain that Sinetar supplied a list of probabilities—one in ten, one in four, one in ten, one in three, one in ten, one in a thousand—and secured Martinez's agreement that if six events bear these probabilities, the likelihood that all six will occur together is one in twelve million.[10]

What is not clear is whether Sinetar told Martinez which six events he had in mind. The California Supreme Court suggested—uncertainly—that he did. But Sinetar says he did not—and both defendant's counsel and a contemporaneous news account agree. Instead Sinetar merely presented Martinez with a chart bearing the letters A through F. To each letter he assigned a probability and then asked Martinez the likelihood that all six events would occur together. Only during closing argument did Sinetar fill in the rest of the chart, adding alongside each

---

[9] The previous three paragraphs draw from phone interviews with Sinetar on June 30, 2005, and Martinez on July 6, 2005.

[10] Petition for Hearing, *supra* n.4, at 4–5, 16; Schmidt, *supra* n.1, at A–1.

letter a characteristic that distinguished both the guilty couple and the Collinses. The chart then looked like this:[11]

| Characteristic | | Individual Probability |
|---|---|---|
| A. | Partly yellow automobile | 1/10 |
| B. | Man with mustache | 1/4 |
| C. | Girl with ponytail | 1/10 |
| D. | Girl with blond hair | 1/3 |
| E. | Negro man with beard | 1/10 |
| F. | Interracial couple in car | 1/1000 |

If this account is correct—if Sinetar added the characteristics to the chart only during closing argument—then Martinez must be absolved of fault for suggesting that the product rule appropriately applies to *these* factors. For forty years he has regretted the "misunderstanding . . . that I was asserting that the factors were independent." The California Supreme Court complained that they were not independent—that bearded men, for example, are more likely than others to wear mustaches, so factor B is not independent of factor E. Martinez agrees that such correlations could cause problems. He meant only to affirm the general operation of the product rule, not to comment on its application in *Collins*. The misunderstanding has made the case a "source of embarrassment" for him—and forty years later, he has yet to bring himself to read the court's opinion. "There's a cautionary tale there for everybody," he says. "It was a mistake on my part to go in without adequate preparation."[12]

But no amount of preparation could have spared Martinez the reckless reporting of the *Los Angeles Times*. The paper's front-page account of the trial declared that "[t]he questions and answers [between Sinetar and Martinez] went something like this"—and then brazenly fictionalized a segment of trial testimony:

Q—What is the probability of a man having a mustache? . . .

A—One in three.

Q—What is the probability of a young woman having blonde hair?

A—One in four. . . .

Q—What is the probability of a Cauca[s]ian woman being seen with a Negro man?

---

[11] The chart and the California Supreme Court's discussion of related testimony are in *Collins*, 68 Cal. 2d at 325 & n.10. I discuss contrary evidence concerning the form this testimony took below at note 13.

[12] *See Collins*, 68 Cal. 2d at 328–29 & n.15. Martinez reflected on the case in our phone conversation on July 6, 2005.

A—One in a thousand.

Q—Then what probability is there that you will find, at a given time and spot, a Negro male with a beard and mustache driving a yellow car in which a blonde woman with a pony tail is riding?

A—Multiplying the probabilities of the six factors together, the chance would be one in 12 million.

This report, which triggered rapid scholarly criticism of Martinez's analysis, defies the account of courthouse newsman Bob Schmidt, who wrote of the trial in the Long Beach *Independent–Press–Telegram* four days after the trial ended—and almost two weeks ahead of the *L.A. Times*. Schmidt reported that while examining Martinez, Sinetar was "[p]revented from talking about the specific facts of the case by" the trial judge. Instead the prosecutor asked, "Suppose situation A happens one in four times, situation B one in 10, ... and situation F one in 1,000. How often are all of those situations likely to be found together?" To this abstract inquiry, Martinez replied, "One in 12 million." Schmidt wrote that "[l]ater, in his argument, Sinetar told the jury that the hypothetical situations might be facts in the case."[13]

But if Martinez never applied the product rule to the facts of *Collins*, then Sinetar must assume full authorship of what the California Supreme Court called his "adventure in proof." Certainly, Sinetar's application of the product rule did not want for boldness. As brash as he was in gathering statistics from the secretarial pool, he showed even more brio in deploying those statistics in closing argument. He advised the jury that he had "tried to make [the statistics] conservative"—that the chance that any other couple was the guilty couple was not merely one in twelve million, but "something like one in a billion." He even invited defense "counsel to use his figures or [the jurors] to use your own." Then, heady with the force of his math, Sinetar reached for the third rail of prosecutorial closing argument: The reasonable-doubt standard, he declared, was "the most hackneyed, stereotyped, trite, misun-

---

[13] The spurious testimony appears in Cohen, *supra* n.7, at 1, 12. It seems likely that Schmidt's account, which appears in Schmidt, *supra* n.1, is correct. In a 1966 article, Charles R. Kingston reproduced Cohen's falsified version and on that basis criticized the prosecution's proof. At the close of his article, Kingston appended an awkward apologia, confessing that he since had spoken with "the defending attorney." Kingston wrote:

> The questions and answers quoted earlier in this article were apparently not involved in the expert's testimony, but were rather hypothetical questions composed by the newspaper reporter on the basis of the prosecutor's summary to the jury. It appears that the expert testified only as to the manipulation of independent probabilities, such as in dice throwing situations, and had no opportunity to testify about the factors relative to the particular case or to be subjected to cross-examination on these issues.

Charles R. Kingston, *Probability and Legal Proceedings*, 57 J. Crim. L., Criminology & Police Sci. 93, 93–94, 98 (1966).

derstood concept in criminal law." Unless jurors take the risk that "on some rare occasion ... an innocent person may be convicted," there would be "immunity for the Collinses, for people who ... push old ladies down and take their money ... because how could we ever be sure they are the ones who did it?"[14]

Throughout Sinetar's adventure in proof, defense counsel Don Ellertson objected valiantly. He alleged that Martinez's testimony was irrelevant and rested on ungrounded assumptions and invaded the jury's province. These stock complaints, however well founded, fell flat before Sinetar's flashy midnight maneuver in calling Martinez. Ellertson realized he had been outmatched. He had expected a far simpler trial. In five years as a deputy public defender, he had tried dozens of cases against Sinetar and his colleagues and knew their prosecutorial wiles. Moreover, he had met many times with the Collinses and thought he knew what to expect at their trial. He had anticipated a simple contest between Mrs. Brooks and Mr. Bass and their vague descriptions of the robbers on the one hand and Janet and Malcolm Collins and their alibi witnesses on the other. Martinez's testimony was something else. "Of course I was not a mathematician myself," Ellertson says today with a folksy twang that disarmed jurors, "and I was a little bewildered...." He objected to Martinez's testimony, but proved unable to stop it. In closing argument, he fell back on that hackneyed, stereotyped, trite, misunderstood concept—and asked the jury to give the Collinses the benefit of every reasonable doubt.[15]

Jurors deliberated eight hours over two days. Outward signs suggested a heated quarrel and frayed nerves. When the foreman reported that the jury might be hung, another juror turned to him in open court and said, her jaw tensing, "You *bet* it may be hung." Her frustration presumably was not with the foreman, but with the lone holdout juror—for the jury had voted lopsidedly to convict from the start. The group had split nine to three on the first ballot, ten to two on the second—and then a single juror stood against the rest, forcing their return the next morning. At last he too voted guilty.

One member of the panel recalls today that she and most of her colleagues judged Sinetar's case compellingly strong. Her most vivid memory is not of Sinetar's proof, however, but of the crime: "I remem-

---

[14] *Collins*, 68 Cal. 2d at 326, 328, 331–32; Brief for Respondent, *supra* n.1, at 47. Sinetar later elaborated in print on his objections to that "obfuscating dirge," the reasonable-doubt instruction. Raymond J. Sinetar, *A Belated Look at CALJIC*, 43 J. State Bar. Calif. 546, 554–55 (1968). Justice Stanley Mosk drew heavily from Sinetar's views in criticizing the statutory formulation of the reasonable-doubt instruction. *See People v. Brigham*, 25 Cal. 3d 283, 295, 297, 298, 315 (1979) (Mosk, J., concurring).

[15] On Ellertson's objections, see *Collins*, 68 Cal. 2d at 326. Ellertson supplied other details in a phone interview on July 19, 2005.

ber thinking how cruel it was that she [Janet Collins] followed an old lady out of the market . . . and stole a purse. . . ." As for the part of the trial that has caused such a fuss, she reports a disappointing indifference: "I don't remember our discussing the professor much when we deliberated. Maybe we were overwhelmed by the numbers."[16] Other jurors, who spoke with reporter Bob Schmidt shortly after trial, suggested similar disinterest. "Jurors said they disregarded Martinez's testimony," Schmidt wrote, "and found the couple guilty on evidence given by other witnesses. . . ."

This fact, if true, would have spoiled a good story. So it died in Schmidt's first account of the trial. The world took note instead of the rest of his story, which appeared on November 29, 1964, four days after the *Collins* verdict. Under the headline "Justice by Computer," Schmidt announced that the law had seen something new that week in Long Beach. As one veteran prosecutor told him, "I feel like the horse that just saw his first Ford."[17]

Filtering slowly across the country, the news from Long Beach touched a nerve. Two weeks later it hit the front page of the *Los Angeles Times* under the headline "Justice Invokes Science: Law of Probability Helps Convict Couple." Within a month, the story went national. *Time* magazine wrote of a daring application of "The Laws of Probability," which it trumpeted as "a totally new test of circumstantial evidence." Legal scholars began writing of the case even before the California Supreme Court's ruling. Because every good story needs a hero, the press lionized Sinetar. The *L.A. Times* chided those "courtroom kibitzers" who had deemed the *Collins* case hard to win. They had "reckoned without 30–year-old Ray Sinetar, a deputy district attorney for only nine months—and Sinetar's knowledge of the Law of Probability." *Time* reported that the Collinses were convicted "because Prosecutor Ray Sinetar, 30, cannily invoked . . . the laws of statistical probability."[18]

---

[16] Several sources help reconstruct the course of deliberations. The California Supreme Court noted their length. *See Collins*, 68 Cal. 2d at 332. Sadly, the court's *Collins* record appears lost. Professor Spencer Neth, who examined the record in 1980, kindly sent me a copy of his handwritten notes. Citing page 303 of the reporter's transcript, he wrote: "1st vote 9 to 3, w/o saying which way. 2nd vote 10 to 2." A member of the trial jury who asked not to be named told me in a telephone interview on August 15, 2005, that the jury was overwhelmingly for conviction all along. She remembers there having been a lone holdout who delayed a verdict overnight. Sinetar's personal trial journal likewise mentions a single dissenter: "Everyone wrong re 'holdout juror'—it wasn't Mrs [] who looked the part. . . . It was Mr. []. . . ." Sinetar also recorded the frustrated courtroom outburst of the fellow juror quoted in the text.

[17] Schmidt, *supra* n.1.

[18] Cohen, *supra* n.7; *Trials: The Laws of Probability*, TIME, Jan. 8, 1965, at 42. Among the early scholarly takes on the case were Kingston, *supra* n.13; William B. Stoebuck,

All this notoriety perhaps doomed the *Collins* verdict. The Court of Appeal had reviewed the case and quietly affirmed, rejecting all of Malcolm Collins's claims of error in an unpublished opinion.[19] (Janet Collins did not appeal.) There the matter might have died. But by the time Malcolm Collins's petition for a hearing reached the California Supreme Court in April 1967, the case was perhaps too big to ignore. The court's grant of a hearing was significant not only to Collins, who was whiling away his sentence in prison, but also to Sinetar, whose lower-court victory hung in the balance.

* * *

Sinetar has never met the man who proved his undoing in *Collins*. That is a shame, for perhaps they would find common ground. Each was born in the Nazi era to émigré Eastern European Jews who had fled either Stalin or Hitler. Each found his way to California in his early youth. Each came of age in the American middle class—Sinetar's father owned a laundry and liquor store, the other's father sold Fords. Each advanced to law school.

There, perhaps, the similarities end. Whereas Sinetar's education was stalled by a youthful malaise that relegated law school behind a stint in the Army, Laurence Tribe bounded through his early schooling, entered Harvard at sixteen, and took his law degree there at twenty-four. When Malcolm Collins's petition for a hearing arrived at the California Supreme Court, Tribe was in the latter half of a clerkship with Justice Mathew Tobriner—and still only twenty-five years old.[20]

Tribe had entered Harvard College as a math prodigy, graduating *summa cum laude* in algebraic topology. At first he enrolled in a doctoral program, but finding math "too lonely a pursuit," he soon abandoned the field for law school. Algebraic topology proved to be poor training for law school, however, and Tribe faltered in his first year. He later gained stride, finished strong, and snagged a clerkship with the liberal lion of the nation's most exalted state court.

When the *Collins* record arrived in Justice Tobriner's chambers, Tribe spied the chance to express long-nagging concerns about courtroom misuse of mathematical evidence. His fear was not merely that

---

*Relevancy and the Theory of Probability*, 51 Iowa L. Rev. 849, 859–61 (1966); *Criminal Law: Mathematical Probabilities Misapplied to Circumstantial Evidence*, 50 Minn. L. Rev. 745, 745–52 (1966).

[19] *People v. Collins* (Calif. Ct. App., Crim. No. 10819 (Mar. 13, 1967).)

[20] Sinetar supplied details of his early years in our phone interview on June 30, 2005. For information on Tribe, see Fred Barbash, *Laurence Tribe Storms Supreme Court, Lets Lampooners Go Free*, Wash. Post, Apr. 23, 1983, at A8; "Laurence H. Tribe," *Newsmakers* (Gale Research, 1988), *reproduced in Biography Resource Center* (Farmington Hills, Mich.: Thomson Gale 2005) (found at http://galenet.galegroup.com/servlet/BioRC).

goal-driven trial lawyers mangled the math. Even when lawyers got the numbers right, he worried that the magic of math overwhelmed mushy but meaningful facts that resist quantification. And he worried that by expressing guilt in quantifiable terms, prosecutors invited jurors to dismiss a certain probability of innocence—albeit a small one—as an acceptable risk of conviction. The beauty of the beyond-reasonable-doubt standard of guilt was that we can call it simply *moral certainty*—that we can advertise our system as demanding the fullest proof that human affairs allow. To Tribe, Sinetar's claim in closing argument that proof beyond a reasonable doubt was a hackneyed concept and that jurors must accept the risk that "on some rare occasion . . . an innocent person may be convicted" endangered one of the noblest features of our trial system.[21]

But Tribe had no need to rehearse these general misgivings about mathematical evidence in his memo to Justice Tobriner, for he felt Sinetar had mangled the math. He set out to expose four errors he saw in Sinetar's probability-based argument of guilt. First, the prosecutor had no studies to back his notions of the frequency of car colors, hair styles, or marriage patterns. His invitation to jurors and defense counsel to supply their own figures made his lack of data plain. And how could anyone generate such data? The state's appellate counsel, Deputy Attorney General Nicholas Yost, sought to defend Sinetar's assertion that his probability estimates were "conservative"—that they erred in the defendants' favor. "Looking out the window," Yost wrote, "[I] cannot but observe that far fewer than 1/10 of the cars are yellow." Answering anecdote with anecdote, Malcolm Collins's appellate counsel, Rex De-George, offered his own curbside count: "[A]ll we have to do is to stand out in the street and see that just about every Negro has either a beard or mustache, or both." But neither Yost nor DeGeorge nor anyone else could survey the population of couples with access to the crime scene on the day Juanita Brooks was robbed.[22]

Second, Tribe noted that despite Professor Martinez's warning that the simple product rule works only when events are independent of one another, Sinetar had carved up his categories in ways that surely risked interdependence. As almost every "Negro man with beard" qualifies as a

[21] Professor Tribe described his role in *Collins* in email correspondence on April 28, 2003, and February 15, 2004. I have drawn the details of his views in this paragraph from his article reflecting on the case and related issues of proof. *See* Laurence H. Tribe, *Trial by Mathematics: Precision and Ritual in the Legal Process*, 84 Harv. L. Rev. 1329 (1971).

[22] Brief for Respondent, *supra* n.1, at 46; Reply Brief, *People v. Collins* (Calif. Ct. App., Crim. No. 10819), at 30–31. This paragraph and the next few, reconstructing Tribe's memo to Justice Tobriner, are based on the analysis in the court's final opinion. *See Collins*, 68 Cal. 2d at 327–31. Tribe recalls that the court's opinion substantially reflected his initial memo.

"Man with mustache," Tribe wrote, Sinetar was wrong to list these characteristics separately.

Then there was Sinetar's unquestioning belief that Mrs. Brooks's and Mr. Bass's descriptions of her attackers were right. What if their car was beige and not yellow or its driver shadowed but not bearded? Sinetar then would have proved that the Collinses were a rare breed—but not that they were Mrs. Brooks's robbers. And how could we ever quantify the likelihood that Brooks and Bass were simply wrong?

Finally there was Sinetar's confusion about the meaning of the one-in-twelve-million figure. Perhaps, Tribe wrote, *if* Sinetar's probabilities are right, *if* we overlook interdependence among them, and *if* the eyewitnesses were accurate, Sinetar has proved that one couple in twelve million will share the robbers' features. But he has not proved, as he claimed to the jury, that "the chances of there being any other couple which fits the description of the Collins[es] on that occasion [are] at [most] one in twelve million." Sinetar had committed what William Thompson and Edward Schumann later termed the "prosecutor's fallacy."[23] He had mistaken the probability that a randomly selected couple would share the robbers' reported features—one in twelve million—for the probability that *any other couple* than the Collinses could be the robbers. The latter figure might be far larger. How much larger depended on all the other evidence in the case and—notably—on how many other couples in the area also shared the robbers' features.

Tribe set out to prove that at least one other couple matching all six of Sinetar's characteristics could have been at the crime scene that day. If we assume a large enough pool of couples, he wrote, the odds of finding another nearby couple sharing the six characteristics loom large. For example, if twelve million couples could have been near the Brooks robbery at the fateful hour, the chance of finding another couple like the Collinses who could have committed the crime grows to forty-one percent. Tribe did not fall into Thompson and Schumann's "defense attorney's fallacy" by suggesting that any such couple was as likely to be guilty as the Collinses.[24] That mistake would ignore all the *other* evidence in the case—the Collinses' cash-strapped lives, Janet's nearby workplace and altered hair, Malcolm's desperate flight from police. But

---

[23] Brief for Respondent, *supra* n.1, at 47 (quoting Sinetar's argument); William C. Thompson & Edward L. Schumann, *Interpretation of Statistical Evidence in Criminal Trials: The Prosecutor's Fallacy and the Defense Attorney's Fallacy*, 11 L. & HUM. BEHAV. 167, 170–71, 175–76, 181–83 (1987).

[24] For the calculations to determine the likelihood of finding another couple with the stated characteristics, see *Collins*, 68 Cal. 2d at 333–35 (Appendix). On the defense attorney's fallacy, see Thompson & Schumann, *supra* n.23, at 171.

Tribe did conclude that Sinetar's six-factor test, standing alone, amounted to far less than he claimed.

What made the prosecutor's errors worse was that the Collinses' trial counsel (and presumably the jurors) plainly lacked the mathematical training to spot them. Tribe refrained from noting that even the Court of Appeal was baffled by the probability evidence. In rejecting Malcolm Collins's claim that the evidence was irrelevant and unfairly prejudicial, the Court of Appeal committed an error even more blatant than the defense lawyer's fallacy. The court looked through a looking glass at Sinetar's probability demonstration and deemed the robbers' distinctiveness to be evidence of the Collinses' *innocence*:

> It appears that the evidence would be more favorable to defendant than to [the prosecution], since the probability of the hypothetical factors occurring would be so remote (1 in 12,000,000) as to render the testimony of the prosecution witnesses (with reference to identifying the persons who perpetrated the robbery) highly improbable.[25]

But the court had missed the concept. A distinctive couple surely *did* rob Mrs. Brooks. No evidence suggested that Mrs. Brooks and Mr. Bass lied or even that they were (badly) mistaken. Contrary to the court's conclusion, therefore, the more "improbable" the guilty couple's characteristics, the worse things looked for the Collinses, who happened to share those characteristics.

Tribe got little more guidance from Rex DeGeorge's briefs on behalf of Malcolm Collins. True, DeGeorge contributed the catchiest rhetoric of the case when he asked if our courts should "be changed to a *green felt jungle* where the dice [are] used to aid the Jury in determining whether a man is innocent or guilty." And he rightly highlighted the risk of interdependence among Sinetar's six characteristics. But DeGeorge's speculation on the nature of that interdependence was too flatly goofy to copy:

> The Court is invited to take judicial notice of the following:
>
> 1) There is a dependence between negro drivers and yellow cars. There are by far more negroes than caucasians driving yellow cars. . . .
>
> 3) There is a dependency between blonds and intermarriage. Blonds and redheads tend to be more adventuresome, more daring, and more likely to choose to be with a negroe [*sic*].
>
> 4) There is a dependency between the way a woman would normally wear her hair and how she would fix it when she goes to carry on a robbery.

---

[25] *People v. Collins, supra* n.19, at 15.

Had such arguments controlled Malcolm Collins's fate, he likely would have served out his time in the obscurity that attends most purse-snatchings. Indeed the California Supreme Court initially voted to deny his petition for a hearing. Here Collins was fortunate that DeGeorge's briefs arrived on Tribe's doorstep, for Tribe persuaded Justice Tobriner of the importance of declaring the non-probabilistic nature of the reasonable-doubt standard. Tobriner in turn persuaded Chief Justice Roger Traynor and Justice Raymond Sullivan, who was assigned to write the court's opinion.[26]

Hoping to lean on Tribe's expertise, Sullivan asked Tobriner's help in drafting the opinion. Tobriner then recruited Tribe to keep a hand in the process even after Tribe left to clerk for Justice Potter Stewart. In the end, the more mathematical parts of Justice Sullivan's opinion and particularly the mathematical appendix drew heavily from Tribe's work. And in the end—on March 11, 1968—the California Supreme Court reversed Malcolm Collins's conviction, exposing Sinetar's technical errors and lamenting that the "sorcerer" mathematics had "cast a spell" over trial jurors.

Immediately, a juror rose in dissent. In the face of the court's smug certainty that Sinetar had snookered the jury—"[u]ndoubtedly the jurors were unduly impressed by the mystique of the mathematical demonstration"—the foreman issued a snappish rejoinder. "Mathematics," he wrote to Justice Sullivan, "and the relation of probability, . . . was not considered as the important item on the conviction of Mr. and Mrs. Collins. . . . [W]e arrived at the conviction only after all the other facts of the case were weighed. . . ." But the foreman's rebuttal came too late. By then, two days after the court's ruling, news of the judgment had spread—and the foreman's protest lay buried, unheard, in the court's files.[27]

Events followed in the judgment's wake. Malcolm Collins, his conviction reversed, received a new trial date of June 17, 1968—one day shy of the fourth anniversary of the robbery of Juanita Brooks. When Sinetar could not assemble his witnesses for retrial, the trial court dismissed the case, and Malcolm Collins went free. As for Janet Collins, she had absconded from parole even as Malcolm's appeal wended its way through the system. After the high court's ruling, she apparently was recaptured

---

[26] For DeGeorge's references to "green felt jungle" and his arguments about interdependence, see *Petition for Hearing, supra* n.4, at 21–22, 28 (emphasis added). DeGeorge presumably borrowed the expression from the title of a 1963 book on casino gambling. *See* ED REID & OVID DEMARIS, THE GREEN FELT JUNGLE (1963). Tribe described his role, as recounted in this paragraph and the next, in email correspondence cited above at note 21.

[27] The foreman's letter is quoted in Professor Spencer Neth's notes of the Supreme Court's *Collins* record, which I described above in note 16.

and returned to prison. No record of her appears after May 29, 1968, when the trial court ordered that Malcolm Collins be permitted to correspond with his wife at the California Institution for Women.[28] Thereafter, presumably freed, she fell from sight.

Yet even as the Collinses slipped from the scene, *People v. Collins* tossed up a storm of academic commentary. Mathematicians and statisticians rushed to defend their disciplines, insisting that all proof is probabilistic, and we ought to be up-front about it and help jurors measure probabilities intelligently. Many legal commentators agreed.[29]

Only one academic voice spoke prominently and powerfully in the *Collins* court's defense. Laurence Tribe, then a young assistant professor at Harvard, wrote "in reaction to a growing and bewildering literature of praise for mathematical precision in the trial process. . . ." Under the title "Trial by Mathematics," borrowed from his own virtually ghostwritten opinion, Tribe rose to defend his unattributed work. Having left Justice Tobriner's chambers a full half-year before the court issued its judgment under a *different* justice's name, Tribe went largely unsuspected as counsel in his own defense. So he made to the world the arguments he first had made to Justice Tobriner—that when we entertain math at trial, we bear the risk of math done badly; that math done badly often goes undetected by lawyers and jurors untrained in math; that quantified evidence can be overbearingly impressive, squashing softer variables; and that by quantifying proof, we necessarily quantify reasonable doubt and declare our tolerance of a known and stated risk of convicting the innocent.[30]

To Sinetar's argument that "life would be intolerable" unless jurors have the courage to convict on strong odds and to risk that "on some rare occasion . . . an innocent person may be convicted," Tribe answered that "the system does *not* in fact authorize the imposition of criminal

---

[28] On April 26, 1968, *Time* magazine reported that "Janet Collins is already out of jail, has broken parole and lit out for parts unknown." *Decisions: Trial by Mathematics, supra* n.1, at 41. All other facts in this paragraph, including the May 29 and June 17 court orders, are drawn from the records of the Los Angeles Superior Court, cited above at note 4.

[29] Among the first statisticians to speak out against the case was William Fairley, who wrote together with lawyer and law teacher Michael Finkelstein. Their 1970 article prompted Tribe's 1971 rebuttal (cited above at note 21), which in turn sparked their reply. *See* Michael O. Finkelstein & William B. Fairley, *A Bayesian Approach to Identification Evidence*, 83 Harv. L. Rev. 489 (1970); Michael O. Finkelstein & William B. Fairley, *A Comment on "Trial by Mathematics,"* 84 Harv. L. Rev. 1801 (1971). Among the first law professors to examine *Collins* critically was Alan Cullison. *See* Alan D. Cullison, *Identification by Probabilities and Trial by Arithmetic (A Lesson for Beginners in How to Be Wrong with Greater Precision)*, 6 Hous. L. Rev. 471, 518 (1969).

[30] Tribe, *supra* n.21, at 1331, 1332, 1334, 1360–62, 1372–75. Tribe has not publicly disclosed his role in *Collins* before now.

punishment when the trier recognizes a quantifiable doubt as to the defendant's guilt. Instead," he wrote, "the system dramatically—if imprecisely—insists upon as close an approximation to certainty as seems humanly attainable in the circumstances."[31]

\* \* \*

Tribe surely won the round of *People v. Collins*. After all, Sinetar had blundered in his math, and Tribe spoke in the ear of power. But the verdict of history is cloudier. For the moral of *Collins* was not that math always "cast[s] a spell" over the trier of fact. The California Supreme Court wrote that math also can "assist[] the trier . . . in the search for truth."[32] *Collins* condemned math done badly, but said almost nothing of the utility of math done well.

In the decades since *Collins*, errors like Sinetar's often have met ready rebuke from appeals courts, sometimes on the direct authority of *Collins* and Tribe's "Trial by Mathematics." Hence when a Michigan prosecutor repeated the first of Sinetar's mistakes and let a dental expert say without foundational data that only one person in millions had teeth to match the murder victim's bite mark, a reviewing court complained that no evidence " 'identified particular features of the bite mark that had a known rate of occurrence.' " Like the proposition "condemned and . . . discredited . . . by the California Supreme Court" in *Collins*, the bite-mark testimony "carried an aura of mathematical precision pointing overwhelmingly to the statistical probability of guilt, when the evidence deserved no such credence."[33]

Likewise, when a Washington prosecutor repeated Sinetar's second mistake and invited the jury to multiply together the probabilities of several unlikely events, a reviewing court wearily reminded him that "[w]here the product rule is used, . . . the events must be shown to be independent, and this record is devoid of foundation evidence establishing independence of these events." Even worse, the court said, the prosecutor committed Sinetar's third error too, for his proposed calculation assumed that the underlying facts took place as eyewitnesses said.

---

[31] *Id.* at 1374. Just two months before Tribe's article appeared—and as if in anticipation of it—two scholars published results of a survey asking judges, jurors, and students to quantify proof beyond a reasonable doubt. Responses varied little among groups. The median judge assigned a probability of 0.88, the median juror 0.86, and the median student 0.91. *See* Rita James Simon & Linda Mahan, *Quantifying Burdens of Proof: A View from the Bench, the Jury, and the Classroom*, 5 L. & SOCIETY REV. 319, 324 tbl.4 (1971).

[32] *Collins*, 68 Cal. 2d at 320.

[33] *Ege v. Yukins*, 380 F. Supp. 2d 852, 870–71, 872, 876, 880 (E.D. Mich. 2005) (quoting state court opinion in this case).

"[T]he argument assumes, for example, that Connie Taff did in fact see a mulatto man, when she may have been mistaken...."[34]

And when a federal prosecutor in Minnesota committed Sinetar's fourth error—the prosecutor's fallacy—he received a similar scolding. An expert had suggested that the chance of randomly matching a questioned hair sample was one in a thousand. The prosecutor deftly converted this claim into proof of the defendant's guilt. Evidence that the defendant's hair matched that in the robber's ski mask was "better than 99.44 percent" proof, he argued to the jury. "[I]t's better than Ivory Soap.... I submit to you that ... it is at the very least proof beyond a reasonable doubt that the unknown hair comes from the same head as the known hair." The reviewing court caught the fallacy: "[T]he prosecutor 'confuse[d] the probability of concurrence of the identifying marks with the probability of mistaken identification.' "[35] That is, the prosecutor had converted the one-in-one-thousand chance that an innocent person, randomly picked, would match a strand of the robber's hair into one chance in one thousand of the defendant's innocence.

All these cases confirmed the central lesson of *Collins*—that math done badly can be grounds for reversal. But what of math done well? How is it that we sometimes hear prosecutors say that only one man in a billion—or ten billion or fifty billion—will match the killer's and the defendant's genetic markers? Today DNA evidence counters any claim that *Collins* forever banished the sorcerer mathematics from criminal courtrooms.

It was not always so. When DNA profiling entered court in the 1980s, judges often balked at its astronomical odds against innocence. To many, the new technique looked suspiciously like Sinetar's exercise in *Collins*. Aided by an expert, a prosecutor listed the guilty man's features—not his car color or facial hair, but his *alleles* at specific chromosomal sites, revealed by the hair or blood or semen he left at the crime scene. The expert then showed that the defendant shared the same alleles at the same sites. To each such match the expert assigned a probability. Then the expert applied the product rule, multiplying the probability of each allelic match to arrive at a one-in-many-millions chance that a different person, randomly picked, would share all the same alleles.

Early courts spied in this new adventure in proof the same four flaws that plagued Sinetar's. First was the lack of foundation for the probability of each match. DNA profiling demands a population database

---

[34] *State v. Copeland*, 130 Wn. 2d 244, 292–93 (1996).

[35] *United States v. Massey*, 594 F.2d 676, 679–81 (8th Cir. 1979) (quoting McCormick on Evidence § 204, at 487 (E. Cleary ed. 1972)).

broad enough to reveal random allelic frequencies. But early DNA analysts worked with narrow and nonrandom datasets. Just as Sinetar had spun his data in the office secretarial pool, the FBI generated its early DNA database by testing *its agents*, who then became the standard by which criminal matches were measured. As one early defense expert deadpanned, this database might be "atypical of the general population."[36]

Then too was Sinetar's second problem—the lack of mutual independence. If certain alleles tend to appear jointly, the product rule will magnify the meaning of a match. Yet in the early days of DNA profiling, scientists could not say with confidence whether mating patterns and population clusters distort allelic mixing. Appeals courts wrestled with the technical demands of "linkage equilibrium" and "Hardy–Weinberg equilibrium" and their elusive standards for assuring independence among alleles.

Sinetar's third error was to overlook the risk that eyewitnesses simply got the robbers' features wrong. Human error can play as big a role in DNA profiling. A claim of contaminated swatches or switched samples is often the defendant's best slip from crushing numeric proof. As one skeptic of DNA profiling observed, "Creating a statistic that is vanishingly small has nothing to do with decreasing the chances of a contamination or mislabeling a test tube."[37]

But the most tempting error of all remained the prosecutor's fallacy, made still more tempting by eye-catching odds against random matching. When the chance of a random match is one in billions or trillions, some prosecutors can't quash the urge to billboard that figure as the chance of innocence.

At first some courts followed the *Collins* court's lead in addressing these dangers: They exposed the flaws in the prosecution's proof and deemed DNA profiling and its fancy math inadmissible. Other courts, friendlier to the new genetic tests, let in evidence of a DNA match, but not of the math with its devastatingly precise calculus of the odds against random matching. Still others let in the math, but required the prosecutor to build into every calculation a cushion to protect the accused against error. After one New York judge heard testimony about

---

[36] *People v. Mohit*, 153 Misc. 2d 22, 35 (N.Y. County Ct., Westchester 1992) (paraphrasing defense expert); Richard Lempert, *Some Caveats Concerning DNA as Criminal Identification Evidence: With Thanks to the Reverend Bayes*, 13 Cardozo L. Rev. 303, 320 n.42 (1991) (noting construction of FBI database).

[37] Jonathan J. Koehler, *One in Millions, Billions, and Trillions: Lessons from* People v. Collins *(1968) for* People v. Simpson *(1995)*, 47 J. Leg. Ed. 214, 222 (1997); *accord* Richard Lempert, *After the DNA Wars: Skirmishing with NRC II*, 37 Jurimetrics 439, 444–54 (1997).

the inbred FBI database and other flaws in the DNA evidence, he did a rough-and-ready recalculation of the prosecution's random-match probability. Rather than one in sixty-seven million, as an FBI analyst suggested, the judge permitted an estimate of just one in 100,000.[38]

These cases represented the growing pains of an era. As DNA typing advanced, some of Sinetar's flaws melted away and with them judges' wariness of the new proof and its math. By the late 1990s scientists neared consensus on allelic frequencies within different racial and ethnic groups and largely resolved fears about interdependence among alleles. True, the third risk remained: Careless or corrupt police still could contaminate crime scenes, and chemists still could cross samples in the lab. But while some experts argued that these risks rendered the one-in-millions random-match probabilities meaningless, courts increasingly disagreed. As one federal district judge in New Hampshire ruled, jurors are capable of discounting astronomical random-match figures once defense experts spotlight the risks of human error.[39]

The same judge dismissed the argument that jurors will repeat Sinetar's fourth error—the prosecutor's fallacy—and mistake the miniscule probability of a random match for the chance of the defendant's innocence. The judge declared himself "confident that the risk of confusion is acceptably small if the concept is properly explained. Moreover," he wrote, expressing a view held by more and more courts, "because [a random-match] estimate can be extremely valuable in helping the jury appreciate the potential significance of a DNA profile match, it should not be excluded merely because the concept requires explanation."[40]

---

[38] *See, e.g., Commonwealth v. Lanigan*, 413 Mass. 154, 162–63 (1992) (deeming proffered DNA evidence inadmissible); *State v. Anderson*, 115 N.M. 433, 444–45 (N.M. Ct. App. 1993) (same); *State v. Schwartz*, 447 N.W.2d 422, 428–29 (Minn. 1989) (advising lower courts that they may admit expert interpretation of DNA evidence but not population frequency statistics); *Rivera v. State*, 840 P.2d 933, 942 (Wyo. 1992) (deeming it "the better practice . . . to not refer to the statistical probability of duplication when introducing DNA test results"); *Mohit*, 153 Misc. 2d at 36–37 (increasing probability estimate from one in 67 million to one in 100,000); *Caldwell v. State*, 260 Ga. 278, 289–90 (1990) (disallowing one expert's probability calculation of one in 24 million, but allowing a second expert's figure of one in 250,000); *State v. Vandebogart*, 139 N.H. 145, 153–57 (1994) (approving trial courts' use of "a highly conservative estimate of the possibility of a random match that resolves all uncertainties in favor of the defendant").

[39] *United States v. Shea*, 957 F. Supp. 331, 344–45 (D.N.H. 1997), *aff'd*, 159 F.3d 37 (1st Cir. 1998); *accord Copeland*, 130 Wn. 2d at 270–71. Even without hearing from defense experts, experimental jurors have fairly accurate intuitions about the likelihood of lab error. *See* Dale A. Nance & Scott B. Morris, *Juror Understanding of DNA Evidence: An Empirical Assessment of Presentation Formats for Trace Evidence with a Relatively Small Random–Match Probability*, 34 J. Leg. Stud. 395, 433 (2005).

[40] *Shea*, 957 F. Supp. at 345.

That was in 1997. Today the risk of the prosecutor's fallacy has all but vanished. By comparing more alleles at more sites, DNA analysts produce random-match probabilities so tiny that prosecutors gain almost nothing through mistranslation. Unless the defendant has an identical twin, the probability of a random match and the probability of finding another matching individual *anywhere* converge—on zero.

* * *

Courtroom math has come far since Sinetar's hand-drawn chart with its secretarial survey results. Still, the story of *Collins* threads a cautionary theme through the DNA case law. For it appears that the difference between casting a spell and casting a light turns on the rigor of the math and the accuracy of the underlying facts. With one eye on *Collins*, judges strain their meager math training to assess the retinue of experts who vouch for the reliability of DNA typing. When the math passes muster, even the overbearingly precise probabilities that so troubled Tribe can find their way into court.

Yet one aspect of trial stays closed to all appeals to probability, however well credentialed. The beyond-reasonable-doubt standard remains rigorously, resolutely unquantified. Probability evidence may help jurors mount that hurdle. But never may a judge advise jurors that if probabilistic evidence has pushed their certitude past a numerical signpost, they may convict without first confronting their certainty *beyond a reasonable doubt* of the defendant's guilt.

For justice at last is no green felt jungle.

*

# 2

# The Death of a Youth and of a Drunkard: A Remarkable Story of Habit and Character in New Jersey

## Peter Tillers*

The fact that at some point in 1943 [Petro Radziwil] may have extended a hand to some family [in Poland] for which he received [from the Nazis], he says, a requirement that he work in a prison factory [in Auschwitz] in Germany [sic], the fact that that occurred in 1943, does not in this Court's opinion, constitute a mitigating factor.—Statement of Judge John Ricciardi, Sentencing Hearing, State of New Jersey v. Petro Radziwil (September 29, 1989).

## 1. Remarkable Facts and Questions in an Unremarkable Case

In many ways the case was unremarkable. It involved a traffic fatality that may have involved drunken driving, a tragic but common occurrence. This unremarkable case—the criminal action of State of New Jersey v. Petro Radziwil, Indictment No. 1257-8-86—was, to be sure, important to the family of the 17 year old male whose death gave rise to the case. On November 25, 2004, a memorial notice appeared in the New York Times:

> MacCORMACK—Keith G. Feb. 5, 1967—Nov. 25, 1984. Killed By Drunk Driver 20 years without you in our lives, but never absent from our hearts.

---

* Professor of Law, Cardozo School of Law, Yeshiva University.

The evidence recounted and discussed here was gathered largely through the efforts of the truly remarkable students in my course in fact investigation at Cardozo School of Law in the fall semester of 2004: Jay Bragga, Starr Brown, Thomas Donohoe, Christopher Fugarino, Thomas Gabriel, Oren Gelber, Meredith Heller, Jason Kadish, Elvira Marzano, Leonid Mikityanskiy, Alexander Paykin, Vincent Rao, and Louis Shapiro. Danielle Muscatello, my former research assistant, also made an important contribution.

Loss so overwhelming, our hearts are broken. Your loving brothers
& sisters, Bryan, Amy, Ali, John, Megan.

The ingredient of personal tragedy, however, does not make *State of
New Jersey v. Radziwil* particularly noteworthy in the eyes of legal
professionals. Thousands of criminal prosecutions each year are occasioned by personal tragedies—murders, rapes, child sexual abuse, and so
on.

*Radziwil* is nevertheless noteworthy. It is noteworthy, first, because
of its surprisingly pristine facts. Evidence in real-world cases is ordinarily messy and usually harbors many uncertainties. The result of such
messiness and uncertainty is that in most appeals there is substantial
uncertainty that the issues submitted on appeal are actually raised by
the evidence in the case. *Radziwil* was seemingly different in this
respect. The evidence and the facts in Radziwil were remarkably unambiguous.

*Radziwil* is also noteworthy because it raises important questions
about an important part of the law of evidence: the relationship between
habit evidence and character evidence. But the questions that *Radziwil*
presents reach beyond the law of evidence. The criminal justice system is
disproportionately populated with unsavory people, unpleasant people,
stubborn people, and strong-willed people. Criminal defendants are frequently both unsavory and unpleasant, and many witnesses—including
prosecution witnesses—share these traits. Prosecutors and criminal defense counsel, although not as a rule unsavory, can be unusually strong-
willed and stubborn, and judges who preside in criminal cases may
become hardened not just to the suffering of victims but also to the
plight of those who cause harm. This combination of character traits has
the making of a toxic brew. There is reason to worry about the capacity
of strong-willed actors, such as police officers and trial judges, to make
sound judgments about the unpleasant and unsavory people—criminal
defendants and witnesses—that they routinely encounter while performing their assigned chores in the criminal justice system. The story of
Radziwil illustrates how personal likes and dislikes, and the prejudices of
actors in the criminal process, can affect the outcomes of criminal
proceedings. The story of Radziwil also raises the question of whether
much can be done to scrub the criminal process clean of the influence of
the biases and emotions of the people who shape that process.

## 2.  Conduct and Character

Guilt or innocence is supposed to depend on what a person does, and
not on what a person is. This precept permeates the criminal law, which
defines misdeeds in terms of intent and action. It also plays a role in the
law of evidence, especially in a doctrine known, variously, as the charac-

ter evidence rule, the character rule, the propensity rule, and—more elaborately—the prohibition against the circumstantial use of character evidence.

The character rule proclaims—broadly speaking—that evidence of a person's character (or propensity) may not be used to prove that person's conduct on a particular occasion. A prosecutor cannot, for example, introduce evidence of a murder defendant's misanthropy to show that the defendant killed her grandfather. The trial would have to focus on matters such as the accused's actions and her feelings toward her grandfather rather than on the her hate-filled disposition toward all humankind. This example, however, does not show that the distinction between character in general and conduct on a particular occasion is clear. Legal rules are never so simple, and the character rule certainly isn't.

One way to try to understand the character rule is to try to understand the legal rules and principles that circumscribe it. One such boundary is the habit rule. This rule permits the use of habit to show conduct on a specific occasion. The habit rule rests on the premise that habit and character are different. But the difference between character and habit is not obvious.

Charles McCormick, who wrote a classic and influential hornbook on the law of evidence, saw a clear distinction between character and habit. Habit, he argued is a recurring response to a specific situation that has become semi-automatic. Courts have quoted and embraced Dean McCormick's explanation on numerous occasions. But the drafter of the 1983 revision of the first volume of Wigmore's monumental treatise on the law of evidence did not find the distinction so easy to make. He nonetheless argued for the admission of habit evidence even if habit is a species of character because habit, he thought, is ordinarily more probative than the kinds of propensity evidence that elicit the characterization "character." He also argued that if the probative value of habit is the key to its admissibility, then fully volitional repetitive behavior should be admissible, if it is probative of the issues in a case.[1]

If habit evidence, is (as the reviser of Wigmore's treatise seemed to think) a species of character evidence, it is not the only kind of evidence the law admits to show action in accord with character. Criminal defendants can offer evidence of pertinent traits of their character to show they did not commit a crime; the bad character of witnesses for truth and veracity can be admitted to suggest they have lied on the stand, and certain kinds of bad acts may be admitted to show a propensity to commit certain sexual crimes. This paper will not, howev-

---

[1] 1A WIGMORE ON EVIDENCE § 93 at 1628–1630 & § 98.1 at 1659–1662 (P. Tillers rev. 1983).

er, examine these permitted uses. My focus is on the distinction between habit and character, and I ask whether courts, though professing to honor the distinction, disguise character as habit by allowing behavior that is not semi-automatic to show conduct on a specific occasion and by allowing circumstantial use of predominantly volitional behavior even when that behavior reveals unattractive character traits. I also ask whether in a specific case where character evidence has probative value, the benefits of character evidence outweigh its dangers. These questions and others are raised by *State of New Jersey v. Petro Radziwil.*

### 3.   Death at Night

Keith G. MacCormack died at about 2:00 a.m.—two hours after midnight—on Sunday, November 25, 1984, in an automobile collision at

FIGURE 1

the intersection of Route 537 and Paint Island Spring Road in Freehold Township, Monmouth County, New Jersey. Keith was a passenger in a car driven by his 18 year-old friend Daleston Cote, Jr. Daleston Cote was driving northeast on Route 537, a two-lane road with narrow shoulders. Daleston had stopped at the intersection of Route 537 and Paint Island Spring Road to make a left hand turn. As Daleston was waiting for two oncoming cars traveling westbound to pass, his car was struck in the rear by another car.

The collision propelled Daleston's car across Route 537 into the westbound lane where it was struck by a car traveling westbound. Keith MacCormack was thrown from the car after the second collision and was killed. His body came to rest on the shoulder next to the eastbound lane of Route 537. Keith was 17 years old at the time of his death.

The car that struck Daleston's car from the rear did not stop. The hit-and-run car and its driver disappeared. No eyewitnesses were able to describe any of the characteristics of the hit-and-run car. However, debris gathered by the police at the scene of the automobile collision, including fragments of a grill, a maroon header panel, and other maroon fragments, revealed that the car driven by the hit-and-run driver was a maroon 1979 Oldsmobile Delta 88. This evidence narrowed the possibilities but left open many others: 1,387 maroon 1979 Oldsmobile Delta 88s were registered in New Jersey in 1984 and more such cars would have been registered in heavily-populated neighboring states.

4.   Seeming Serendipity and Skill in a Criminal Investigation

On May 7, 1986, an attentive Freehold Township police officer with an excellent memory—Officer Donald Burlew—made an interesting discovery. He saw a 1979 Oldsmobile Delta 88 in the nearby town of Jackson, New Jersey, and noticed that the car had a new front end rather than the front end assembly that such cars normally come with. He took the license plate number of this Olds 88 and established that the registered owner was Carl Hobson. Officer Burlew returned to Jackson on May 9, 1986, and spotted the vehicle again. He stopped the vehicle and questioned the driver, who turned out to be Ginger Hobson, Carl Hobson's wife. Although Ginger Hobson told Officer Burlew that Carl was out of town at the moment, she did say Carl had acquired their Olds 88 from an auto body shop. Investigation later established that Carl Hobson had purchased the Olds 88 from Diorio Auto Body Shop in January 1985. The Diorio Auto Body Shop had acquired the Olds 88 from Laffin Chevrolet on November 29, 1984, and Laffin Chevrolet had acquired the Olds 88 from Petro Radziwil on November 28, 1984. In 1984 Radziwil lived in South River. Route 537 lies approximately half-way between South River and Rova Farms, a place that plays an important part in our story.

Burlew's work had established that Radziwil's car was the kind of car that might have rear-ended Daleston Cote's car on November 25, but this fact did not rule out the possibility that one of the other 1,387 maroon 1979 Olds Delta 88s, or a similar car from out of state, was the hit-and-run car. But a phone conversation with Carl Hobson on May 13, 1986, added crucial information. Hobson told Burlew that after acquiring the Olds 88 from Diorio Auto Body Shop in January 1985 he had repaired the damaged front end of the car and that he had thrown the parts that he had removed on a junk pile in his back yard. He also said that he had found and retrieved those discarded parts and that he would be happy to deliver them to the Freehold Township Police Department the next day. He testified that he did exactly that at 8:00 a.m. the next morning.

One of the items that the police said Carl Hobson turned over to them was a support for a small section of a plastic grill that had been made for use on a front end of a 1979 Olds Delta 88. That broken-off support matched a part of a plastic grill that the Freehold Township police had found among the debris at Route 537 and Paint Island Spring Road on November 25, 1984. Now it no longer mattered that 1,387 maroon 1979 Olds Delta 88s were registered in New Jersey in 1984 or that more such cars were registered in nearby states. The match between the broken-off support that Hobson delivered to the Freehold Township Police Department and the plastic grill fragment that the Freehold Township police had found at the scene of the automobile collision—together with evidence that Radziwil was the owner of Carl Hobson's Olds 88 on November 25, 1984—apparently established, practically conclusively, that the Olds 88 Radziwil had once owned was the car that rear-ended Daleston Cote's car. The thesis that Radziwil (rather than someone else) was driving his Olds 88 when his Olds 88 rear-ended Daleston Cote's car was effectively clinched by Radziwil's subsequent statement to the police that he never let anyone else drive his car.

But the case against Radziwil was not yet complete. The prosecutor wanted to charge Radziwil with aggravated manslaughter.[2] To make that charge stick the police and the prosecutor had to produce evidence that Radziwil had a reckless state of mind on the night of November 25, 1984. To prove that Radziwil had this state of mind at 2:00 a.m. on November 25, 1984, the prosecution sought permission and was allowed to introduce evidence of Radziwil's customary drinking practices.

---

[2] Radziwil was also charged with "death by auto." But his conviction for that crime was merged into his conviction for aggravated manslaughter, and for present purposes we can disregard the indictment for this lesser crime.

### 5.   A Well–Established Drinking Habit

An essential element of the crime of aggravated manslaughter under New Jersey law was that the perpetrator have the *mens rea*—the state of mind—of "extreme indifference to human life" at the time the perpetrator committed the act or acts causing the death of another person. It was also the law in New Jersey—as the appellate courts reaffirmed in this very case—that a trier of fact is free to infer such indifference on the part of a driver of a car that causes the death of another person if the trier concludes (beyond a reasonable doubt) that the driver of the car was intoxicated at the time that the car that he or she was driving precipitated that death.

Radziwil's trial for criminal homicide began on January 13, 1987. To prove that Radziwil was intoxicated and, thus indifferent to human life at the time of the accident, the prosecutor offered and the trial court admitted evidence that Radziwil routinely got drunk on Saturday nights at a place called Rova Farms. In particular, at Radziwil's 1987 trial the prosecutor offered and the trial judge admitted the testimony of Bernie D'Zurella, a Rova Farms bartender. The Appellate Division of the Superior Court of New Jersey later described the bartender's testimony this way:

> [T]o prove that defendant was intoxicated at the time of the accident, the prosecutor offered testimony by Bernie D'Zurella, the bartender at Rova Farms from 1981 to the end of 1985, that defendant came to Rova Farms just about every weekend until the end of November 1984 and that he always got drunk shortly after arriving. D'Zurella also said that defendant would regularly become loud and obnoxious and that he would be forced to escort him outside the bar.

D'Zurella did not testify that he recalled seeing the defendant intoxicated on Saturday November 24 or Sunday November 25, 1984. Indeed, although D'Zurella initially resisted being pinned down, he eventually testified that he did not remember seeing Radziwil at Rova Farms during the evening of November 24, 1984, and that he did not remember seeing Radziwil in an intoxicated state on that particular night. It is possible that the bartender was worried about being personally liable under New Jersey's dram shop doctrine. In any event, the bartender's testimony about Radziwil's customary drinking practices was the only evidence submitted at the trial that tended to show that Radziwil was intoxicated at the time of the automobile collision on November 25, 1984.

The jury convicted Radziwil of aggravated manslaughter. Radziwil appealed. On appeal New Jersey's Appellate Division said that questions relating to the evidence used to show Radziwil's intoxicated state at 2:00

a.m. on November 25, 1984, were the "only real issue" on appeal because "[t]he evidence that defendant was the driver of the hit-and-run vehicle which caused the accident resulting in Keith MacCormack's death was overwhelming." The Appellate Division added: "Indeed, this point was virtually conceded in defense counsel's summation." The Appellate Division described the central question on appeal this way:

> The significant issue presented by [Radziwil's] appeal is whether evidence that a defendant regularly became intoxicated every weekend at a particular bar is admissible as evidence of a habit to prove that defendant was intoxicated at the time of the automobile collision which resulted in his conviction for aggravated manslaughter and death by auto.

The Appellate Division rejected Radziwil's challenge to his conviction. In an opinion that was later "substantially" adopted by New Jersey's Supreme Court, the Appellate Division held that the bartender's testimony about Radziwil's practice of drinking of excessive amounts of alcohol on Saturdays at Rova Farms over a period of years amounted to evidence of habit and was therefore admissible. Like the trial judge, the Appellate Division rejected the defense's claim that Radziwil's pattern of drinking amounted to a propensity or a character trait. The Appellate Division further held that the bartender's testimony about Radziwil's drinking practices on Saturdays and weekends at Rova Farms was sufficient—by itself—to support the jury's implied finding that there was no reasonable doubt that Radziwil was intoxicated at the time of the automobile collision that killed Keith MacCormack—at 2:00 a.m. on November 25, 1984.

The courts of New Jersey also rebuffed the defense's contention that the evidence of Radziwil's pattern of drinking was unduly prejudicial. In its explanation for this conclusion, the Appellate Division emphasized that the bartender's testimony had, it thought, substantial probative value. The Appellate Division also quoted a passage from McCormick's hornbook that ends with the following words:

> By and large, the detailed patterns of situation-specific behavior that constitute habits are unlikely to provoke such sympathy or antipathy as would distort the process of evaluating the evidence.[3]

The story of the Radziwil case tests this proposition.

## 6.  The Lives of Immigrants

Petro Radziwil was born at an unfortunate time, September 15, 1922, not long before the onset of the Great Depression in Europe. Radziwil was born in a part of Poland that he called "White Russian

---

[3] C. McCormick, Evidence § 195 at 575 (3d ed. 1984).

country." (Today we would say that Radziwil was born in a part of Poland that was ethnically Belarus.) Radziwil was 17 years old when Stalin and Hitler carved up Poland in 1940 pursuant to the Molotov-Ribbentrop Pact. Petro's mother died the same year. He was 18 years old when Germany invaded the Soviet Union in June of 1941. He was 22 years old on VE Day, the day that World War II ended in Europe in May of 1945. His father died in 1946.

Petro Radziwil emigrated to the United States in 1952. He was then 30 years old. Radziwil's native language was Russian. When Radziwil arrived in the United States, he almost surely spoke very little English. (He had little formal education, attending school only until he was eight years old.) After arriving in the United States, Radziwil settled in northern New Jersey, a portion of the Eastern Seaboard that had large populations of Russian, Polish, and other Eastern European immigrants.

Rova Farms, where Radziwil is alleged to have regularly have gotten drunk, was the result of one wave of Eastern European immigration. In 1926 Russian immigrant communities in the United States gathered for a meeting in Philadelphia and established the Russian Consolidated Mutual Aid Society of America–or ROOVA. In the early 1930s branches and members of ROOVA established Rova Farms Resort, Inc., a joint-stock company which promptly acquired 1400 acres in Jackson, New Jersey. Rova Farms was to be a cultural and social center for Russian immigrants in the United States. From the 1940s through the early 1960s Rova Farms flourished; it ran a large variety of cultural activities (such as a Tolstoy library and a children's school); it was a popular vacation resort for Russian immigrants and their children, and it hosted popular bands and acts that performed before audiences numbering in the thousands.

It is not surprising that Rova Farms became a focal point of Petro Radziwil's social life. Radziwil's facility with English was poor. His native language was Russian. At Rova Farms he could find the company of other Russian-speaking immigrants. It is not clear when Radziwil started spending time at Rova Farms, but he probably began soon after his arrival in the United States. Sometime in the early 1970s Petro Radziwil even lived and worked at Rova Farms.

As Russian immigrants and their children assimilated and moved to other parts of the United States, Rova Farms began a slow but inexorable decline. Today Rova Farms retains only 40 of the 1400 acres it once had. Although Rova Farms is still used by some Russian immigrants and their descendants for festive occasions such as weddings, its main activity now consists of a restaurant and a bar. Outdoor areas are used for activities such as flea markets.

St. Vladimir Church – Russian Orthodox Church Adjoining Rova Farms

FIGURE 2

Despite Rova's decline, Radziwil continued to spend most of his leisure time there. That he did so is understandable. Radziwil led a life that can fairly be characterized as solitary and hardscrabble. His parents

Outdoor Area at Rova Farms in 2004

FIGURE 3

were both dead. He was unmarried. He had no children. He had a sister somewhere in the United States but he had little or no contact with her. Radziwil lived by himself, mainly in rented apartments or rooms. His work could not have given him much satisfaction. Because he had practically no formal education and spoke poor English, he could only get jobs as a laborer. For the last 21 years of his working life, he worked as a cable extruder operator in a wire plant. Here he operated a mechanical device—an extruder—that turned metal such as copper into cable. Radziwil took pride in his work, but the pay was low and the work was hard and dangerous.

Although Radziwil must have regarded Rova Farms as a place of refuge, he did not go to Rova Farms only to see friends and associates. Rova Farms had a bar as well as a restaurant (and other facilities) on its premises. Petro Radziwil did a lot of drinking at Rova Farms from 1981 through 1984 with a small circle of Russian-speaking friends or associates. He very probably did a lot of drinking at Rova Farms for many years before that.

### 7.  An Obnoxious and Dangerous Drunkard?

Although Radziwil's life in the United States from 1952 until the mid–1980s can fairly be described as hard and bleak, probably very few of the participants in and observers of Radziwil's 1987 trial saw him as a sad or pathetic figure. By the end of the trial most of those people probably instead thought of Radziwil mainly as both a repulsive and dangerous old man.

The tone was set by Bernie D'Zurella, the Rova Farms bartender who testified against Radziwil. D'Zurella gave the following testimony:

Q.  [by the prosecutor] Let me ask this, how was he in the bar?

A.  He drank a lot. I seen him numerous occasions mostly all the time drunk.

Q.  Did he drink at the bar?

A.  No, sir, because I flagged him from the bar. He get drunk, got loud, obnoxious with me and the customers and we'd have to escort him outside.

. . .

Q.  So do I understand your answer that ever [every] time you remember him being there he was drunk or got drunk?

A.  Yeah because most of the time he'd start fighting with me every time he was there, you know.[4]

---

[4] In the sentencing hearing following the verdict, only Radziwil's trial lawyer expressed pity for him, although it is impossible to know whether he meant what he told the presiding judge:

You know, Judge, when I walked out of here on the 15th or 16th of January [1987], I was tired, but it was not just physical or mental fatigue ... [T]here was a very draining experience for me because this is unlike any other criminal case and Mr. Radziwil is unlike any other criminal defendant, because while his activities are criminal, they are defined as such by the legislature. This type of offense is qualitatively different than any other type of crime. We have a person who obviously has ... a disease. Society has chosen to deal with it ... by harshly punishing those convicted for the serious offense for which this defendant is convicted of, there is no doubt, but Mr. Radziwil has a disease. ... Mr. Radziwil is a sick person who needs help. ... I quite honestly believe Mr. Radziwil when he tells me to this day he has no recollection of this accident. ... [H]e was and is a very frightened, very confused, very lonely, old man. ...

Regardless of whether the defense counsel actually believed what he said, the prosecutor was having none of it:

[The record of Radziwil's prior convictions and violations] indicates that the guy has a problem, and he is, he is sick. There is no question of that. I am not sitting here and saying he isn't sick. ... [But] he is dangerous, and that is why I stand up before this Court and ask for the maximum. Not because he is sick. I might feel sorry for him. I don't, but I might. But he is dangerously sick....

The record the prosecutor referred to included two convictions for disorderly conduct, and a conviction in 1953 for being a Peeping Tom.

The bartender's testimony about Radziwil's behavior, of which this is only a small sample, was apparently persuasive enough to convince the trial judge that Radziwil was *unforgettably* obnoxious and quarrelsome. When the question arose at trial whether Radziwil's drinking practices were regular enough to qualify as habit, the trial judge reasoned that the bartender's testimony that Radziwil's invariable proclivity to become loud and quarrelsome lent credence to the bartender's claim that he remembered that Radziwil got drunk almost every weekend over a period of four years. The judge said:

> And it was interesting to note when [the bartender] said I can't forget him. That clearly means and adds credibility to the fact that he does remember this particular defendant. And when I asked him why you can't forget him, he said because he's drunk and he always becomes obnoxious, etcetera, and so I remember him. He said you can't forget people like that.

Indeed, Radziwil's own lawyers seemed to see him as an obnoxious drunkard. In an interview on November 25, 2004, one of Radziwil's appellate lawyers said, "You have to remember that this was a long time ago and there's not much that I remember. What I do remember is that he was a terrible drunk."

The people participating in Radziwil's trial saw him not only as an obnoxious person or chronic drunkard; they also saw Radziwil as a dangerous menace. The trial judge made both formal findings and side comments to this effect.

The view that Radziwil was a menace is not unsupported by evidence. In addition to the accident for which he was tried, Radziwil was by his own admission an alcoholic, and by 1984 Radziwil's driver's license had been suspended for 22 years for driving while intoxicated, a result of six convictions for driving while intoxicated, and neither the suspensions nor the convictions prevented him from driving.

Yet until the Cote's accident Radziwil had either been a very lucky or a safe driver. At a sentencing hearing he told the trial judge:

> I never make accident for all my life. I drive since 1947. I never make one accident with another car, me.

This seems to have been the truth. Although the government's pretrial investigation established that Petro Radziwil had been convicted six times for driving while intoxicated and had had his license suspended, the state uncovered no evidence that contradicted Radziwil's claim that before November 25, 1984, he had never been involved in an automobile accident. Petro Radziwil, despite his abuse of alcohol, had apparently driven a motor vehicle for 37 years–32 years in the U.S. and five years in post-war Germany—without being involved in even a fender-bender. Until the automobile collision on November 25, 1984, Radziwil was seemingly a safer-than-average driver.

But at the trial no one even mentioned Radziwil's accident-free driving record, and only Radziwil noted it at a sentencing hearing. The hypothesis that Radziwil had been a dangerous driver, and would remain one if not locked up, seems to have been accepted as following inexorably from his drinking history. Despite Radziwil's protestations, no one seems to have wondered whether he really was more dangerous than an ordinary driver. Our association between drunken driving and unsafe driving is so strong that the judge, lawyers and jurors in this case took it as a received truth.

### 8.   Is There a Devil in This Detail?

Since Radziwil's aggravated manslaughter conviction turned on the testimony of Bernie D'Zurella, it turned on D'Zurella's credibility. Radziwil's counsel and D'Zurella had the following exchange:

Q.  Do you know who Mr. Radziwil was with on November 24, 1984?

A.  No, when he comes into Rova he's usually by himself. . . .

Q.  So he doesn't bring a friend?

A.  He hangs around, there is a bunch of—I don't know how to put it, but a bunch of bums, alcoholic that hang out there too. So he hangs out with all the bums outside that I usually see him with.

Q.  Radziwil is a bum, you mean he's a bum?

Mr. Fagen [prosecutor]: Judge.

THE COURT: Sustained.

A bit later the following exchange took place:

Q.  He's a pain, you said?

A.  Yes, very much.

Q.  You didn't like him?

A.  I liked him.

Q.  You liked—

A.  I had nothing against him. It's just that when you're working and something is aggravating, you know—

Q.  You used to talk to him and that was aggravating too?

A.  No, sir, it wasn't aggravating.

What should the jury make of this? D'Zurella's distaste for Radziwil is plain; indeed, from his description of Radziwil's behavior he seems to have detested him. How could he say he liked him? One might think that contradictions like this would shatter D'Zurella's credibility.

There were other inconsistencies and ambiguities in D'Zurella's testimony that should have raised alarm bells about D'Zurella's credibility. A cloud of inconsistencies and ambiguities enveloped D'Zurella's testimony about the time he closed the bar on November 24 and about the time he left Rova Farms that night. For example, at the 1987 trial D'Zurella testified that he did not remember seeing Radziwil at Rova Farms during the evening[5] of November 24, 1984, and he denied having any recollection of seeing Radziwil in an intoxicated state on November 24, 1984. D'Zurella further testified that on November 24—a Saturday— he closed the Rova Farms bar between 5:30 and 6:00 p.m. (on a Saturday night!) and that he left Rova Farms that night between 6:30 and 7:30 p.m. On cross-examination D'Zurella backtracked somewhat on this last point and testified that he left "[a]t nine, ten o'clock." Yet later in the trial he amended his testimony further by saying that he left "give or take a little time, 8:30 to eight thirtyish, eight, something around there."

There was good reason for the jury to question D'Zurella's credibility.[6] But the jury rejected whatever doubts it had. Given what D'Zurella had told the jurors about Radziwil's "habits" and the view that drinking behavior gave them of Radziwil, inconsistencies and ambiguities in D'Zurella's testimony seemed of little moment even though D'Zurella's word was all they had to establish Radziwil's behavior on the night in question.

### 9.  Obnoxious Drunks and Good Kids

Daleston Cote and Keith MacCormack were 18 and 17 years old, respectively, at the time of Keith's death; physically speaking, they were

---

[5] However, apparently to the prosecutor's surprise, D'Zurella testified that he *did* remember seeing Radziwil at the Rova Farms during the *day*; he testified that the prosecutor's reference to the Saturday following Thanksgiving "kind of recalls it [that Saturday] into my memory." The prosecutor responded, "I mean you wouldn't be able to say that definitely Mr. Radziwil was there on that particular day, would you?," but D'Zurella replied, "I think he was in there [in the bar at Rova Farms]." (Nonetheless, D'Zurella testified that he did not remember seeing Radziwil at Rova Farms in the evening of November 24th.)

[6] Given D'Zurella's testimony about the time he closed the bar, the jury, if it had been thinking carefully, might well have wondered how it was possible that Radziwil was intoxicated at 2:00 a.m. on the following morning, a full eight hours after the closing of the Rova Farms bar. But this reasonable question and doubt may have been defused by D'Zurella's testimony that liquor could be purchased elsewhere on the Rova Farms premises, even after the closing of the Rova Farms bar. This last piece of testimony, however, left the question of what D'Zurella could have meant when he testified (several times) that he was the *only* bartender at Rova Farms. This puzzle was never explored by defense counsel.

in the prime of their lives. Radziwil was not in the prime of his life in the 1980s. He was 62 years old when the fatal collision occurred, 64 years old when his case for criminal homicide came to trial, and 66 years old when he was re-sentenced in 1989. Radziwil spoke broken English, and suffered from black lung disease. He would die on July 10, 1994.

The physical contrast at trial between the 64 year old Radziwil and the 20 year old Daleston Cote must have been stark. The difference between Radziwil's appearance and the image the jury had of the deceased Keith MacCormack must have seemed equally great. At the trial the jury was told that Keith was 17 years old at the time of his death. The trial judge, the prosecutor, and some witnesses repeatedly referred to Keith either as a "young man" or "young boy." Evidence presented at the trial revealed that Keith was six feet tall and weighed 180 pounds at the time of his death. Although Radziwil did not testify at his trial, Radziwil must have made a much less favorable impression on the jury. By the time of his trial Radziwil was almost certainly the chronic drunkard he had been portrayed as being and had been for some years. Surely his drinking had taken a heavy physical toll. An appellate lawyer for Radziwil recalled in November of 2004, "You have to know that everyone believed that Radziwil was guilty and a drunk. He was poor and downright near being homeless from what I remember. Everyone wanted and would have liked to see him found guilty."

Although the prosecution succeeded in portraying Radziwil as a quarrelsome and dangerous drunkard, Radziwil was not without redeeming features. But most of Radziwil's favorable qualities came out only after the trial, in the two sentencing hearings that followed the trial. For example, in one of the sentencing hearings there was evidence that Radziwil, whether an alcoholic or not, had worked hard and had supported himself without interruption for decades. Even the trial judge had to concede that Radziwil was a conscientious worker. Furthermore, Radziwil apparently revered his parents. In the second sentencing hearing Radziwil seemed as concerned with defending his parents from what he thought were accusations in the press as he was with defending his own behavior:

> Something never talking over here in the court, because I have about after two months in the jail, paper [newspaper?] make alcoholic my father, mother, all relationship [relatives?]. My alcoholic. And I am, too.

> My father never smoke, never drink a glass of beer all his life and he died 1946. Mother die in 1940. They now make you mother and father alcoholic.

. . .

Put in [news]paper. My father—I say in his life I never seen him where I live with him when he drink glass of beer. He never smoke. Never drink. That's it. Yeah.

Radziwil clearly believed that the press had insinuated that his parents had been drunkards and he tried to defend the honor of his long-dead parents. (It is also clear that Radziwil had a limited command of English, could not communicate clearly, and had little capacity to defend himself in a forum as foreign as a court of law, even in an informal sentencing hearing.)

Even some of the evidence presented at the trial suggests that Radziwil was not as obnoxious as the Rova Farms bartender would have had people believe. Although the bartender called Radziwil's drinking companions "bums" and "alcoholics," Radziwil was at least sociable enough to have drinking companions. Furthermore, Radziwil seems to have had a "girl friend": D'Zurella—the Rova Farms bartender—testified that Radziwil's girl friend sometimes stayed overnight at Rova Farms with Radziwil.

Evidence from an unlikely source also suggests that the unfavorable picture painted in 1987 of Radziwil's character was an exaggeration. Michael Schottland, a New Jersey trial lawyer, represented Keith MacCormack's mother Elizabeth MacCormack in a wrongful death action she brought against Rova Farms. Schottland was present during the taking of Radziwil's deposition in East Jersey State Prison in 1991, along with Rova Farm's counsel and an interpreter. In an interview on July 6, 2005, Schottland said that although Radziwil was bitter about having been imprisoned, his manner was pleasantly "Eastern European," even "courtly." Schottland added that he thought that the trial judge, Judge Ricciardi, had given Radziwil an excessively harsh sentence.

If the arrows thrown at Radziwil in his 1987 trial were too sharp, perhaps more arrows should have been directed at Daleston Cote and Keith MacCormack. Stripped of the patina of youth, the behavior of Daleston Cote and Keith MacCormack on the night of November 24 and 25, 1984, was in one respect very similar to the behavior that Radziwil was said to have routinely engaged in at Rova Farms: On the night of the fatal collision—the night of November 24, 1984—Daleston Cote and Keith MacCormack had gone drinking with their buddies.

Just before the collision that killed Keith MacCormack, Daleston's car was stopped on Route 537, apparently in preparation for a left hand turn, a sharp left turn of approximately 140°. (See FIGURE 1.) The time was approximately 2:00 a.m. What was Daleston's car doing on Route 537 at that time of night? Where were Daleston and Keith going? Where were they coming from? Some of the answers to these questions are known. Daleston testified that when his car was hit from behind he and

Keith were on their way to Keith's house. They had left the house of a friend, Eric Wallace, another teenager, at 12:30 a.m. After leaving Wallace's house, they had gone to look for a fast food restaurant, Daleston testified. Not finding one open, they had gone to the house of another friend, Darren. Not finding Darren home—or not being able to rouse Darren from his slumbers—Daleston and Keith decided that Daleston should drive Keith home. They were on their way to Keith's house when the accident happened.

Daleston also told the jury that he and Keith had been at a small party at the home of a teenage friend, Eric Wallace, from 8:00 p.m. on, and he admitted that alcohol had been consumed there. In his original statement to the police, however, Daleston had denied that he had been at the Wallace party. Later—at the trial in 1987—he explained his lie to the police by saying that he had not wanted to get his friend Eric into trouble, particularly since Eric's father was a clergyman. Daleston further testified that he did not know if Keith had drunk any alcohol at Eric Wallace's party and that he himself had not been drinking.

Daleston's denial that he had been drinking does not ring true. The police officer who arrived at the scene of the automobile collision at approximately 2:15 in the morning of November 25 testified that when he interviewed Daleston at the scene of the collision he smelled alcohol on Daleston's breath. After Daleston was taken to the hospital the same officer testified that he took a sample of Daleston's blood. This was done at approximately 3:30 a.m. A test on the sample showed that Daleston's blood alcohol content (BAC) was .035%. Daleston wanted the jury to believe that the source of his BAC was three seven ounce "nips" of Budweiser that he had drunk the night before at 7:00 p.m., but consumption of 21 ounces of beer could not possibly account for a BAC of .035% eight-and-one-half hours later. The conclusion that Daleston had been drinking at Eric Wallace's party and then lied about his drinking is almost inescapable. Keith MacCormack had also almost certainly been drinking at Eric Wallace's house. A test on a blood sample extracted from Keith's corpse during an autopsy showed a BAC of .07% according to the testimony of the examining pathologist. Neither Daleston nor Keith were old enough to drink legally in New Jersey at the time, nor was Eric Wallace who hosted the party, for the drinking age in new Jersey at the time was 21.

If Daleston perjured himself when he lied about his drinking behavior at his friend's party, might he also have lied about the circumstances of the accident? Would any such perjury, for example, raise doubts about Daleston's contested assertion at the trial that his left-hand turn signal was on while he was waiting to turn left? Of course it would. But although Radziwil's trial counsel did touch on one or two of the inconsistencies in Daleston Cote's statements about his drinking and Keith's drinking on the night of the accident, Radziwil's counsel mentioned those inconsistencies only in passing, and he did not mount a serious challenge to Daleston Cote's credibility by emphasizing and exploring the varied ways in which Daleston might have lied about his and Keith's drinking behavior. We may never know what motivated Radziwil's counsel to try the case as he did. But it is possible that character images—images of the character of Daleston Cote, Keith MacCormack, and Petro Radziwil—led (or misled) Radziwil's counsel to pull his punches during his cross-examination of Daleston Cote.

During the criminal proceedings against Radziwil there emerged starkly asymmetrical images of Radziwil, on the one hand, and Cote and MacCormack, on the other hand. Yet Radziwil may not have been a worthless alcoholic bum and Daleston Cote and Keith MacCormack may not have been exemplary young men. The generally-favorable images of Daleston Cote and Keith MacCormack probably made the unfavorable image of Petro Radziwil more intense. The starkly-unfavorable image of Radziwil darkened the heart of at least one key participant in the criminal proceedings against Radziwil and it probably clouded the judgment of at least one other important actor.

### 10.   The Trial Judge and Mr. Radziwil

In pretrial argument about Radziwil's counsel's unsuccessful demand for a nonjury trial the prosecutor said:

> But the big argument, as I hear it now, it's not going to be on your [the judge's] mind, the big argument then [for a bench trial] is a jury would be inflamed. And I submit to the Court that a jury is not going to be inflamed by the proofs of this case any more than it would be in any other criminal case and certainly not anymore than a court would. Thank you.

The prosecutor's words were unwittingly prophetic.

*The trial judge proclaims the irrelevance of Auschwitz*

During the sentencing process, probably in speaking to the probation officer who prepared the presentence report, Radziwil claimed that he had been sent to Auschwitz because of an unsuccessful effort to save a family—possibly a Jewish family—from persecution by the Nazis.

Judge Ricciardi's response to Radziwil's claim of having done a heroic act in the face of Nazi oppression was curt. He said:

> The fact that at some point in 1943 [Radziwil] may have extended a hand to some family for which he received [from the Nazis], he says, a requirement that he work in a prison factory [Auschwitz] in Germany [sic], the fact that that occurred in 1943, does not in this Court's opinion, constitute a mitigating factor. That is a long time

ago and there is no indication as to the extent that he gave whatever help he says he gave, what that help was at all.

At his trial for criminal homicide Radziwil had been portrayed as a quarrelsome and worthless drunkard. At his second sentencing hearing he tried to challenge this devastating picture of his character by showing that he had at least done one extraordinarily good thing in an otherwise possibly worthless life. His attempt was dismissed out of hand. Discredited characters are not easily rehabilitated.

*The trial judge and Radziwil experience a failure of communication*

As is evident from Radziwil's attempt to defend his parents' character discussed above, Radziwil may have had trouble understanding English, and he clearly had trouble speaking understandable English. Consider a further example, this one taken from a pretrial hearing to determine the admissibility of statements made by Radziwil to the police. Radziwil testified as follows:

Q. [by prosecutor] Do you remember the police ever telling you had certain rights in connection with not taking the breathalyzer [after stops or arrests prior to 1984], do you remember that?

A. [by Radziwil] Yes, I take it.

Q. Did you ever refuse to make it, did you ever refuse to take the breathalyzer?

A. In Jackson [New Jersey] when I was asleep there about three hundred feet when this man and wife, I come to him and the police right from me, I go left, police—They come, stop, you drink. I say no. I say like this—

THE REPORTER: Your Honor, I don't understand the witness.

THE COURT: Neither can I.

A. Makes a ticket, I refuse.

Q. Refused to take the breathalyzer. Didn't they tell—did they read you rights before you refused to take the breathalyzer?

A. I never saying I never drunk; I say I stayed on one feet. The police make refuse.

Despite Radziwil's obvious difficulty in communicating, neither Judge Ricciardi nor Radziwil's counsel ever moved to provide an interpreter. The trial judge saw no need: at one point he said that Radziwil was only pretending to have difficulty understanding and speaking English and that Radziwil was a "faker." Whether counsel failed to move for an interpreter because he shared this view, we do not know. Certainly much of Radziwil's testimony at pretrial and sentencing hearings suggests language difficulties rather than trickery, for it is hard to see what Radziwil could gain by failing to get his points across. And when a civil action was later brought against Rova Farms, the lawyer for Rova Farms saw the need for an interpreter. It may be that the judge's image of Radziwil as an obnoxious drunkard shaped his view of why Radziwil spoke English poorly, or it may be that Radziwil's poor English reinforced the image of an obnoxious drunkard; or both or neither of these conjectures may be true. Whatever the situation, Radziwil got no sympathy from the trial judge, and Radziwil may have failed to fully understand the testimony against him and to communicate everything he knew that might have supported his defense.

### The trial judge punishes Radziwil

After the jury found Radziwil guilty of aggravated manslaughter, Judge Ricciardi sentenced Radziwil to imprisonment for twenty years, the maximum allowable sentence for the crime that Radziwil was found to have committed. The trial judge also ordered that Radziwil be ineligible for parole for ten years, the maximum permissible period of parole ineligibility under the then applicable New Jersey law. This sentence was imposed in 1987 when Radziwil was 64 years old. Although the Appellate Division of the Superior Court of New Jersey (and, later, the Supreme Court of New Jersey) affirmed Radziwil's conviction for aggravated manslaughter, the Appellate Division vacated the sentence, finding that Judge Ricciardi had erred in his findings of aggravating factors. However, Judge Ricciardi, on remand, did not accept the Appellate Division's strong hint that a twenty year sentence for Radziwil was excessive: He again imposed a sentence of twenty years imprisonment, and he again ordered that Radziwil be ineligible for parole for ten years.[7]

## 11.  A Civil Action

On November 14, 1986, Elizabeth MacCormack commenced a civil action for the wrongful death of her son Keith MacCormack. The named defendants were Petra [sic] Radziwil; Rova Farms; Deleston [sic] Cote, Jr.; Jan Cote, the owner of the car that Daleston Cote was driving on November 25, 1984; and Barbara Castor, the hapless driver who slammed into the car that had been pushed by a hit-and-run driver into her lane. The MacCormack complaint averred that (i) Radziwil's negligent and drunken driving contributed to Keith MacCormack's death; (ii) Rova Farms and its employees contributed to Keith's wrongful death by serving alcoholic beverages to Radziwil after he was visibly intoxicated; and (iii) Daleston Cote, Jr., and Jane Cote contributed to Keith's wrongful death as a result of their negligent operation and maintenance of the motor vehicle that Daleston was driving. Radziwil's answer to the complaint denied that Radziwil was intoxicated and it denied that

---

[7] Radziwil did have the services of an interpreter at the second sentencing hearing.

Radziwil was involved in the collision. In a deposition taken in East Jersey State Prison in 1991 Radziwil testified that he had not been involved in the collision on the night of November 25, 1984. In their answers to the complaint Radziwil and the other defendants responded in part by averring that Keith MacCormack's own negligence had caused his death. Radziwil's answer contained a cross-claim that averred that Daleston and Jan Cote's negligence had been a contributing cause of Keith MacCormack's death. Radziwil's insurer settled with Keith's mother, Elizabeth MacCormack, prior to trial for $15,000. Rova Farms settled with Elizabeth MacCormack for $110,000 after plaintiff's counsel wrung a concession out of D'Zurella, the Rova Farms bartender in 1984, that he had closed the bar at Rova Farms not at 5:30 or 6:00 p.m.—as he had testified at the criminal trial—but sometime thereafter; he did remember seeing Radziwil at Rova Farms that night; and he did remember seeing Radziwil at Rova Farms in an intoxicated state that night. The Rova farms bartender, however, persisted in asserting that he had not served Radziwil any alcohol that night.

What's important about the civil action is not the claims made or the result, but the differences between the evidence that was developed in the civil action and the evidence that was submitted in the criminal case. One wonders whether Radziwil was perjuring himself when he swore he was not involved in the collision, whether he was telling the truth or whether his memory of the accident was a blank. One also wonders how the jury in the criminal case would have reacted had Radziwil's counsel made a more forceful argument that Daleston's drinking or negligence contributed to the accident, and one wonders whether D'Zurella's changed recollections would have affected anything. One also wonders how difficult it was for defense counsel to wring concessions from D'Zurella during the criminal proceedings against Radziwil, criminal proceedings that took place when D'Zurella might have been sued under New Jersey's dram shop law but wasn't, and when D'Zurella was already cooperating with Mrs. MaCormack's counsel.

## 12. Loose Ends

Once the Rova Farms bartender had given his testimony in Radziwil's 1987 trial for aggravated manslaughter, it seemed apparent to practically everyone that Petro Radziwil was a dangerous drunk whose drunken driving had killed a young man. Janet Flanagan, a deputy attorney general for New Jersey, later told the New Jersey Supreme Court that the Rova Farms bartender saw Radziwil drunk more than 200 times. In the criminal proceedings against Radziwil for criminal homicide the minds and energies of the professional actors—the prosecutor, the trial judge, and the defense counsel—were concentrated on Radziwil's recurring drinking behavior. It is possible that this preoccupation with Radziwil's chronic drinking and drunk driving not only hardened the trial judge's heart but also diverted the judge, defense counsel, and jury from other matters bearing on Radziwil's culpability.

There was evidence and discussion at trial about the possibility that Daleston Cote's left-turn signal was not blinking as he waited to turn at the intersection of Route 537 and Paint Island Spring Road, and there was evidence and discussion about the possibility that the headlights and taillights of the Daleston Cote car had not been on. But beyond this, no one really explored the possibility that the accident might have been caused by a sober driver. Route 537 and Paint Island Spring Road meet at a dangerous intersection. An investigation conducted in 2004 by Cardozo Law School students, one of whom had professional experience as a traffic and road engineer, indicated that because of the changing slope of Route 537 as it approaches Paint Island Spring Road, a driver in a car approaching Route 537 and Paint Island Spring Road from the west would first be able to see a car at the intersection of Route 537 and Paint Island Spring from a distance of slightly more than 200 feet.

Looking southwest on Route 537 from the intersection of Route 537 and Paint Island Spring Road

FIGURE 4

The speed limit on Route 537 was 50 miles per hour in 1984. If the line-of-sight measurements that the Cardozo student investigators made are approximately correct, a sober driver traveling east on Route 537 at 50 m.p.h. might not have been able to react quickly enough and brake forcefully enough to bring his car to a stop without hitting a car parked in the eastbound lane of Route 537 at Paint Island Spring Road. This would be almost certainly true if it were dark and the car at the intersection did not have its lights on. Moreover, the photograph in FIGURE 4 suggests—and evidence introduced at the trial and measurements by student investigators in 2004 confirm—that the shoulder at the intersection on Route 537 was not wide enough to allow a car to avoid a collision by passing on the right.

Thus the driver of the hit-and-run car may have been sober. It is, furthermore, arguable—though not beyond doubt—that even if the driver of the hit-and-run car was intoxicated, the intoxicated state of the hit-and-run driver was not a contributing cause of the death of Keith MacCormack in the sense that the accident and Keith MacCormack's death would have resulted regardless of the driver's insobriety.

*Was Radziwil really the driver of the hit-and-run car?*

The case against Radziwil proceeded on the assumption that Radziwil was driving the vehicle that caused the accident. The Appellate Division said that there was "overwhelming" evidence that Radziwil was the driver of the hit-and-run vehicle and noted that Radziwil's trial lawyer "virtually conceded" during closing argument that Radziwil was the driver. Indeed, Radziwil's trial lawyer gave up on this question long before that. Before the trial began, he told the trial judge, "I think quite frankly the State will be able to prove there was an accident with [Radziwil's] vehicle."

But Radziwil steadfastly denied being the driver of the hit-and-run car. Radziwil's protestations that he was "not there" apparently puzzled his own lawyers and was not believed by his trial counsel. In Radziwil's second sentencing hearing the following exchange took place:

THE COURT: ... Ask [Mr. Radziwil] if there's anything he would like to say to me before I sentence him. ...

INTERPRETER: He says—he said he doesn't know what you want him to say and that he's just stating that he doesn't know of the accident. And what he said before then, it wasn't him.

He just said that his lawyer told him that he would answer all the questions and the only thing that he would get is probation. That's what he was told by his attorney at that time.

And then he said that his lawyer said that he was driving and he wasn't allowed to speak.

Is it possible that Radziwil was telling the truth and that he was not the driver of the hit-and-run vehicle?

At first sight this hardly seems possible, for Carl Hobson seemed to have nailed this issue for the government when a part he had saved from his front end work and given to the police—a "small support piece"— yard precisely matched a section of a broken plastic grill that the Freehold Township police had retrieved at the accident scene. However, Hobson's story, though not implausible, raises questions that perhaps should have precipitated some investigative activity. One might, for example, wonder why Carl Hobson was moved to save the damaged body parts that he said he removed from his Olds 88.9[8] In 2004 a student investigator from Cardozo Law School was interested in this very question and called Carl Hobson's listed phone number in Jackson, New Jersey. The man who answered identified himself as Carl Hobson. When asked about the parts he said, according to the student, that he had not given the Freehold Township Police any parts from an Olds 88. When the student called the same number the next day, the phone was not answered but there was a message from the phone company saying the number was out of service.

On another occasion another a Cardozo Law School student who was investigating a different issue related to the case received a telephone call from a person claiming to be a police officer with the Freehold Township Police Department. This caller told the student investigator, "You better stop looking for [the police report] or you'll find yourself in a whole pile of shit." A few hours later the same person called again and apologized for his earlier call, explaining that he had thought that the student was investigating something else. (This intrepid student investigator was not intrepid enough to ask the police officer what that "something else" was.)

What was going on? If Hobson did not give any parts from the Olds to the police, only one explanation seems possible: The police found both the support piece and the piece it matched at the accident scene, the police persuaded Hobson to testify that he had turned the support piece over to the police, and at trial the matching pieces were offered as conclusive evidence of Radziwil's involvement. Accusations of such seri-

---

[8] An investigation in 2004 suggested that at one point Carl Hobson's property had a garage with room for 21 cars. Perhaps Hobson dealt with junk cars or was in the business of repairing cars and for this reason saved old auto parts. But this possible explanation for Hobson's discovery of old car body parts in his back yard was moot at the trial—because at trial Radziwil's counsel did not suggest there was anything suspicious about Hobson's supposed discovery.

ous prosecutorial and police misconduct—perjury and subornation of perjury—are often made but rarely true. However, when police or prosecutors are convinced they have the right person but a weak case such actions are not unheard of. We will never know if such misconduct occurred here. But whether or not such misconduct did occur, the possibility that the trial judge and counsel were too quick to dismiss Radziwil's claim that he was not the driver involved in the collision is a real one. Of course, even if there was a frame-up here, a guilty man may have been framed. Furthermore, even if Radziwil genuinely believed that he was not involved in an automobile collision on November 25, 1984, Radziwil may have been guilty: A severely-intoxicated person can easily forget what happened when he was drunk.

### 13.   Habit and Character[9]

"Character," McCormick wrote "is a generalized description of a person's disposition, or of the disposition in respect to a general trait, such as honesty, temperance or peacefulness. Habit.... denotes one's regular response to a [specific] situation. If we speak of a character for care, we speak of the person's tendency to act prudently in all the varying situations of life.... A habit, on the other hand, is the person's regular practice of responding to a particular kind of situation with a specific type of conduct.... The doing of habitual acts may become semi-automatic, as with the driver who invariably signals before changing lanes."[10]

Was Radziwil's purported practice of going to Rova Farms on weekends and drinking until drunk a description of his character or a habit? In fact, it seems neither. It does not describe a generalized attitude or an aspect of personality nor does it seem to be a feature of Radziwil's persona that applies generally across situations. But it is equally hard to characterize Radziwil's drinking practices as a habit, at least as McCormick uses the term. There is no reason to think that Radziwil's drinking was semi-automatic behavior that hardly crossed the threshold of consciousness in the way flicking a turn signal may be, nor does it seem that when Radziwil visited Rova farms something about the scenery or company there impelled him to respond by drinking when he would not have drunk if he were sitting with his bottle at some other location. Yet the New Jersey courts felt compelled to choose, and they chose to call Radziwil's drinking behavior a habit. They probably felt compelled to choose because the dominant view treats traits like alcoholism and drug addiction as if they were traits of character, and does not

---

[9] I am indebted to Rick Lempert for many helpful suggestions, but I am particularly indebted to him for his extensive suggestions for this section of my paper.

[10] McCormick § 195 (5th Ed. 1999 J.W. Strong, ed.).

allow a factfinder to infer drinking behavior or drug use on a specific occasion simply from the fact of addiction. The alcoholic is, after all, often sober; and the drug user only intermittently gets high. Only by treating Radziwil's Saturday night drinking behavior as habit, seeing in its week after week repetition the same guarantee of behavior on the night in question that one gets from knowing that the driver who changed lanes has in the past always used his turn signal, could the court reconcile admitting this seemingly probative evidence with its past precedents.

But we need not be imprisoned by old dichotomies and need not characterize Radziwil's drinking as either character or habit. Rather we can see it for what it was; namely,—if the bartender is to be believed—regular behavior reflecting a serious addiction, behavior so regular that if Radziwil was at Rova Farms the night of the accident he is unlikely not to have been drinking. This is true even if we suspect that no matter where Radziwil was on a Saturday night it is likely he was drinking. The evidence is thus relevant, and not just relevant but in all likelihood highly probative of Radziwil's behavior, and so presumptively admissible. In this sense, it is like habit after all.

But the evidence about Radziwil's drinking practices is like character in an important respect. The law is wary of character evidence not just because it is often of low probative value, but also because it may produce verdicts motivated by bad reasons: The miser may be found guilty of embezzlement not because he embezzled but because he is a miser, or the ruffian may be found guilty of assault not because he attacked the victim in the case but because the jury is convinced that he has surely at some time attacked someone. Radziwil may have been found guilty of aggravated manslaughter not because he was clearly drunk—beyond a reasonable doubt—when he hit Daleston Cote's car or even because it is certain that he did hit Cote's car, but rather because it is easy to imagine someone like him hitting some car while drunk and killing someone.

Classic habit evidence, on the other hand, rarely excites passions or clouds judgment. Always using a turn signal, or taking two stairs at a time, or turning to the obituaries first, or having a cigarette after sex may elicit approval or disapproval, but it will rarely lead to a positive or negative judgment of a whole person. Rather it keeps attention focused on the likelihood the action in question occurred as one party says it did, which, in a trial, is where attention is supposed to be. In calling Radziwil's Saturday night drinking at Rova Farms a habit, the courts that passed on its admissibility assimilated it to a category where prejudice is ordinarily not an issue.

Ironically, the very relevance of Radziwil's drinking behavior may have made it more prejudicial than ordinary prejudicial but marginally relevant character evidence. The probative value of Radziwil's Saturday night drinking routine demanded attention; it was at the center of the prosecutor's case, and its centrality in the case may have made it seem central to Radziwil's personality. Certainly no one saw Radziwil as a courtly European gentleman, as a hard worker, a possible holocaust hero, or someone who loved his parents and was concerned with their reputations even after they were in their graves. The trial judge's words to Radziwil and his sentencing decisions suggest he saw only evil in Radziwil, and Radziwil's attorney may have been blinded to possible weaknesses in the state's case by his view that his client was the kind of person who committed the crime with which he had been charged. Trials are trials of human beings. Judges, jurors and attorneys are going to judge the merits of the people they confront regardless of what the law provides. Evidence law can and does try to refocus actors' attention to what happened in the case. But when highly probative evidence is also highly prejudicial, separating judgments of what happened from judgments of the people involved is often an impossible task.

Was justice done in Radziwil's case? With respect to the sentence he received, probably not. With respect to his involvement in the collision and his insobriety at the time, perhaps yes, but we will never know. Given who Radziwil was, it may be that the trial judge, the prosecutor, the jurors, and the police would not even care.

### Epilogue

Petro Radziwil died before completing his prison sentence. He died on July 10, 1994. He was 72 years old.

Judge John Ricciardi died on March 23, 2000. His obituary stated:

In surveys conducted by the Law Journal in 1993 and 1999, lawyers who practiced before Ricciardi graded him high in case-management and courtroom efficiency but low in demeanor, that is, in how he treated lawyers and litigants. His demeanor rating in last year's survey—2.83 on a 1-to-5 scale—was the lowest in Monmouth County and the sixth lowest of all judges in the state.[11]

A second judge, who ruled against Radziwil in the New Jersey Supreme Court, had his own story:

Call it a quirk in scheduling or a twist of fate, but on Oct. 23—a year to the day after he began a one-year recusal from sitting on drunken

---

[11] Maria Armental, Ricciardi, *Stern but Efficient Judge in Monmouth County, Dies at 61*, New Jersey Law Journal (April 3, 2000).

driving cases—State Supreme Court Justice Robert Clifford was back in the driver's seat.

Clifford sat on a case involving the admissibility of evidence that the defendant is a habitual drinker, [the Radziwil case]. . . .

Last October, Clifford was stopped by Princeton Borough police for driving 46 miles an hour in a 35–mile-an-hour zone. At a hearing on Oct. 23, 1989, Clifford apologized for driving while intoxicated and refusing to take a Breathalyzer test, and volunteered to recuse himself from cases involving driving-while-intoxicated or related charges for at least the year that his driver's license was suspended. He also said that he would avoid drinking.[12]

Fortunately Justice Clifford never killed anyone, and the admissibility of evidence about his drinking was never an issue.

---

[12] Suzanne Riss, *Boy That Year Went Fast*, New Jersey Law Journal p. 6 (November 1, 1990).

*

# 3

## *United States v. Woods*: A Story of The Triumph of Tradition

### Edward J. Imwinkelried

Paul Woods was barely eight months old when he died. At the time of his death, he was a foster child in the care of Mrs. Martha Woods, the wife of an Army sergeant. The Woods' home on Aberdeen Proving Ground, a federal reservation, was Paul's second foster placement. He had spent the first five months of his life with one foster family, and during that period he never suffered any breathing problems. However, shortly after he was moved to the Woods' home, he mysteriously began experiencing breathing difficulties. Paul was initially treated at Kirk Army Hospital, transferred to Walter Reed, but later entered The Johns Hopkins Hospital where he eventually died. Paul had suffered a fatal cyanotic episode—he stopped breathing. The question was why he had stopped breathing. One possibility was that someone—perhaps Martha— was guilty of smothering him to death. Another possibility, though, was that he suffocated because of some unknown disease. The year was 1969, and the expression, "sudden infant death syndrome," had just been coined.[1] None of the physicians at Kirk, Walter Reed, or Johns Hopkins had been able to pinpoint a cause of death. However, even in 1969 physicians realized that unexplained deaths, particularly among the very young, can occur.

But Dr. Vincent DiMaio did not think that Paul's death was acciden- tal. Rather, after studying the case, DiMaio became convinced that Paul had been murdered. Dr. DiMaio was someone to be reckoned with. In 1970, his opinion helped convince a federal grand jury to indict Martha

---

[1] According to J. B. Beckwith, *Defining Sudden Infant Death Syndrome*, 157 Arch.Pe- diatr.Adolesc.Med. 286–90 (2003), a definition of SIDS was first adopted by the Second International Conference on the Causes of Death in Infants in 1969. *See also* Candus Thomson, *Perspective*, The Baltimore Sun, Aug. 8, 1999, at 1C ("The term SIDS was coined in 1969 . . . .").

Woods for Paul's murder.[2] DiMaio's medical education included an M.D. from S.U.N.Y. Medical Center, a pathology internship at Duke University Hospital, a pathology residency at the Kings County Medical Center in Brooklyn, and a forensic pathology fellowship at the Office of the Maryland Chief Medical Examiner. During a good part of the investigation in *Woods,* Dr. DiMaio was a major in the Army Medical Corps, assigned to the Armed Force Institute of Pathology, in Washington, D.C. By 1972, the date of the trial in *Woods,* he had had seven years of specialized training in pathology and had established himself as one of the country's leading forensic pathologists. His testimony had figured prominently in several homicide trials and had been instrumental in putting many of those defendants behind bars for murder.

DiMaio was—and is[3]—a credit to his profession. He was no prosecution hack. While he believed that Paul Woods had been murdered, his testimony at the 1972 trial was blunt and honest. Dr. DiMaio acknowledged that he could not be certain that Paul's death was homicidal. He was also willing to quantify his uncertainty; he testified that although there was a 75% chance that someone had smothered Paul to death, there remained a 25% chance that the cause of death was some unknown disease. He even went to the length of conceding that the forensic evidence alone did not prove Martha's guilt beyond a reasonable doubt!

Given that concession, if DiMaio's testimony had been the prosecution's only evidence, Martha Woods might never have stood trial. Even if his testimony alone had been enough to persuade the federal grand jury to file charges, in all probability the defense would have won a dismissal at the conclusion of the prosecution case-in-chief; as a matter of law, it would have been clear that no rational jury could find Martha guilty beyond a reasonable doubt. The prosecution desperately needed other evidence to corroborate DiMaio's opinion. The defendant's background seemed to furnish compelling evidence.

As a military dependent, Martha Woods lived on Aberdeen Proving Ground. She had qualified as a foster parent in the Maryland system. Paul was not the first child placed in Martha's custody. For 25 years, in one way or another, she had been taking care of children, both her own as well as the children of relatives and friends. According to a string of prosecution witnesses, during those 25 years, nine children—Judy Woods, Charles Stewart, Mary Huston, Carol Huston, John Wise, Lilly

---

[2] United States v. Woods, 484 F.2d 127 (4th Cir. 1973), *cert. denied,* 415 U.S. 979 (1974).

[3] Dr. DiMaio is presently the Chief Medical Examiner for Bexar County, San Antonio, Texas. Coincidentally, as a federal inmate, Mrs. Woods was later transferred to a federal prison and, in 2002, she passed away at the Federal Medical Center Carswell in Fort Worth, Texas.

Stewart, Eddie Thomas, Marlan Rash, and Paul Sadler—had experienced at least 20 cyanotic episodes while in Martha's custody. Seven of these children had died. The case against Martha became curioser and curiouser: None of these children had suffered any cyanotic episodes while they were in a hospital away from Martha, and none of the treating physicians had been able to definitively identify a medical cause for the fatal episodes. There were too many episodes to be dismissed as mere accident, and common sense seemed to dictate that if someone was smothering these children, it was Martha. Martha seemed to be a serial killer who for some reason—perhaps anger at their crying—regularly smothered children in her care. Considering these facts, a layperson might have had no doubt that she was guilty; the only question might have been why the killings had been allowed to go on for so long. Even if a jury had been a bit skeptical after listening to DiMaio's testimony, surely the other evidence would seal Martha's fate.

In short, *Woods* should have been an easy case for the prosecution—right? Wrong! The rub was that under Anglo–American law in 1972, it was not at all clear that the testimony about the 20 other incidents was admissible against Martha. Even Martha's later appeal from her conviction occurred in 1973, two years before the Federal Rules of Evidence took effect, so the common law governed. At federal common law, the issue raised by the *Woods* case was a matter of first impression. Understanding *Woods*, and why it was a difficult case for the common law, requires a journey back to the emergence of the common law rules governing uncharged misconduct and their subsequent elaboration by American courts.

## SETTING THE STAGE FOR *WOODS*: THE CONFUSION IN THE AMERICAN LAW GOVERNING THE ADMISSIBILITY OF UNCHARGED MISCONDUCT EVIDENCE

Early English precedents such as the 1810 decision in *Rex v. Cole*[4] imposed only one restriction on the use of evidence of an accused's uncharged misconduct: The prosecution could not offer testimony of an accused's bad acts to prove the accused's bad character and then without more treat the accused's bad character as circumstantial proof that he

---

[4] Julius Stone, "The Rule of Exclusion of Similar Fact Evidence: England," 46 Harv.L.Rev. 954, 959, 961 (1933) ("Phillips, in 1914, illustrating the rule that no evidence ought to be admitted to any point other than the disputed facts or points in issue ... cites Rex v. Cole, where it was apparently held by all the judges that 'in a prosecution for an infamous crime, an admission by the prisoner that he had committed such an offence at another time and with another person and that he had a tendency to such practices, ought not to be admitted.' This brief passage in Phillips constitutes the entire report.... Rex v. Cole in 1810 established the principle that evidence which merely showed that the defendant had a propensity to do the sort of acts with which he was charged was not admissible. This is a very narrow principle of exclusion....").

was likely to have committed the charged offense.[5] As thus stated, the rule protects against several dangers. Both of these inferential steps pose significant probative risks. To begin with, if the jury is allowed decide whether to infer bad conduct from prior misdeeds, the prior bad acts may not only distract the jury's attention from the charged crime, but also revulsion at the earlier conduct may lead the jury to resolve doubt against rather than in favor of the defendant.[6] After inferring the accused's bad character, the jury must use the accused's character as proof of conduct on the charged occasion. At this second step, the jury may overvalue the testimony. Although the psychological research on the issue is now mixed, there is a strong argument that a person's general disposition or character is a poor predictor of conduct on a particular occasion. However, these dangers can be largely mooted when the prosecution has an alternative, noncharacter theory of logical relevance. Hence, according to the original, orthodox English rule, although the prosecution could not treat an accused's uncharged crimes as circumstantial proof of guilt of the charged crime, the prosecution was allowed to introduce the misconduct for any relevant, noncharacter purpose. The character evidence prohibition did not apply when the prosecutor could articulate a legitimate noncharacter theory of logical relevance.

Before 1840 the American cases dealing with the admission of uncharged misconduct evidence followed the English inclusionary approach. The American courts, for example, routinely received uncharged misconduct when it was logically relevant on a noncharacter theory to prove the accused's guilty knowledge. The rule was "inclusionary" in the sense that evidence suggesting bad character was automatically inadmissible only when it was offered for the forbidden character (or propensity) inference; any noncharacter theory was presumptively acceptable. However, in the United States, by the middle of the 19th century, this approach to character evidence began to break down. The American courts started describing the character evidence doctrine as if it were a general exclusionary rule with a limited number of exceptions.

One of the watersheds in the American law of uncharged misconduct was the New York Court of Appeals' 1901 decision in *People v. Molineux*.[7] Judge Werner authored the influential lead opinion in that case.

---

[5] Norman Krivosha, Thomas Lansworth & Pennie Pirsch, *Relevancy: The Necessary Element in Using Evidence of Other Crimes, Wrongs, or Bad Acts to Convict*, 60 Neb.L.Rev. 657, 664 (1981); Julius Stone, *Propensity Evidence in Trials for Unnatural Offenses*, 15 Aust.L.J. 131, 132 (1941).

[6] For a general review of these arguments and supporting cases and other authorities see 1 EDWARD J. IMWINKELRIED, UNCHARGED MISCONDUCT EVIDENCE (§ 2:19 (rev. 2003)).

[7] 168 N.Y. 264, 61 N.E. 286 (1901); Thomas J. Reed, READING GAOL REVISITED: ADMISSION OF UNCHARGED MISCONDUCT EVIDENCE IN SEX OFFENDER CASES, 21 Am.J.Crim.L. 127, 174 n. 265

The judge observed that the "exceptions" permitting the introduction of uncharged misconduct "cannot be stated with precision"[8] but then went on to catalogue a list of recognized "exceptions": motive, intent, absence of mistake or accident, identity, and common scheme or plan. A careful reading of Werner's opinion shows that it does not mandate the exclusionary approach. Nevertheless, his opinion gave great momentum to the exclusionary approach in the United States. By consistently describing the alternative theories of logical relevance as "exceptions," he reinforced the conception of the doctrine as a firm exclusionary rule with a finite number of exceptions, promoting the mindset, soon enshrined in the law of New York and other states, that there is a general rule of inadmissibility.

In part, *Molineux* was so influential because Judge Werner's opinion contained such an excellent collection of the published opinions that judges throughout the country had occasion to consult and cite his opinion. *Molineux* was also attractive to judges because it served to reduce the potentially difficult legal analysis to an algorithm, inspiring the widely used MIMIC mnemonic for uncharged misconduct: The evidence is admissible only to prove M(otive), I(ntent), M(istake or accident), I(dentity), or C(ommon scheme or plan). Moreover, the approach struck a responsive chord in American jurisdictions committed to the so-called rule of lenity, which mandated strict construction of penal statutes. As part of their libertarian philosophy, many American courts had announced that any ambiguity in a penal statute must be resolved in the accused's favor. The same attitude prompted courts to resolve ambiguity in the case law in the accused's favor by rejecting novel theories of independent logical relevance.

But even at the height of the ascendancy of the exclusionary approach in America, 18 states retained the orthodox, British inclusionary approach. For instance, in its 1924 decision in *State v. Bassett*,[9] the New Mexico Supreme Court championed the inclusionary view. The court declared that:

> These various statements of the so-called exceptions to the general rule are but statements that any evidence which tends to show the guilt of the person on trial is admissible, regardless of the fact that it may show the guilt of the defendant of another crime.[10]

---

(1992) ("Molineux has been cited hundreds of times by courts in most U.S. jurisdictions in support of the uncharged misconduct rule. It is frequently cited by the courts today, 88 years after its rendition")

[8] 168 N.Y. at 293, 61 N.E. at 294.

[9] 26 N.M. 476, 194 P. 867.

[10] 194 P. at 868.

Commentators such as Wigmore and Julius Stone, who in 1938
wrote what came to be regarded as the definitive article on the topic,
inveighed against the approach.[11] They condemned the exclusionary
approach as spurious and heretical. Yet, the exclusionary approach
weathered those attacks and persisted as the prevailing view in America.
This state of the law served as the backdrop for *Woods*.

## THE BATTLINES DRAWN IN *WOODS*

The character evidence prohibition was at the heart of the legal
battle in *Woods*. At trial, the defense insisted that the introduction of the
testimony about the other children was a blatant violation of that
prohibition.[12] On appeal, Martha was ably represented by Robert Cahill,
now a Baltimore County Circuit judge, who vigorously pressed the
character evidence argument. The prosecution countered that the testimony was logically relevant to disprove accident and prove *actus reus*,
but the defense quite correctly pointed out that there was no federal
precedent squarely holding that that use of uncharged misconduct was a
legitimate, noncharacter theory of admissibility.

One can only imagine the prosecutor's frame of mind on the eve of
trial. In light of the character evidence prohibition, the prosecutor knew
that he could not stand up in court and ask the trial judge to admit the
evidence to establish the type of person the defendant was. That would
have played into the defense's hands and virtually guaranteed that the
judge would invoke the prohibition and exclude the testimony. However,
the prosecutor had to be thinking that the defendant was a monster, and
that if he did not stop her, she would surely kill again.[13] To stop these

---

[11] Julius Stone, *The Rule of Exclusion of Similar Fact Evidence: America*, 51 Harv.
L.Rev. 988, 1027 (1938).

[12] Arguments attributed to the parties at trial and before the Circuit Court for the 4th
Circuit are taken from the briefs and reply briefs of the party. Specific citations are
available from the author upon request. *See generally* 4th Cir. 72–2217 (1973).

[13] Richard Boller, an old friend and teacher of the author, faced a similar situation. He
was the trial attorney for the prosecution in United States v. Flesher, 37 C.M.R. 669
(A.C.M.R. 1967). There the defendant was charged with sodomizing a minor. The victim
did not testify. The key evidence was photographs depicting the victim committing oral
sodomy on an adult male. The photographs had been discovered during a lawful search of
the defendant's residence. However, the photograph did not show the adult's face. To
convict, Boller had to introduce the photographs. However, the victim would not take the
stand to authenticate them; and since the defendant invoked his privilege against self-
incrimination, Boller could not elicit the foundational testimony from the defendant. Boller
creatively marshaled circumstantial evidence to authenticate the exhibit. First, he called a
photography expert:

The expert made a detailed forty-hour examination of all pictures and the camera and
concluded they were true photographs (R. 106) and not composites; in his opinion no

serial killings, the prosecution would have to successfully invoke two venerable traditions of American law.

### The Grand Tradition of Common Law Reasoning

Even a cursory reading of the briefs filed in *Woods* demonstrates that the two sides were urging the court to take radically different approaches to common law reasoning.

For its part, the defense argued that the fact pattern in *Woods* did not fit within any "recognized" "exception" to the supposed general rule of inadmissibility. The defense generally characterized the then existing exceptions as "circumscribed" and "limited." *Woods*' attorney conceded that the recognized exceptions included disproof of claims of accident, but the defense brief understandably read the cases approving that exception narrowly:

> This exception is appropriate in cases where the defense rests upon the defendant's contention that even though he did the acts charged, he did them accidentally, or he did them without the intent necessary to constitute a crime. (citations omitted). The defendant in the present case has steadfastly denied any acts contributing to the death of Paul Woods, accidental or otherwise, thus, there was no need for the government to prove that her acts were not accidental.[14]

The defense supported this argument by noting that its research had uncovered no American case law allowing the introduction of uncharged

---

one had removed or cropped figures and substituted others, and therefore the photographs were pictorial records.

*Id.* at 671. Second, Boller established that the premises shown in the photographs were Flesher's. *Id.* One photograph depicted the torn wallpaper at Flesher's house. *Id.* at 672. Third, although the photograph did not show the adult's face, the adult's right hand displayed a bruise or blemish on his right hand. *Id.* The defendant had a matching bruise. Finally, the adult shown in the photographs had sparse chest hair but unusually hairy legs. *Id.* at 673. The distribution of hair on the defendant's body was similar. *Id.* Since the case was so unique, Boller could not cite any cases explicitly holding that similar testimony was adequate to authenticate a photograph. However, he argued that cumulatively, the testimony provided sufficient circumstantial authentication. *Id.* at 672–74. The court sustained the argument.

The author distinctly recalls Boller's class discussion of *Flesher* at the Basic Class at The United States Army's Judge Advocate General's School at the University of Virginia in 1971. Then Major Boller was one of the author's instructors in military evidence. Boller was incredibly intense when he described the need he felt to convict the defendant—to incapacitate a monster and prevent him from victimizing other young children. The prosecutor in *Woods* undoubtedly experienced the same feeling. Boller described racking his brain to find a way to introduce the vital photographs, just as the prosecutor in *Woods* must have desperately sought a way to defeat the obvious character evidence objection to the testimony about the other victims of cyanotic episodes.

[14] Reply Brief of Appellant at 9, United States v. Woods (4th Cir. No. 72–2217 May 1, 1973).

misconduct evidence for the specific purpose of establishing the actus reus in a criminal case.

The defense emphasized that the prosecution was asking the court to approve a "new" and "novel" exception. Nor surprisingly, in the defense view the very novelty of the prosecution theory was sufficient justification to reject the theory and reverse the trial judge's ruling. This case was simple in the extreme. There was a list of permissible uses of uncharged misconduct evidence; and no matter how cleverly the prosecution attempted to "wiggle the facts," the prosecution testimony did not "fit" any exception enumerated in the list.

The prosecution's brief was in stark contrast, pressing multiple arguments on the court. One argument was that if there was a general rule of inadmissibility subject to exceptions, and if none applied, the facts in *Woods* called for the recognition of a new "exception." The evidence in question was so highly probative that its exclusion would amount to an affront to common sense, for the evidence created a "compelling" inference that the charged victim's death was not accidental. The occurrence of so many accidental cyanotic episodes to children in the accused's custody was "very unlikely" and "improbable." The defense was asking the court to believe that a truly "extraordinary" coincidence had come to pass.

More importantly, the prosecution made a frontal assault against the common law exclusionary approach that had emerged in the United States. The government argued that it was wrong-minded to force the prosecution to "pigeonhole" its evidence into the rigid parameters of an exception, and urged the court to abandon the conception of the character evidence prohibition as a firm exclusionary rule subject to a finite number of "mechanically" applied exceptions.

Although the defense had argued that it could find no case law supporting the prosecution's theory, the prosecution uncovered a nine-year old First Circuit case[15] that gave it some comfort. Acknowledging that "this subject is frequently thought of in terms of the well-established exceptions, such as those relating to identity, design, or intent.... ," the prosecution argued that it was sounder to focus on the general "principle" underlying the so-called exceptions. Simply stated, the prosecution may not introduce testimony about an accused's prior crimes to initially prove the accused's subjective bad character and then treat the accused's personal character as circumstantial evidence that the accused committed the charged offense. Character evidence offered for any other purpose was admissible. The list of "exceptions" was not only incomplete and not "exhaustive"; more fundamentally, the various "exceptions" were merely "illustratory" (*sic*) of the broader principle

---

[15] Dirring v. United States, 328 F.2d 512 (1st Cir.), *cert. denied*, 377 U.S. 1003 (1964).

which permitted noncharacter theories of logical relevance. If this sounds like the original English common law, it is no coincidence. Nor is it surprising that the relevance of the English precedent itself became an issue on appeal.

### The Tradition of Drawing on Foreign Legal Precedent

The prosecution's brief forcefully argued for the wisdom of relying on English precedents and twice acknowledged that it was relying on "old" English cases such as the late 19th century decision in *Makin v. Attorney General*[16] and the early 20th century decision in *R. v. Smith*.[17] *Smith* is the celebrated "brides of bath" case. Smith's wife was found drowned in her own bath. Her life was insured in Smith's favor. The court permitted the prosecution to introduce evidence that two other women who had lived with Smith had been discovered drowned in their bath tubs. The facts in *Makin* were strikingly similar to those in *Woods*. There the defendants were a husband and wife, charged with murdering a baby in their care. The baby's body was discovered buried in their garden. The defendants admitted that the manner of burial was irregular and unlawful, but they claimed that the child died through natural causes. The court allowed the prosecution to present evidence that the bodies of 12 other infants in the Makins' custody had been found buried on various premises occupied by the Makins.

The *Woods* prosecution argued not only that earlier American decisions had approvingly cited cases such as *Makin* and *Smith*, but also that the English precedents reached a sensible result. On the one hand, they respected the policy underlying the character evidence prohibition by forbidding the prosecution from treating the accused's uncharged misconduct simply as proof of the accused's bad character. On the other hand, they permitted the introduction of evidence that was highly probative on the key issue of whether the death in question was accidental or the result of an *actus reus*. Just as Lord Redding had concluded in *Smith* that trial judge had "rightly admitted" the uncharged misconduct testimony, the prosecution argued that the *Woods* trial judge had "properly allowed" the evidence of the other cyanotic episodes.

The defense responded in its reply brief by urging the court to eschew the English decisions, disparaging the English precedents as "divergent." The defense wrote that "long ago" English courts had taken a position affording the accused "less stringent" protection. The defense asserted:

---

[16] Makin v. Attorney General, [1891–94] All E.R.Rep. 24.

[17] R. v. Smith (1914–15) All E.R. 262.

A prime example of the mischief that can result from ... the ...
English rule is the "Brides of Bath" case, R v. Smith, (1914–15) All
E.R. Rep. 262. ... That case was a common scheme case, wherein
the defendant married several women in sham ceremonies, had
them will their property over to him and then drowned them in the
bathtub.

In the defense view, the *Smith* case should have addressed only the
question of whether the facts fit within the parameters of the recognized
exception for common scheme; the case erred in venturing beyond such
exceptions and suggesting that there is a broader principle, permitting
the prosecution to resort to any noncharacter theory. The defense then
cited a number of American precedents, which it claimed "squarely"
rejected the English view.

## THE FOURTH CIRCUIT'S DECISION IN *WOODS*

Judges Winter, Field, and Widener constituted the three judge panel
of the Court of Appeals for the Fourth Circuit that decided *Woods*.
Judges Winter and Field voted to affirm over a spirited dissent by Judge
Widener.[18]

### *The Dissent*

Judge Widener's dissenting opinion implicitly rejected the relevance
of English precedent by not mentioning it, even though the prosecution
brief was replete with citations to those precedents and the majority
opinion discussed those precedents. Widener also adopted the defense's
argument as to how the uncharged misconduct doctrine should be
conceived. To defeat an objection, the prosecution must "fit" its evidence
with one of "a number circumscribed exceptions." The American courts
had previously "recognized" the legitimate exceptions. After demonstrating to his own satisfaction that the prosecution testimony in *Woods* did
not satisfy the requirements for any of the existing exceptions, Judge
Widener found that "the total lack of authority" supporting an exception
for proof of the *actus reus* was fatal to the prosecution's position.

### *The Majority Opinion*

The majority opinion was quite different. Judge Winter, who authored the opinion, cited three English precedents, including *Smith* and
*Makin*,[19] and in one instance, the conception of the plan theory of

---

[18] United States v. Woods, 484 F.2d 127 (4th Cir. 1973), *cert. denied,* 415 U.S. 979
(1974). Quoted language from the opinions in *Woods* may be found here. References to
specific pages where cited arguments were asserted are available by request from the
author.

[19] Makin v. Attorney General of New South Wales, [1894] A.C. 57 (P.C. 1893), Regina
v. Roden, 12 Cox Cr. 630 (1874), and Rex v. George Joseph Smith, [1914–15] All E.R.Rep.
262.

admissibility, relied exclusively on British authority as precedent supporting his position.[20]

Under the American exclusionary approach, Judge Winter would
have found for the prosecution because he interpreted the accident
theory far more broadly than the defense or Judge Widener:

> The evidence may have been admissible under the lack of accident
> exception, although ordinarily that exception is invoked only where
> an accused admits that he did the acts charged but denies the intent
> necessary to constitute a crime, or contends he did the acts acciden-
> tally. [I]n State v. Lapage, 57 N.H. 245, 294 (1876), there was
> dictum that under certain circumstances where several children of
> the same mother had died, evidence of the previous deaths ought to
> be admissible because of the unlikelihood of such deaths being
> accidental.[21]

However, Judge Winter refused to conclude his analysis there. He
quickly added: "While we conclude that the evidence was admissible
generally under the accident ... exception[], we prefer to place our
decision upon a broader ground."

The remainder of his opinion developed two broader grounds. One
was that the list of exceptions "is not complete." Unlike Judge Widener,
Judge Winter balked at treating the uncharged misconduct doctrine as a
closed system. More importantly, however, Judge Winter questioned
whether the "exception" terminology was apt for at least some of the
noncharacter theories of logical relevance. The very use of that terminology was potentially misleading. The judicial task is "not merely one of
pigeonholing...." "Simply fitting evidence of this nature into an exception heretofore recognized is, to our minds, too mechanistic an approach." Judge Winter then prescribed an approach for trial judges.
Initially, the judge must ensure that the uncharged misconduct possesses
genuine relevance on a noncharacter theory; the evidence must be "be
relevant for any purpose other than to show a mere propensity or
disposition on the part of the defendant to commit the crime...." If the
evidence is so relevant, there is no need for the judge to pause to decide
whether that noncharacter theory fits within any existing "exception."
Rather, the judge's next step is to assess the prosecution's "actual need
for the other crimes evidence [on that theory] in the light of the issues
and the other evidence available to the prosecution...." Having gauged
the probative worth of the uncharged misconduct, the trial judge must
"balanc[e]" the countervailing consideration of the prejudicial character

---

[20] *Makin* and *Roden, supra* note 19, were the only cases Winter cited on this issue.
Winter cited those authorities in footnote 7 of his opinion.

[21] *Woods, supra,* note 18, at 134.

of the testimony. More specifically, the judge should evaluate "the degree to which the jury will probably be roused by the evidence to overmastering hostility." Even when the uncharged misconduct evidence is logically relevant on a noncharacter theory, "the trial judge may exclude the evidence if its probative value is outweighed by the risk that its admission will create a substantial danger of undue prejudice to the accused."

## FORWARD TO THE PAST: THE MAJORITY OPINION AS A TRI-UMPH OF TRADITION

The *Woods* decision is significant for several reasons. The most obvious is that the majority helped change American law governing the admissibility of uncharged misconduct evidence and, although not using the phrase, identified a new basis for admissibility, "the doctrine of objective chances."[22] Other act evidence is relevant and admissible when it tends to establish the objective improbability that an untoward event had an innocent cause or that an accused's association with an event is coincidental. No formal statistical evidence is required to show this, at least in the usual case. Rather, the law allows jurors to draw on their knowledge of the common course of events to assess the objective probability of the litigants' competing claims about the disputed events. (Indeed, in many jurisdictions, the judge's pattern instructions direct the jury to employ that very type of reasoning.[23]) The evidence is admissible because the doctrine of chances does not require the jury to infer either that the accused has a bad character or character trait or that this character or trait led the accused to commit the charged crime. The doctrine of chances has become a mainstay for introducing evidence of an accused's uncharged misconduct in situations ranging from child abuse cases to drug prosecutions.

In endorsing doctrine of chances reasoning, the *Woods* majority reached a result unprecedented in federal law. As both the defense brief and the dissent correctly observed, there were then no American precedents specifically holding that the doctrine of chances is sufficient to defeat a character evidence objection. The paradox is that the *Woods* majority decided to reject the defense contentions and reach this novel outcome precisely because the majority was faithful to the oldest traditions in American law.

---

[22] For a more in depth discussion of this doctrine, *see* Imwinkelried, *supra*, note 6.

[23] *E.g.,* 2 Kevin F. O'Malley, Jay E. Grenig & William C. Lee, Federal Jury Practice and Instructions: Criminal (§ 12.02 (5th ed. 2000)) ("You are expected to use your good sense in considering and evaluating the evidence in the case. [G]ive the evidence a reasonable and fair construction in light of your knowledge of the natural tendencies and inclinations of human beings").

In its brief in *Woods,* the defense proposed an inward looking approach to evaluating the issues, urging the court to ignore the English precedents in a way that reflected a disregard, just short of disdain, for foreign authority.[24] The defense also urged a freezing of American precedent in a situation where both logic and justice appeared to cry out for an extension of admissibility. In rejecting the approach proposed by the defense, the *Woods* majority upheld two of the longstanding traditions in American law. One is an occasional, cosmopolitan willingness to consider foreign precedents, at least to the extent of discussing them in footnotes and regarding them as some authority. The majority might well have reached the same result without the benefit of the insights in the British decisions. However, unlike the dissent, which completely ignored the British decisions, the majority displayed a willingness to listen to and respect what other courts have to say.

The other tradition is the Grand Tradition of common law reasoning. True to that tradition, the majority refused to conceive of the uncharged misconduct doctrine in "mechanistic" terms. In its brief, the government explicitly asked the court to focus on the principle underlying the doctrine, and the majority did so. Judge Winter began his legal analysis by enunciating the core principle: "evidence of other crimes is not admissible to prove that an accused is a bad person and therefore likely to have committed the crime in question." Having identified that principle, the majority then reasoned in classic, common law fashion, following Llewellyn's view that every "rule" is animated by a principle or reason and that "where the reason stops, there stops the rule."[25] Llewellyn called this the "Grand Tradition."

The majority went beyond the received law. The majority did so because given the nature of the principle underlying the character evidence prohibition, it made, as the prosecution argued, no sense to admit uncharged misconduct testimony only when a party can "pigeonhol[e]" the testimony into a previously recognized exception. Rather, the uncharged bad act evidence should be presumptively admissible if it is logically "relevant for any purpose other than to show a mere propensity or disposition on the part of the defendant to commit the crime...." Reasoning in the Grand Tradition dictated the conclusion that the inclusionary conception of the uncharged misconduct doctrine is perfectly consistent with the character evidence prohibition. As Justice Winter remarked, "the range of relevancy outside the [character] ban is almost

---

[24] The defense derided "the divergent English rule" and asserted that the English precedents had produced "mischief" in the jurisprudence.

[25] Karl Llewellyn, THE BRAMBLE BUSH 157–58 (1951); *see also* Paul J. Mishkin & Clarence Morris, ON LAW IN COURTS: AN INTRODUCTION TO JUDICIAL DEVELOPMENT OF CASE AND STATUTE LAW 89 (1965).

infinite." If so, it would be silly to think of the doctrine as a closed system with a finished list of legitimate noncharacter theories of relevance. The doctrine is perforce a work in progress; and, as in *Woods,* a court must be prepared to determine whether even a previously unprecedented theory possesses genuine noncharacter relevance and is, therefore, beyond the reach of the character evidence prohibition. The *Woods* majority was prepared to do so and rightly found that the theory of objective chances passes muster.

The *Woods* majority's affirmation of these two traditions could not have been more timely. The majority's decision coincided with the beginning stages of two major developments in American law. One development was the growing globalization of legal practice. As globalization progresses, American courts can hardly afford a disdainful attitude toward foreign precedents. In an increasingly international legal environment, that attitude is becoming outdated and unacceptable.

The other development was the then imminent adoption of the Federal Rules of Evidence. The *Woods* majority rendered its decision in September 1973. At that time, the draft proposed rules were still pending before Congress. Indeed, the majority took comfort from the fact that the language of proposed Rule 404 lent support to its position. The *Woods* majority's invocation of Grand Tradition common law reasoning conveyed an important message to other federal courts that would soon be construing evidence statutes. The majority's reference to the Federal Rules was apt, for common law reasoning in the Grand Tradition is to case law as purposive interpretation is to statutes. A court reasoning in the Grand Tradition looks beyond the narrow factual parameters of prior decisions and attempts to discern the principle or policy rationale that prompted the decisions by the earlier courts. Similarly, a court interpreting legislation purposively looks beyond the statute's literal text and endeavors to identify the policy considerations which animated the legislative action. As a general proposition, neither narrow readings of cases nor literal interpretations of statutes necessarily promote the policies which should inspire judicial decisions as well as legislative intervention. Thus, by reaffirming the Grand Tradition in a common law setting, the *Woods* decision served as a useful reminder for the courts that would soon be tasked with construing the Federal Rules to promote policies often similar, if not identical, to those which had previously driven common law evidence decisions.

In sum, the story of the *Woods* case is a story about the tradition of judicial reasoning. The *Woods* chapter is part of a larger story about the third branch of our government. The larger story portrays a judiciary committed to pursuing the public interest and sufficiently open-minded to realize that it does not always possess all the answers to questions about the public interest. For that matter, it may not always be the government institution that should resolve a particular public policy matter. But when it comes to evidence law and justice in specific cases, no branch of government is better positioned to decide wisely than our courts. *Woods* is thus a tale about doing justice in an individual case. During Mrs. Woods' lengthy, six-month trial, a theory new to American law, which has come to be called the doctrine of chances, was used to admit evidence that was unique in the way it shed light on what probably had happened. The trial jury found that evidence persuasive. In the words of her prosecutor, then Assistant U.S. Attorney Charles Bernstein, "The facts won out."

The jury found Mrs. Woods guilty on eight counts of mistreatment of a minor, assault, attempted murder, and first degree murder. Her sentence included a term of life imprisonment on the murder count. The Fourth Circuit affirmed the trial court's evidentiary rulings and the verdict at trial, and the Supreme Court later denied certiorari. Justice was served, and American evidence law was refined. Most importantly, Martha Woods had no further victims. How many lives were saved? Realistically, perhaps none, for even had her trial ended in an acquittal, she might never again have been entrusted with the care of a foster child. But people move; and in an era before computerized records became ubiquitous, social work agencies might not even have attempted to track people seeking to foster parent. So one cannot be sure. In the 25 year period prior to her 1972 trial, though, Martha Woods may have been responsible for eight deaths. She lived another 30 years, and passed away at the Federal Medical Center Carswell in Fort Worth, Texas in 2002.[26]

---

[26] June 14, 2005 telephone call by Professor Imwinkelried to the Records office of the Bryan Federal Prison Camp in Texas at (979) 823–1879.

\*

# 4

# Of Misshapen Stones and Compromises: Michelson and the Modern Law of Character Evidence

## Christopher B. Mueller*

## Introduction

*Michelson v. United States* is best known for its detailed exposition of the rules governing character evidence and for its closing paragraph, in which Justice Jackson described the rules governing character evidence as "archaic" and "paradoxical," but concluded that tinkering would bring more risks than gains. So rather than remove "one misshapen stone" from a "grotesque structure," he instead left intact a doctrine that give an "irrational advantage" to one side "offset by a poorly reasoned counterprivilege" for the other, finding it a "workable even if clumsy" scheme.[1]

The opinion, written in Jackson's plain-talking style, is a pleasure to read, and the language speaks almost as much to the modern mind as it spoke to the people of his own day, more than two generations ago. Perhaps its most engaging aspect is its frankness in acknowledging tensions that exist in the law and its pragmatic attitude that "if it ain't broke don't fix it," coupled with the recognition that changing one aspect of the law might have unintended and adverse consequences.

* Henry S. Lindsley Professor of Procedure and Advocacy, University of Colorado School of Law. I want to thank the University of Colorado Law School for research support for this project, and I want to thank Laura Sturges, class of 2005, for her research on this project. Finally, I want to thank David Kaye for consulting with me on the Bayes issues discussed in this paper, and Roger Park and my longtime colleague and co-author Laird Kirkpatrick for reading the manuscript and making valuable suggestions, and Richard Lempert for careful editing work and substantive suggestions. Needless to say final responsibility for any errors in this work rests with me.

[1] Michelson v. U.S., 335 U.S. 469 (1948).

Moreover, Justice Jackson paints a masterful picture in *Michelson* that captures the rules relating to character evidence as they existed, not only in 1948 when the opinion came down, but in most respects today as well. Although *Michelson* was decided at a time when federal courts largely followed the lead of the states on matters of evidence law, the opinion has had enormous and enduring impact as *authority* on what the law is.[2]

*Michelson* involves not one but three evidence stories, which are progressively more interesting and important. First is the story of Solomon Michelson, the defendant in the case, and the crime that he apparently committed. Not much is known about him, but it seems that his crime was small potatoes, and but for the case that bears his name, he would long since have been forgotten. Second is the story of Justice Robert Jackson, the last person appointed to the Court without a law degree and a jurist of extraordinary ability and influence. Among other things, he wrote with remarkable clarity and an unrivaled ability to turn a phrase. Third is the story of the law of character evidence, which Jackson's opinion in *Michelson* captures and summarizes and which continues to be controversial. This essay follows all three stories, beginning with the case and its protagonist.

## I. The *Michelson* Decision

The decision in *Michelson* arose out of the trial of a 58–year-old secondhand jewelry dealer named Solomon Michelson, who lived in the Brighton Beach area of Brooklyn[3] and worked in the Bowery in lower Manhattan,[4] where he and other jewelry dealers rented counter space.[5] Michelson was charged with attempting to bribe Maurice Kratter, an IRS agent who had been investigating Michelson's tax returns for the years 1942 and 1943. The two met several times at Michelson's place of

---

[2] According to Westlaw, as of September 2005 *Michelson* had been cited more than 2,600 times.

[3] His address was 3152 Brighton Sixth Street, located in the Brighton Beach Area on the Boardwalk along the ocean. The address now houses the Winter Garden Club that serves Russian food and has an elaborate floor show featuring singing and dancing, "during which puffs of perfumed smoke are blasted into the high-energy crowd" (a prix fixe dinner includes two shots of vodka).

[4] Michelson's business address is given as 74 Bowery Street, which is now the home of the New York Jewelers Exchange. Janet's Diamonds advertises a business at that address today.

[5] Most of the facts in this account come from the Supreme Court opinion or from the Second Circuit opinion in the case, which are cited throughout this article. Some of the facts are found in a contemporaneous news story. See "$5,000 Tax Bribe Charged," New York Times, July 30, 1946 (reporting that Maurice Kratter "made a routine inspection of the records of Michelson's organization and discovered large sums of undeclared income that would have resulted in" tax obligations exceeding $25,000; Michelson was released on $5,000 bail).

business, and Kratter thought that Michelson owed $25,000 in taxes, which suggests that he had unreported income of at least $28,409, and that his total income was substantially higher.[6] While perhaps less than truly wealthy, Michelson must have been well to do by the standards of his day.

After these meetings, it appears from the prosecutor's case that Michelson and Kratter spoke by phone several times and ultimately agreed to meet in a guest room of the St. George Hotel in Brooklyn on July 17, 1946.[7] The point on which the case turned was whether, as Michelson claimed, Kratter demanded to be paid off or, as the government claimed, that it was all Michelson's idea—that it was a bribe. Clearly Michelson was set up because the room was wired, but the stenographer who was taking down the conversation could not make out much of what was said. Kratter testified that Michelson knocked on the door, and that on entering he placed a package containing $5000 in cash on the dresser. In that day, this sum was enough buy a new Chrysler Imperial automobile.

Considering the simplicity of the case, there were lots of witnesses, and the pivotal question was close, because the first two-day trial ended in a hung jury. The second trial led to conviction, and Michelson was fined $3,500 and sentenced to prison for a year and a half. On the government's side was Agent Yung of the IRS, whom Kratter enlisted to help him handle the Michelson file (Kratter himself was a newcomer in the IRS). On the defendant's side was Michelson's accountant Abraham Osterfeld. Michelson also called five character witnesses to testify to his good character (Susan Kirk, David Oppenheim, and others identified in the opinions only by last names: Gerstein, Smith, and Weitzman).

Michelson took the stand in his own defense, as he almost had to do, given the nature of the case. He acknowledged on direct examination that he had been convicted 19 years earlier for possessing counterfeit watch dials. Nevertheless, his five character witnesses testified in their

---

[6] For 1942, the top marginal tax rate was 88%, and if Michelson owed that much in taxes and was in that bracket, his unreported income would be the figure set out above. The lowest marginal tax rate was 19%, but he surely was not in that bracket (which ended at $2,000).

[7] At the time a grand hotel located at 100 Henry Street in Brooklyn Heights, the St. George overlooked Manhattan and the Brooklyn Bridge and boasted an indoor salt-water swimming pool. It burned down in 1995, and now the address is a student residence hall. The modern (and much smaller) St. George on nearby Clark Street is a boutique hotel. The website for the student residence claims that the old hotel was "a beacon for celebrities and athletes," and that part of The Godfather was filmed there, namely the scene in the bar where Luca Brasi (Lenny Montana) was murdered by Sollozzo (Al Lettieri), who ice-picks Brasi's hand to the bar, and Tattaglia (Victor Rendina), who strangles him with a garrote.

own ways that Michelson had a good reputation for honesty, truthfulness, and being a law-abiding citizen. Ostensibly to impeach these witnesses, the prosecutor asked three of them on cross-examination whether they had heard that Michelson had been arrested twenty-six years earlier for receiving stolen goods (at that time he would have been 32 years old). The defense objected, and questioned the suggestion that Michelson had been arrested at all.[8] The court initially sustained the objection, but then changed its mind and told the jury that the question went to the "standard of opinion of the reputation of the defendant," which was being "tested," but that the jury was "not to assume" that the incident "actually took place." In the petition for certiorari, Michelson's lawyer made the point that there is "perhaps no kind of merchandise which, when stolen, is more likely to be received by a dealer innocently than second-hand jewelry."

On appeal to the Second Circuit, Michelson argued that the court ought not to have allowed questions about the arrest. Wigmore, who died five years before the Supreme Court decided *Michelson,* had criticized roundly the practice of cross-examining character witnesses about reports or rumors of prior acts by the defendant, and a distinguished panel in the Second Circuit (Judges Frank, Swan, and Carrie) quoted Wigmore's statement with approval, and said that it wished the Supreme Court would adopt what it described inaccurately as the Illinois rule, allowing questions only on "offenses similar to those for which the defendant is on trial."[9] Nevertheless the Second Circuit felt compelled to defer to settled traditions allowing broader cross-examination.

When his case reached the Supreme Court, Michelson's attorney stopped short of advocating what is actually the Illinois rule (barring all cross-examination on prior acts), and did not urge adoption of the appellate panel's preference to limit cross-examination to acts by the accused that might bear on the underlying charges. Instead, following classical principles of advocacy, Michelson asked for the smallest corrective measure that would allow his client to prevail. He argued that the

---

[8] On appeal, the defense argued that there was no evidence that the defendant had been arrested for receiving stolen goods, but the government brief said an arrest record so indicates. Compare Petition for Writ of Certiorari, p. 24 (stating that defendant testified on direct that "he had had no other trouble," other than the one conviction, "since he had been in the United States," and that nothing elsewhere in the record shows "any arrest of defendant on a charge of receiving stolen goods") (February 16, 1948) with Brief for the United States, p. 10 (stating that the prosecutor "submitted a photostatic copy of the 1930 license application containing a notation of the 1920 arrest") (October 1948), both filed in Michelson v. U.S., 335 U.S. 469 (1948).

[9] U.S. v. Michelson, 165 F.2d 732, 735 n.8 (2d Cir. 1948), citing Wigmore and *Aiken v. People,* 55 N.E. 695 (Ill. 1899). In fact, the Illinois rule expounded in *Aiken* barred (and still does bar) questioning defense character witnesses about *any and all* prior bad acts by the defendant, whether similar to the charged offense or not.

cross-examiner should not be allowed to ask about *arrests,* and stressed that this particular arrest was too old to be relevant. As a fallback, he urged that the trial judge had erred in assuming that he lacked discretion in this area.

In the famous opinion in *Michelson,* the Supreme Court refused to budge in the directions urged by the defense and the Second Circuit. *Even though* the question "have you heard" asks the character witness about hearsay ("rumors and reports"), and *even though* these "do not affect his conclusion," and *even though* the particular arrest raised on cross happened twenty-six years earlier, and *even though* the charges leading to arrest were unlike the charged crime, *nevertheless* asking about the arrest made sense because, the Court said, character testimony about being honest and law-abiding is *itself* "broader than the charged crime," and "receiving stolen goods" was "as incompatible with" being honest and law-abiding as offering a bribe would be. So even questions unrelated to the charged offense can test whether the reputation of a defendant really is as good as a witness has said.

The rule of the case is even harder than that: *Michelson* states that even events that happened half a lifetime earlier, some twelve years *before* at least one of the character witnesses had *even met* the defendant, were fair game—a point softened slightly by language indicating that the court has discretion to cut off inquiry about "an event so remote, unless recent misconduct revived them." Since two of Michelson's character witnesses had already known him for six years when he was first arrested, allowing the question was not, in the Court's view, an abuse of discretion. In dissent, Justices Rutledge and Murphy said they would have adopted the Illinois rule, meaning that they would not allow questions asking whether the witness "had heard" about other acts, and would not allow questions about *arrests* because they have no "substantial bearing" on reputation.

*Michelson* grew out of the rationalist tradition. It assumes that answers to hard legal questions can be derived by thinking carefully and valuing experience, and it exudes a level of confidence that searching inquiry leads to the truth and that today's answer is likely to be the answer tomorrow too. It is not a "realist" opinion reflecting a notion that the law springs from the mind of the judge (hence might change tomorrow), nor is it an "oracular" opinion that is thought to be valid simply because *someone* must determine the law, and the Supreme Court is the one. It is both pragmatic and conservative in that it sees existing law as part of a workable dynamic equilibrium that could be upset if any part of the law is altered. Cautious pragmatism and a certain conservatism were part of Justice Jackson's judicial creed.[10] Thus *Michelson*

---

[10] Robert H. Jackson, The Struggle for Judicial Supremacy: A Study of a Crisis in American Power Politics 315 (1941) (the Court "is almost never a really contemporary

describes and refuses to unsettle a system of rules that had found expression in English Treatises for a hundred years and more.[11]

## II. *Michelson's* Author: Justice Robert H. Jackson

Justice Jackson was the last person appointed to the Supreme Court without a law degree.[12] He was among the forty or so Justices who came to the Court with no prior judicial experience (other examples include Justices Brandeis, Douglas, Warren, White and Rehnquist). Jackson learned his profession in an apprenticeship program with a law firm and from a mentor in the firm. During his brief time in law school (a year in Albany New York), he preferred watching oral arguments in the Court of Appeals to sitting in class and reading casebooks. Jackson went on to found his own small firm in Jamestown New York, enjoying considerable success (he earned $30,000 a year in the middle of the depression) with a practice that served mainly individual clients.

A lifelong Democrat, Jackson involved himself in Woodrow Wilson's presidential campaign, and was rewarded by being put in charge of patronage appointments in New York, but he had misgivings about entering public service. Although he became friends with Franklin Roosevelt, who worked in the Wilson administration, Jackson turned down an offer of a state position when Roosevelt became governor of New York. When Roosevelt became President, Jackson turned down another opportunity to enter public service, declining the position of General Counsel for the Works Progress Administration. Jackson found the program ideologically unattractive ("getting something for nothing"), but the Depression convinced him that the concentration of capital in the hands of large corporations was a grave threat to democracy, and in 1934 he accepted a position as assistant general counsel for

---

institution," as life tenure for judges keeps "the average viewpoint" on the Court "a generation apart" from the viewpoint of Congress; the judiciary "is thus the check of a preceding generation on the present one; a check of conservative legal philosophy upon a dynamic people, and nearly always the check of a rejected regime on the one in being").

[11] The rule has been discussed in English and American treatises for almost 200 years. See, e.g. 2 Thomas Starkie, EVIDENCE (2d ed. 1828); Burrill, ON THE NATURE, PRINCIPLES AND RULES OF CIRCUMSTANTIAL EVIDENCE 524–525, 531 (1859); 2 Simon Greenleaf, Evidence § 25 (2d ed. 1844); STEPHEN'S DIGEST OF THE LAW OF EVIDENCE 111–112 (1867); James Thayer, A PRELIMINARY TREATISE ON EVIDENCE AT THE COMMON LAW 525 (1898).

[12] The ensuing account is drawn from THE SUPREME COURT JUSTICES ILLUSTRATED BIOGRAPHIES (1789–1993) 406–410 (Clare Cushman, ed., Supreme Court Historical Society 1993); Eugene C. Gerhart, AMERICA'S ADVOCATE: ROBERT H. JACKSON (1958); Jeffrey D. Hockett, NEW DEAL JUSTICE, THE CONSTITUTIONAL JURISPRUDENCE OF HUGO L. BLACK, FELIX FRANKFURTER, AND ROBERT H. JACKSON (1996); Mr. Justice Jackson, FOUR LECTURES IN HIS HONOR (1969). For a list of Jackson's opinions, see Bibliography, *The Judicial Opinions of Justice Robert H. Jackson in the Supreme Court of the United States, October 6, 1941–October 9, 1954,* 8 Stan. L. Rev. 60 (1955).

the Bureau of Internal Revenue. Two years later he moved to the antitrust division of the Department of Justice, where he wanted to help reinstate what he considered traditional doctrines of encouraging free competition and smaller economic units.

Jackson was uneasy with what he considered to be the New Deal philosophy of working with business under the National Recovery Act, which collapsed when the Court found it unconstitutional. Pressed by Roosevelt to back his Court-packing plan, Jackson offered a tepid defense (stressing his hope that the legislative and judicial branches could find ways to cooperate), and did not argue the "party line" that the Court was an inefficient institution because it had too few judges. Still, Roosevelt appointed Jackson Solicitor General in 1938, and later appointed him Attorney General, and he apparently told Jackson that he wanted him to serve as Chief Justice. That was never to be. Instead, Jackson took his seat as Associate Justice when Chief Justice Hughes retired, and Justice Stone shifted over to become Chief Justice.

On the Supreme Court for 13 years (1941–1954), except for a year-and-a-half hiatus when he served as prosecutor in the War Crimes trial in Nuremberg, Justice Jackson authored 148 opinions, plus 46 concurrences and 115 dissents. His work on the Court is best remembered among historians and scholars for his role in four cases: Early in his tenure, Justice Jackson authored the Court's opinion in *Wickard v. Filburn,* which was important in removing roadblocks that the Court had erected in blocking New Deal legislation during the depression era.[13] In 1943 he wrote the opinion in the *Barnette* case discarding a holding penned by Justice Frankfurter just three years before, and holding instead that school children could not be forced to recite the pledge of allegiance to the flag.[14] Coming as it did in the middle of the Second World War, this decision was an act of courage not just by Jackson, but by the Court as well. In the very next year, in another act of courage, Justice Jackson dissented from the opinion in the Japanese Internment case, writing that "if any fundamental assumption underlies our system, it is that guilt is personal and not inheritable."[15] Finally, toward the end of his tenure, in 1952, Justice Jackson famously concurred in the steel seizure case, where he laid out a systematic approach to the problem of defining presidential powers that is much admired to this day.[16]

---

[13] Wickard v. Filburn, 317 U.S. 111, 63 S.Ct. 82, 87 L.Ed. 122 (1942).

[14] West Virginia State Board of Education v. Barnette, 319 U.S. 624 (1943); Minersville School District v. Gobitis, 310 U.S. 586 (1940).

[15] Korematsu v. U.S., 323 U.S. 214 (1944) (dissent).

[16] Youngstown Sheet & Tube Co. v. Sawyer, 343 U.S. 579 (1952) (President has "maximum" power when acting pursuant to "express or implied" authorization by Congress, but if Congress has neither granted nor denied authority the President "can only

Two other opinions authored by Justice Jackson had important impacts on trial practice and became standard teaching vehicles in casebooks read by thousands of law students. One is Jackson's opinion in *Michelson*, the subject of this essay. The other is his concurrence in *Hickman v. Taylor,* which recognized the existence of work product protection *despite* the fact that the Civil Rules made no provision for such protection. In *Hickman,* it was Justice Jackson who framed the issue from the standpoint of the litigating lawyer: He wrote that he could "conceive of no practice more demoralizing to the Bar than to require a lawyer to write out and deliver to his adversary an account of what witnesses have told him."[17]

Jackson is also remembered for some pithy and downhome phrases. Consider the following: "If it is interstate commerce that feels the pinch, it does not matter how local the operation which applies the squeeze."[18] "We are not final because we are infallible, but we are infallible only because we are final."[19] "Might does not make right even in taxation."[20] "There is a danger that, if the Court does not temper its doctrinaire logic with a little practical wisdom, it will convert the constitutional Bill of Rights into a suicide pact."[21] "I see no reason why I should be consciously wrong today because I was unconsciously wrong yesterday."[22] And finally, "The naïve assumption that prejudicial effects can be overcome by instructions to the jury all practicing lawyers know to be unmitigated fiction."[23]

Justice Jackson is, however, best known not for what he wrote while on the Court, but for his controversial decision to leave the Court in order to serve as Chief Prosecutor in the Nuremberg War Crimes Trials, which kept him in Germany from June 1945 through October 1946.[24]

---

rely upon his own independent powers," although there is a "zone of twilight" in which Congress and the President have "concurrent authority," and when President takes measures "incompatible with" the will of Congress, his power is "at its lowest ebb" because it depends on his constitutional powers "minus any constitutional powers of Congress").

[17] Hickman v. Taylor, 329 U.S. 495 (1947) (concurring opinion).

[18] U.S. v. Women's Sportswear Mfg. Association, 336 U.S. 460, 464 (1949).

[19] Brown v. Allen, 344 U.S. 443, 540 (1953).

[20] International Harvester Co. v. Wisconsin Department of Taxation, 322 U.S. 435, 450 (1944).

[21] Terminiello v. Chicago, 337 U.S. 1, 37 (1958).

[22] Massachusetts v. U.S., 333 U.S. 611, 639–640 (1948).

[23] Krulewitch v. U.S., 336 U.S. 440, 453 (1949) (concurring opinion).

[24] Justice Jackson did not, however, play any role in the story recounted in the film "Judgment at Nuremberg" (1961). The movie is a fictional account of trials of German

Not only did he successfully prosecute 20 Nazi war criminals, many of whom were hanged or sentenced to life in prison, but he led the negotiations that created the tribunal and formulated the procedures to be followed. In that role, Jackson was acutely aware that winners set the rules, and he urged that while international law was being "first applied against German aggressors," it must condemn "aggression by any other nations including those which sit here now in judgment." His opening statement at the trials admirably framed the reasons for the extraordinary proceedings:

> The privilege of opening the first trial in history for crimes against the peace of the world imposes a grave responsibility. The wrongs which we seek to condemn and punish have been so calculated, so malignant, and so devastating, that civilization cannot tolerate their being ignored, because it cannot survive their being repeated. That four great nations, flushed with victory and stung with injury stay the hand of vengeance and voluntarily submit their captive enemies to the judgment of the law is one of the most significant tributes that Power has ever paid to Reason.[25]

It is at least possible that his experience in Nuremberg made Jackson more inclined to interpret the Bill of Rights narrowly when he returned to the Court. One scholar has suggested that Jackson saw the collapse of the Weimar Republic and the rise of Nazism in terms of a failure to crack down adequately on radicals.[26]

Justice Jackson is also known for his disputes with Justice Black, which were at times not only ideological but personal, and for not taking a firm position in the battle between Justices Black and Douglas on the one hand, and Justice Frankfurter on the other hand, on the question whether the particular protections of the Bill of Rights should be incorporated the Due Process Clause of the Fourteenth Amendment. Justice Jackson was never wholly convinced of the wisdom of going in either direction, and so on this point he occupied an uncertain middle ground.

In 1954 Jackson suffered a heart attack and was urged to reduce his activities, but he returned to the bench six weeks later to be present when the Court announced its unanimous decision in the *Brown* school desegregation case. He died suddenly five months later.

---

judges and doctors that took place in Nuremberg *after* the trial of German military officers, where Robert Jackson was the chief prosecutor. The model for the American judge Dan Heywood, played by Spencer Tracy, was Justice James Brand of the Oregon Supreme Court, who presided at the earlier trials.

[25] Telford Taylor, THE ANATOMY OF THE NUREMBERG TRIALS: A PERSONAL MEMOIR 161 (1992).

[26] Henry J. Abraham, JUSTICES AND PRESIDENTS: A POLITICAL HISTORY OF APPOINTMENTS TO THE SUPREME COURT 178 (new and revised ed. 1999).

III. *Michelson* and the Modern American Law of Character Evidence

Before the adoption of the Federal Rules of Evidence in 1975, the Supreme Court played little role in developing evidence law, apart from its jurisprudence in the areas of criminal procedure and a few Sixth Amendment cases dealing with issues of confrontation. With only a few exceptions, the Court did not begin to apply the Confrontation Clause to issues relating to hearsay until the 1960s, and it was in the 1960s and 1970s that the Court resolved the most important issues of burden of proof and presumptions operating against the accused in criminal cases.[27]

Before 1975, federal courts in diversity cases applied either state or federal evidence law and were directed to apply the rule that favors admissibility in the event of conflict, although federal courts did develop their own common law traditions in federal criminal cases. In the Jackson era, the Court dealt several times with the coconspirator exception, with the spousal testimonial privilege, and with state secrets, and the year before Jackson's retirement the Court dealt with the business records exception.[28] That was about it.

As Jackson commented in *Michelson*, the law of evidence as it relates to proving character "developed almost entirely at the hands of state courts," and the Supreme Court itself "has contributed little to this or to any phase" of evidence law.[29] The same comment applies across the board to the whole of the law of evidence. Thus *Michelson* was the

---

[27] In 1965, the Court first applied the Confrontation Clause to the states. See Pointer v. Texas, 380 U.S. 400 (1965). Before that, the Court approved a few hearsay exceptions, but balked in one case. See Mattox v. U.S., 146 U.S. 140 (1892) (dying declarations); Mattox v. U.S., 156 U.S. 237, 244–250 (1895) (prior trial testimony); Kirby v. U.S., 174 U.S. 47 (1899) (cannot use third-party conviction to prove that property was stolen); Snyder v. Massachusetts, 291 U.S. 97 (1934) (dying declarations and documentary evidence). The first modern case deciding that confrontation limits the use of hearsay is California v. Green, 399 U.S. 149 (1970). The cases on burden of proof in criminal cases came in the 1970s. See In re Winship, 397 U.S. 358 (1970); Mullaney v. Wilbur, 421 U.S. 684 (1975); Patterson v. New York, 432 U.S. 197 (1977). The big decisions on criminal presumptions came in 1979. See Sandstrom v. Montana, 442 U.S. 510 (1979); County of Ulster v. Allen, 442 U.S. 140 (1979).

[28] See Krulewitch v. U.S., 336 U.S. 440 (1949) (refusing to extend coconspirator exception to post-conspiracy utterance; Jackson concurred but complained that conspiracy law was out of hand); Lutwak v. U.S., 344 U.S. 604 (1953) ("War Brides" case known for holding that spousal testimony privilege does not apply where defendant married the witness to keep her from testifying; Jackson and Frankfurter thought marriage was valid and privilege should apply); Reynolds v. U.S., 345 U.S. 1 (1953) (upholding government's claim of privilege covering report on crash of military plane; Jackson, Black and Frankfurter thought government should have produced underlying report for *in camera* inspection); Palmer v. Hoffman, 318 U.S. 109 (1943) (refusing to apply business records exception to accident reports offered by railroad as a defense against FELA claims).

[29] Michelson v. U.S., 335 U.S. 469, 486 (1948).

first significant evidence case that the Court decided while Jackson was on the Court, and it fell to him to write the opinion.

## A.  Did *Michelson* Get the Big Picture Right?

In many respects, *Michelson* does get things right, and the decision is often cited not for its narrow holding, but for broader propositions— character evidence is generally inadmissible against the accused, and ordinarily only the defense can open this subject.

Many parts of the law recounted in *Michelson* remain black letter law today. These include (a) barring the prosecutor from offering proof of a defendant's bad character to show that he behaved accordingly, (b) allowing a defendant to prove his innocence through witnesses who testify to his good character, including the general trait of law abiding-ness, (c) allowing prosecutors to cross-examine character witnesses about rumors that undercut the picture they paint, including talk about arrests, provided only that the cross-examiner has a good faith basis for such questions, and (d) requiring courts, if the defense so requests, to tell the jury that anything suggested by such cross-examination can be used only in assessing the character witnesses and cannot be used as evidence of defendant's guilt. FRE 404 and 405 largely incorporate these principles, although they allow character witnesses to give not only reputation testimony, but personal opinions as well (in which case cross-examination can inquire into *knowledge* of bad acts).

In another sense, however, the big picture suggested by *Michelson* is misleading. In fact, prosecutors can often prove various aspects of defendant's character during their case-in-chief. As students of evidence soon learn, prosecutors can prove specific instances of conduct when they have relevance beyond their tendency to show character, as when they indicate intent, planning, "modus operandi" or identity. Equally impor-tantly, a defendant who testifies in a case—*regardless* whether he says anything about his character—may be cross-examined about specific acts that are relevant to truthfulness, including convictions for major of-fenses (felonies) that do not *directly* relate to truthfulness. In this respect defendants are, to be sure, treated neither better nor worse than other witnesses, except for the telling fact that defendants risk being convicted if juries misuse prior misdeeds by treating them as proof of guilt, or if they convict in anger because of them. And of course defendants can be cross-examined on prior bad acts that contradict anything they say on direct about the course of their lives. Particularly dangerous is blanket testimony describing an innocent past ("I've never been in trouble before"), which opens the door to questions about and extrinsic evidence of all sorts of bad acts that conflict with this picture.

## B.  What's Missing from *Michelson?*

Three basic points about character evidence are not addressed in *Michelson.* The first is the standard for proving past acts when prosecutors seek to use them for permissible purposes like intent. It wasn't until 40 years after *Michelson* that the Supreme Court decided in the *Huddleston* case that in federal litigation other bad acts only have to be proved by a preponderance of the evidence—not by proof beyond a reasonable doubt, nor even by clear and convincing evidence (the standard many courts had adopted).[30] Second, there is the question whether the judge or the jury should decide whether the defendant committed a particular prior crime or other bad act. In *Huddleston,* the Court held that the jury decides this point, subject only to the power of the judge to reject the evidence if it is so weak that it cannot reasonably form the basis of a conclusion that the act was committed. Finally, *Michelson* did not consider the question whether a prior acquittal bars the government from proving the underlying criminal act. Forty-two years later the Supreme court held it did not, again in an opinion that binds only federal courts.[31]

## C.  Was *Michelson* Right on the Narrow Point It Decided?

Read with care, *Michelson* actually decides only that a prosecutor may cross-examine defense character witnesses who give broad testimony that the accused is law-abiding by asking them whether they have heard about bad acts by the accused, even of the acts do not bear on aspects of character that might have led the accused to commit the charged crime. Such acts are fair game even if they happened prior to the time when the witness came to know the defendant. And the cross-examiner can ask about prior arrests, even though being arrested for a crime does not mean that one has committed any crime.

I think *Michelson* is wrong on these points. Take first the more critical aspect of the holding—that cross-examination can delve into acts unrelated to aspects of character that connect with the charged offense. In theory, the cross-examination is still relevant in two ways. First, it tests the knowledge of the testifying witness about the reputation that she describes or (today) the opinion that she offers. If a reputation witness has not heard of the acts in question, then arguably the community judgment reflected in the reputation testimony is ill-informed. If an opinion witness does not know about the acts, then arguably she is ill-informed. Second, cross-examination tests the judgment of either the community or the witness. If the acts are "talked about" or the witness "knows about" them, then the favorable reputa-

---

[30] U.S. v. Huddleston, 485 U.S. 681 (1988).

[31] Dowling v. U.S., 493 U.S. 342 (1990).

tion or opinion testimony is called into question: How could the community or the witness consider the defendant law-abiding if his misbehavior is known?

Still, the wiser answer is that even a broad endorsement of character is helpful only insofar as it suggests that the defendant did not commit the charged offense. Hence a mistake or omission on the part of the community or the witness on some point unrelated to a relevant aspect of character lacks salience—it has virtually no bearing on the likelihood that reputation or opinion is right, *in any way that matters*, in appraising the character of the defendant.

*Michelson* also seems wrong in allowing cross-examination on "arrests," even if the deed that occasioned the arrest bears on an aspect of character that connects with the charged offense. If Solomon Michelson had been arrested for attempting to "fix" a traffic ticket five years before he allegedly bribed the agent, the idea that knowledge of this arrest bears on the credibility of reputation (or opinion) testimony stretches credulity. Part of the reason is that arrest is a poor proxy for the act itself. More importantly, it is doubtful that people in a modern community would, even if well informed, know that a person had been arrested. Most people today do not live in small towns where such information might once have been generally available. In *Michelson* itself the venue was New York City, where surely even on the day the case was decided, little pieces of Michelson's past would not likely be known to his friends. Even convictions (which generate more publicity than arrests) are not likely to be known widely, absent extraordinary circumstances. Hence it is doubtful that a favorable reputation should be discounted if the community does not speak of the arrest, or that a favorable opinion should be discounted if the witness does not know of the arrest.

Similarly *Michelson* was too generous on the matter of questions relating to events in the distant past. Of course failing to take into account an event might indicate that relevant data is being ignored, and perhaps a positive appraisal is open to doubt if it persists despite negative events, but it would be astonishing if events 26 years ago, or even five years ago (unless it was something like murder or child abuse) were still a matter of knowledge or conversation, and it stretches credulity to suppose that such events would still bear significantly on an assessment of character.

Modern cases stress that the trial judge can control the scope of questioning defense character witnesses about prior acts, a point that *Michelson* acknowledged. Some decisions take this opening to restrict cross-questions that seem abusive and counterproductive. Courts have come up with at least one hard-edged rule, which is that prosecutors should not ask "guilt-assuming" questions. They should not ask charac-

ter witnesses whether their favorable opinion would change if they knew
that defendant had committed the charged crime. This rule is all to the
good: Allowing such questions involves a kind of logic-chopping that
undermines the whole idea of proving good character. In effect the
question asks jurors to assume the opposite of what the character
testimony indicates, and then asks them whether a person who has done
what the question supposes could have such character. A technique
better calculated to destroy the presumption of innocence is hard to
imagine.

Another constructive principle would block questions about events
that the witness would not likely know about, which would include most
prior arrests. And some courts have held, rightly in my view, that a
character witness who gives specific testimony relating to a specific trait,
such as peacefulness, cannot be cross-examined about conduct by the
accused that does not relate to this trait.

### D.   What's Different in Modern American Law?

The American law of character evidence has changed in some ways
since *Michelson*. One obvious change is that in all but about a dozen
states an accused's character may now be proved through opinion
testimony and not just reputation. This change makes sense because
reputation testimony is usually opinion thinly disguised. Except in
unusual cases, most of us, if asked about the reputation of someone we
know, would be hard-pressed to recall more than a few conversations in
which we heard any talk about that person, and our own judgments
usually rest on personal observation and watching interactions with
others. Those judgments should be expressed directly as opinion. The
only reason to allow reputation testimony is that sometimes our opinions
are affected by what we hear, and opinions then convey a mixture of
personal knowledge and recollections of what some have said. Even here,
however, the opinion of the witness is likely to drive the testimony more
than anything that could be called "reputation." For this reason the
drafters of the Federal Rules and most state codes thought the distinction between reputation and opinion was artificial, and elected to admit
both.

The change accommodating opinion testimony has *not* led courts to
admit expert testimony on character, although some scholars advocate
moving in this direction. Courts do, however, admit expert testimony
describing "syndromes" and "social frameworks," which can suggest
inferences about character, the only real difference being that syndromes
and frameworks are generic rather than personal. Hence many courts
allow testimony that battered women feel helpless to leave spouses,
which suggests that a particular woman who did not leave her husband
may have been beaten, notwithstanding her failure to flee. Such testimo-

ny is not far from an opinion that this woman's character is such that she would not leave a man who was beating her, and of course the testimony is admitted for this very reason.

Perhaps the biggest legal change since *Michelson* relates to trials for sexual assault or child molestation. In the federal system and some states, concerns over these crimes have given rise to rules of character evidence that apply only in prosecutions for such crimes. These rules, unknown at common law and not originally codified in the Federal Rules or in state counterparts, let prosecutors prove a defendant's prior sexual assaults or molestations in order to show that he committed the charged crime, even when the evidence supports this conclusion only through the propensity inference—he did it before, so he probably did it this time. The only check on such evidence is that trial judges retain authority to exclude such evidence when its probative value is substantially outweighed by its prejudicial effect

## IV.   Do We Have It Right Now?

### A.   Modern Critiques of the Law of Character Evidence

Not surprisingly, given that *Michelson* maintained the status quo while proclaiming its irrationality, the law of character evidence continues to draw supporters and critics. It's worth considering the main lines of criticism and the main defenses in some detail.

The primary criticism has two branches. The first branch stresses that our rules err in resting on the belief that character evidence (especially prior acts) is highly probative of conduct. Drawing on psychological literature, critics claim that "character" as we generally understand it sheds little light on conduct on a given occasion. Situational factors, it is argued, have more impact on decisionmaking and behavior than character. The experiments that support these contentions are problematic when it comes to formulating sound evidence policy for reasons identified by Professor Park, who points out that most of the experimental evidence involves nonviolent and noncriminal behavior, as researchers focus mainly on things like honesty, which is far removed from activities like drug dealing or sexual assault.[32]

Setting aside this objection for the moment, one implication of the psychological research is that it may well be a mistake to admit proof of prior acts under FRE 404(b) to show things like plan or intent, and also a mistake to allow the use of prior bad acts under FRE 608 or prior convictions under FRE 609 to show untruthful disposition. The argument is that proof that a person once dealt drugs has little bearing on whether, for example, he intended to sell drugs on a particular occasion,

---

[32] Roger C. Park, *Character at the Crossroads,* 49 Hastings L. J. 717, 728–736 (1998).

and proof that a person lied on a job application by inflating his resume has little bearing on whether he is testifying truthfully.

Other studies suggest a middle ground between theories resting on character (or disposition) and theories resting on situational factors. This middle ground accepts the idea that people have basic natures (or characters) that are more or less constant, and that character shapes viewpoint and perspective and affects conduct in important ways. But it also holds that these dispositions or traits interact with situational factors to shape behavior, meaning that manifestations of character in one situation may say little about likely behavior in another. These intermediate theories of the relationship between character and behavior suggest intermediate rules on proving character—like a rule that character evidence should be admitted only when there is special reason to think it is relevant. We should, for example, admit opinion testimony if it is deeply grounded in extended acquaintance with the person, and we should admit proof of prior acts if circumstances closely resemble those of the case at hand, paying less attention to physical or mechanical parallels and more to psychological parallels.

The second branch of this primary criticism sees our intuitions and understandings of the effect of character on conduct as inherently untrustworthy. The thought is that lay observers are prone to what psychologists call "attribution error," meaning essentially that it is our human tendency to put too much weight on character in appraising another's conduct (although we view *our own* misconduct as reflecting the situation rather than our shortcomings). Once again, this view brings into question the wisdom of admitting prior acts under FRE 404(b), and the wisdom of allowing the impeaching use of bad acts under FRE 608 and convictions under FRE 609. If, for example, we hear that a defendant hit his child, and the question is whether he later started a fight in a bar, we as external observers may be too quick to connect the one with the other and conclude that the defendant is the kind of hot-headed person who would, and so probably did, start the bar fight. But concluding that the father is hot-headed from the fact that he hit his son may reflect our lack of understanding of the context. We might have characterized the father in a different way if we had known that when he hit his son he was laboring under economic or workplace stress, or had been taking lip from the rebellious son in an altercation over the son's drug use. Similarly, if we hear that the defendant forged a check, we may be too prone to think he is lying on the stand, attributing the forgery to a dishonest character, rather than to desperation and financial stress. In short, the lay observer is too quick to attribute conduct to character, not considering situational factors. Some scholars dissent from these suggestions, however, and argue that there is no reason to think that jurors cannot properly appraise character evidence.

Somewhat related to this view is the approach taken by Professors Taslitz, Orenstein, and others.[33] These scholars argue not so much that our law of character evidence needs changing, but that what we really need is expert testimony that informs juries of the implications of social contexts, behavioral patterns, and the experiences and psychology of the person in question. If we had a richer context in which to appraise behavior, they argue, we would appraise it better. We should tap the knowledge of psychologists and other social scientists who can explain, for example, why rapists commit rape, and we should listen to a psychiatrist who might explain that someone charged with stealing welfare checks has a personality "characterized by an unusually high degree of passivity and dependency," which could be explained by recounting parts of her "life history, interviews, tests, and other data," that could in turn be encapsulated in a professional diagnosis. A psychologist might testify, for example, that such a person is "compliant and generally avoids conflicts that threaten the stability of her emotional attachments," leading to "unusual gullibility" that accounts for otherwise baffling behavior. Modern movement in the direction of admitting such evidence is good as far as it goes, the argument runs, but courts should go further and let experts relate their findings and knowledge specifically to the case at hand, which most courts do not allow. Equally important, we should listen more to psychologists who can help us understand the degree to which tendencies or traits in our psyche or mentation affect attitudes, purposes, and decisions about persons charged with a crime.

There is yet another, completely different but equally serious, criticism of the law of character evidence. This one also proceeds along two fronts. To begin with, we should pay more attention to the data on recidivism. Professor Imwinkelried has argued that recidivism rates for sexual offenses are far lower, for example, than recidivism rates for other crimes, hence that the principle embodied in FRE 413, allowing prosecutors to prove prior sexual offenses in trials for later sexual offenses, does not make sense.[34] Citing earlier statistics indicating that recidivism rates for sexual offenses are about the same as rates for other violent crimes, Professor Reed reached the opposite conclusion, arguing that we should

---

[33] See especially Andrew E. Taslitz, Myself Alone: *Individualizing Justice Through Psychological Character Evidence*, 52 Maryland L. Rev. 1 (1993); Aviva Orenstein, *No Bad Men!: A Feminist Analysis of Character Evidence in Rape Trials*, 49 Hastings L. J. 663 (1998).

[34] Edward J. Imwinkelried, *Undertaking the Task of Reforming the American Character Evidence Prohibition: The Importance of Getting The Experiment Off on the Right Foot*, 22 Fordham Urb. L. J. 285 (1995) (recidivism rate for rapists is 7.7%; among violent crimes, only homicide has a lower rate; sexual offense crimes are the wrong place to loosen the rule against prior acts).

be more generous in acknowledging the relevance of prior crimes in criminal cases across the board.[35]

Professor Park has opened up a second front in this debate. He argues that recidivism rates are relevant in appraising the probative worth of proof of other crimes, but he stresses that what we really want to know is slightly different, and he warns of problems in appraising recidivism rates. He points out that recidivism in crimes like arson, larceny, burglary, and drug dealing is higher than recidivism for sexual assaults, but he suggests that we should not be as interested in recidivism *rates*, but in what he calls "comparative propensity." He focuses *not* on the proportion of offenders in any particular category (such as rape or burglary) who commit the same crime again, but on the proportion of those caught committing a crime who have committed it before, which is not the same thing. For example, in the case of rapists, we can compare the percentage of people who are caught committing rape after having raped before with the percentage of people who rape after having committed some other offense, and with the percentage of people in the population at large who commit rape. He suggests that the relatively low recidivism rate for rape (7.7% according to one study) masks the fact that people arrested for rape are more than ten times more likely to have committed a prior rape than some other crime, and 163 times more likely to have committed a prior rape than persons with no criminal histories.[36] Park concludes that proof of prior crimes, even crimes with low recidivism rates, can be highly probative.

When we consider not just recidivism rate but also the relative proportion of first offenders as against repeat offenders committing any particular crime, it is possible to compute mathematically the probative value of proof that a defendant committed a prior similar offense. For illustrative purposes, suppose we know that a large proportion of burglaries are committed by people who committed prior burglaries, and we know as well that the base rate of burglars in the general population is low. Using Bayes' Theorem, we can appraise numerically the impact that proof of defendant's prior burglary should have in a case in which the jury, after evaluating the other evidence in the case, believes that there is about a 50% chance that defendant is guilty. Assume for purposes of this example that 25% of those who commit burglary have committed prior burglaries, which is a figure related to the recidivism rate (about 40%, according to recent data) but also related to the number of people

---

[35] Thomas J. Reed, *Reading Gaol Revisited: Admission of Uncharged Misconduct in Sex Offender Cases,* 21 Am. J. Crim. L. 127 (1993) (rapists are "as likely to be rearrested for other violent crimes as for another rape," and their rate for sexual offenses is "much closer to the average serious crime recidivism rate" than we thought; we should admit such acts more broadly).

[36] Roger C. Park, *Character at the Crossroads,* 49 Hastings L. J. 717, 738–741 (1998).

who "enter the field" by committing burglary for the first time. Assume as well that only one person in a thousand in the general population has committed burglary before, a proportion that approximates the probability that a person innocent of the charged crime would have committed other burglaries.

On these assumptions, Bayes' Theorem indicates that proof that defendant committed a prior burglary raise the new assessment of guilt to 250:1 (a probability of guilt exceeding 99%). Alternatively, if there were no other credible proof (no fingerprints, for example, and no credible eyewitness testimony), conceivably the jury would think, before learning of defendant's prior burglaries, that the odds of his guilt were only 1:1000. Then proof of the prior burglaries should raise their estimate of guilt to 1:4, which represents an increase in the likelihood of guilt, while obviously falling short of proving guilt beyond a reasonable doubt and in fact leaving innocence as more likely than guilt.[37] If, however, the jurors thought that prior acts were more probative of guilt than in fact they are, then the jurors might vote to convict on the basis of this overestimation.

The other branch of this criticism also stresses the importance of social science, but emphasizes the danger of making false assumptions about base rates. Professor Lempert and his colleagues argue that the appropriate comparison is *not* with the rate of burglary in the general population or even the population of arrestees, but with the prior burglary rate among innocent defendants who go to trial. Positing that the police often "round up the usual suspects" in investigating crimes and that prosecutors are more likely to pursue weak cases if they have evidence of prior acts that courts will admit, Lempert and his coauthors argue that the proportion of people with criminal histories who are *actually charged* with a crime like burglary is *much higher* than the proportion of people in the general population who have committed burglaries before. If 25% of *guilty* burglary defendants have prior burglary offenses and 12.5% of *innocent* burglary defendants have such records, and if prior odds of guilt (before admitting proof of prior burglaries) are even (1:1), then proving the prior burglaries should raise the odds of guilt to the level of 2:1 (a probability of 67%), which means that guilt is more likely than not, but which certainly does not prove guilt beyond a reasonable doubt. But thinking about the rate of burglary in the general population, rather than the rate among innocent defendants who are actually charged and tried, leads one to a multiplier of 250 rather than two, suggesting the demonstrably false conclusion that the odds of guilt

---

[37] Bayes' Theorem leads to these results. For accounts of this theorem, see Mueller and Kirkpatrick, EVIDENCE § 7.18 (3d ed. 2003); Richard R. Lempert, Samuel R. Gross, James S. Liebman, A MODERN APPROACH TO EVIDENCE 228–239 (3d ed. 2000). For more details, see David H. Kaye, *Quantifying Probative Value*, 66 Boston U. L. Rev. 761 (1986).

are more than 99%. Lempert and his colleagues argue that further complexities arise because plea bargaining may weed out more guilty than innocent defendants, so those defendants who actually stand trial are even more likely to be innocent than the 2:1 (or 67%) figure suggests.

One scholar has sought to answer the argument that selection bias skews the probative worth of prior misconduct. If police are more likely to arrest and prosecutors are more likely to charge people with records than people without them, this fact skews the comparison with the population at large only if innocent people with records are more likely to be arrested and charged. But that may not be right. Police and prosecutors are doing exactly what they ought to do if they arrest and charge on the basis of evidence that bears on guilt. And as Professor Sanchirico argues, it is doubtful that prosecutors would charge anyone for whom there is little independent evidence. In short, the base rate problem might not exist or might be smaller than supposed.[38]

Finally, there are other criticism of the law of character evidence that proceed from differing doctrinal perspectives. Some urge that our cherished basic rule—character evidence is inadmissible to prove conduct—is misleading or worse, because prior bad acts are often provable for various purposes, such as showing intent, identity, or modus operandi. On the larger point made by these arguments, there is little disagreement: Everyone recognizes that admitting prior crimes for any of these purposes necessarily invites a kind of propensity inference. But from this basic observation, the arguments go in radically different directions: Some argue that we should revise the rule to reflect more honestly what actually happens, which might lead to admitting specific instances of conduct more often. Others say we should revise the rule to bar mention of prior acts where their relevancy depends on some form of propensity inference.

One criticism that commands broad respect in the academy focuses on the use of other acts to challenge credibility under FRE 608 and 609. For years commentators have argued that other acts, even when they involve deception (like perjury or lying on employment applications), have little bearing on the question whether a witness is testifying falsely. At least some studies support this criticism.

The argument is that lying is highly context-specific, an argument that appeals to common experience. In particular, a person accused of a

---

[38] Chris W. Sanchirico, *Character Evidence and the Object of Trial,* 101 Colum. L. Rev. 1227, 1257–1258 (2001) (also answering suggestions that only innocent persons with prior records would go to trial by suggesting that guilty defendants might be horrified by incarceration, or might find the difference between a deal and likely punishment to be small enough to make trial worth the risk).

crime who testifies in his own defense has strong motives to lie if he is guilty. As Professor Friedman argues in urging an end to the use of convictions and bad acts to attack veracity in this setting, the likelihood the accused would lie on the stand has little to do with his past behavior.[39] While one can argue that past behavior has little bearing on the likelihood that *any* witness is truthful (because lying is more a function of situation than character), the real concern is criminal defendants. They are most vulnerable to unfair prejudice because they alone risk conviction and punishment.

In *Michelson*, for example, Solomon Michelson was asked whether he omitted from a license application the fact of his previous arrest for receiving stolen property, so the arrest entered the case not only to impeach his character witnesses, but also to impeach Michelson himself. In this setting, the justification was not that the arrest showed he was a liar, but that failing to mention it on the application suggested as much. This evidence, however, adds little to our assessment of Michelson's veracity. He may have been lying when he testified in his defense, but it is hard to believe that his failure to mention a conviction on a license application years earlier tells us much about this probability.

## B.   Is the Law Really That Bad?

Let us consider first whether the basic rule requiring exclusion of character evidence, and particularly bad acts by the accused, is justified. That rule rests mainly on three points. First, we fear that juries will misuse character evidence to convict "bad people" *because* of their previous bad deeds or their dreadful natures. Second, we think juries overvalue character evidence, placing too much weight on it as pointing toward guilt of the charged crime. Third, we consider it unfair to burden an accused, who stands trial for a specific offense, with the task of defending against other charges, or for that matter defending his life.

Do these reasons seem ill-founded or inadequate? The first two reasons implement, in lay terms, the idea that ordinary men and women are likely to commit "attribution" error, a well-supported psychological concept discussed above. The second reason also expresses the idea that admitting bad character evidence would cause *anyone* (not just juries) to care less about mistakenly convicting a defendant when he is shown to have an evil character or has behaved terribly on other occasions. It is hard to quarrel with this notion.

The third reason, which is that the accused should not be required to defend his whole life, reflects concerns rooted both in pragmatism and our sense of justice. Even without invoking the specter of inquisitorial

---

[39] See Richard D. Friedman, *Character Impeachment Evidence: Psycho–Bayesian [!?] Analysis and a Proposed Overhaul*, 38 U.C.L.A. L. Rev. 637, 638 (1991).

justice, we find it shocking to imagine a prosecutor behaving in the manner described in Camus' *L'Etranger,* proving that a defendant charged with shooting a man on the beach didn't cry at his mother's funeral in order to show that he intended to kill the man on the beach.[40] Do we really want to invite a jury to conclude from such evidence that the defendant is hard-hearted or to force him to take the stand and review in detail his relationship with his mother and why he didn't cry when she died?

It is true, as Professor Gross argues, that prosecutors often characterize defendants harshly by arguing in summation, for example, that the evidence shows that "defendant is a cold-blooded killer." But there is a huge difference between arguing that "defendant is a cold-blooded killer because he killed in the past, so you should find that he killed in this case" and arguing that the evidence shows that "defendant killed in this case, which makes him a cold-blooded killer." And our judges are supposed to stop prosecutors in their tracks when their rhetoric is too demeaning or flies too far beyond their proof, and they risk reversal if they don't.[41]

If these traditional arguments are not enough to justify the rule excluding bad acts by the accused, consider some responses that might be made to arguments that recidivism rates justify admitting more proof of bad acts. These arguments may not be so persuasive if Professor Lempert and his colleagues are right about the relevant comparisons. But suppose we agree that comparisons with the base rate in the general population are the right way to look at such proof. A similar argument is made every day in paternity suits, where a "paternity index" can show that the defendant is probably the biological father. This index rests on the difference between the probability that defendant would pass the paternal gene to a child and the likelihood that a "random man" drawn from the population would do so. In the same fashion, epidemiological evidence ("gold standard" in toxic exposure cases) rests on the difference

---

[40] See Renee Lettow Lerner, *The Interaction of Two Systems: An American on Trial for An American Murder in the French Cour D'Assises,* 2001 Univ. Ill. L. Rev. 791, 822 (2001) (the first phase of trial in the Cour d'assises reflects "interest in the psychology and personal circumstances" of the defendant, whose "life history and personality are explored over the course of a day or two," since the French "do not share American concerns about character evidence and poisoning the well," and prefer "to get as full an understanding as possible of the person on trial") (the information does not go "to a lay jury alone, but to a mixed panel with professional judges" who warn lay jurors about the danger).

[41] See Samuel R. Gross, *Make-Believe: The Rules Excluding Evidence of Character and Liability Insurance,* 49 Hast. L. J. 843 (1998); Albert W. Alschuler, *Courtroom Misconduct by Prosecutors and Trial Judges,* 50 Tex. L. Rev. 629, 642 (1972) (describing cases tolerating language characterizing defendants as "animalistic" and a "type of worm," but reversing where the prosecutor called the defendant a "cheap, scaly, slimy crook" or a "junky, rat, and sculptor with a knife").

between the proportion of unexposed people who suffer an ailment as against the proportion of exposed people who suffer the ailment.[42]

Why don't these examples demonstrate the value of statistical analysis in proving the probative worth of evidence of other acts? One reason is that in toxic tort and paternity cases we don't worry about proof beyond a reasonable doubt. The more important reason is that the numbers in paternity cases and epidemiological studies do not even *purport to tell us* anything about volitional behavior. Assigning a number, based on sociological comparisons, to the probability that someone with a prior record will again rob or kill or rape seems altogether another matter precisely because the question is volition: What has a particular person *chosen* to do? As Professor Mendez argues, in criminal cases we want to know how this defendant's prior conviction affected this defendant's conduct on this occasion, and the numbers do not even purport to answer this question.[43] No doubt the numbers tell us something, at least if we can overcome problems with base rates (a very big if), but they cannot answer or even address the question that criminal trials must answer, which is whether this person (who did it before) decided to do it this time.

In defending the American law of character evidence, and criticizing changes that would admit more such evidence, commentators have advanced four additional arguments. One stresses that the psychological and social science literature shows, if anything, that we already admit too much. Professor Mendez has argued that prior acts and estimations of character in the form of reputation and opinion are unreliable predictors of behavior.[44] Among social scientists, the conversation and debate on this subject is not over, and there is reason for caution. The question what character is and what it portends for any particular circumstance goes to the heart of what it means to be human, and philosophers, psychologists, and psychiatrists have discussed these matters and offered theories for centuries, not to mention authors and playwrights. The modern conversation seems to suggest that what we might call character is really some kind of interior force that might to some extent "control" us (an idea associated with Freud), but philosophers as disparate as Aristotle and Sartre have considered character to

---

[42] See Christopher B. Mueller and Laird C. Kirkpatrick, EVIDENCE § 7.19 (3d ed. 2003) (describing paternity index), and see Christopher B. Mueller, *Daubert Asks the Right Questions: Now Appellate Courts Should Help Find the Right Answers,* 2003 Seton Hall L. Rev. 987, 1010–1018 (2003) (exploring statistical significance of epidemiological proof).

[43] Miguel A. Mendez, *Character Evidence Reconsidered: "People Do Not Seem to be Characters,"* 49 Hastings L.J. 871, 874 (1998).

[44] See Miguel A. Mendez, *The Law of Evidence and the Search for a Stable Personality,* 45 Emory L. J. 221 (1996).

be very much a function of personal choice and purposeful cultivation. As Professor Tillers argues, the persistence of such disparate views helps explain why we have not (maybe cannot) reach enduring conclusions on the value of character evidence to prove conduct.[45]

A second argument supporting the rule excluding proof of the character of the accused stresses that we need the rule to support our ideal of a presumption of innocence. Even in a regime that excludes character evidence, that presumption is arguably in tension with the mere circumstance of being charged and put literally on the defensive. From the standpoint of a juror, the defendant in a criminal case is already isolated in a graphic way: He is the only one charged with anything, and he has no role in the case except to try to undercut and refute the evidence offered against him. Enforcing the rule against character proof is arguably a necessary aspect of implementing the presumption of innocence.

A third argument, which defends roughly our current system, is advanced by Professor Leonard. He suggests that the law of character evidence is concerned not only with achieving accurate results (its principal aim), but with other goals. He argues that trials must give litigants a "catharsis," meaning a transformative emotional impact. Because our understanding of the human condition includes beliefs that character shapes conduct, a regime that excluded all proof of character would be unacceptable, and the contrary regime admitting all character proof passing a minimal relevancy standard would be unwise because of doubts raised by psychologists, and perhaps unconstitutional as well. Professor Leonard stakes out a middle ground that differs from present law in not specifying the form that such proof should take and in letting prosecutors respond to defense evidence of good character only by impeaching character witnesses or refuting the picture of character they portray.[46] Whether or not "catharsis" is the best term for it, most would agree that defendants should emerge from the awful experience of a trial, in which life or liberty is at stake, with a feeling that they have been heard and treated fairly. In addition, trials should at least *seem* just and fair to the citizenry at large. Arguably our character rules serve this end.

Finally, an ambitious modern defense of roughly the existing law of character evidence argues that it resembles tort and criminal law in aiming through the creation of incentives to affect behavior outside of

---

[45] Peter Tillers, *What's Wrong with Character Evidence?*, 49 Hast. L. J. 781, 812–830 (1998) (rejecting argument that we must bar character evidence to maintain a vision of humans as autonomous; describing character as a self-organizing principle).

[46] David P. Leonard, *The Use of Character to Prove Conduct: Rationality and Catharsis in the Law of Evidence*, 58 U. Colo. L. Rev. 1, 39 and 56–57 (1987)

court. Professor Sanchirico distinguishes between "trace evidence," (not only physical clues, but eyewitness accounts) and "predictive evidence" (prior acts and character traits), and argues that admitting trace evidence and barring predictive evidence—both features of our law—enhance the incentive functions of criminal law. The argument for barring predictive evidence (including proof of character) is that a person thinking about committing a crime is more deterred if he knows that what he has already done won't count against him if he is mistakenly arrested than if he thinks that it will. In the latter instance, a decision to "go straight" is less attractive, and crime becomes more attractive. Surprisingly, Professor Sanchirico concludes that letting defendants prove good character does not provide an important incentive function because it benefits people with "impressive friends and a clean record" who don't need proof of good character, and admitting prior crimes to impeach defendants and other witnesses does, on balance, serve the incentive purpose because it allows for the better evaluation of "trace" evidence.[47]

## C.   What Can We Change?

With so many vigorous criticisms and suggestions for change, one might think that reform is just around the corner. But it doesn't seem likely, for several reasons. First, changes that would help criminal defendants seem unlikely, if only because there seems to be no political gain in being "soft on crime," and the visible momentum that produced FRE 413–415 is very much in the opposite direction Second, the Evidence Rules Committee has given no sign that it wants to tackle something as central to criminal cases and as conflicted as the rules on proving character. Finally, there is *Michelson* itself. The opinion has endured for nearly sixty years without significant change, and Justice Jackson's description of this "workable even if clumsy scheme," and the reluctance to "upset its present balance," have stood all those years as counsels of caution from a Court that has chosen not to revisit the larger body of law described in that case.

Still, there are a few changes toward which reformers might aspire:

Without changing a word in the Federal Rules, it would be possible to reject the holding of *Michelson* that prosecutors can cross-examine defense character witnesses on arrests, and possible to bar questioning on acts by the accused that do not bear either on the particular trait to which the witness has testified (some courts already take this view) or on the trait involved in the charged crime. A court faithful to the text and purpose of FRE 404 and 405 could easily conclude that arrests are *not* "specific instances of conduct" by the accused within the meaning of

---

[47] Chris W. Sanchirico, *Character Evidence and the Object of Trial,* 101 Colum. L. Rev. 1227, 1263 (2001).

FRE 405(a), and that the text of those provisions supersedes *Michelson* on these points. And a court faithful to the letter and purposes of FRE 404 and 405 could conclude that cross-examination on acts bearing no relation to the trait described in the testimony is impermissible.

Arguably we should go further. Barring cross-examination of defense character witnesses about prior bad acts, as Illinois has done, would, in my judgment, be another step in the right direction.[48] Confining the cross-examiner to questions asking the witness how well he knows the defendant, by reputation or personally, would adequately test the character witness. But any change in this direction would require amending FRE 404 and 405.

More importantly, we should amend FRE 608 and 609 to block impeachment of the accused by questions about prior bad acts and convictions. These provisions are already sensitive to risks in this area. FRE 608 gives judges broad discretion in determining what questioning to allow and confines cross-examination to acts that are "probative of truthfulness or untruthfulness," and FRE 609 applies a "reverse 403" balancing standard when prosecutors want to ask defendants about prior felonies (apart from those involving "dishonesty or false statement"). Unfortunately these protections are not enough.

What is gained from such questions is far outweighed by what is lost in admitting prejudicial evidence and keeping defendants from testifying. If there is a concern that defendants with long records of criminality will appear as innocents who are caught unjustly in the system if they testify but keep their past hidden, it would be possible to advise juries to make no assumption one way or another about the past life of the defendant, and evidence of prior criminal history would remain admissible if a defendant advanced a claim of having led a blameless life or a claim like being ignorant of drugs, that his criminal record directly refutes.

Commentators are on the right track, I think, in suggesting some fine-tuning of the system. Again without amending FRE 404 and 405, we could instruct trial judges to require situational similarity between prior crimes and charged offenses when the former are offered to prove things like intent and planning, or where relevance rests on a propensity

---

[48] See People v. Roberts, 479 N.E.2d 386, 390 (Ill. 1985) (cannot "question character witnesses regarding specific acts of misconduct"); People v. Hannon, 44 N.E.2d 923, 924 (Ill. 1942) (cannot cross-examine character witnesses about rumors of prior acts); Aiken v. People, 55 N.E. 695 (Ill. 1899) (cannot ask witnesses who testified to defendant's good reputation as a "peaceable and law-abiding man" whether they had heard he "violated the criminal law," as specific acts are inadmissible to rebut character evidence); People v. West, 617 N.E. 2d 147, 151 (Ill. App. 1993) (cannot ask character witnesses about prior acts); People v. Hunt, 270 N.E.2d 243, 247 (Ill. App. 1971) (reputation cannot be "impeached by proof of particular acts" on cross).

inference. More care might also be taken to prevent impeachment or other uses of stale crimes.

Finally, FRE 413–415 should be replaced by a rule that allows evidence of prior sexual assaults or acts abusing children only when they are so distinctively similar to the charged offense that one can be reasonably confident that the prior behavior provides by itself substantial reason to believe the defendant is guilty of the crime charged. Alternatively these rules could be simply repealed. Under both the common law and the Federal Rules as initially enacted, innumerable courts admitted prior acts in those settings when similarities to the crime charged suggested relevance.

## CONCLUSION

*Michelson* remains a classic case in the pantheon of important evidence decisions. Its broad outline of the common law rules of character evidence and their underlying justifications has been extraordinarily influential. *Michelson* shored up these rules and served as a model for the Federal Rules, which departed only slightly from the *Michelson* account. Among modern opinions, *Michelson* achieved in almost sixty years a place of honor that is matched by only a handful of other decisions. While *Michelson* is flawed on points of detail, including its actual holding, the opinion in its broader contours is more durable, and even the searching light of modern scholarship has not uncovered enough flaws to dislodge it. Whether these contours should remain in place will likely occupy scholars for many more years.

Neither the man Solomon Michelson, nor his crime nor his story, is highly significant. But the story of the American law of character evidence, as it unfolded in the case and was recounted in the decision, is central in the American law of evidence. In assessing the law of character evidence, we must turn to psychology, social science more generally, politics and even philosophy. The debate over these rules involves precedent, logic, formal models, psychological experiments and theories, criminal justice statistics, legislative and judicial politics, our beliefs and understandings about the ways that police and prosecutors and defendants and juries behave, and a heavy dose of pragmatism. Ultimately the debate forces us as humans to confront what it means to be human.

Unlike Solomon Michelson, Justice Jackson was a towering figure— a man who rose to the Supreme Court without graduating from law school, who virtually invented the modern law of war crimes and of trials for war crimes, and who brought to bear on the American law of character evidence brilliance tempered with caution and pragmatism. His classic description of this body of law as "archaic" and "paradoxical" shows that he knew it was convoluted. What he didn't know was how convoluted the debate over this law would become.

*

# 5

# The Story of Rule 410 and *United States v. Mezzanatto*: Using Plea Statements at Trial

## Christopher Slobogin*

In 1975 Congress simultaneously adopted Federal Rule of Evidence 410 and Federal Rule of Criminal Procedure 11(e)(6), both of which prohibited, in virtually identical language, evidentiary use of withdrawn guilty pleas and statements made during failed plea negotiations.[1] Twenty years later, in *United States v. Mezzanatto*,[2] the United States Su-

---

* Stephen C. O'Connell Professor of Law, University of Florida Levin College of Law. The author would like to thank Amy Fletcher and Toby Olvera for their research assistance.

[1] Today Federal Rule of Evidence 410 states:

Except as otherwise provided in this rule, evidence of the following is not, in any civil or criminal proceeding, admissible against the defendant who made the plea or was a participant in the plea discussions: (1) a plea of guilty which was later withdrawn; (2) a plea of nolo contendere; (3) any statement made in the course of any proceedings under Rule 11 of the Federal Rules of Criminal Procedure or comparable state procedure regarding either of the foregoing pleas; or (4) any statement made in the course of plea discussions with an attorney for the prosecuting authority which do not result in a plea of guilty or which result in a plea of guilty later withdrawn. However, such a statement is admissible (i) in any proceeding wherein another statement made in the course of the same plea or plea discussions has been introduced and the statement ought in fairness be considered contemporaneously with it, or (ii) in a criminal proceeding for perjury or false statement if the statement was made by the defendant under oath, on the record and in the presence of counsel.

The original rule did not include the language "with an attorney for the prosecuting authority" or exception (i), both of which were added in 1979. Federal Rule of Criminal Procedure 11(e)(6) went through the same permutations. Compare Pub.L. 94–149, § 1(9) (1975) with 89 Stat. 371, 372 (1979). In 2002, the latter rule was converted to Rule 11(f) and simply states: "The admissibility or inadmissibility of a plea, a plea discussion, and any related statement is governed by Federal Rule of Evidence 410." See Adv. Comm. Notes, Fed. R. Crim. Proc.11.

[2] 513 U.S. 196 (1995).

preme Court held that a criminal defendant may waive the protection provided in these rules. This is the story of those rules and that case.

The story behind the adoption of Rule 410 and its sister rule of criminal procedure is byzantine, but is worth telling because it exemplifies how Congress uses evidentiary rules to promote public policy, in this case a policy bolstering plea bargaining. Of dubious legality as late as 1958, the practice of exchanging reduced charges or sentencing recommendations for guilty pleas proved remarkably resilient. By 1971 the Supreme Court, in its opinion in *Santobello v. New York*, felt compelled to call plea bargaining "an essential part" of the criminal process that was "highly desirable for many reasons,"[4] among them its efficient avoidance of trial (today over 90% of all resolved federal criminal cases are disposed of through bargaining) and its ability to generate information about other criminals (which figures in perhaps 40% of all federal bargains). Apparently of the same mind, Congress wanted to encourage plea bargaining by assuring defense attorneys that their clients' admissions during that process would not come back to haunt them if negotiations with the prosecutor fell through. Rules 410 and 11(e)(6) (which is now Rule 11(f) and simply cross-references to Rule 410) were the result.

The story behind *Mezzanatto* is also of interest, because its holding that the prosecutor may condition plea negotiations on a waiver of the exclusionary rule embodied in Rule 410 and Rule 11 turns out to be extremely important to the practice of plea bargaining and to the rules of evidence. Admittedly, at the time it was handed down and for several years thereafter, *Mezzanatto* was a relatively "quiet" case. The decision is not heavily referenced in the annals of evidence law, if only because it appears to be more about plea bargaining than the rules of evidence. And even for criminal procedure buffs, it has not occupied a conspicuous place in the legal firmament; only a few authors, most of them students, have focused their attention on it.

Yet, slowly but surely, *Mezzanatto* is becoming a big deal. Using *Mezzanatto* as a springboard, the lower courts have put a serious dent in Rule 410, to the point where waiver of its protections is now the norm, and the options of defense attorneys who go to trial after failed negotiations are severely restricted. Indeed, today an argument can be made that *Mezzanatto* is the most important decision on plea bargaining since *Santobello*.

The opinion's significance for evidence rules is almost as profound, because it affects them in two different ways. First, *Mezzanatto* helped establish new ground rules for interpreting the federal evidence provisions, by making clear that their plain meaning does not always govern.

---

[4] 404 U.S. 257, 261 (1971).

Second, it was the first case in which the Court explicitly recognized that evidence rules, including those meant to further societal goals, could be waived by individual litigants, a precedent that has far-ranging implications for criminal and civil law practice.

I.  The Congressional Effort to Encourage Plea Bargaining—Rule 410 and Rule 11(e)(6).

The idea of preventing trial use of communications made during attempts to plead guilty did not originate in 1975 with the promulgation of Rule 410. Beginning as far back as the late nineteenth century, numerous cases, from a variety of states, prohibited the use of withdrawn guilty pleas in later proceedings. While almost as many cases decided to the contrary—on the ground that permitting a defendant to escape the consequences of his earlier admission of guilt "compounded crime"—in the 1927 decision of *Kercheval v. United States*[5] the Supreme Court sided with the first group of courts. There the defendant asked to withdraw his guilty plea after finding out he would receive a much higher sentence than the prosecutor had promised during negotiations; the trial court granted the request, but then allowed the fact of the plea to be introduced at trial. Writing for a unanimous Supreme Court, Justice Butler concluded that such a practice should no longer occur in federal court. Citing an earlier lower court case, Justice Butler stated, " 'The withdrawal of a plea of guilty is a poor privilege, if, notwithstanding its withdrawal, it may be used in evidence under the plea of not guilty.' "[6]

Of course, a withdrawn guilty plea is not the same as a statement made during plea negotiations. A plea or plea offer might be withdrawn for all sorts of reasons having only indirect import about guilt, including, as occurred in *Kercheval*, a realization that the judge is not going to go along with the prosecution's sentence recommendation. Furthermore, a proffer of a guilty plea does not necessarily entail an admission of crime; a defendant who maintains his innocence is still allowed to plead guilty. Statements that support the plea, in contrast, are often explicitly incriminating.

As plea bargaining became more prevalent, however, many courts did not think this distinction important. A sizeable number of decisions prohibited trial use of both the plea and any statements made during negotiations or to the plea-taking court. At the same time, a number of other state courts refused to exclude either pleas or plea statements, or were willing to exclude only withdrawn pleas and plea offers, an approach followed by the few state codes that addressed the issue.

---

[5] 274 U.S. 220 (1927).

[6] Id. at 224 (quoting White v. State, 51 Ga. 284, 289 (Ga. 1874)).

It was against this backdrop that Congress began its efforts to draft Rule 410. Those efforts were anything but smooth. As Professors Wright and Graham note in their treatise, "Rule 410 has easily the most convoluted legislative history of any of the Evidence Rules."[7] Because that treatise already lays out that history in some detail, only enough will be said here to set up the *Mezzanatto* case.[8]

The preliminary draft of Rule 410, issued by the Advisory Committee on the Rules of Evidence in 1969, parroted existing state statutes by prohibiting only withdrawn pleas or plea offers. By 1971, however, lobbyists from the antitrust defense bar—to be distinguished from the regular criminal defense bar, which rarely gets what it wants—pushed for an expansion of the rule to include a prohibition on the use of plea *statements* as well as pleas. As a result, the Advisory Committee added a sentence to the proposed rule simply stating "Evidence of statements made in connection with any of the foregoing pleas or offers is not admissible," which meant that such statements could not even be used in subsequent perjury prosecutions.[9]

That move immediately triggered a negative reaction by the Justice Department, as well as by the powerful Senator John McClellan. McClellan was so bothered by the new language that he threatened to curtail the Supreme Court's rule-making power if it was not removed. But the Advisory Committee, chaired by Third Circuit Court of Appeals judge Albert B. Maris, stood firm, and it soon sent the revised version of 410 on to the Supreme Court for its consideration. At that point, Deputy Attorney General Kleindienst got into the act, sending a letter to Chief Justice Warren Burger urging that use of plea statements be removed from Rule 410's prohibition. The Advisory Committee again responded strongly, however, and in 1973 the Court approved the Committee's version.

The Rule then moved to the Subcommittee on Criminal Justice of the House Judiciary Committee. Here the Justice Department mounted a new attack. Realizing that deleting all reference to plea statements was probably a lost cause, it argued that the rule should at least permit use of statements for subsequent perjury prosecutions and for impeachment of defendants who take the stand and contradict those statements. But the Department failed again. Not only did the House subcommittee refuse to adopt the Department's suggestions but, in early 1974, both

---

[7] Charles Alan Wright & Kenneth W. Graham, 23 FEDERAL PRACTICE & PROCEDURE § 5341 (1977).

[8] Most of the following account comes from Wright & Graham, ibid.

[9] 51 F.R.D. 315, 355 (1971).

the full Judiciary Committee and the House of Representatives approved the Supreme Court's language.

The Justice Department did not give up, however. The Senate had not yet had its say on the rule and the indefatigable Department renewed its pitch for an impeachment exception in this new forum. Here, aided by Senator McClellan, it finally achieved success: the Senate Judiciary Committee added language that permitted the introduction of "voluntary and reliable statements made in court on the record" both for impeachment purposes and in false statement and perjury prosecutions, and the full Senate endorsed that language.

The Department's victory was not complete, however. Since most useful incriminating statements are made during plea negotiations *before* the defendant pleads guilty for the record, the Senate's version did not advance the Justice Department's cause as far as it might have liked. Furthermore, in the House–Senate Conference Committee, the House members refused to go along with the Senate's language. The compromise reached by the Conference Committee in the face of this resistance was to adopt the Senate's version of Rule 410 but postpone its effective date until August 1, 1975, at which time it would be superseded by Federal Rule of Criminal Procedure 11(e)(6) to the extent there were any inconsistencies.

So it all depended on what happened with Rule 11(e)(6), which the Supreme Court had promulgated and transmitted to Congress on April 22, 1974, along with other proposed amendments to the Federal Rules of Criminal Procedure. When that rule, which used language identical to the House's original version of Rule 410, was considered by the House Subcommittee on Criminal Justice in the spring and fall sessions of the Congress, the Justice Department again pushed for the impeachment and perjury exceptions for use of statements made in open court. Why it persisted in this endeavor is not entirely clear; as Wright and Graham's treatise points out, the Department's survey of its staff around the country suggested that the plea statement issue "was of comparatively little concern to federal prosecutors." But the persistence paid off. In June, 1975, the House Judiciary Committee grudgingly agreed to add an exception for false statements and perjury prosecutions. Warning that such an exception "may discourage defendants from being completely candid and open during plea negotiations and may even result in discouraging the reaching of plea agreements," it nonetheless admitted that the exception was necessary "to protect the integrity of the judicial process from willful deceit and untruthfulness."[11]

Even this concession was a small one, however. Only those statements made under oath in court could be used, and only in prosecutions

---

[11] H.R. Report No. 94–247, 94th Cong., 1st Sess., 1, 23 (June 3, 1975).

for perjury or making false statements. The Committee still refused to adopt an impeachment exception, even the limited exception proposed by Justice that focused on use of in-court statements. The full House ended up adopting this version of Rule 11(e)(6).

For the Justice Department there was still one last chance, the Senate. Here the Department's friend, Senator McClellan, tried to scuttle the House's version by proposing that Rule 11(e)(6) be eliminated entirely, which would have had the effect of substituting the Senate's version of Rule 410 allowing use of plea statements (or at least not prohibiting their use). McClellan argued, in the words of an earlier Senate report, that the House approach was "unjustified," because it would allow defendants to "lie with impunity." The logic must have been persuasive, because the full Senate passed McClellan's proposal without debate. McClellan and the Justice Department had finally succeeded.

But only for short time. The Conference Committee rejected the Senate's version of Rule 11(e)(6). In its place, it adopted the House version recognizing only the false statements/perjury exception, and only when the plea statements are made in open court, under oath, with counsel present, language the full Congress eventually adopted. Given the Conference Committee's earlier equation of Rule 410 with whatever was decided about Rule 11(e)(6), that meant that Rule 410 read the same way. Four years later, in 1979, Congress added another, very limited exception that permitted use of a plea statement introduced by the *defendant*, as well as any other statements in the plea discussion that "ought in fairness be considered contemporaneously with it."[13] The relevant language of Rule 410 has not been changed since that time.

Thus, despite numerous efforts by the Justice Department and its congressional allies, Congress specifically rejected even a limited impeachment exception. As a matter of logic, therefore, it also rejected use of plea statements as general rebuttal evidence or in the prosecution's case-in-chief. But it was soon clear that the issue was not settled. The Justice Department knew that there is more than one way to skin a cat.

II.   The Government's Efforts to Encourage Truth–Telling—*Mezzanatto* and Its Progeny

The problem that Congress wrestled with did not go away. As the Senate Judiciary Committee noted, defendants could take advantage of

---

[13] See 77 F.R.D. 507, 610–11 (1978). A second amendment added in 1979 narrowed the scope of Rules 410/11(e)(6) to statements made to the prosecuting attorney, in an effort to avoid use of the rules to exclude confessions made to police during interrogations. Id. This significant change raises several issues, but is beyond the scope of this piece. See generally United States v. Herman, 544 F.2d 791 (5th Cir. 1977).

Rule 410 by saying one thing during negotiations (usually inculpatory) and, if those talks failed, take the stand and say something else at trial (usually exculpatory). The natural prosecutorial reaction to this scenario was to require those defendants who wanted to deal to *waive* their Rule 410 protection, sometimes just in the the event they took the stand and sometimes for any purpose. The former practice became standard in a number of jurisdictions, including the Ninth Circuit, where in 1991 Gary Mezzanatto was charged with possession of a pound of methamphetamine with intent to distribute. It is time now to turn to his story.[14]

## A. The Arrest

Mezzanatto is a native of San Bernardino, California. Shortly after high school, he joined the military and completed a tour of duty in Vietnam, where he received medals for combat duty. He left the service in 1973, and two years later married Leticia Rosas, with whom he had three children. For over fifteen years after he left the service he worked as an electrician's assistant, a job he held first with Kaiser Steel and then with Santa Fe Railroad. But at the time of his arrest, he had been laid off from the latter job for more than a year, and his only employment was with a man named Gordon Shuster, a colorful figure who turned out to be Mezzanatto's demise.

Mezzanatto met Shuster through a "mutual friend," a drifter whose given name was Brent Vincent, but who went by "Uncle Bob." Uncle Bob was himself a shadowy individual, a man with no permanent employment or address whom Mezzanatto met at about the time he lost his job at the Santa Fe Railroad and separated from his wife. Although at trial Mezzanatto refused to admit that Uncle Bob had anything to do with the methamphetamine trade, at other times he has acknowledged that his friend earned his living trafficking in drugs. Mezzanato also admits that, partly because of his connection with Uncle Bob, he started using methamphetamine and dealing in small amounts. As he put it, "everybody was smoking something back then—pot, meth, you name it. I sold a little on the side and that was it." Until 1991, he had never been arrested.

---

[14] Unless otherwise indicated, the following account comes from telephone interviews with: Gary Mezzanatto on June 27, June 28 and July 25, 2005; Shane Harrigan (the prosecutor in Mezzanatto's case) on July 1 and July 24, 2005; Merle Schneidewind (the defense attorney during the plea negotiations) on July 1, 2005; and Mark Lippman (Mezzanatto's appellate attorney) on June 10, 2005. Unsuccessful efforts were made to reach Richard Chier, Mezzanatto's trial attorney, and Tristan Moreland, the undercover agent involved in the case. References to statements at trial and additional facts come from Transcript of Proceedings in United States of America, Plaintiff v. Gary Craig Mezzanatto, Defendant, No. 91–0739–G–Criminal, U.S. Dist. Ct., So. Dist. Calif. 173–75 (Dec. 17, 1991) (hereafter Mezzanatto Transcript).

But he had been working for Shuster for some six or seven months under circumstances that, to some observers, might have suggested deeper involvement in the drug trade. Shuster lived a good hour and a half from Mezzanatto, in a trailer in a very rural area accessible only by a dirt road. Strewn around the property were various outbuildings, which contained a wide array of items, including containers with chemicals in them. The government would later establish at Mezzanatto's trial that these chemicals were of the type needed to manufacture methamphetamine.

The San Diego Narcotics Task Force zeroed in on Shuster in July, 1991. They placed his property under surveillance for a couple of weeks. By August 1, they were ready to move in. The arrest was carried out by a number of officers, led by John McKee and including Tristan Moreland, who often worked undercover for the Task Force.

Mezzanatto was not at Shuster's at the time. But while still on Shuster's property, Moreland let Shuster know that cooperation would soften his treatment by the government, and Shuster immediately provided Moreland with Mezzanatto's name and agreed to lure him into police clutches. With Moreland sitting across the table from him, Shuster contacted Mezzanatto through his pager (which was under a fictitious name). It took seven or eight conversations throughout the day, together lasting about 40 minutes, but by the last one Mezzanatto had agreed to deliver a package to a "friend" of Shuster's who wanted to buy it for $13,000.[15]

Late that night, after one unsuccessful attempt to meet at a place called the Rainbow Club, the three of them (Shuster, Moreland and Mezzanatto) connected at a Sizzler restaurant. Shuster introduced Mezzanatto to his "friend," and Mezzanatto asked "Where do you want to do this thing?" Moreland assured him there were no police around, at which point they all walked over to Mezzanatto's car in the parking lot. Moreland got in the passenger seat, with Shuster standing alongside him, while Mezzanatto sat in the driver's seat.

Mezzanatto then pointed to a package on the floor of the car. Moreland opened it and went through several layers of wrapping before determining from the aroma that the contents were methamphetamine. According to Moreland, he also told Mezzanatto how "clean" the drugs looked, and asked him how long it would take to get another pound.

---

[15] Harrigan never presented any testimony about what Shuster said on the phone (on the assumption it would have been hearsay) but rather asked Moreland what he "directed" Shuster to say. While Moreland said he directed Shuster to order a pound of methamphetamine for $13,000, Mezzanatto claimed Shuster only told him to bring the "package," for which he would get "13 big ones." Id. at 31 (direct examination of Moreland); 92–93 (cross-examination of Moreland); 197–98 (direct examination of Mezzanatto).

Mezzanatto responded, according to Moreland, that it would take about six hours, two to drive back home, two to pick up the product and another two to drive back down. Mezzanatto claims, on the other hand, that nothing specific was said about the contents of the package and that he only offered to get more "stuff," without specifying driving times. Both parties agree, however, that Mezzanato then pulled out from the ashtray a glass pipe (later found to contain methamphetamine residue) and asked if Moreland wanted a "hit." Moreland declined, and walked away, purportedly to get the money to consummate the deal. He then pulled off his yellow bandana, a pre-arranged signal for other officers to close in and arrest Mezzanatto. While the police tackled Shuster (apparently in an effort to mislead Mezzanatto about his informant status), Mezzanatto was handcuffed and placed in the squad car.

## B.  The Plea Negotiation

Three months later, on October 17, 1991, Mezzanatto and his attorney, Merle N. Schneidewind, met with the Assistant United States Attorney prosecuting the case, Shane Harrigan, who was accompanied by McKee and Moreland. The meeting took place in the federal prosecutor's office adjacent to the federal courthouse in San Diego. It was requested by Schneidewind, who was interested in cutting a deal for his client. Harrigan, who had been an attorney for 8 years and a prosecutor for four, was hoping to get information on other individuals involved in the methamphetamine trade. Consistent with routine practice in the federal prosecutor's office for the Ninth Circuit, Harrigan started by stressing the importance of telling the truth during negotiations and noting that, if the negotiations fell through, the state would be free to use Mezzanatto's plea statements to impeach him at trial and in any subsequent perjury prosecution (although not in its case-in-chief on the drug charges). As he later explained, Harrigan believed that such an arrangement was crucial in "proffer" situations such as this; "without a hammer, there is no incentive to be truthful" about who else was involved in crime and the evidence to support it.

Schneidewind says he also explained the waiver arrangement to Mezzanatto. According to Mezzanatto, however, the explanation didn't take. Mezzanatto remembers that he was "clueless" about the negotiation process and its pitfalls. His principal impression was that if he gave himself up he might get a deal from the prosecutor.

Even so, the decision to talk was not easy for him, for a couple of reasons. First, he went into the negotiations thinking that the mandatory minimum for his offense was five years. One of the first things he learned from Harrigan was that the actual mandatory minimum was ten years. He was also worried that cooperation with the authorities would lead to repercussions from Shuster's associates. Although Mezzanatto says he never saw Shuster's cronies because he was always asked to leave when they showed up, he figured they probably knew who he was.

Schneidewind convinced him, however, that going to trial would be a mistake. So, although Mezzanatto began the plea discussion with the statement that he feared for his own life and the lives of his family, he went on to admit that he had been acting as a small-time drug broker for Shuster, and that he had also engaged in similar deals with "Uncle Bob," from whom he obtained the package in his car on the day of his arrest. He also conceded that he knew Shuster ran a drug lab in his home and that he had handled some glassware used for manufacturing methamphetamine, after initially denying both facts.

So far so good, it would seem. But all of a sudden, things fell apart. Wanting to minimize his association with Shuster, the next thing Mezzanatto said was that he had not visited Shuster's home during the week prior to his arrest. McKee promptly countered with the observation that he had seen Mezzanatto's car at Shuster's home the day before the arrest. At that point, Harrigan accused Mezzanatto of lying and terminated the meeting.

Mezzanatto's slip seems a slim reason for ending a meeting that might have produced bigger game. Indeed, McKee was upset with Harrigan because he thought Mezzanatto might have had some useful information about suppliers. But Harrigan's decision to end the negotiation was based on a number of considerations. To begin with, he had Mezzanatto dead to rights. The evidence against him was strong, and a guilty plea wasn't needed to convict him. More importantly, he was leery of Mezzanatto, for a number of reasons. First, the defense had come forward to negotiate at the "11th hour" just a few days before trial was to start, often a sign of desperation likely to produce concocted stories in an effort to avoid a jury conviction and a longer sentence. Second, Mezzanatto's vacillations about various incriminating details did not bode well for getting accurate information from him; he seemed willing to admit to his lies only after his story became obviously inconsistent or was contradicted. Third, Harrigan was "incredulous" over Mezzanatto's insistence that he was new to the drug game, given his ability to produce a pound of meth on quick notice. Finally, the information Mezzanatto was providing about other players was vague; at one point, Harrigan remembers expressing dismay over having to miss a Braves/Pirates playoff game over the paltry revelations Mezzanatto was giving him. All of this raised concerns about Mezzanatto's ability to provide significant investigative leads or credible testimony against others. So his lie about his pre-arrest contact with Shuster was merely the proverbial straw.

Mezzanatto admits that he never had much to give the prosecution except his own admission of guilt; the government already had Schuster, of course, and seemed to know about Uncle Bob as well. As Mezzanatto put it, "the government is going to go with the guy who talks first," which meant he was out of luck as far as having anything of value to offer the government. When he walked into the negotiating room, he said, "I was the bad guy and I didn't even know it." He says Harrigan kept on asking for people "who sold pounds, not ounces," but that he, Mezzanatto, didn't know anybody like that except Shuster. "Harrigan's job was to clean up the streets. If I couldn't offer him anybody big, I was going to jail for at least ten."

In hindsight, Mezzanatto says he still would have talked to the prosecutor—even though he now knows that Shuster led the police to him and that he had nothing to offer but his own story about being a small-time dealer, which the prosecutor was not about to buy. When asked if he now understands what a waiver of Rule 410 permits, he responded that it allows the government to use plea statements of someone like him if "they can already prove what I'm saying"—if, in other words, it has other evidence corroborating the defendant's negotiation statements. When his misimpression about Rule 410 waiver is corrected, it dawns on him: "Then I guess my getting on the stand opened the door." Finally, fifteen years later, he gets it.

## C.  The Trial

Once it became clear to Mezzanatto he was going to trial, he ditched his attorney. Although Schneidewind was an accomplished lawyer with over twenty years experience, he was also a state-paid public defender, and Mezzanatto's jail mates advised him to get a "real" attorney from private practice. Independent of that, he'd lost confidence in Schneidewind, who was telling him he couldn't win at trial and that even a plea without a deal would likely result in a lesser sentence than the judge would hand down after a conviction by a jury. But Mezzanatto just couldn't see spending ten years in prison for what he had done. "That was ridiculous." He now admits that Schneidewind had given him good advice, and that he probably should have stuck with him and pleaded guilty. But at the time he wanted a new attorney.

His choice was Richard Chier, who worked out of Los Angeles, with an office on the Avenue of the Stars, Wilshire Boulevard. Despite his fancy address, Chier was relatively new to criminal practice, with a four-year track record. Many of his decisions during the trial were questionable, but in fairness to him, he had a tough case.

The trial took place in the federal courthouse adjacent to where the plea negotiations had occurred. It was a three-day affair, presided over by Earl B. Gilliam, a judge since 1957. Harrigan's case consisted of three witnesses: Moreland and McKee, who described the arrest and the events leading up to it, and a chemist who testified that the substance in the package that Mezzanatto handed to Moreland was methamphetamine.[16] Harrigan rested the state's case-in-chief the morning of the second day of trial. Chier's first and only witness was Mezzanatto, whose testimony took up most of the rest of the second day.

Chier undoubtedly knew the old defense attorney's saw that, unless the defendant is innocent or a real charmer, putting him on the stand is not a good idea. That rule would seem ironclad when the defendant has made incriminating statements during plea negotiations and waived his Rule 410 protection against impeachment. But Chier let Mezzanatto testify anyway, with predictably disastrous results. Now aware of the surveillance records, Mezzanatto admitted that he had been at Shuster's home the day before the arrest. But the rest of his story was hard to swallow.

He began his direct testimony by describing how, after being laid off, he met Shuster through a "mutual friend" (he did not mention Uncle Bob by name). Shuster soon asked him to help out around his property in Fallbrook (the location of Shuster's eventual arrest). The initial job was to set up a power source, since the property had none. But eventually, Mezzanatto said, he simply became a "handyman," doing chores around the lot such as cleaning up and fixing equipment, sometimes for just a few hours, sometimes for longer periods of time. He said Shuster paid him $100 a day, up to $300 a week.

The work had nothing to do with drug manufacturing, or at least, Mezzanatto testified, he didn't think it did. Shuster first told him he was shipbuilder (and showed him a place in San Marcos with a 70–foot boat). He later revealed to Mezzanatto that he was a special agent for the CIA, involved in making plastic explosives. And finally, Mezzanatto said Shuster convinced him he was working on a plan to recycle gold from ocean water, and got Mezzanatto to invest $3,000 of his savings in the project. All of this was designed to suggest that Mezzanatto was not the sharpest knife in the drawer. As Chier would put it in his closing argument:

> [Mezzanatto] is not an enormously intelligent guy, he is not a well-educated person. He is not a cynical person, ... he is just, basically, a working stiff. A guy that is gullible and easily misled.

So this was the picture painted during Mezzanatto's direct testimony: Mezzanatto didn't think Shuster was a drug manufacturer, but rather an explosives expert. And when Shuster handed a package to Mezzanatto the day before the arrest, and told him to take it and put his

---

[16] Interestingly, it was McKee, the police officer, rather than the chemist who asserted that the chemicals found at Shuster's could be used to manufacture methamphetamine.

address on it, Mezzanatto did so because he was the dependent sort who did what people in authority told him to do, and because he figured Shuster wanted explosives out of the area for some reason. And when Shuster called him the next day to bring the "package" for his friend, Mezzanatto thought he was delivering explosives. He admitted to making most of the statements Moreland said he made in the car on the day of his arrest, but explained that he was merely offering Moreland a friendly "hit," not a sample from the package (which he thought contained explosives), and that his comments about getting other stuff for Moreland were merely designed to "play along with Shuster's deal," which had little to do with him.[17]

On cross-examination, Harrigan contested each of these assertions. As a riposte to Mezzanatto's professed ignorance of Shuster's drug activity, Harrigan emphasized the presence of the chemicals on Shuster's property, the fact that Mezzanatto had registered his pager under a false name, and the fact that Mezzanatto had purchased, at Shuster's behest, equipment that could be used as a vacuum pump of the type needed to manufacture methamphetamine. He questioned why Mezzanatto would put his address on a package of explosives that, if misplaced, would thus be sent back to the home in which his wife and children lived. Harrigan also asked Mezzanato why he suggested that Moreland take a hit when that act would position a lighted match directly over the package, supposedly full of explosives, on Moreland's lap. During closing argument he emphasized the fact that the wrapping material for the package contained a bag from a store near Mezzanatto's, not Shuster's, home. Surely the jury was also wondering why Shuster would give Mezzanatto explosives one day and ask for them back the next, why Mezzanatto would continue to think explosives were part of the deal when he saw a white substance in the package, and why he would say he could get more "stuff" when Shuster, the supposed explosives manufacturer, was standing right there next to Moreland.

With all of this ammunition, Harrigan probably didn't need to mention the October 17 plea negotiations. But he did. During cross-examination of Mezzanato, without any on-point objection from Chier,[18] Harrison called Mezzanatto's attention to the plea meeting, got him to admit that during that meeting he stated that he had obtained the package from Uncle Bob, and asserted that Mezzanatto had also said he knew the package had contained methampethamine (to which Mezzanatto responded that he had only meant to say that he had *since* found out

---

[17] Mezzanatto reiterated this claim on cross-examination: "This is Gordon's deal. I am playing along. I don't even know what is happening."

[18] At this point, very early in the cross-examination of Mezzanatto, Chier seemed to be concerned only about whether an account of the meeting by Mezzanatto would be hearsay.

the contents of the package). Later in the cross-examination, this time with Chier making several objections but none of them referencing Rule 410,[19] Harrigan got Mezzanatto to admit that he had said nothing about the CIA or explosives at the October 17 meeting and asserted (with Mezzanatto denying the assertion) that Mezzanatto had admitted he knew Shuster was manufacturing meth.

Then, after Mezzanatto had stepped down, Harrigan called Moreland again, this time as a rebuttal witness who could describe the October 17 meeting in more detail. Moreland testified that Mezzanatto had "decided he wanted to cooperate with the government," that he had been told his statements could be used in false statements prosecutions and for impeachment, that he knew that the package seized on the day of the arrest contained methamphetamine, that he had helped handle some of the glassware for the drug manufacturing process, and that he had lied about being present at Shuster's house the day before the arrest. On cross, Chier tried to minimize the damage by pointing out that Moreland had no detailed notes of the October 17 meeting, that the notes he did have were dated December 5th (a month and half later), and that Mezzanatto had been "in a turmoil" after finding out that the mandatory minimum was twice as long as he had thought, and thus in no shape to tell a coherent story. He also got Moreland to concede that even the feds had initially thought Shuster might be making explosives; when asked about whether there was "some original interest" in Shuster's site for that reason, Moreland stated, rather sardonically, "I would say for about a minute and a half, yes."[20] But these efforts were merely a pinkie in the dam.

Given this devastating impeachment, why did Chier put Mezzanatto on the stand? As one might expect, the answer is more complicated than

---

[19] Chier correctly objected, without citing Rule 410, that "[d]iscussions as part of a case settlement are by policy excluded from evidence," Mezzanatto transcript, *supra* note 14, at 235, but then elaborated by citing relevance concerns, Rule 408 (regarding use of statements from *civil* settlement negotiations) and "Kastigar" (the latter objection referring to the rule that government must show an independent source for evidence that appears to be derived from immunized or inadmissible evidence). Id. at 236. After Chier's mention of Rule 408, Judge Gilliam, apparently bemused by the multiple, inapposite objections, overruled Chier and stated "You keep thinking, don't pay attention to what we are doing." Id. Chier's confusion about how to handle evidence about the negotiation meeting was also apparent when, during Moreland's cross-examination, Chier himself started asking questions about the plea meeting! He was only stopped in this effort when Harrigan suggested, at a sidebar, "I don't want to try your case, but it is not going to help you." Id. at 99. And toward the end of the trial Chier seemed to admit he was at sea on the issue. Id. at 303 ("I just discovered the . . . I don't know how this happened. My life has been made extra hard for me, until Mr. Harrigan clued me in today.").

[20] One wonders why Chier did not mention this admission of Moreland's during closing argument. It was the only external support for Mezzanatto's seemingly outlandish explosives story, at least the only support that got into evidence.

is suggested in the appellate opinions. Chier's investigator, Manny Lopez, had managed to track down the owners of the property on which Shuster lived, two elderly folks by the names of Bernard and Lorene Cook. According to Chier's offer of proof, both would have testified that they too had been taken in by Shuster's CIA/explosives story. The idea was to paint Shuster, in Chier's words, as a man with considerable "charm, persuasion, salesmanship, force of personality."[21] All of this (added to Moreland's concession that the government was looking into the explosives story as well) would have perhaps made Mezzanatto's testimony sound less fantastic to the jury. The combination of Shuster's wiliness and Mezzanato's density, Chier hoped, would lend credibility to Mezzanatto's account. Unfortunately for that theory, Judge Gilliam determined that the Cooks' testimony was irrelevant since they had never communicated their beliefs about Shuster to Mezzanatto.[22]

The Cooks probably would not have helped much anyway. The jury returned a verdict of guilty in less than a hour. Judge Gilliam felt compelled to comment that it was "one of the quickest juries I have ever had, and I have been at this for 28 years.... I don't think I have ever had a jury come back quite so fast." He subsequently sentenced Mezzanatto to 170 months—over 14 years—in prison. The term was well over the statutory minimum because of Mezzanatto's perceived fabrications at trial (still another reason not to take the stand). Of course, Mezzanatto could have been tried for perjury as well, but that prosecution never took place; it wasn't necessary given the sentence enhancement.

D.  Appeals to the Ninth Circuit and the U.S. Supreme Court

Mezzanatto appealed to the Ninth Circuit, where the case was heard by a three-judge panel consisting of Chief Judge J. Clifford Wallace and Judges Cynthia H. Hall and Joseph T. Sneed—except that Sneed was not present in the courtroom; sick at the time, he was represented by a box on the podium (out of which no voice issued during the entire argument). Harrigan appeared for the state, while Mezzanatto acquired his third attorney when Chier opted not to do the appeal: Mark Lippman, a lawyer with just a few years experience in trial and appellate litigation, was assigned the task of arguing the defense side. The principal focus in the briefs was whether the protections of Rule 410 could be waived.

---

[21] Chier made these points at sidebar in arguing unsuccessfully for the relevance of the Cooks' testimony.

[22] One may also ask why Chier didn't subpoena Shuster. He may have decided that Shuster, who was cooperating with the government, would have contradicted everything Mezzanato said and, given his "charm," done a much better job of denial than Mezzanatto did.

At oral argument, however, Lippman wasn't sure he'd even get to the merits. First, Chier's objections had been so diffuse that the court could have chosen to handle the case under the plain error rule, a tough standard to meet where a statutory, rather than a constitutional, violation is involved.[23] Although Lippman was able to finesse the default issue, he did get a number of questions about whether, assuming admission of the plea statements was error, that error was harmless—an easier test to overcome than the plain error standard, but still one that, if met, would have allowed the panel to find against Mezzanatto on the ground that guilt was clear even without the impeachment. Ultimately, however, the judges dropped this line of inquiry. Harrigan, who is sure he could have convicted Mezzanatto even without the impeachment evidence, didn't forcefully argue the harmless error point.[24]

Chief Judge Wallace was more adamant about Lippman's arguments on the merits, however. At one point, he stared angrily at Lippman and simply stated, "He waived it!" That sentiment permeated his eventual opinion in the case, which argued that if defendants can waive constitutional rights like the fourth amendment, they certainly should be able to waive Rule 410's provision. As Wallace put it, "It would be difficult to conclude, for example, that the policy of quickly and cheaply resolving cases is more important than the policy of securing ourselves in our 'persons, houses, papers, and effects.' "[25] Harrigan, on the other hand, recalls that the judges' questions of him were "softball." Although Judge Hall persisted in comparing the waiver condition imposed on Mezzanatto to an unconscionable contract, the general tenor of the questions was such that, after they were done, Harrigan wagered Lippman lunch that the government would win.

So Harrigan was "shocked" when the panel found for Mezzanatto, 2–1, with Wallace dissenting (although Harrigan dutifully bought Lippman lunch soon thereafter). Judge Sneed, he of the voicebox, wrote the panel's opinion, which asserted that "[t]o allow waiver of these rules would be contrary to all that Congress intended to achieve. If these rules were subject to waiver, candid and effective plea bargaining could be severely injured." Sneed called Wallace's equation of constitutional rules and Rule 410 a "false equality." While cases permitting waiver of constitutional rights are an "inescapable feature of courts interpreting the Constitution by defining the right being asserted," the Federal Rules of Evidence were promulgated by the Supreme Court and Congress.

---

[23] FED.R.CR.P. 52(b) (permitting review of unobjected to error only if "substantial rights" are involved).

[24] And in its opinion the panel concluded the error was not harmless. United States v. Mezzanatto, 998 F.2d 1452, 1456 (9th Cir. 1993).

[25] Id. at 1457 (Wallace, J., dissenting).

"Given the precision with which these rules are generally phrased, the comparative recentness of their promulgation, and the relative ease with which they are amended, the courts can afford to be hesitant in adding an important feature to an otherwise well-functioning rule." Finally, Sneed noted the "weak bargaining position" of defendants in Mezzanatto's situation, suggesting that his waiver was of questionable validity.[26]

Matters might have ended there; Mezzanatto was ready to plead guilty, and figured he'd get about eight years. But the Department of Justice thought the Ninth Circuit's decision would be a good one to appeal to the Supreme Court, given the rising number of proffers by defendants and concomitant imposition of waiver conditions by federal prosecutors. And just a few months after the Ninth Circuit handed down *Mezzanatto*, the Seventh Circuit came down with an opinion that decided the waiver issue in favor of the government, creating a split between the circuits.[27] Although most certiorari petitions are denied, this one was granted.

Lippman had never argued in front of the Supreme Court, and he admits it was "stressful" preparing for the arguments. He arrived in Washington a week beforehand, and mooted the case several times with the ACLU, which thought the case important even though it normally doesn't take on non-constitutional litigation. As the appellee, he argued second, after Miguel Estrada, the attorney from the Solicitor General's office (the entity that usually argues for the United States in such cases). Lippman's memory is that, from the moment he took the podium, it was clear Chief Justice Rehnquist was hostile to Mezzanatto's case; he'd shake his head every time Lippman made a point, and usually come back with a rejoinder. Justices Scalia, Kennedy and Ginsberg engaged Lippman as well, while Justices Souter and Stevens were much more active with Estrada. Justice Thomas, who would write the majority opinion, was mute as usual.

Estrada later gained considerable notoriety when he was nominated by President George W. Bush for the U.S. Court of Appeals for the District of Columbia and then withdrew after two years of concerted Democratic opposition. He was poised and articulate in the face of a flurry of questions from the bench. His central argument was that Rule 410 existed to protect defendants, and therefore, like the rights to silence, jury trial, counsel and other rights, ought to be waivable by

---

[26] Id. at 1455–56 (majority opinion). Wallace asserted, on the other hand, that Mezzanatto's waiver was knowing and voluntary. Id. at 1456.

[27] United States v. Dortch, 5 F.3d 1056, 1067–1068 (7th Cir. 1993). Two other circuit courts of appeal were in agreement with the Ninth Circuit. United States v. Acosta–Ballardo, 8 F.3d 1532, 1536 (10th Cir. 1993); United States v. Lawson, 683 F.2d 688, 692–94 (2d Cir. 1982).

them. He also made a useful distinction between "charge bargaining" and "cooperation bargaining." In the former situation, the defendant is trying to get a reduction in charge in exchange for pleading guilty. In such cases, Estrada noted, the prosecutor only needs to meet with the defense attorney, not the defendant, and thus Rule 410 was less likely to be relevant. But in cooperation cases, the defendant purportedly has information that can be useful to the government; since undercover agents and others may rely on it to their detriment, the government needs assurances of accuracy, which a Rule 410 waiver can help provide.[28]

Lippman's argument was three-pronged. First, Mezzanatto's waiver should not be recognized because Rule 410 is aimed at creating a "fair" procedure, and thus should be considered unwaivable. This was the focal point of virtually the entire exchange between him and the bench, with most of the justices suggesting that litigants have always been allowed to forego the protection of evidentiary rules (the hearsay prohibition was the justices' favorite example), and Lippman gamely trying to convince them that Rule 410/11(e)(6) was different, more like the rest of Rule 11 (which requires that the judge ensure the defendant's guilty plea is knowing and voluntary). In his brief, he also argued that permitting prosecutors to demand Rule 410/11(e)(6) waivers would scare defendants away from the bargaining table and thus undermine plea bargaining, at the same time it would allow prosecutors to elicit admissible incriminating statements from defendants whom they know are desperate to obtain the sentencing benefits of a guilty plea but with whom they have no intention of settling.

Justice Thomas, writing for the seven-member majority, had answers for each of these contentions. First, he noted that most rights, even constitutional ones, are waivable, and should be considered sacrosanct only when they are "fundamental to the reliability of the fact-finding process," a trait not easily associated with a rule that excludes voluntarily-made incriminating statements.[29] Second, Thomas noted that plea bargaining in the Ninth Circuit, where *Mezzanatto* originated and which had followed a waiver policy for some time, obtained at least as many pleas as other circuits, and that, in any event, precluding such waivers might inhibit *prosecutors* from coming to the table. Finally, Thomas stated, instances of prosecutorial bad faith and deception should be dealt with on a case-by-case basis rather than through a blanket ban

---

[28] It is not entirely clear how Rule 410 achieves this goal, however. Most defendants probably think either that the negotiation will be successful or that, if it isn't, they won't take the stand; thus, to their way of thinking, this kind of waiver can't hurt them even if they lie.

[29] 513 U.S. 196, 204.

on waivers. He also noted that the Court had never found coercion existed simply because a defendant is given a hard choice between legitimate alternatives.

While Thomas' opinion could be read to permit Rule 410 waivers for any purpose, three justices in the majority (Ginsburg, O'Connor and Breyer) signaled they would be more hesitant to permit defendants to waive protection against use of such statements outside the impeachment context at issue in Mezzanatto's case. They feared that allowing broader waivers would be much more likely to deter defendants from negotiating. The dissent, authored by Justice Souter, more realistically recognized that, as Estrada acknowledged during oral argument, defendants are usually in no position to turn down a plea offer, given the differential between the sentence after a guilty plea and the sentence after trial.[30] Souter also pointed out the illogic of the concurrence's intimation that *Mezzanatto* could be limited to impeachment cases; once waiver is recognized as legitimate, Souter asserted, prosecutors can insist that plea statements be admissible at any point during trial and "there is nothing this Court will legitimately be able do about it." Finally, he predicted that such waiver demands would become so broad that eventually they would amount to waivers of trial, because attorneys who agreed to them would not be able to suggest their clients' innocence without triggering use of their plea statements.

That latter prediction has come to pass. Most courts that have considered the issue have approved waiver agreements permitting use of *any* statements, including even preliminary "proffers," for *any* rebuttal of the defense's case, including impeachment of defense witnesses other than the defendant and statements by the defense attorney, and some courts have explicitly allowed plea statements to be used in the prosecution's case-in-chief.[31] Consistent with Justice Souter's prediction, *Mezza-*

---

[30] The huge differential between guilty plea and trial sentences is well-known. Michael M. O'Hear, *Remorse, Cooperation, and "Acceptance of Responsibility," The Structure, Implementation, and Reform of Section 3E1.1 of the Federal Sentencing Guidelines*, 91 Nw. U. L. Rev. 1507, 1513–15 (1997) (noting pre-Federal Sentencing Guidelines data showing that defendants who pleaded guilty received sentences 30 to 40 percent lower than had they gone to trial, and describing how the Guidelines attempted to implement such a "plea discount" through Section 3E1.1).

[31] At least five circuits have upheld broad Rule 410 waivers. United States v. Barrow, 400 F.3d 109 (2d Cir. 2005) (upholding use of proffer statements and omissions to rebut defense attorney's assertions during opening argument and cross-examination, even when they do not directly contradict the attorney's assertions); U.S. v. Rebbe, 314 F.3d 402, 406–07 (9th Cir. 2002) (proffer statements admissible in prosecution's case-in-rebuttal even when defendant does not testify, if defendant "presented any evidence or made any arguments and/or representations at trial that were inconsistent with his proffer statements"); United States v. Young, 223 F.3d 905 (8th Cir.2000) (affidavit executed by defendant during plea negotiations admissible in government's case-in-chief); United States

*natto* is well on the way to making Rule 410 and Rule 11(f) "dead letters." The Justice Department, so unsuccessful in Congress, has prevailed in the courts.

III. *Mezzanatto's* Legacy for the Rules of Evidence

*Mezzanatto's* impact on plea bargaining has overshadowed its implications for the rules of evidence, which are more subtle. To understand these implications, it is worth looking a bit more closely at how the majority arrived at its result. The plain wording of Rule 410 does not permit waiver of the type involved in *Mezzanatto*. But Justice Thomas asserted that prior caselaw had established that most evidence rules are "presumptively waivable" even when they don't explicitly speak of waiver. He concluded, "[b]ecause the plea-statement Rules were enacted against a background presumption that legal rights generally, and evidentiary provisions specifically, are subject to waiver by voluntary agreement of the parties, we will not interpret Congress' silence as an implicit rejection of waivability."[32]

In short, *Mezzanatto* permits courts to go beyond the plain meaning of the federal rules. It was the first Supreme Court case to read into an evidence rule a provision that is not there. As Professor Jonakait has stated:

> *Mezzanatto* teaches an important lesson for interpretations of the Rules of Evidence.... *Mezzanatto* convincingly demonstrates, if it had not been clear before, that the Federal Rules of Evidence cannot simply be treated as a self-contained code in which the text alone embraces the answer to all evidence questions. Sometimes we must look beyond the words of the Rules to understand evidentiary doctrine.[33]

*Mezzanatto* is also important because, Justice Thomas' assertions about precedent notwithstanding, it is the first case in which the

---

v. Krilich, 159 F.3d 1020 (7th Cir.1998) (upholding introduction of a proffer statement to impeach the defendant's witnesses and to rebut arguments suggested by defense counsel in his cross-examination of the Government's witnesses); United States v. Burch, 156 F.3d 1315, 1321–23 (D.C. Cir. 1998) (plea statements admissible in case-in-chief).

[32] 513 U.S. 196, at 203–04. Of course, Congress had not been *entirely* silent on the issue. Rule 410(i) clearly endorses one form of waiver: it does not apply when the defendant decides to use plea statements at trial. According to normal rules of statutory interpretation, that provision could be interpreted to "occupy the field" in terms of when waiver is allowed. The *Mezzanatto* majority itself noted that "an express waiver clause may suggest that Congress intended to occupy the field and to preclude waiver under other, unstated circumstances" (citing Crosby v. United States, 506 U.S. 255 (1993) and Smith v. United States, 360 U.S. 1 (1959)).

[33] Randolph, N. Jonakait, *Texts, or Ad Hoc Determinations: Interpretation of the Federal Rules of Evidence*, 71 Ind. L.J. 551, 571 (1996).

Supreme Court *explicitly* recognized that the protections of the evidence rules may be waived. The question now is which evidence rules can be "mezzanattoed." Perhaps the most likely such provision is Rule 408, the civil analogue to Rule 410.[34] Conditioning settlement talks on a waiver of that rule's protections could be said to provide the same incentive for truth-telling at trial that *Mezzanatto* attributes to a Rule 410 waiver. But there are indications that the Court would even permit waivers when reliability might thereby be sacrificed. Indeed, *all* of the justices in *Mezzanatto*, not just those in the majority, acknowledged that the hearsay prohibition may be waived by the parties, apparently even when the hearsay in question is clearly unreliable.

Perhaps the justices were not worried about the latter scenario because they assumed that parties will not engage in such waivers unless the evidence is relatively harmless to both sides. But *Mezzanatto* obviously allows a waiver that permits introduction of evidence clearly harmful to one side. Given *Mezzanatto*'s apparent approval of this dynamic, all sorts of waiver opportunities are created for the enterprising prosecutor. For instance, the logic of *Mezzanatto* might permit a prosecutor to make plea negotiations conditional on a relinquishment of Rule 404's protection against proof of prior crimes to prove character. Or perhaps the prosecutor could impose a waiver of the limitations on impeachment evidence found in Rules 608, 609 and 610. One might argue that the protections behind these rules are not waivable because they are *"fundamental* to the reliability of the fact-finding process," to use Justice Thomas' language. But are they *really* fundamental, given that all of them have been discarded in whole or in part by at least some jurisdictions?[35] At the least, *Mezzanatto* has opened the door for such arguments, and it is only a matter of time before prosecutors routinely make them.

## IV. Epilogue

In the meantime, what has happened to Gary Mezzanatto? He was released from federal prison on March 14, 2003, at the age of 53. He is driving trucks and trying to stay out of trouble. He didn't go back to electrician work because, as he says, he wants to make the transition

---

[34] Rule 408 provides, inter alia, that "([e]vidence of statements made in compromise negotiations is . . . not admissible.").

[35] See McCormick on Evidence 54, § 190 (4th ed., 1992) (noting that "although a majority of courts limit cross-examination concerning acts of misconduct as an attack upon character to acts which have a significant relation to the credibility of the witness" [as under Federal Rule 608(b)], "[s]ome courts permit an attack upon character by fairly wide-open cross-examination upon acts of misconduct which show bad moral character and can have only an attenuated relation to credibility") & id. at 55, § 191 (noting that the "definitions of crimes for which a conviction shall be ground of impeachment vary widely among the states that have not adopted Federal Rule of Evidence 609").

from prison life "slow and easy." He is seeing Leticia again, and visits with his children, all in their twenties, almost every weekend.

As to his crime, he swears virtually everything he said at trial was an accurate description of what he thought at the time of his arrest. He says he was an easily confused, easily misled small-timer, outsmarted by the more sophisticated Shuster. He also explains that his most damning incriminating actions—continuing with the transaction in the car once he knew for sure the package contained drugs and telling Moreland he could get more "stuff"—were the result of only slowly realizing he was involved in a major drug deal, feeling "squeezed" between Moreland and Shuster once he "put two-and-two together," and deciding to "play along." He doesn't have explanations for the wrapping in the package that came from near his home, and is even willing to say that he didn't really believe Shuster was an explosives expert. But he insists that he was always just a courier, not a manufacturer or a big time seller. He fell hard because Shuster got to the police first and saved himself by making Mezzanatto look like a bigger fish than he was. (Shuster, it turns out, ended up with a significantly reduced sentence and no jail time for cooperation in this and other cases[36]).

Harrigan, on the other hand, is convinced that Mezzanatto was more that a two-bit player. Anyone who could claim to produce a pound of meth on short notice, he says, "had to have been involved" in the game for awhile. He adds that it's a "shame" that Mezzanatto decided not to hand over more names to the police at the plea negotiations, because that cooperation would have reduced his sentence substantially.

There are several morals to Mezzanatto's story. Here are a few:

1. If you're involved in criminal activity with others, find out as much as you can about your colleagues in crime without letting them know anything about you. If things start falling apart, this information differential will put you in the driver's seat when it comes to dealing with the government. (Ironically, the leaders of a criminal group are most likely to be able to pull this kind of thing off; thus Mezzanatto got 14 years while Shuster virtually walked).[37]

---

[36] However, according to the Federal Bureau of Prisons, Shuster was arrested again for manufacture of methamphetamine on March 17, 2000, and is now serving a sentence that does not terminate until 2017. Phone conversation with records office, Lompoc Prison, 3600 Guard Rd., Lompoc, Calif. 93436, on July 22, 2005; see also, Federal Bureau of Prisons website, at www.bop.gov/iloc2/InmateFinder, last visited July 22, 2005.

[37] But see Linda D. Maxfield & John H. Kramer, *Two Sentencing Commission Staff Reports on Substantial Assistance*, 11 Fed. Sent. Rep. 1, 10 (July/August, 1998) ("The oft-cited 'truth' that drug conspiracy members at the top of the organization are more likely to secure reduced sentences due to substantial assistance than those lower in the criminal organization is not supported by these exploratory data.")

2.   If you're a defense attorney representing a client who wants to trade information for a reduced charge or sentence, don't let your client talk to prosecutors unless and until you have some indication from the government that it thinks the client's information is significant enough to warrant a formal prosecutorial request for leniency (called a "5K1.1 letter" in federal court, after the provision in the federal sentencing guidelines that allows a reduction in sentence for substantial assistance to authorities). If the information is sufficiently useful, the government may even be willing to forego a rule 410 waiver to get it. If it is not significant (and remember the government gets to decide that), don't let your client talk to the prosecution. This prohibition applies even to a "proffer" meeting under a so-called "Queen-for-a-Day" arrangement, because that label is very misleading; today many prosecutors require broad Rule 410 waivers even for these preliminary attempts to find out what the defendant knows.[38] At best, negotiations in such situations (that is, when the government concludes the client's information is trivial) will net you the same result as a simple admission of guilt, communicated without any help from the client. At worst, assuming the prosecution conditions a deal on a modern Rule 410 waiver (i.e., one that allows the prosecution to use plea statements for any type of rebuttal), any incriminating admissions made by your client will reduce your chances of succeeding at trial to virtually nil.

3.   It follows that if you're a defense attorney representing a client who has made incriminating statements after waiving Rule 410 protection, be *sure* to make a deal. Given the differential between sentences imposed after a trial conviction and a conviction by plea, you don't want to go to trial. Ask Gary Mezzanatto.

## SUGGESTED READINGS

Jonakait, Randolph, N. Texts, or Ad Hoc Determinations: Interpretation of the Federal Rules of Evidence, 71 Ind. L.J. 551, 571 (1996).

Manekas, Jason. Case Comment, United States v. Mezzanatto, 29 Suffolk L. Rev. 338 (1995).

Naftalis, Benjamin A. "Queen for a Day" Agreements and the Proper Scope of Permissible Waiver of the Federal Plea–Statement Rules, 37 Colum. J.L. & Soc. Probs. 1, 7–8 (2003).

---

[38] For example, the standard proffer agreement of the United States Attorney's Office for the Southern District of New York currently provides: "[T]he Government may also use statements made by Client at the meeting to rebut any evidence or arguments offered by or on behalf of the Client (including arguments or issues raised sua sponte by the District Court) at any stage of the criminal prosecution (including bail, all phases of trial, and sentencing) in any prosecution brought against Client." Reproduced in Benjamin A. Naftalis, *"Queen for a Day" Agreements and the Proper Scope of Permissible Waiver of the Federal Plea–Statement Rules*, 37 Colum. J.L. & Soc. Probs. 1, 7–8 (2003).

Rasmusen, Eric. Mezzanatto and the Economics of Self–Incrimination, 19 Cardozo L. Rev. 1541 (1998).

Seigle, Christopher P. Note: United States v. Mezzanatto, 32 Tulsa L.J. 119 (1996).

United States v. Barrow, 400 F.3d 109 (2d Cir. 2005).

Wright, Charles Alan & Kenneth W. Graham, 23 Federal Practice & Procedure § 5341.

# 6

# The Story of Swidler & Berlin v. United States: Death and the Privilege

## Kenneth S. Broun

The body of Deputy White House Counsel Vincent W. Foster, Jr. was found at Fort Marcy Park in suburban northern Virginia on July 20, 1993. The United States Park Police officially designated the death a suicide and that conclusion was eventually confirmed in reports of two Independent Counsel. Nevertheless, the controversy over what actually happened to Mr. Foster still churns in books, articles and on websites.[1] The writings and internet entries range from relatively objective accounts to bizarre conspiracy theories. Arguably, the events surrounding Mr. Foster's death are surpassed in intrigue only by those surrounding the assassinations of Presidents Lincoln and Kennedy.

In addition to the rich historical lore created over the years since Mr. Foster's death, the tragedy also left a legacy of an important United States Supreme Court case dealing with the application of the attorney-client privilege after death of the client, *Swidler & Berlin v. United States*.[2] The *Swidler & Berlin* case is significant not only because of its

---

[1] Three of the books achieved fairly wide circulation: Dan E. Moldea, A WASHINGTON TRAGEDY (1998) (finding errors and questions arising from the investigation but clearly concluding that the death was a suicide); James B. Stewart, BLOOD SPORT (1996) (also concluding that the death was a suicide; the book focuses on the investigation of President and Mrs. Clinton's involvement in the Whitewater Development Corporation and related matters); Christopher Ruddy, THE STRANGE DEATH OF VINCENT FOSTER (1997) (written by a former New York Post reporter who questioned the validity of the conclusion that death was suicidal almost from the beginning; the author concludes that there was a massive coverup of the real facts).

[2] 524 U.S. 399 (1998). Mr. Foster's death was involved in a second United States Supreme Court case not concerning the attorney-client privilege and not the subject of this story. In National Archives and Records Admin. v. Favish, 541 U.S. 157 (2004), the Court declared that, under the Freedom of Information Act, Vincent Foster's surviving family

holding that the privilege survives the death of the client but also because of its implications for the application of the privilege even when the client is still alive.

## The Death of Vince Foster

The only things absolutely certain about the Vincent Foster matter are that Mr. Foster is dead and that his body was found in Fort Marcy Park. Questions have been raised about virtually every other detail of his death, including where in the park his body was found, the position of the body after death, the amount of blood found at the scene, whether he had or didn't have briefcase with him, his mood on the day of this death and dozens of other facts.[3]

Mr. Foster was a long-time Arkansas friend of both President and Mrs. Clinton. A well-known and widely-respected lawyer, he had been Hillary Clinton's partner in the Rose Law Firm in Hot Springs, Arkansas. Mr. Foster had acted as attorney for both in connection with various transactions including some that eventually became part of the Whitewater affair. He had been active in the 1992 presidential campaign and was part of the President's initial White House legal team.

No suicide note was found. A torn note, probably written by Foster at some point during the last weeks of his life, contained comments that gave some clues as to his state of mind including the ending phrase that he "was not meant for the job or the spotlight of public life in Washington. Here ruining people is considered sport."[4] Although there were conflicting opinions as to the true nature of Mr. Foster's mental state, he

---

members had a right to personal privacy with respect to Mr. Foster's death-scene images that outweighed any public interest in disclosure.

[3] The factual account of the context of the *Swidler & Berlin* case contained here is taken from a number of sources and largely contains matters not in dispute. Reference will ordinarily not be made to a particular sources. The sources used included: *Hearings Relating to Madison Guaranty S & L and the Whitewater Development Corporation— Washington, DC Phase: Hearings on the death of Vincent W. Foster, Jr. before the Senate Comm. on Banking, Hous., and Urban Affairs*, 105th Cong. (1994) (Report of the Independent Counsel Robert B. Fiske, Jr., In re Vincent W. Foster, Jr. (June 30, 1994) [hereinafter FISKE REPORT]); Office of Independent Counsel in re: Madison Guaranty Savings & Loan Assn., Report on the Death of Vincent W. Foster, Jr. (1997) [hereinafter STARR REPORT]; Moldea, A WASHINGTON TRAGEDY, *supra* note 1; Stewart, BLOOD SPORT, *supra* note 1; Ruddy, THE STRANGE DEATH OF VINCENT FOSTER, *supra* note 1. Parts of this discussion also draw on information learned from an interview on July 21, 2005 with James Hamilton, who was the lawyer Foster consulted and the lawyer who argued the case against disclosure in the Supreme Court.

[4] Starr Report, *supra* note 3, at 107. James Hamilton, the lawyer whose notes relating to his interview with Mr. Foster nine days before his death were the subject matter of the *Swidler & Berlin* case, believes that this note was written in the evening of the day that Mr. Foster spoke to him. Author's interview with James Hamilton, July 21, 2005.

certainly had been stressed by the work load at the White House. By many accounts, he suffered anguish as a result of the so-called Travelgate matter, where long-time members of the White House Travel Office had been accused of wrongdoing and ultimately dismissed. His role in that matter and in other aspects of his job had been criticized, most notably by editorials in the Wall Street Journal.

Even the many people who concur in the opinion that the death was a suicide acknowledge that serious mistakes were made in the investigation. Among those mistakes were questions of access to Mr. Foster's office immediately after his death. The U.S. Park Police, who conducted the initial investigation, did not order Mr. Foster's office sealed until the day after his death. Reports, apparently erroneous, circulated that documents had been removed from the office by White House staffers on the night of his death. In any event, two days after Vincent Foster's body was found, Chief White House Counsel Bernard Nussbaum, in the presence of law enforcement officials but without their participation, removed files from Foster's office. It was later revealed by the White House, that at least some of the documents involved the Whitewater Development Corporation and related matters.

What has become known historically as "Whitewater," in the simplest of terms, involved investments made by President and Mrs. Clinton when he was governor of Arkansas and she was a partner in the Rose Law Firm.[5] Questions were raised during the campaign for the presidency in 1992 concerning the legality and ethics of the Clintons' participation in those matters. However, despite efforts by some hostile to Clinton to keep the matter in the news, press attention to Whitewater had largely dissipated at the time of Mr. Foster's death. His death and the removal of files concerning the matter from his office by persons associated with the Clintons brought the Whitewater controversy crashing back into the national limelight.

Pressure from the press, public and Congress ultimately resulted in the appointment in January, 1994 of an Independent Counsel, Robert B. Fiske, Jr., to investigate the Whitewater matters. Fiske reopened the investigation of Foster's death. On June 30, Fiske issued a report confirming that Foster had committed suicide.

But in the eyes of the some of the press and some members of Congress, the Fiske report raised even more questions about the death than it answered. The Senate Committee on Banking, Housing and

---

[5] The term "Whitewater" is used in this story to include the entire investigation into the activities of the President and Mrs. Clinton in connection with various matters including Whitewater Development Corporation, Madison Guaranty Savings & Loan Association and Capital Management Services. There are several full accounts of this matter, including the STARR REPORT, *supra* note 3 and Stewart, BLOOD SPORT, *supra* note 1.

Urban Affairs conducted its own inquiry into the Park Police's investigation of the death. The Senate Committee investigation also concluded
with a finding based on "overwhelming evidence" that Foster had died
from a self-inflicted gun-shot wound. Still the questions did not go away.
Indeed, the fires seemed to have been fueled to a high intensity; second
guessing abounded. Fiske was replaced as Independent Counsel by
Kenneth W. Starr, who was given authority to continue the investigation
of the broader Whitewater matter. As Mr. Starr noted in his report on
Mr. Foster's death, his investigation included the circumstances of that
death:

> Due to continuing questions about Mr. Foster's death, the relation-
> ship between Mr. Foster's death and the handling of documents
> (including Whitewater-related documents) from Mr. Foster's office
> after his death, and Mr. Foster's role or involvement in other events
> under investigation by the OIC [Office of the Independent Counsel],
> the OIC reviewed and analyzed the evidence gathered during prior
> investigations of Mr. Foster's death and conducted further investiga-
> tion.[6]

One of the events of the Foster death investigated by Mr. Starr was
a meeting Mr. Foster had with attorney James Hamilton at Hamilton's
home on Sunday morning, July 11, 1993—nine days before his death.
Mr. Hamilton, who was a partner in the Washington law firm of Swidler
& Berlin, was a friend of the Clintons and had worked with Mr. Foster in
vetting possible United States Supreme Court nominees. Before meeting
with Mr. Foster, Mr. Hamilton read and made notes on a report issued
by the White House with regard to the Travel Office matter. During his
meeting with Mr. Foster, Mr. Hamilton took an additional three pages of
handwritten notes. On December 4, 1995, a federal grand jury, at the
request of the Independent Counsel, issued subpoenas to Mr. Hamilton
and the Swidler & Berlin law firm seeking Hamilton's notes relating to
his meeting with Vincent Foster as well as documents concerning his
representation of the Foster family after Mr. Foster's death. Mr. Hamilton and the firm moved to quash or modify the subpoenas based on the
claim that submitting the requested information would violate the attorney-client and work-product privileges.

An evaluation of the subsequent legal history of this matter, including the opinion of the United States Supreme Court, must be assessed in
light of the unique circumstances involving the office of Independent
Counsel and the Whitewater affair. The intensity of the opposition to the
Clintons and the fear that Clinton was, in the opinion of his critics, not
only a bad president but an evil person was matched by a feeling at least
equally as strong that the Clintons were victims of a witch-hunt perpe-

---

[6] STARR REPORT, *supra* note 3, p. 8–9.

trated by a far right-wing conspiracy. Statements from the lips of their trusted confidant, Vincent Foster, could go a long way toward shedding light on the guilt or innocence of the first family with regard to a variety of alleged wrongdoing. The special prosecutor was willing to bet that such statements would, at least, shed light on his investigation of the Clintons. The Clintons' defenders were undoubtedly convinced that if Kenneth Starr got the information, he would try to use it to reflect badly on the President and his wife.

## The Legal Background

The attorney-client privilege—which provides that a client may prohibit the disclosure of confidential communications with his or her lawyer—is the most venerable of all of the evidentiary privileges. Its origins are deep in the English common law and the early American cases. Despite attacks from some quarters, beginning almost two centuries ago with scathing criticisms by the utilitarian philosopher Jeremy Bentham,[7] the privilege has maintained its protective powers to this day. The rationale usually given for the protection afforded is utilitarian: protecting the client's confidential communications to an attorney fosters the free flow of information between lawyer and client.[8] More recently, other, more humanistic reasons for protecting attorney-client conversations have been articulated. Some writers have sought to justify the privilege based upon privacy considerations or related concerns for protecting private enclaves that promote individual autonomy in making important personal decisions. Others emphasize the connection between the privilege and the right of individuals in a free society, with egalitarian pretensions, to "resist the power of the state to compel information in certain instances."[9]

Case and statutory law have, almost unanimously, made the privilege absolute in the sense that, once it applies and is not waived, a client's communications to his or her attorney are protected regardless of the need for the information in an individual case. The United States Supreme Court has opined with regard to the attorney-client privilege that "an uncertain privilege . . . is little better than no privilege at all."[10] However, despite its absolute power once correctly invoked, the privilege

---

[7] Bentham, RATIONALE OF JUDICIAL EVIDENCE (1827), 7 The Works of Jeremy Bentham 473, 474, 477, 479 (Bowring ed. 1842).

[8] Bentham's principal attack on the privilege was also utilitarian. He believed that the innocent had nothing to fear from disclosure of their conversations with attorneys, so the privilege could only aid the guilty.

[9] Charles Alan Wright and Kenneth W. Graham, Jr., FEDERAL PRACTICE AND PROCEDURE § 5422, at 675–76 (1986).

[10] Upjohn v. United States, 449 U.S. 383, 393 (1981).

is neither certain nor eternal. Numerous exceptions—most prominently one that denies the privilege to communications in furtherance of crime or fraud—will prevent its application. Furthermore, the privilege will be lost if not invoked by the client at the appropriate time.

Although arising more frequently in the imagination of legal scholars than in the courts, the issue of the survival of the privilege after the death of the client has been the subject of speculation for many years. The courts have consistently applied an exception to prevent application of the privilege in one circumstance arising after the death of the client. The privilege is held not to apply in cases involving the validity or interpretation of a will or other dispute arising between parties claiming by succession from the client after his or her death. One theory behind the exception is that disclosure of the communications is most likely to reflect the will of the client. Another is simply that all of the survivors claim through the client and that therefore one survivor ought not to be able to claim the privilege as against another. But the need for an exception in such circumstances, arguably implies that the privilege survives in other cases. Several state courts have held that death does not terminate the privilege in other instances. Only one case, prior to the Court of Appeals decision in *Swidler v. Berlin,* held to the contrary.[11] One court went so far as to apply the privilege under circumstances where the deceased had told his attorney that he had committed a crime for which another man was on trial.[12] A substantial minority, close to half, of the states have dealt with the issue of the privilege's survival in their codification of the privilege by providing that the personal representative of the client may claim the privilege. The privilege would have to survive the death of the client in order for such provisions to have meaning. One state, California, specifically provides that the privilege exists only until the estate is finally distributed and the personal representative discharged.[13]

---

[11] Cohen v. Jenkintown Cab Co., 357 A.2d 689 (Pa. Super. 1976) (balancing test used to determine applicability of privilege after death of the client).

[12] State v. Macumber, 544 P.2d 1084 (Ariz. 1976). The conviction was vacated on other grounds. On remand, the deceased client's mother waived the privilege but the testimony of the attorney was excluded as hearsay. State v. Macumber, 582 P.2d 162, 166–67 (Ariz. 1978).

[13] Calif. Evid. Code, § 954. Although the code section itself is not explicit, the Law Revision Commission Comment states:

The privilege may be claimed by a person listed in Section 954 . . . only if there is a holder of the privilege in existence. Hence, the privilege ceased to exist when the client's estate is finally distributed and his personal representative is discharged. Under the existing law, it seems likely that the privilege continues to exist indefinitely after the client's death and that no one has authority to waive the privilege.

*Swidler & Berlin* gave the United States Supreme Court the opportunity to settle, at least for the federal courts, the interesting issue of posthumous survival of the attorney-client privilege. But the case's significance is not limited to that rather esoteric point. The case gave the Supreme Court an opportunity to stake itself out with regard to the strength of the protection of lawyer-client communications—whether protected for utilitarian or humanistic reasons—in the face of a substantial need for information in the judicial process.

Federal Rule 501 provides that privileges "shall be governed by the principles of the common law as they may be interpreted by the courts of the United States in the light of reason and experience."[14] *Swidler & Berlin* presented a situation where the Court's interpretation of the common law had implications not only for parties to a lawsuit or the defense of a criminal action but for the very foundations of the American Republic. If Vincent Foster's statements to James Hamilton implicated the president or his wife in criminal activity, the integrity of the United States government was at stake. *United States v. Nixon,*[15] involving a claim of presidential privilege, permitted balancing where the interests of the presidency clashed with the interests of an investigation into wrongdoing by a president and his advisors. Arguably, although a different privilege was involved, *Swidler* presented no less of a policy justification for balancing the need for the information with the strength of the privilege. Putting the question in the light most favorable to the position of the Independent Counsel: Does the utility of protecting lawyer-client confidences justify forever keeping secret the statements of a deceased client to his lawyer when the disclosure of such statements might not only assist the investigation of a crime, but help protect the republic from official corruption? If the Court were to interpret the common law as providing that the privilege applies and survives in its absolute form, information presumably believed by the Independent Council to be possibly crucial to the continuing integrity of our government would be lost.

On the other hand, a decision to terminate the attorney-client privilege on the death of the client or to balance the privilege against the needs of future courts for the information—generally or in criminal cases alone—might weaken the privilege to a point where utilitarians would realistically fear a limitation on communication between lawyer, and client and the humanistically oriented would see an invasion of a private enclave unprecedented in our legal history.

---

[14] FED. R. EVID. 501.

[15] 418 U.S. 683 (1974).

## The Lower Court Proceedings

The Chief Judge of the United States District Court for the District of Columbia, John Garrett Penn, who was appointed to the Federal District Court for the District of Columbia in 1979 by President Carter, took the matter concerning Mr. Hamilton's claim of privilege under advisement and asked to view Hamilton's notes *in camera*. After reviewing the notes, Judge Penn, ruled that the notes were protected under both the attorney-client and work-product privileges. His brief opinion emphasized the application of the work-product privilege, applying a balancing test to find that no need by the grand jury trumped the "privileges." The Independent Counsel appealed Judge Penn's ruling to the Court of Appeals for District of Columbia Circuit.[16]

The Court of Appeals panel, in a 2–1, vote reversed the District Court's ruling and sent the matter back for re-examination in light of the majority's decision.[17] The majority decision was written by Reagan appointee Judge Stephen F. Williams, who was joined by Judge Patricia M. Wald, one of the most liberal members of the Circuit Court, whom President Carter had appointed to that court the same year Judge Penn joined the district court bench. Judge David S. Tatel, a Clinton appointee, dissented.

The majority found, as have many of the commentators and courts, the justification for the privilege to be instrumental or utilitarian, noting that the provision of legal assistance "can only be safely and readily availed of when free from the consequences or apprehension of disclosure."[18] The majority also noted the common assumption among the courts that the privilege survives the death of the client. However, the court noted that most of the posthumous cases have involved the exception that abrogates the privilege where both sides claim under the estate of the client. Of particular interest to the majority were the many commentators, including the drafters of the Restatement of the Law Governing Lawyers, who have suggested limitations on the privilege after the death of the client. For example, the court noted the argument in the Wright and Graham treatise that favoring survival of the privilege requires "imputing a 'Pharaoh-like concern' " to the clients. Although referring to such a view as a "bit of an exaggeration," the court found

---

[16] The trial court granted the motion to quash the subpoena with regard to all of the documents sought by the Independent Counsel, including the notes relating to the interview and documents relating to Mr. Hamilton's representation of the Foster family after Mr. Foster's death. The Independent Counsel appealed the court's ruling only with regard to the notes relating to the interview with Mr. Foster. Author's interview with James Hamilton, July 21, 2005.

[17] In re Sealed Case, 124 F.3d 230 (D.C. Cir. 1997).

[18] *Id.* at 233, quoting Hunt v. Blackburn, 128 U.S. 464, 470 (1888).

that, if balancing were confined to the realm of criminal litigation, "we should expect the restriction's chilling effect to fall somewhere between modest and nil."

The court recalled the language of the *Upjohn* cases that an uncertain privilege "is little better than no privilege at all." Despite this reference, it applied a balancing test to the application of the privilege in the case before it:

> Although witness unavailability alone would not justify qualification of the privilege, we think that unavailability through death, coupled with the non-existence of any client concern for criminal liability after death, creates a discrete realm (use in criminal proceedings after death of the client) where the privilege should not automatically apply. We reject a general balancing test in all but this narrow circumstance.[19]

The majority noted that the creation of an exception for post-death criminal matters "produces none of the murkiness that persuaded the Court in *Upjohn* and *Jaffee* to reject the limitations proposed there."

The guidelines for balancing the need for maintaining the protection of the privilege against the need for the information were vague: the protection should be abrogated only in criminal proceedings and then only as to communications "whose relative importance is substantial." The statements "must bear on a significant aspect of the crimes at issue, and an aspect as to which there is a scarcity of reliable evidence." The court suggested that there would "normally" be little basis for intrusion on confidentiality where there is an abundance of disinterested witnesses with unimpaired opportunities to perceive and unimpaired memory.

The court also rejected the application of the work product privilege in its absolute form, finding no such blanket protection for attorney's notes. In so ruling, the court distinguished instances in which an attorney interview is conducted as part of a litigation-related investigation from an initial client interview such as conducted by James Hamilton in this instance. In this latter instance, the majority believed that the contest suggests that "the lawyer has not sharply focused or weeded the materials" so that the "super-protective" envelope reserved by Fed. R.Civil P. 26(3) for "mental impressions" should not apply, but no case was cited to directly support this position.

The dissent, written by Judge Tatel, would have applied the attorney-client privilege in its absolute form. As did the majority, Judge Tatel relied on an instrumental rationale for the privilege noting in part that encouraging individuals to disclose to matters to their lawyers candidly and fully "allows the legal profession to help individuals understand

---

[19] In re Sealed Case, 124 F.3d at 234.

their legal obligations and facilitate voluntary compliance with them."
The dissent noted the virtually unanimous assumption that the privilege
applies after the death of the client except in testamentary situations. To
apply the privilege after death recognizes, contrary to the majority's
assumptions, that people care deeply about posthumous decisions. Judge
Tatel set forth a litany of instances of instances in which individuals
such as Andrew Carnegie and Henry Ford cared about how posterity
would view them. His references to the concern for posthumous reputations would be repeated at length and with great vigor by both the
petitioner's and the various *amici* when the matter went before the
Supreme Court on certiorari. Judge Tatel, perhaps with reference to an
address Vincent Foster had given at a University of Arkansas Law
School commencement in May 1993[20] and the fragmented note found in
his brief case evidencing his own concern for his reputation, noted that
"this case seems a particularly inappropriate one in which to abrogate
the common law's posthumous protection of the attorney-client privilege."

On petition for rehearing *en banc,* Judge Tatel, now joined by Judge
Douglas H. Ginsburg, a Reagan appointee and one of the Circuit Court's
more conservative members, continued his dissent noting that the
court's balancing test would have implications beyond criminal cases in
the District of Columbia. Judge Tatel expressed the belief that clients
anywhere in the country would have "no way of knowing whether
information they share with their lawyers might someday become relevant to a federal criminal investigation in Washington, D. C." Judges
Tatel and Ginsburg also rejected the argument made by the Independent
Counsel concerning the lack of empirical support for the proposition that
abrogating the privilege after the client's death will chill client communication. In a point later to be echoed by the Supreme Court, their opinion
argued that, in light of the consistent common law holdings on the
question, the Independent Counsel "bears the responsibility of producing
evidence" with regard to the absence of an effect on client communications. "Without convincing evidence that abrogating the privilege will do
no harm to client communications, this court should not abandon
centuries of common law." Although recognizing that there is a loss of
information in this instance as in any other in which the privilege
applies, the dissent observed that the common law "long ago determined

---

[20] In the speech, Foster had expressed deep convictions concerning a lawyer's reputation:

"I cannot make this point too strongly, there is no victory, no advantage, no fee, no
favor, which is worth even a blemish on your reputation for intellect and integrity.
Nothing travels faster than an accusation that another lawyer's word is no good. . . .
Dents to the reputation in the legal profession are irreparable." Stewart, Blood Sport,
*supra* note 1 at 255–56.

that the benefits gained by recognizing the privilege posthumously outweigh whatever damage might flow from denying information to the trier of fact in any particular case."

Judge Tatel had not addressed the work-product privilege in his earlier dissent, relying simply on his view that the matter was covered by the attorney-client privilege. However, in his opinion on the denial of a rehearing *en banc*, he expressly rejected the distinction drawn by the majority between litigation-related interviews and an initial interview such as involved here. The dissent opined that if the holding of the court were to stand, "lawyers will simply stop taking notes at early, critical meetings with clients." Although no judge hearing this litigation could have been unaware of the case's inflammatory political context, Democratic and Republican appointees, known liberals and known conservatives, were on both sides of the issues. The differences among the judges seems not to have reflected feelings toward the Clinton administration, but rather deep divisions on how far the privilege should extend and the validity of empirical justifications for claims of absolute privilege, mirroring similar divisions in the academy.

## The Starr Report

The court of appeals decision was issued on June 20, 1997. As early as December, 1996, Starr had issued public statements predicting that his conclusion in the investigation of Foster's death would be the same as that reached in the earlier investigations—Vincent Foster committed suicide in Fort Marcy Park on July 20, 1993. Starr's formal report on the Foster death was not released by the Court of Appeals for the District of Columbia until Oct. 10, 1997, but the final release of the report only confirmed what Starr had previously made public.

Starr's report sought to deal with all of the questions that had been raised by the press, various conspiracy theorists and members of Congress. The conclusions were based on extensive interviews of witnesses and expert analysis of every conceivable aspect of the case. Despite the continuing rantings of some, it is difficult to argue with the conclusions reached. Not only was the investigation seemingly as complete and thorough as possible, it is difficult to imagine that this Independent Counsel would have hesitated to expose any possible wrongdoing on the part of the President, those close to him or anyone else.

What is clear from the timing of the Starr report on Foster's death is that the Supreme Court decision was no longer about the investigation of Foster's suicide. That matter had been resolved to Starr's satisfaction. Politically, it was about Whitewater or Travelgate and any information that Foster may have disclosed to Hamilton with regard to those matters. Legally, it was about the strength of the attorney-client privilege in today's world.

## The Petition for Certiorari

James Hamilton and the firm of Swidler & Berlin petitioned for certiorari on two issues: whether the attorney-client privilege was subject to a balancing test after the death of the client and whether handwritten notes taken during an initial interview with a client should receive the virtually absolute work product protection otherwise afforded to an attorney's mental impressions.

Like Judge Tatel's opinion with regard to the attorney-client privilege, the petition emphasized the concern for the freedom of communications between clients concerned about their mortality and their attorneys: "By denying the full protections of the attorney client privilege to ... people [including the elderly, the suicidal, those engaged in hazardous lifestyles, and others concerned about mortality], the decision discriminates against the aged, the diseased, and the distraught—against society's most vulnerable."[21] The petition argued that the damaging effect of the decision below is not ameliorated by the court's attempt to limit disclosure to criminal litigation—"a client's concern for family, friends and associates surely will extend to their potential criminal as well as civil liabilities."

The petition pointed to the conflict between the Court of Appeals decision and the prevailing state cases, citing numerous criminal and civil cases in which the evidence of communications between a deceased person and that person's attorney was excluded. The petition noted that the only contrary authority was from a mid-level state appellate court.

The primary emphasis in the petition was on the impact of a balancing test on attorney-client communications—referring, as had both the majority and dissenting opinions below, to the language of *Upjohn* that an "uncertain privilege is little better than no privilege at all." The petition added, "[t]he balancing approach the court of appeals adopted is particularly damaging to the attorney-client privilege because potential violations of the law (including those by persons who survive the client's death) are a frequent subject of attorney-client conversations."

With regard to work product, the petition emphasized the absence of a real distinction between an initial interview and those conducted during the course of litigation. The petition argued that "to adopt a conclusive presumption that initial interview notes do not reflect the

---

[21] Petition for Writ of Certiorari at 7–8, In re Sealed Case, 327 U.S. App. D.C. 145, (1997), *rev'd sub nom.* Swidler & Berlin v. United States, *cert. granted,* 66 U.S.L.W. 3639 (U.S. March 30, 1998) (No. 97–1192).

lawyer's mental impressions ignores both the reality of the practice of law and reality of this case."

An amicus brief was filed by the National Association of Criminal Defense Lawyers, American Corporate Counsel Association and National Hospice placing special emphasis on "the importance the living attach to their reputations after death." The brief quoted from the Bible,[22] Longfellow[23] and Shakespeare,[24] among other sources, and made reference to the lives of Alfred Nobel, the inventor of dynamite and founder of the Nobel Prize and the late Justice Hugo Black and their concerns for their posthumous reputations.[25]

The same sentiments, without the biblical or literary references, were contained in briefs in support of the petition filed by the American College of Trial Lawyers and American Bar Association. All of the amicus briefs, and especially these latter two, expressed concern with the court of appeals decision with regard to the work product as well as the attorney-client privilege.

The brief of the Independent Counsel in opposition to the petition emphasized the need to avoid delay in "an important grand jury investigation which touches on vital matters of public concern."[26] The respondent's brief argued that the client's interests in his own reputation and in protecting friends and associates does not justify nondisclosure of information after death. The argument was based, in part, on the notion that the client could be asked to divulge the underlying facts if he were still alive. The client must testify truthfully and while he may have a privilege against self-incrimination, that privilege would cover only his own crimes, not the crimes of others or facts merely harmful to his

---

[22] Brief for Amici Curiae National Association of Criminal Defense Lawyers, American Corporate Counsel Association, and National Hospice Organization in Support of Petitioners, Swidler & Berlin v. United States, 524 U.S. 399 (1998) (No. 97–1192), at 11. "All these were honored in their generations, and were the glory of their times." Apocrypha 44:7.

[23] Id. at 12. "Lives of great men all remind us/We can make our lives sublime/And, departing, leave behind us/Footprints on the sands of time." (A Psalm of Life st. 7.)

[24] Id. at 12. King Richard the Second, act 1, sc. i, l. 182: "Mine honor is my life; both grow in one; Take honor from me and my life is done."

[25] Id. at 13. Nobel, criticized as a "merchant of death," became so obsessed with his posthumous reputation that he wrote his last will, bequeathing most of his fortune to "a cause upon which no future obituary writer would be able to cast aspersions." Kenn Fant, ALFRED NOBEL, 207 (Ruuth trans. 1993). Black, on the eve of his death, in what was termed "Operation Frustrate the Historians," directed that his Court papers be destroyed. Roger K. Newman, HUGO BLACK, 621–22 (1994).

[26] Brief for the United States in Opposition at 7, Swidler & Berlin v. United States, 524 U.S. 399 (1998) (No. 97–1192).

reputation. The brief also argued that sensitivity to reputation has never limited the abrogation of the privilege in testamentary cases.

In addition, in points that would ultimately be answered by the Supreme Court's majority opinion, the petition stressed the nonexistence of empirical support for the utility of a posthumously applied privilege as well as the specter of the exclusion of statements that could free an innocent person.

The brief in opposition to the petition contained only a single, short paragraph on work product.

Certiorari was granted on March 30, 1998.

## The Briefs in the United States Supreme Court[27]

In their briefs on the merits, the petitioners and the *amici* continued to hammer away at the concern that a client is likely to have for his reputation and the well-being of his friends and relatives and the chilling effect that such concerns would have on communications between attorney and client if the court of appeals decision were to stand. Vincent Foster's concern for his reputation was expressed in the note found after his death and his seeking of assurances from James Hamilton as to the privileged nature of their conversations. People, especially Vince Foster, care a great deal about their privacy after death.

The petitioner and virtually all of the *amici* continued the same theme with regard to the work-product privilege—attorney notes should be absolutely privileged whether taken in a litigation-related interview or in an initial interview such as the one between Mr. Foster and Mr. Hamilton. The petitioner's brief ends with the sentence:

> As Judge Tatel's dissent correctly observed, the court of appeals' "two new holdings—one chilling client disclosure, the other chilling lawyer note-taking—will damage the quality of legal representation without producing any corresponding benefits to the fact-finding process."[28]

The brief on the merits filed by the Independent Counsel made perfectly clear that he was arguing not simply for an affirmance of the court of appeals decision. He argued plainly that the "attorney-client privilege does not apply in federal criminal proceedings when the client

---

[27] The petitioners were supported by amicus briefs on the merits from the same organizations that had support the petition for certiorari. The National Association of Criminal Defense Lawyers, American Corporate Counsel Assoc. and National Hospice Organization were joined in their brief on the merits by Trial Lawyers for Public Justice and the American Psychiatric Association.

[28] Brief for Petitioners, Swidler & Berlin v. United States, 524 U.S. 399 (1998) (97–1192), at 38.

is deceased.''[29] The balancing test articulated by the court of appeals was not part of the respondent's position on certiorari. Rather, the essence of the respondent's argument was that balancing the likely chilling effect on now-deceased clients as a class, said to be marginal, against the intrusion on the grand jury's generalized need for relevant evidence should result in the abrogation of the privilege.

With that significant exception, respondent's brief closely tracked the majority's reasoning below. Although the cases have assumed the survival of the privilege, most commentators have opposed it. Most of the posthumous cases are will contests, where there is no protection for the communications because of the testamentary exception.

> The testamentary rule is important, if not decisive, in assessing the appropriate rule for criminal cases. The public's need for determining whether a crime has been committed (and if so, by whom) warrants at least parity of treatment to that afforded the interest in resolving will contests with precise accuracy.[30]

Petitioner had sought to distinguish the testamentary exception cases as simply a reflection of the testator's intent irrespective of embarrassing disclosure. The respondent countered that if it were fair to presume intent in that situation, it was also fair to presume that the client would have wanted to provide relevant information to the grand jury.

The Independent Counsel raised the "profound" problem of the statement made by a now deceased client to an attorney that would exonerate another person now charged with a crime. The respondent rejected the possibility of a narrow constitutional exception applicable to criminal defendants only. There is no basis "for granting a criminal defendant greater power than a grand jury to override a witness' common-law privilege."[31]

Independent Counsel also made the point that, especially with regard to the deceased client, recognition of the privilege assists only the client who would have committed perjury. In essence, a client who intended to tell the truth would not be chilled in his conversation with his attorney because he would testify to exactly the same matters.

---

[29] Brief for the United States, Swidler & Berlin v. United States, 524 U.S. 399 (1998) (97–1192), at 9.

[30] Brief for the United States, *supra* note 84, at 17.

[31] *Id.* at 25. The Independent Counsel cited language from United States v. Nixon, *supra* note 15 at 709, "To ensure that justice is done, it is imperative to the function of courts that compulsory process be available for the production of evidence needed either by the prosecution or by the defense."

The respondent conceded that roughly half the states provide for the personal representative of the estate to claim the privilege, thus supporting the view that the privilege survives the death of the client. However, the brief argued, the vesting of the right to claim the privilege in the personal representative means that the privilege exists only until the estate is closed.

Only a little over two pages of the Independent Counsel's brief was directed to the work-product issue. It stressed the need for the information in light of the potential witness's unavailability.

## The Oral Argument

The argument for the petitioner was made by James Hamilton—the principal lawyer/actor in the drama. He started his argument by confirming, based on personal knowledge, the facts that appeared in the record by way of affidavit: Mr. Foster and Mr. Hamilton spoke alone for two hours. Hamilton took notes on the conversation. "Before we began, Mr. Foster asked me if the conversation was privileged and, without hesitation, I said that it was."

Mr. Hamilton's primary point was that any balancing test that leaves the existence of the attorney-client privilege after death in doubt would have a significant chilling effect on client candor, particularly as to those who expect to die soon. People care about their reputations and the fate the family and friends after death.

A significant portion of Mr. Hamilton's portion of the oral argument was taken up with the issue of state statutory provisions with regard to the end of the privilege—especially where the state gives the power to claim the privilege to the client's personal representative. Justice Kennedy observed that such statutes mean that the privilege ended with the termination of the administration of the estate, using California as an example. Other members of the Court suggested that providing that the privilege be claimed by the personal representative is, by implication, a proviso that it expires when the estate ends. Mr. Hamilton responded by referring to the statutory provisions for the lawyer to claim the privilege as well as the personal representative. He also noted that California is the only jurisdiction that specifically provides for the termination of the privilege after the closing of the estate and added that the administrator would be able to assert the privilege even if this case were in California because the estate had not yet wound down.

Justice O'Connor raised the issue of the disclosure of information where evidence is sought to show that a third person is not guilty of a crime. Hamilton answered that there may be constitutional considerations in that instance, giving rise to Justice Scalia's interjection, "there goes your absolute rule."

The Independent Counsel's argument was made by Brett M. Kavanaugh. Mr. Kavanaugh began his argument by referring to the opinions of commentators who had expressed the view that permanently walling off a critical category of evidence could lead to extreme injustice. He emphasized the point suggested by Justice O'Connor to Mr. Hamilton—the possibility of harm to a person whose innocence might be established by a client's confession to his or her attorney. Justice Stevens pointed out that even the petitioner would not necessarily carry the survival of the privilege to that extreme.

Mr. Kavanaugh noted that the most likely scenario for posthumous application of the privilege is the testamentary contest, already excepted from the privilege. Justice Souter pointed out that the testamentary exception is based upon the client's likely intent. Mr. Kavanaugh replied that the client may also want to disclose his information to the grand jury.

Questions were raised as to who has the burden of showing that the privilege applies or does not apply in the posthumous situation. Counsel responded that, because privileges are in derogation of the need for information, the burden should be on those seeking to establish the privilege. He added that he would confine the balancing to a criminal case but rejected the balancing provided for in the court of appeals decision. Mr. Kavanaugh argued, as had respondent's brief, that the balancing had already been done by the court of appeals—the grand jury's needs outweighed the benefits of the privilege's protection.

There was only the briefest mention of the work product point in the oral arguments for each side. At this point, the parties were putting all their eggs in the attorney-client basket. The Supreme Court's opinion followed suit.

## THE SUPREME COURT OPINION

The United States Supreme Court, in a 6–3 decision, avoided the necessity of dealing with either the work-product issue or the question of whether further balancing needed to be done in this case. The majority opinion held that the privilege survived the death of Vincent Foster in its absolute form.[32]

Chief Justice Rehnquist writing for the majority took the same instrumental view of the privilege as did the court of appeals, citing *Upjohn* for its statement that the privilege is intended to encourage "full and frank communication between attorneys and their clients and thereby promote broader public interests in the observance of law and the administration of justice."

---

[32] Swidler & Berlin v. United States, 524 U.S. 399 (1998) (The decision was 6–3, with Justices O'Connor, Scalia and Thomas dissenting).

The opinion analyzed existing case law as providing that the privilege survives in a case such as this one. The case before the Court was clearly not within the testamentary exception, the rationale for which is a furtherance of the client's intent. The majority opinion noted both the scholarly opinion recognizing of the survival of the privilege other than in the testamentary instance and the criticism of that view. However, largely adopting the views of the petitioners and the *amici*, Chief Justice Rehnquist found weighty reasons counseling in favor of posthumous application. He noted that clients may be concerned about reputation, civil liability, or possible harm to friends or family. "Posthumous disclosure of such communications may be as feared as disclosure during the client's lifetime."

The Chief Justice dismissed the Independent Counsel's argument that survival of the privilege would encourage only a client intending to perjure himself. The opinion pointed out that the Independent Counsel's argument assumes that the privilege is analogous to the Fifth Amendment's protection against self-incrimination. Chief Justice Rehnquist noted that the privilege serves much broader purposes. A client may consult a lawyer for any number of reasons that do not involve criminal liability, "These confidences may not come close to any sort of admission of criminal wrongdoing, but nonetheless be matters which the client would not wish divulged."

The opinion found the potential for loss of evidence more apparent than real. It noted that, in this case, Vincent Foster, "perhaps already contemplating suicide may not have sought legal advice from Hamilton if he had not been assured the conversation was privileged."

The majority rejected even the limited balancing in criminal cases that the court of appeals sought to establish, noting that balancing "*ex post* the importance of the information against client interest, even limited to criminal cases, introduces substantial uncertainty into the privilege's application." It distinguished the established exceptions to the privilege, such as crime-fraud and the testamentary exception, as consistent with the purpose of the privilege in encouraging communication between attorney and client.

Perhaps most significantly, the Court distinguished its earlier cases in which it had urged that privileges be strictly construed because they are "inconsistent with the paramount judicial goal of truth seeking."[33] The earlier cases involved privileges that were not recognized by the common law. In this case, the Court was asked not simply to construe the privilege but "to narrow it, contrary to the weight of the existing body of case law." Chief Justice Rehnquist's opinion puts the burden of

---

[33] *Id.* at 410, citing United States v. Nixon *supra* note 39 (executive privilege) and Branzburg v. Hayes, 408 U.S. 665 (1972) (journalist's privilege).

showing an absence of impact on a client's willingness to communicate squarely on those who would limit the impact of the privilege, stating:

> It has been generally, if not universally, accepted, for well over a century, that the attorney-client privilege survives the death of the client in a case such as this. While the arguments against the survival of the privilege are by no means frivolous, they are based in large part on speculation—thoughtful speculation, speculation none-theless—as to whether posthumous termination of the privilege would diminish a client's willingness to confide in an attorney. In an area where empirical information would be useful, it is scant and inconclusive.[34]

The Chief Justice conceded that Federal Rule of Evidence 501's dictate to look to "the principles of the common law ... in the light of reason and experience" does not mean that a rule should endure for all time. Here, however, the Independent Counsel has "simply not made a sufficient showing to overturn the common-law rule embodied in the prevailing case law."

Justice O'Connor, joined by Justices Scalia and Thomas, dissented. The dissenting opinion takes the same utilitarian view of the privilege, but reaches a different conclusion in a posthumous situation, finding that the potential impact on the free flow of information between attorney and client is outweighed, at least in some circumstances, by more urgent needs. The dissent would hold that either a criminal defendant's right to exculpatory evidence or a compelling law enforce-ment need may, where testimony is not otherwise available, override a client's posthumous interest in confidentiality. The attorney-client privi-lege exists to facilitate legal services and should only operate where necessary to achieve its purpose. Although a deceased client may retain an interest in confidentiality, that interest is greatly diminished after death. Where, as in this case, there is a heightened urgency for the information the privilege should give way.

Justice O'Connor summed up the dissent's position, stating:

> Where exoneration of an innocent criminal defendant or a compel-ling law enforcement interest is at stake, the harm of precluding critical evidence that is unavailable by any other means outweighs the potential disincentive to forthright communication. In my view, the cost of silence warrants a narrow exception to the rule that the attorney-client privilege survives the death of the client[35]

---

[34] Id.

[35] *Id.* at 416.

## The Aftermath

Whitewater and Travelgate are now part of history unless revived during a campaign by now Senator Hillary Clinton for the presidency. Both controversies ended with a thud rather than a bang. The subsequent impeachment and trial of President Clinton involved matters occurring separately from those situations and, in any event, well after Mr. Foster's death. The cause of the death of Vincent Foster remains a subject of controversy only for an unknown number of conspiracy theorists talking to each other on the internet. The reports of two Independent Counsel finding beyond any reasonable doubt that his death was a suicide disposed of the issue for most of the public and the mainstream press. Whatever was said by Vincent Foster to his attorney on the morning of July 11, 1993 will be known only to his attorneys and to the judges who reviewed the memoranda *in camera*. We do not know whether the confidences Foster shared with James Hamilton would have prolonged or changed the outcome of the Whitewater, Travelgate or Foster death controversies, but to think they would is pure speculation. If they did, it would have been, as the Supreme Court ultimately held, at a price affecting the policies giving rise to our most venerable evidentiary privilege.

Although the factual controversies surrounding the case of *Swidler & Berlin v. United States* may have effectively ended, the impact of the decision on the attorney-client privilege remains. The Supreme Court's opinion in the case reaffirmed the privilege in its absolute form and again endorsed its utilitarian justification. In these respects, the case affirms the *status quo* for future decisions with regard to the attorney-client privilege. The burden is on those who would narrow its scope and application.

Most lawyers probably applauded the holding in *Swidler & Berlin* and its utilitarian justification. Despite the absence of strong empirical evidence reinforcing the notion that the privilege encourages free discourse between lawyer and client, practitioners are likely to feel instinctively that it does. As argued by the petitioner and the *amici* in *Swidler & Berlin,* many clients may care as much about disclosure after death as before, especially those who may be contemplating suicide. But we really don't know.

Lawyers, particularly litigators, no doubt breathed sighs of relief at the holding that there would be no balancing of the privilege against the need for information in criminal prosecutions.[36] The view announced in

---

[36] James Hamilton views his petition for certiorari in the *Swidler & Berlin* case as a "matter of principle," especially with regard to the need to abrogate the balancing test that had been established by the Court of Appeals. Author's interview with James Hamilton, July 21, 2005.

*Upjohn* and *Jaffee* that "an uncertain privilege is little better than none at all" is that of most lawyers who might otherwise feel obliged to share the uncertainty with uneasy clients. Not many criminal defense lawyers would want to trust trial judges to ensure the confidentiality of client communications if judges had discretion not to do so. Given the political climate in which the *Swidler & Berlin* case was decided, the temptation to err on the side of disclosure, would for some judges, have been enormous. But given the Court's acceptance of the utilitarian justification for the privilege, its absolute application in *Swidler & Berlin* seems, in retrospect, a foregone conclusion.

State cases decided after *Swidler & Berlin* have followed the Supreme Court's lead. But *In re Miller*,[37] a North Carolina case in which the court purports to follow *Swidler & Berlin,* in fact reaches a different result in so far as it partially abrogates the posthumous application of the privilege. *Miller* involved an alleged murder by arsenic in which the victim's wife and her lover were the principal suspects. The wife's lover consulted an attorney and then committed suicide. The prosecutor sought to compel the lawyer to file an affidavit detailing his conversation with the deceased. The deceased's widow, presumably learning of her husband's infidelities for the first time after his suicide, was willing to waive the privilege. The court held not only that the privilege survived, but also that it could not be waived by the personal representative of the deceased's estate under North Carolina probate law. However, the court held that the privilege would apply only if the conversation concerned the legal rights of the client, and not some other person, and then only if there was a need to protect the client's concerns for his criminal or civil liability or harm to reputation or loved ones. The court observed that in *Swidler & Berlin* the Supreme Court had treated the need to protect against damage to these interests of the deceased as the reason for recognizing the survival of the privilege. The court remanded so that the trial judge might consider an affidavit setting forth counsel's recollection of the conversation with his client in light of these principles.[38]

The rationale of the *Miller* case is faulty. The court confused protecting communications between attorney and client for the purpose of fostering free communications with the Fifth Amendment privilege, which applies only if the information is in fact incriminating. At least in survival cases, North Carolina is now in the odd position of having to look at the contents of communications between lawyer and client rather

---

[37] 584 S.E.2d 772 (N.C. 2003).

[38] *Id.* at 787–90. On remand, the trial judge determined that one paragraph of counsel's affidavit disclosed a conversation that concerned the action of the deceased's lover rather than his own actions and was therefore not covered by the privilege. The trial judge's ruling was upheld on appeal. In re Miller (2) 595 S.E.2d 120 (N.C. 2004).

than at the circumstances of the communication. Nevertheless, one can sympathize with the struggle of the court in *Miller,* just as Chief Justice Rehnquist sympathizes with the plight of Independent Counsel in *Swidler & Berlin,* calling the arguments "by no means frivolous." Recognizing an absolute privilege might well have denied the court evidence needed to convict a guilty person. Furthermore, unlike the living client situation, the court's interpretation of the state's probate law prohibiting waiver by the personal representative, would prevent any appeal to the client's concern for justice. The loss of the evidence is eternal.

The *Swidler & Berlin* case has not been without its critics, one text referring to the "haste in which the case was decided" and its purportedly "misleading or erroneous statements about the state of law."[39] Others have expressed concern at the absolute as opposed to qualified application of the privilege in situations where attorney communications would protect an innocent defendant or where information was essential to law enforcement purposes. Perhaps the most creative criticism has come from Professor Michael Stokes Paulsen who argued that there should be a special exception where the client committed suicide to prevent the disclosure of information.[40]

If one rejects the view that the primary justification for the attorney-client privilege is utilitarian, the case for an absolute privilege weakens. Under the utilitarian view that the privilege encourages free communication between lawyer and client, an uncertain privilege is little better than no privilege at all. However, if one looks at the purpose of the privilege as the protection of privacy or as the protection of the autonomy of an individual to make decisions after receiving professional advice, the need for absolute protection after death is less certain. The privacy or autonomy of the individual can be protected to a significant extent, but can give way to other urgent needs without a derogation of the fundamental principles.

### The Future

Despite some academic musings in favor of a privacy or autonomy rationale for privilege, the utilitarian view that the privilege promotes

---

[39] Charles Alan Wright & Kenneth W. Graham, Jr., Federal Practice and Procedure, § 5498 (Supp. 2005). The "misleading or erroneous" statement referred to is the Court's claim that its view is supported by the "great body of caselaw." 524 U.S. at 404. The authors find the statement "misleading because of the limited scope of the common law privilege and paucity of cases in which the claim for a perpetual privilege was a holding rather than dicta." *Id.* at note 16.2. *See* discussion of the Court of Appeals reference to Professor Wright and Graham's main volume views on survival of the privilege in the text accompanying notes 45 and 46, *supra.*

[40] Michael Stokes Paulsen, *Dead Man's Privilege: Vince Foster and the Demise of Legal Ethics,* 68 Ford. L.Rev. 807 (1999).

free discourse between attorney and client will likely prevail after *Swidler & Berlin*. To be sure, there may be a watering down of the privilege in some respects. For example, some have argued that the use and application of the crime-fraud exception has grown to such an extent that the privilege may have little meaning in the criminal context. In most instances, however, the absolute privilege is here to stay, both before and after the client's death, although an exception might emerge should a case arise where the disclosure of a dead client's confidences could free an innocent person. Chief Justice Rehnquist's suggestion of the application of a constitutional right to evidence argument in such a case, supplemented by the well-articulated concerns of Justice O'Connor, provides a firm basis for such an exception. But except for evidence that might free an innocent criminal defendant, *Swidler & Berlin* seems to create a privilege eternal—unless the doctrine of waiver comes more prominently into play.

The question of waiver played a prominent part in the oral argument of both counsel in *Swidler & Berlin*. During the petitioner's argument, Justice Scalia raised the point that no one here can act, but that a living client could waive the privilege and then commented:

> But what's extraordinary here is, you're saying there is nobody—no matter how severe the public interest is on the other side, there is nobody who can say enough is enough, in these circumstances the information ought to come out. Even if you yourself thought that the information was really crucial to you, you would have to say, nobody can let it out. That's extraordinary.[41]

Mr. Hamilton responded, "Justice Scalia, in this particular situation I do believe the personal representative of Mr. Foster's estate could waive the privilege."

Both parties were asked about the state of the law of waiver. Some twenty states provide that the personal representative of the deceased can claim and therefore waive the privilege. Counsel and the court discussed at some length the question of whether that meant that the right to claim the privilege ended with the closing of the estate. Although the Independent Counsel argued that the state statutes clearly had that effect, opposing counsel was not so certain, noting that the attorney could also raise the privilege on behalf of the client. Only California specifically provides that the privilege ends with the closing of the estate.

It is possible that the states and perhaps the federal courts or Congress will consider the question and provide more specifically for waiver. California's solution is one approach, although it is based on concern for civil liability rather than any of the other concerns that

---

[41] Swidler & Berlin v. United States, No. 97–1192, 1998 WL 309279 (U.S), at *15–16.

might trouble a client before confiding in his or her lawyers. Another possibility is to give the right to claim or waive the privilege to a personal representative irrespective of whether the estate has formally been closed. If the issue comes up after the estate is closed, a special personal representative could be appointed. At least some human assigned to represent the deceased would have the power to exercise what he or she could guess would have been the client's intent. It is an imperfect solution, but it may come as close to the satisfying the purposes of the privilege as any.

## Conclusion

Perhaps the conspiracy theorists would have been satisfied if they had some idea of what was troubling Vincent Foster when he consulted James Hamilton, but probably not. Perhaps further light would have been shed on the Whitewater or Travelgate scandals if Foster's confidences had not been respected, but probably not. More likely the disclosures would have simply added a little more fuel to either fire. But at least those investigating the case might have had more insight into the complex and puzzling issues involved in those controversies.

Nevertheless, even weighing those benefits, the principles behind protecting the confidences of clients, whether for utilitarian purposes or those involving considerations of privacy or autonomy, seem better served by the *Swidler & Berlin* decision than they would have been by the opposite result. Whether there is further gloss on the posthumous application of the privilege through application of the waiver doctrine will have to await future developments.

# 7

## The Story of *Upjohn Co. v. United States*: One Man's Journey to Extend Lawyer–Client Confidentiality, and the Social Forces That Affected It

### Paul Rothstein*

The attorney-client privilege protects information a client provides an attorney in confidence for the purpose of securing legal advice. But suppose the client is not a person but a corporation and can only speak through its agents and employees. What then are the contours of the privilege? If the corporation's attorney asks an employee for information relating to pending litigation or other legal matters, is the conversation privileged? Some courts said that no communications to a corporate attorney were privileged unless they came from members of the corporate control group, loosely those people who had authority to direct the attorney's activities in connection with legal matters. Other courts said that the identity of the communicator was less important than the subject matter of the communication, and that even the communications of a lower level employee to corporate counsel would be protected, if they pertained to the employee's duties, if they were relevant to the corporation's need for legal advice, and if the employee had been directed by appropriate corporate authority to speak to counsel on the matter.

Suppose that you were counsel to a major corporation, and you wanted to investigate a matter that might have serious legal ramifications for your company, where many of the facts were in the possession of lower-echelon field employees. How would you proceed? What communications would you expect to be protected? Would you fight the matter all the way to the Supreme Court if the lower courts ordered you to

* Professor of Law, Georgetown University Law Center.

share with the Internal Revenue Service (IRS) your notes of confidential communications between you and these employees? Gerard Thomas proceeded with great care to build the strongest case possible for claiming the privilege, and when two lower courts refused that claim, he appealed—successfully—to the United States Supreme Court, forever changing what corporate communications are privileged and the way corporate law is practiced. The case was *Upjohn Co. v. United States*, 449 U.S. 383 (1981).

## THE CASE AND ITS DRAMATIS PERSONAE

Gerard Thomas today is just over 80 years old. At 6 ft. 2 inches, he still cuts a handsome figure, topped with an impressive mane of white hair.[1] Officially retired less than five years ago from his private law firm in Kalamazoo, Michigan, Thomas is still found at meetings there on a fairly regular basis. He remains married to the same woman, after all these years. She, like his friends at the office, calls him "Gerry". He dotes on his two grown daughters and a son—none of whom are lawyers—and eight grandchildren, two of whom just graduated from college.

There is something Clark Kent-ish about Thomas. A true gentleman, he is polite, soft spoken, and courtly. It is hard to believe that twenty-odd years ago he doggedly faced down the IRS, winning such a dramatic expansion of attorney-client privilege in the process, that even today he is deemed a hero by the legal community.

Indeed, the IRS probably thought from his demeanor that Thomas would be a push-over. They were wrong. If you listen closely when he talks, there are glimpses of the man of steel within. This veteran WWII infantry corporal didn't win two battle stars and a purple heart for nothing.

At the time of the fight with the IRS, Thomas was General Counsel, Vice President, and Secretary of the great American pharmaceutical firm, the Upjohn Company. He was also on the boards of several of its subsidiaries. Headquartered in Kalamazoo, where Thomas still lives, Upjohn had world-spanning operations in over 150 countries, requiring Thomas to travel from time-to-time to consult with overseas employees. The attorney-client victory he won in the Upjohn case involved his communications with some of these overseas employees—communica-

---

[1] My descriptions of Gerard Thomas, his involvement in the case, and other matters related to the case, are based on my personal interviews with Thomas and others connected with the case, and on court records, press accounts, corporate documents, and information from government filings, some obtained through the Freedom of Information Act, as well as more traditional legal and internet sources. David Sinkman, my student research assistant, aided me in various ways, and I am grateful for his help.

tions the IRS badly wanted to discover in order to determine Upjohn's tax liability.

The precise issue in the case was whether the company's attorney-client privilege covered written and oral exchanges between Thomas and lower-echelon Upjohn employees—field employees in various parts of the world who, unlike certain officers and directors, were not part of the company's "control group". It was undisputed, owing to previous cases, that an attorney's communications with members of the control group itself, being most like an individual client's communications with her attorney in the non-corporate context, were privileged, assuming other privilege requirements were met.

Thomas prevailed in the Supreme Court. The lower-echelon communications were held sacrosanct, ushering in an era of increased confidentiality and reliance on attorneys by the business community. Whether a lawyer was an "in-house" lawyer, like Thomas, or one hired externally by the corporation made no difference.

The *Upjohn* decision has particular resonance today, when corporate fraud and the role of lawyers in facilitating or preventing it, is so much on the front burner. Recent abuses by executives in charge of such leviathons as Enron Corp., Tyco, MCI–Worldcom, and Health–South, have resulted in massive corporate bankruptcies and huge financial losses to employees, shareholders, and investors. Individual, institutional, and governmental retirement funds have been decimated. The entire national economy has suffered. Enron alone is estimated to have cost investors over 63 billion dollars. Does an expansive corporate attorney-client privilege impede discovery of fraud and enable lawyers to help engineer legal circumventions? Or does it encourage companies and their employees to lay the facts fully before the attorney so she can advise them to stay within the law? The Supreme Court in *Upjohn* believed the latter to be a more significant effect, saying:

> The narrow scope given the attorney-client privilege by the court below not only makes it difficult for corporate attorneys to formulate sound advice when their client is faced with a specific legal problem, but also threatens to limit the valuable efforts of corporate counsel to ensure their client's compliance with the law. In light of the vast and complicated array of regulatory legislation confronting the modern corporation, corporations, unlike most individuals, constantly go to lawyers to find out how to obey the law, particularly since compliance with the law in this area is hardly an instinctive matter. [For just one example,] the behavior proscribed by [the antitrust laws] is often difficult to distinguish from the gray zone of socially acceptable and economically justifiable business conduct.[2]

---

[2] *Upjohn,* 449 U.S. at 392 (internal quotation marks and citations omitted).

Government enforcers and regulators have a less charitable view of lawyers and recently have taken some counter-measures. We shall return to this later.

Thomas' involvement with the events giving rise to *Upjohn* began in 1976. Independent accountants conducting a routine audit had alerted Upjohn that some of Upjohn's subsidiaries abroad or their employees may have made payments to foreign officials or governments in order to secure or facilitate business for Upjohn. Since Upjohn's foreign subsidiaries were in many respects independent entities, Upjohn's International Division first looked into the matter without Thomas' direct participation. But that inquiry did not come up with much. Since there were some aspects that might affect Upjohn on a broader basis, Thomas got more intimately involved.

He does not remember precisely how it first came to his personal attention that Upjohn's subsidiaries might be involved in questionable payments, or how he initially felt. It is likely he was notified by the company's chief financial officer, who may have approached him at the water cooler, in the hall, or over lunch in the executive dining room. A more formal memo would have followed. Several things undoubtedly flashed through Thomas's mind. That American companies and their subsidiaries were making such payments was not news. The practice was beginning to be discussed in business circles and, very disparagingly, by the press. Congress was considering legislation to curb the payments, and something called the Foreign Corrupt Practices Act was eventually passed, but too late to affect this case. However, there already were laws on the books that made such payments potentially illegal at home and abroad.

Thomas obviously knew the realities. Foreign governmental entities often purchased American products, including pharmaceuticals, for their populations, or required that official permission be obtained to sell through other channels. Formal or informal fees, legally authorized or not, were frequently exacted as a prerequisite to doing such business. International competition for these lucrative marketing opportunities was intense. Many companies or their employees believed that paying informal "fees" was necessary for American firms to stay competitive. In some instances it was not clear whether the payments were illegal bribes, or a form of "customary law"—that is, an informal license fee that was an accepted part of doing business in the country. Just as formally prescribed license fees could be properly paid, so could these, the argument went—particularly in a country where there was little formal law or where the line between formal law and customary practice was blurry. Some of these informal payments might appear to be part of the understood "salary" for otherwise low-paid or unpaid officials, much like the theoretically optional but universally expected tip one gives to waiters in a restaurant. There were other ambiguities as well: Was treating an official to dinner at a fine restaurant, or giving him or his family a small gift, improper? Would it be considered impolite not to do so? How large or lavish must a dinner or gift be to be improper? But not everything was in the gray area. Clearly, there were circumstances where everyone should realize that a payment because of its size, expected benefit, or recipient, was flat out wrong.

Thomas also knew that this was the immediate post-Watergate era. A candidate for U.S. President named Jimmy Carter was running on a platform calling for a "return to ethics," and it was all but certain he would win. American politicians and corporate executives were facing public anger over secret political contributions and corporate bribery at home and abroad. The press, public, and government investigators were keen to discover more Watergate-like scandals. "Bananagate", for example, revealed that the United Fruit Company, the world's predominant supplier of bananas, was bribing officials in tropical countries where bananas were grown. United Fruit and other companies were found to have maintained unaccounted-for "slush" funds—likened to President Nixon's famous slush fund that had financed the Watergate break-in. These corporate slush funds were used to bribe and make under-the-table political contributions to domestic and foreign politicians. Companies were getting into trouble with the IRS and the Securities and Exchange Commission (SEC), for not properly disclosing the payments or their true nature to regulators, for deducting them from income, and for failing to report or identify them (or the foreign and domestic civil and criminal liabilities they potentially entailed) to investors, as required by American law. Currency regulations and foreign laws were also being violated. If Upjohn were making payments to foreign officials, it would be viewed very much askance, to say the least.

Thomas called a meeting with Ray ("Ted") Parfet, Jr., Upjohn's Chairman of the Board, and others in the company. In a move to fend off possible legal trouble as well as a public relations nightmare, they launched an internal investigation into these questionable payments. It would cover the preceding several years through to the present. Thomas was in charge. He was assisted by an in-house staff of three or four lawyers, a secretary, and a couple of part-time paralegals. Because foreign payments could affect Upjohn's federal securities and tax obligations, Thomas called upon the old-line patrician Washington D.C. law firm of Covington & Burling, specialists who over the years had assisted Upjohn's legal department in federal matters. They could now help structure the investigation and help prepare oral and written questions to ask the foreign employees.

Thomas says these questions were structured not as much to preserve a possible future attorney-client privilege claim, as to get the facts so that Upjohn and their subsidiaries could comply with domestic and foreign legal requirements.

The investigation included written questionnaires and letters sent to "All Foreign General and Area Managers". They were signed by Parfet. These questionnaires addressed "possibly illegal payments to foreign government officials" and solicited all information relating to any such payments. The letters informed the managers of Thomas' leading role in conducting the investigation and instructed that all responses should be sent directly to him. Because the inquiry was "highly confidential" the managers were told to restrict the information to as few Upjohn employees as necessary. By thus underlining the role of Thomas, his status as exclusive recipient of responses, the legal purposes of the investigation, the restricted confidential nature of the communications, and the employees' authorization by the corporation to speak to its counsel, Thomas and Covington enhanced the likelihood that the communications would be held privileged in any future challenge, as well as the likelihood employees would make significant disclosures.

Another part of the investigation included live interviews, mostly conducted by Thomas personally, of the foreign managers and thirty-three other employees. He traveled to approximately fifteen or twenty different developed and underdeveloped countries—places in Mexico, Central and South America, Europe, Asia, and Africa—to speak with employees who made or knew of payments. The trips, often arduous, lasted for weeks or even months. Once, in Egypt, Thomas was jailed overnight for not having the right medical inoculations. Coming from a company that manufactured them, he should have been more savvy. But he had overlooked the fact that, because he stopped to do interviews in Kenya before going on to Egypt, he needed more shots than if he had come straight from the U.S. He was told he was being taken to a Holiday Inn, but it turned out to be a jail. The only resemblance to a Holiday Inn was the guards' green blazers, Thomas says. He was more than a little frightened by their machine guns and the fact that an Ethiopian in his cell said he had been there for days for a similar infraction

Thomas wanted to do most of the oral interviews personally. This certainly would increase the credibility of any future claim of attorney-client privilege, but he says that was not his only purpose. As in the written questionnaires, he wanted to assure the employees that they could be forthright with him, despite any self-damaging revelations, because the company would do all it could to protect them. His subsequent fight for confidentiality, all the way to the Supreme Court, suggests his promise was not empty.

Thomas's approach in the interviews emphasized that the company valued its employees, had always treated them fairly, regarded them in many respects as family, and would be loyal. He told them he knew they had been trying to help the company, but that now the company needed their assistance in the investigation. He says today that for the most part, employees trusted the company. It had been founded near the turn of the century by an honorable pillar of the Kalamazoo community, Dr. William Erastus Upjohn, who had achieved wealth by inventing the friable pill, the key to modern pharmaceuticals.[3] Dr. Upjohn, himself the son of a respected local doctor, went on to become one of the country's great philanthropists. The Upjohn family remained involved in the ownership and management of the company, and continued and expanded the great philanthropic tradition of Dr. Upjohn. The company, Thomas says, always put a high value on integrity, and the employees knew that. So they cooperated. No doubt, "Gerry" Thomas's extremely personable nature had a lot to do with it.

Many of the employees abroad told him that, if you were doing business in their country, you *must* pay somebody, especially in the social services and health field. They said often there was no real government to deal with. Doing business was prevented by *somebody* unless "palms were greased". In many instances, he was told, it was hard to tell whether someone seeking payments and in a position to impede business was a governmental agent or a private party. Yet the legality of the payment under both foreign and U.S. law might hinge on that.

Some of the payments he was told about seemed relatively insignificant. In Mexico, for example, "government" drivers of company employees would get lost or delayed unless an amount, ranging from $2 to $20 was added to the charge under the table. In some countries, he was told, one had to be careful not to "tip" too much, or "you would look ignorant". Frequently, the amount had to be big enough for the recipient to divide with others. Sometimes payments were "in kind". For example, company employees may have had to see that someone in a key position got a telephone installed in their home.

But many of the stories he heard undoubtedly involved more significant payments, to people as low on the chain as purchasing agents, or as high as the head of a major governmental department, or even higher, in more questionable circumstances. Thomas does not feel free to talk about those. But he says he told the employees that the questionable payments must stop.

---

[3] A friable pill is dissolvable, made of compacted powder. Previously, pills were unyieldingly hard, passing through the bodily system undissolved. Medicines had to be administered in liquid form. Dr. Upjohn's marketing to doctors involved sending a hammer and two pills on a board—one friable, one not—and inviting the doctor to hammer them both. One would smash into powder, one would dent the board. The logo of the Upjohn Company for many years was a tiny depiction of this hammer-and-board experiment.

Some of the employees Thomas interviewed had felt that they shouldn't bother their employer about the payments made to grease the wheels of business. They felt they were protecting Upjohn. If told, the company might have to halt the practice, costing it business and putting it at a competitive disadvantage. But many of these same employees seemed relieved that the company had now found out and wanted to know more.

There was a feeling on the part of some of those Thomas interviewed that "everybody does it—it is a part of the culture of this country—penalties against it are not enforced—you cannot practicably apply U.S. standards here." It may also be supposed that at least some employees themselves benefited, as employees, from the increased sales, in terms of commissions, promotion, or the like. There was little suggestion, though, that any employees got direct kickbacks.

Upon their return to the United States, Thomas and his staff put together provisional materials about the payments based on his notes of the interviews and the answers to the written interrogatories. (It is the privileged status of these notes and answers that subsequently became the main subject of the *Upjohn* case. But we are getting ahead of the story.)

The SEC was investigating foreign payments generally, and may have gotten wind of the fact that Upjohn might be involved. Under SEC disclosure regulations, such payments, and potential legal liabilities connected with them, had to be clearly reported and identified in shareholder and other material. Few companies, including Upjohn, had done so, often being ignorant of the payments or their true nature. Some companies, however, were purposely covering up.

Thomas and Covington & Burling consulted and decided that early disclosure to the SEC of what Upjohn's investigation had found would mitigate whatever penalties the SEC might ultimately impose on them for violation of these reporting requirements over the last several years. Stanley Sporkin—subsequently General Counsel of the Central Intelligence Agency and later a Federal District Judge in Washington, D.C—was the head of enforcement at the SEC at the time. He had instituted a policy encouraging early cooperation and disclosure by a company, of possible law infractions, even in advance of any SEC investigation. He would reward such self-reporting with a reduction or elimination of any penalties the company might eventually face. He felt this would supplement his own resources, greatly expanding the number of potential violations the SEC could feasibly and economically investigate. In addition to generally publicizing his policy, he went so far as to send letters to companies he suspected of violations, urging them to investigate and report on themselves. Sporkin, known as a "Washington *wunderkind*," is credited with the first large-scale program encouraging such self-investigation and self-reporting. It has since been widely copied and expanded by other agencies. Today, Sporkin—an enthusiastic and tirelessly energetic person— has retired from the bench and is practicing in a Washington, D.C. law firm that, perhaps ironically, is handling the bankruptcy of Enron.

After substantial input by Covington & Burling and others in Upjohn, a summary report of some of Thomas's findings, based on some of his notes and some of the interrogatory answers, was produced and submitted to the SEC on the appropriate official forms, with a copy to the IRS. It included only summaries of those transactions the lawyers representing Upjohn felt were relevant. The company's disclosures appeared to be motivated in part by Sporkin's promise of more lenient treatment for voluntary compliance and Thomas's own conviction that early disclosure is best.

The SEC ultimately seemed satisfied with this material, after some supplemental disclosures.

The IRS, however, took a firmer stance and soon began investigating the tax consequences of the questionable payments. For example, were payments deducted from Upjohn's income when they should not have been? As part of its inquiry, the IRS demanded production of "all files relevant to the investigation conducted under the supervision of Gerard Thomas to identify payments to employees of foreign governments and any political contributions made by the Upjohn Company or any of its affiliates." The IRS also specifically asked for the answers to the written questionnaires and all memos or notes of all Thomas's interviews. At first the requests were made only in letters and discussions with Thomas and Covington & Burling. Upjohn declined to produce the answers and interview materials, claiming that the attorney-client privilege protected them, but the company offered to make people they had interviewed available for interrogation about the facts that they knew (as opposed to what they told attorneys about them), not a large concession since such information is not protected by the attorney-client privilege anyway.

The IRS then turned up the heat, issuing a "summons" for the refused information. A special statute and accompanying regulations permit this IRS summons procedure. Only a few agencies can issue such summonses. They are supposed to be issued only in connection with civil investigations (which, so far, this was) but are not invalidated by the fact that, as here, the possibility of using the information summoned in subsequent criminal proceedings has not been ruled out. Tax infractions can lead to either civil or criminal proceedings, depending upon how aggravated and intentional they prove to be.

Technically, an IRS summons is issued and signed by the special agent in charge of the investigation. In this case, the special agent was David Nowak, a tough, uncompromising, no-nonsense enforcer of fearsome reputation who was not satisfied with the voluntary disclosures that had been made by Upjohn. His summons was addressed to Thomas and Upjohn by name. They refused to comply with it. Under the statute, the special agent can then go to the Federal District Court to get the summons enforced with a court order that, if violated, results in punishment.

On August 31, 1977, Agent Nowak requested the United States District Court for the Western District of Michigan to enforce the summons and compel production of the documents. As customary, the caption of the case prominently bore Agent Nowak's name as the party seeking enforcement, and the names of Gerard Thomas and Upjohn as the parties resisting enforcement. This is the case that ultimately went to the Supreme Court.

In the District Court in cases of this kind, a Magistrate—an assistant to the District Judge—normally hears the case first. The Magistrate listens to witnesses, examines documentary evidence, and considers points of law raised by both sides, and then makes a recommendation to the District Judge, supported by detailed reasoning, concerning whether or not to enforce the summons. The District Judge can adopt, reject, or modify the recommendation. Sometimes the Judge takes additional evidence, or sends the case back to the Magistrate to hear more evidence or make additional findings or clarifications. After the District Judge finally rules, a dissatisfied party can appeal to the Court of Appeals, and thereafter to the Supreme Court, if the Supreme Court thinks the issue is important enough.

Upjohn and Thomas were represented before the Magistrate by local Michigan counsel and Covington & Burling, since Upjohn's in-house lawyers did not try cases. However, some in-house lawyers on Thomas's staff who had participated in strategy sessions were at counsel table and on the papers. The lawyers argued attorney-client privilege, work-product, and some minor points of statutory and regulatory authority. The privilege against self-incrimination was not invoked because corporations and corporate officials have no such privilege covering corporate documents.

Agent Nowak explained in testimony before the Magistrate why he was not satisfied with only the disclosures Upjohn had voluntarily made to the IRS (basically the summaries of some of the transactions Upjohn's investigation had discovered that had been given to the SEC). Like any tough law enforcer, Nowak did not want to take Upjohn's word for which transactions and details were relevant and what their import was:

**Q.** [By Government Attorney]: Why do you feel that you should have these documents...rather than take the Upjohn Company's assurance as to what the relevance of those documents [is]?

**A.** [By Nowak]: Well, I feel that those files may contain evidence that would indicate that there is in fact a tax implication involved in payments which the company has alleged have no U.S. tax implication. These files may contain leads or other evidence that would have a relationship to those payments that the company does admit have a U.S. tax implication. I believe that it would—if it served no other purpose—it would help me corroborate the company's position that there is no tax impact, if that is what the facts would show upon my investigation of the files.

Thomas himself appeared as the other principal witness. He testified regarding the physical events of the investigation, including his trips and the sending of the questionnaires. He characterized his interview notes as follows:

My notes would contain what I considered to be the important questions, the substance of the responses to them, my beliefs as to the importance of these, my beliefs as to how they related to the inquiry, my thoughts as to how they related to other questions. In some instances they might even suggest other questions that I would have to ask, or things that I needed to find elsewhere. They were more than just a verbatim report of my conversation with the—a report of my conversation in the interviews.

He reiterated that Upjohn would voluntarily make current employees available to the IRS for questioning except for those Upjohn deemed totally irrelevant. But Upjohn declined to absorb travel expenses the IRS might incur in such interviews. Moreover, some of the people involved were former employees that Upjohn could no longer produce. But none of this would necessarily prevent the IRS from using its own resources and auspices to obtain interviews. Interviewing witnesses would of course be more difficult and expensive than examining the documents, and the IRS could not be sure the witnesses would be as frank as they had been in Thomas' inquiry.

The Magistrate ruled in the government's favor, giving several grounds: the privilege applies only to communications of the control group, and anyway the limited disclosures to the SEC and IRS had the effect of waiving the privilege as to almost everything that had been communicated, whether that was intended or not.[4] The District Judge

---

[4] The Magistrate also ruled that the work-product doctrine did not apply to material requested in an IRS summons, but if it did, it was overcome by the IRS's need for the information.

summarily adopted the Magistrate's opinion in all respects and ordered production of the allegedly protected material.

On Thomas's and Covington's recommendation, Upjohn appealed to the Court of Appeals for the Sixth Circuit, which rejected the lower court's finding of waiver, holding that waiver only occurred as to information actually given to the IRS and SEC—a very narrow waiver that sounds like it should have been good news for Upjohn.

But the Court of Appeals agreed with the lower court that the privilege did not apply "to the extent the communications were made by officers and agents not responsible for directing Upjohn's actions in response to legal advice"—virtually all the communications at issue here—because these communications, being made by people not in the corporate "control group," were not made as part of any attorney-client relationship. The Court of Appeals was worried that extending the privilege further, as some Courts of Appeals had done, would encourage upper-echelon management to ignore unpleasant facts and would create a broad "zone of silence."[5] So, although Upjohn may not have waived its privilege, as to most of the material there was no privilege to be waived to begin with. This was a crushing loss.

Upjohn had been roundly defeated twice: in the trial court, and in the appeals court. A lesser man than Thomas might have caved. But he knew there was one last chance to preserve the confidentiality of the information he had collected, and he convinced the company to take it. That last chance was to persuade the United States Supreme Court, first, to take the case, and second, to address the merits of the case and reverse the Court of Appeals' decision.

Upjohn's strongest argument for taking the case was that a conflict of authority existed among lower courts on the question of who in a corporation may make privileged communications to the corporation's attorney. In advancing this argument, Upjohn stressed the legal profession's urgent need to know precisely the scope of the attorney-client privilege in the corporate context.

---

[5] The Court of Appeals also agreed with the lower court that work-product protection did not apply. The decision did not directly address whether someone other than top executives in Upjohn might be considered in a control group of sorts—e.g., regional managers who might have authority to act on legal advice relating to their own regions. This possibility had been recognized by some decisions. Nor did the decision discuss whether investigating foreign payments was more a business function than a professional legal function, which would strip communications related thereto of attorney-client privilege. This possibility has been considered in other unrelated cases, particularly where the lawyer wears two hats, as Thomas did; that is, holds a legal position and a business position in the company. The investigation here had been constructed in a way that would maximize the claim that legal concerns were foremost.

Thomas and Covington were pleased but not really surprised when the Supreme Court "granted certiorari"—that is, agreed to hear the case—because it is well known that the Justices like to resolve important conflicts among the Federal Circuits. Resolving such conflicts is one of the most important functions of the Court and a primary reason the Court gives for reviewing lower court decisions.

## UNDERCUTTING AN ANCIENT PRIVILEGE

To understand the Supreme Court's ultimate decision on the *merits* of the case, we first need to review a few basics about the privilege.

The attorney-client privilege provides that, with certain exceptions, confidential communications between an attorney and her client are not to be received as evidence in judicial and similar proceedings. Originally based on a notion of the lawyer's honor (a gentleman would not reveal the confidences of another), today the privilege is supported on other grounds. Combined with the roughly parallel ethical obligation of attorneys not to disclose client information in venues outside of those covered by privilege, the privilege is believed to encourage clients to truthfully reveal to the attorney everything the client knows that might bear on the legal advice sought by the client, regardless of whether the advice is sought to prepare for litigation or for other legal purposes. The lawyer's ability to provide sound legal advice is thought to provide a number of social benefits that more than compensate for any loss of evidence—not the least of which is that the lawyer may be able to avert illegal action by the client. It is also argued that courts and other public entities make better decisions if they are presented with fully informed legal arguments, and when clients tell their lawyers everything, sounder legal documents and transactions also result.

From at least the early 19th century on there have been scholars who have wanted to abolish or restrict the privilege, including the celebrated philosopher Jeremy Bentham, who, in *Rationale of Judicial Evidence* (1827), authored a particularly scathing critique. However, the privilege has withstood most assaults. Its roots are deep. They stretch back at least to the reign of Elizabeth I, and some scholars think the privilege may be traced as far back as the Roman Empire, where the notion that a lawyer could not be a witness against his client was an accepted principle.

Courts developed the attorney-client privilege for the individual client. The rise of the modern corporation has created enormous problems in identifying the client for purposes of the privilege. Unlike an individual person, a corporation is an artificial body lacking the human dignity and personal rights that the privilege seeks to protect. While attorneys generally rely on the individual client as the sole source of information about their case, a corporation has many individual workers, from the factory worker to the door-to-door salesman to the chief executive, each with his or her own story to tell. As corporations grew in size and complexity during the 20th century, information and responsibility were dispersed across the globe. Thus questions arise in the corporate context that do not exist with individual clients. As a result, American courts have struggled, particularly since the 1960s, to define the scope of this privilege as it relates to corporations. While it is generally agreed that in most circumstances only those who run the corporation can claim (or waive) the privilege, there has been substantially less agreement on the range of protected communications. Before *Upjohn*, courts and commentators frequently asked, "Does the privilege protect communications between every employee and the corporation's lawyers? Or does the privilege only protect communications between executives and corporate counsel? Or is the answer somewhere in-between?"

In a landmark 1962 utilities antitrust case known as *Radiant Burners*, Chief Judge Campbell of the United States District Court for the Northern District of Illinois ruled that letters from corporate officers and employees sent to the corporation's lawyers were not privileged and must be produced during discovery. Judge Campbell reasoned that the attorney-client privilege was (1) historically and fundamentally personal in nature and (2) the lack of confidentiality inherent in a corporate hierarchy diminishes the force of the privilege. As a result, he ruled against extending the privilege to corporations. Prior to Judge Campbell's decision, courts made no distinction between individuals and corporations in applying this privilege. All that was required for the privilege was that the information furnished to the attorney by any officer or employee must be given in confidence and without the presence of a third person.

The legal backlash to Judge Campbell's decision was swift. The Court of Appeals for the Seventh Circuit reversed the ruling. *Radiant Burners, Inc. v. American Gas Assn.*, 320 F.2d 314 (1963). Citing a number of early U.S. and English cases, this court, sitting *en banc*, held that a corporation is entitled to the same treatment as any other client. The court stressed the need to encourage full disclosure by clients to their lawyers, reasoning that such communication is essential for a lawyer to be effective as counsel. Although Judge Campbell's decision was overturned and most courts and legislatures showed little inclination to embrace his decision, his opinion struck a cord with many commentators and sparked a fierce legal debate.

Challenged by Judge Campbell's reasoning, courts were forced to fall back on a utilitarian rationale for the privilege, as articulated by the Seventh Circuit in *Radiant Burners*, to support their extension of the privilege to corporations. But Judge Campbell had alerted them that there are serious arguments against a corporate privilege. The response of some was a compromise of sorts: the control group test, first developed in *City of Philadelphia v. Westinghouse Electric Corp.*, 210 F. Supp. 483 (E.D. Pa. 1962), only months after Judge Campbell's decision. As put forth in *City of Philadelphia*, the control group test enabled courts to extend the privilege to corporations, but in a sharply limited form. Under this test, a communication is protected if the person speaking or writing is in a "position to control or even to take a substantial part in a decision about any action which the corporation may take upon the advice of the attorney." This *control group* test was quickly accepted around the country. In fact, the drafters of the Federal Rules of Evidence recommended the control group test in their original proposal for the Rules.

The development of the control group test was driven by several concerns. First, extending the privilege to statements made by all witnesses seemed contrary to the Supreme Court's decision in *Hickman v. Taylor*, 329 U.S. 495 (1947). Under *Hickman*, an attorney's mental impressions and free exchanges between clients and lawyers are protected but the knowledge of witnesses to disputed events is not protected, and they must provide all relevant information. Given the structure of the modern corporation, many employees with relevant or incriminating information are not corporate executives and thus are arguably more like witnesses than clients. The control group test was intended to limit the privilege to only those who were most like "clients," i.e., those who could act on the attorney's advice—the senior executives—rather than to protect all workers who knew damaging information (arguably more like "witnesses").

A second concern that the control group test took into account was a corporation's ability to manipulate an expansive attorney-client privilege so as to protect embarrassing or incriminating documents. Unlike an individual, a corporate client could structure its procedures so as to privilege much of its documentation relating to routine transactions by addressing it to counsel. Thus, the control group test was intended to remove routine intra-corporate communications from the privilege's protection. Commentators noted, however, that there were other features of the attorney-client privilege that could partially mitigate this problem. For example, communications and documents, to be privileged, must have been created in connection with the rendition of legal services rather than for business or criminal purposes. Nevertheless, a broad attorney-client privilege for corporations is of legitimate concern, in that it can deprive courts of vast amounts of information.

Third, the control group test took into account the need for a bright-line rule. Uncertainty about the exact limits of the privilege would erode full communication between clients and their lawyers because of fears that the conversation would eventually be disclosed. By limiting the privilege to the small group of senior managers who control decision-making, the control group test was intended to allow corporations to identify easily those whose communications were protected by the privilege. Some commentators noted, however, that uncertainty about who is within the control group was inevitable. A broader test embracing all employees might be more certain. Leaving the matter open without any test is what produced the uncertainty.

The control group test was greeted with widespread acceptance and was applied in all federal courts until 1970 when the Court of Appeals for the Seventh Circuit challenged this approach in *Harper & Row Publishers, Inc. v. Decker,* 423 F.2d 487. The Seventh Circuit, apparently again indulging its inclination in favor of a corporate attorney-client privilege that it had manifested in *Radiant Burners*, adopted a broader test for determining the scope of the corporate attorney-client privilege. It focused on the subject matter of the employee's communications rather than on the position of the employee who was communicating the information. Under the subject matter test, an employee's communication with the corporation's lawyer is privileged when made at the direction of a superior and when the subject matter upon which the attorney's advice is sought concerns the worker's employment.

The reasoning behind this broader interpretation was clear. Opponents of the control group test argued that only by extending the privilege to low-level employees could attorneys adequately advise their corporate clients. To restrict the privilege only to communications by top-level executives was to ignore the realities of corporate life because executives often lack the information needed by attorneys to formulate sound legal advice.

The subject matter test's emphasis on ensuring effective legal advice won many adherents, and when the Supreme Court granted certiorari in *Harper & Row* it was thought that the choice between the control group and subject matter tests would soon be made. However, the Court, being shy one member, divided four to four on the issue, resulting in a summary affirmation without opinion, of the Seventh Circuit's decision. *Decker v. Harper & Row Publishers, Inc.,* 400 U.S. 955 (1971), rehearing denied 401 U.S. 950 (1971). In law, a split decision furnishes no guiding precedent. It did, however, lead the drafters of the Federal Rules of Evidence to drop their proposal to add the control group test to the Rules, leaving the matter open. Congress thereafter decided not to include specific rules of privilege in the Federal Rules, with the result that further elucidation of the scope of the federal corporate attorney-client privilege was relegated (along with federal privileges generally) to case-by-case development by the courts.

Federal courts in the 1970s usually adopted either the control group or the subject matter test, though some courts applied variations or even a synthesis of the two. The best-known elaboration of the subject matter test was *Diversified Industries, Inc. v. Meredith*, 572 F.2d 596 (1978), where the Court of Appeals for the Eighth Circuit required that for a lower level corporate employee's communications to be privileged, they must be made at the direction of the employee's superiors and must cover information within the employee's duties. In addition, the court required that the communication be made for the purpose of getting legal services for the corporation and be kept confidential within the corporation. The court reasoned that these requirements would limit the privilege to legitimate attorney-client communications as opposed to regular business dealings, thus taking care of some of the concerns that had led courts to adopt the control-group approach.

This brings us to the Court of Appeals for the Sixth Circuit's decision in *Upjohn*, which was a classic application of the control group test. The court spoke about the difficulties of extending the attorney-client privilege to Upjohn's lower-echelon employees because the privilege's protections were based on the "intimate relationship" between an individual and his lawyer. The court also questioned the effectiveness of the subject matter test, voicing concern that corporate counsel would become the dumping ground for incriminating facts and that corporate executives would be able to shield themselves from information about possibly illegal transactions. In the specific context of *Upjohn,* the court also noted the severe burden that the questioning of large numbers of foreign citizens would place on the IRS. Concluding that the subject matter test would create the potential for a broad "zone of silence," the court applied the narrower control group test and held that the bulk of the questionnaire answers, letters, and interviews in *Upjohn* did not meet it.

The court's "shielding" or "dumping" point deserves a closer look, because it is a mainstay in cases that rejected the subject matter test. The worry is that if communications with field employees are privileged, corporations will be encouraged to structure things in such a way that illegal conduct could be planned or perpetrated by lower echelon employees and discussed by them with corporate lawyers—who might aid the effort or at least keep quiet about it. The information would be funneled to the lawyer and stop there, or be routed through counsel to other lower level employees needed for the scheme, without informing, and hence shielding, upper management. People outside the business would have trouble discovering it. Nor could they discover whether the lawyer told upper management about it. Senior executives could thereby insulate themselves from the wrongdoing and would have "plausible deniability".

They could turn a blind eye with impunity. They would have little incentive to take corrective measures.

But, it may be asked, wouldn't the crime-fraud exception to attorney-client privilege curtail privilege in this nefarious scenario? Wouldn't a requirement that a lower-level employee must be authorized by someone in authority, to communicate with the lawyer tend to mitigate the problem of management deniability? Isn't such a requirement an integral part of the subject-matter test? For example, in *Upjohn* itself, the Chairman of the Board authorized Thomas's inquiry and directed the employees to communicate with Thomas on the matter. Surely Thomas would have to report back to executives on the results. Thus, it is hard to see how the executives could have shielded themselves. Nevertheless, there is something to the court's concern. How major a problem it is, and how determinative it should be, was part of the debate that was the backdrop for the next stage in *Upjohn*: the Supreme Court decision.

## THE SUPREME COURT DECISION IN *UPJOHN*

Thomas sat in the audience during the argument in the Supreme Court. He liked it that no one in the audience knew who he was or that he was the central character behind the arguments they were witnessing. What he and the audience saw were two of the nation's top Supreme Court advocates squaring off against each other. Both were well known to the Justices as fine lawyers, having appeared before them many times. The two therefore had a certain caché with the Court.

Arguing for the government was Lawrence Wallace, a senior career attorney with the U.S. Solicitor General's Office. That office, known as "the Government's Law Firm," handles virtually all the federal government's work before the Supreme Court, and many other important government appellate cases. The Solicitor General has been called the "Tenth Justice" because of the extra credibility that office has in the eyes of the Court. Wallace had worked, ironically, for Covington & Burling immediately following law school. A few years later, he joined the Solicitor General's Office, intending to stay two or three years, but wound up staying 35 years, as deputy to ten Solicitors General, through the administrations of eight presidents beginning with President Lyndon Johnson. He had a steady diet of Supreme Court cases. At six feet tall and 200 pounds, with a machine-gun-like, slightly pedantic, extraordinarily confident delivery, Wallace was truly formidable.

On Upjohn's and Thomas's side was Covington & Burling's Dan Gribbon. Slim, wirey, distinguished, of moderate height, with sparse hair, Gribbon is described by Wallace as "having a style of argument that was at once friendly, warm, personable, and supremely competent", and by Thomas as "physically looking exactly the way a Washington lawyer and partner at Covington & Burling should look". Thomas was struck by the fact that Gribbon, during his oral argument, seemed to welcome—indeed, enthusiastically embraced—the toughest, potentially most damaging and difficult questions from the Justices—*especially* ones that revealed the Achilles heels of his case. Thomas would cringe at such a question, thinking all is lost. "I am very glad you asked me that question," Gribbon would say, and genuinely seem to mean it. He would go on to painstakingly and thoroughly answer the question. He knew that any question represents a problem in the mind of the Justice who asks it, and could well be a deciding factor. Thus he viewed questions as golden opportunities to get inside the minds of the Justices and resolve their problems favorably. His advance preparation, including mooting before other lawyers in the firm, always seemed to have anticipated the question and supplied him with the best answer possible. Thomas reports that Gribbon's performance was stunning. Thomas knew that Gribbon's daughter, a law student, was in the audience and must have felt very proud of her dad. Today she is a federal judge.

The Supreme Court reversed the Court of Appeals' decision, holding that the "control group" test applied by the Court of Appeals was too narrow and overlooked the needs of the lawyer to gather information from whomever within the corporation has the information necessary to enable the lawyer to render fully-informed and therefore sound legal advice—which sound advice serves the public interest in a number of ways. Justice (later Chief Justice) Rehnquist who wrote the opinion for the Court mentioned the need for predictability and certainty as an important reason for discarding the control group test. Nevertheless, to the disappointment of many lawyers and scholars the decision in its concluding passages declined to (in its own words) "lay down a broad rule or series of rules to govern all conceivable future questions in this area" and instead said courts should determine the issue on a case-by-case basis.

Although the *Upjohn* case presented legal questions almost identical to those that had divided the Court in *Harper & Row* a decade earlier, this time the Supreme Court had little trouble with the issue, unanimously rejecting the control group test as applied by the Court of Appeals below. Wallace (the advocate from the Solicitor General's Office) reports that he did not think the case was that open-and-shut, and was surprised not to garner even a single vote among the Justices.

In the first part of the opinion, Justice Rehnquist established that the purpose of the attorney-client privilege was to encourage complete and honest communication between attorneys and their clients. He cited cases dating as far back as the 1880s, concluding that this purpose applied equally well regardless of whether the client was an individual or a corporation.

He then turned his attention to flaws in the control group test. First, he criticized the control group test for failing to further the original aims of the attorney-client privilege. The control group test's emphasis on the employee's ability to act on legal advice from counsel did not provide enough protection to encourage a sufficient flow of important information to the attorney. Rather, it inhibited it by restricting the privilege to a small group within the corporation. The Court reasoned that without vital facts possessed by non-control group employees, the corporation would be left without effective legal counsel. Second, the Supreme Court faulted the control group test's "Hobson's choice": the lawyer could either interview non-control group employees without the protection of the attorney-client privilege or refrain from interviewing them, leaving the company with only a partial understanding of the facts of the case. Even if a lawyer could formulate a legal opinion without talking to low-level employees, "the control group test made it more difficult to convey full and frank legal advice" to the lower level employees who would put the policy into effect. Third, the decision criticized the control group test for its unpredictability, pointing out that contrary decisions in cases applying the control group test showed the test's inherent arbitrariness concerning who is in the control group. The Court reasoned that some degree of certainty is essential to encourage the free flow of information and that without this knowledge the privilege would be ineffectual.

The final part of the Court's analysis applied these principles to the facts in the case. The Court restated what it considered to be the key facts: the communications were made by Upjohn employees to counsel at the direction of corporate superiors; Upjohn needed the communications as a basis for legal advice; the employees were sufficiently aware that they were being questioned so that the corporation could receive legal advice; the communications concerned matters within the scope of the employees' duties; and Upjohn kept the communications highly confidential. The Court concluded that protecting the communications was consistent with the underlying purposes of the attorney-client privilege.

On the other side of the scales, Rehnquist gave relatively short shrift to the notion that a broad privilege hinders the discovery of truth by making evidence unavailable. He noted that all it renders unavailable is the communications themselves, which would probably not be made if privilege did not cover them. So there would be little net loss. This is because the privilege does not prevent discovery of the underlying *facts*, even though they may have been recounted in the communications. The IRS could still summon or subpoena the employees themselves to get the facts; it could just not learn what they *said to the lawyer* about the facts. While independently questioning the witnesses might be relatively difficult or expensive, it is no more so than if the communications had never been made. Indeed, Rehnquist seemed hostile to the notion that difficulty and expense to the government are valid considerations at all when discussing the privilege.

Some commentators have since wondered whether Rehnquist was too facile in this whole argument that extending the privilege entails little loss to discovering truth. The fact is, communications sometimes are—and perhaps were in this case—made for other reasons than privilege. And questioning witnesses independently is not entirely satisfactory. They may not be as truthful with investigators as with the lawyer, and it might be useful both substantively and for impeachment purposes for the government to have the statements made to the lawyer.

At any rate, based on his reasoning, Justice Rehnquist held, for the Court, that the privilege extended to communications of the lower echelon employees here. But he strictly limited the decision to *Upjohn's* facts. This was meant to prevent lower courts from thinking that the Court implicitly embraced the subject matter test as elaborated in *Diversified Industries*. The Court also did not make any attempt to set forth rules or guidelines for determining the scope of the corporate attorney-client privilege. This was striking given the growing acceptance of the subject matter test in the federal courts and the fact that Chief Justice Burger, behind the scenes, was pushing for the Court to adopt a modified subject matter test as indicated in his concurring opinion. The opinion of the Court, however, was confined to a narrow holding that the control group test did not govern the development of the law of the attorney-corporate client privilege, and left future development to the lower courts.[6]

Some have faulted Rehnquist's opinion on the grounds that, in failing to adopt a concrete test, and in mentioning a number of pivotal features of the communication that might not always be ascertainable at the time of the communication, Rehnquist promotes the very uncertainty he decried—uncertainty of application of the privilege, that will discourage full and frank communication. But others felt these same things constitute strengths: The pivotal features that the communications should have if they are to be privileged, gives clear indication to communicators of what will likely be and not be privileged. Refusing to adopt a definitive test leaves desirable flexibility to determine, in an extraordinary case, that the privilege is being used to provide too great a zone of silence or for other improper purposes.

---

[6] The decision also held that work-product protection applies to IRS summonses, and that the lower court had applied the wrong standard for overcoming such protection. The Supreme Court said mental impressions of the attorney may never be discoverable or may be discoverable only on a significantly heightened standard of need. The Court felt that it need not be more specific because its ruling on attorney-client privilege was largely dispositive of the case.

## SUBSEQUENT EVENTS AND EFFECTS OF *UPJOHN*.

### Subsequent Developments in the Case.

Rehnquist's decision technically remanded the case to the lower courts for proceedings consistent with the decision. No one remembers precisely what happened on remand, since they all felt the ball game was over after the Supreme Court decision. There are no records of any subsequent judicial proceedings in any lower court concerning the case. To the best anyone can recollect, the IRS saw the handwriting on the wall after the *Upjohn* decision, and got together with Upjohn to settle the case. The available evidence suggests that, since the Supreme Court's decision effectively privileged most of the communications at issue, the settlement was based on the portions of material voluntarily disclosed by Upjohn for which no privilege had been claimed, and on IRS interviews with some witnesses on their personal knowledge that was not covered by privilege. The IRS and Upjohn agreed that a relatively modest payment would be made by the company with essentially no adverse impact on the company or any of its employees. They agreed, as Upjohn had done with the SEC, that policies would be adopted by Upjohn (which had already substantially been done) to prevent similar problems in the future. Henceforth foreign payments would have to meet certain legal parameters and be handled in a certain way on tax returns. Thomas recalls that much of this mirrored what the IRS by this time had worked out with other companies regarding foreign payments.

### Subsequent Developments in the Law of Corporate Attorney–Client Privilege.

Despite Rehnquist's care in *Upjohn* only to negate a test centering on the control group and not to set forth any alternative test, lower federal courts (and those state courts that choose to follow *Upjohn*)[7] have tended nevertheless to read the opinion as establishing something very akin to the *Diversified Industries* version of the subject matter test for all cases in which a claim of federal corporate attorney-client privilege is raised. The Supreme Court should not be surprised. Rehnquist's enumeration in *Upjohn,* of the significant features of the privileged Upjohn communications—corresponding almost identically to the features deemed controlling under the subject matter test in *Diversified Industries*—could have been expected to be elevated to the status of a "test" by lower courts, who are, as a rule, eager for guidance, generally timid,

---

[7] A dwindling number of state courts still apply a control group test. The Uniform Rules of Evidence, recommended to the states by the National Conference of Commissioners on Uniform State Laws and by the American Bar Association, incorporated the subject-matter test into its attorney-client privilege provision, after the *Upjohn* decision by means of an amendment, upon which I was advisor.

and anxious to stay well within any parameters set by the Supreme
Court.

### Effect of Upjohn on Corporations and Corporate Law Practice.

Corporate lawyers generally agree that after *Upjohn* there was more
confiding in corporate attorneys (both in-house and outside counsel),
which enhanced their ability to obtain information and render good legal
advice, sometimes enabling them to spot and stop illegal conduct more
easily, as Justice Rehnquist hoped. Indeed, the Thomas saga proves this
can and does happen. The degree to which it does is an open question.

Although *Upjohn* remains intact today, some lawyers believe that
recent and accelerating trends among legislators, regulators, other enforcement authorities, and corporations themselves, threaten to undermine the decision's intended effectiveness in encouraging the flow of
information to corporate lawyers. These trends—many of them expressly
designed to penalize or circumvent claims of attorney-client privilege—
became intensified after *Upjohn* and seem at least in part to be a
reaction to the broad scope *Upjohn* gave the privilege. Enforcement
agencies and some politicians felt that something must be done about
the way the privilege impedes the discovery and investigation of corporate wrongdoing—particularly after the 2001 Enron scandal fueled vot-
ers' thirst for punishing corporate miscreants. The public believed—with
some justification—that lawyers had contributed to the problem or at
least had kept quiet out of allegiance to their clients. Regarding as
difficult any direct attempts to overturn *Upjohn* or the attorney-client
privilege generally, Congress, regulators, and law enforcement agencies
instead began increasingly to adopt measures to get around them. These
measures and some corporate trends exacerbating them fall into four
categories:

(1) *The Sarbanes–Oxley Act.* In 2002, in direct response to Enron
and associated debacles, Congress enacted the Sarbanes–Oxley Act,
named after the primary legislators who sponsored it. Among other
provisions, the Act empowers the SEC to adopt rules regulating lawyers
who handle SEC matters for publicly traded companies or companies
registered or filing with the SEC. This covers most major American
companies and any lawyers who advise on or handle matters that might
potentially involve the SEC—a wide range of matters indeed, because of
broad SEC disclosure requirements. Almost any matter of substance a
lawyer might handle for such a company probably has potential disclosure implications, and thus subjects the lawyer to the SEC regulations.

The SEC has now adopted regulations pursuant to this statutory
authorization. Some of these permit or require a lawyer to do certain
things if she becomes aware of credible evidence of a material past,
future, or ongoing illegal act by or within the corporation that would

constitute fraud or a securities, fiduciary, or similar violation. She *must* report it "up the ladder" within the corporation—that is, to the Chief Legal Officer or even the Chief Executive Officer or the Board of Directors[8] if necessary—and request a response. This mandatory "up the ladder" disclosure is designed to overcome the problem of isolating top executives from wrongdoing that decisions adopting the "control group" view thought was endemic to the broader "subject matter" view ultimately embraced by *Upjohn*. The "up the ladder" reporting would not violate the privilege or customary legal ethics notions of confidentiality, because it is reporting within the client, not to the outside, but it could worry employees speaking to lawyers.

If the response from the top of the ladder is unsatisfactory, the lawyer *is allowed if she wishes* to report the wrongdoing and the unsatisfactory response to the SEC. This provision is intended to relieve her of customary malpractice liability for breaching confidentiality. Such reporting to someone *outside the client* would seem to violate both the privilege and the confidentiality requirements contained in the ethics rules of many jurisdictions—at least if the wrongdoing is past rather than current, continuing, or proposed, which might be within the crime-fraud exception to the privilege. Since lawyers are licensed to practice in a particular jurisdiction, that jurisdiction's local ethics rules would normally govern counsel. But the new SEC regulations supersede state ethics rules, at least until there is a successful challenge to such superseding on constitutional grounds. Some state ethics rules, rules recommended by the American Bar Association, and the Restatement's Law of Lawyers, have also recently been amended to allow, or even sometimes require, reporting by lawyers to outside persons or entities, of serious wrongdoing by clients. Some of these provisions apply only where the wrongdoing may·involve death or bodily injury, but some go beyond this to substantial financial or property harm, or, specifically, business fraud or securities violations (in the wake of Enron).

How do all these new disclosure provisions—and particularly those under Sarbanes–Oxley—affect the premise of *Upjohn* that employees will frankly communicate with the corporate attorney if they are covered by the corporation's privilege? Would the employees talking to Gerry Thomas have been less forthcoming if they thought Thomas might reveal what they said to corporate superiors or to law enforcers under these new

---

[8] The trend in the post-Enron era, sparked by legal reforms and by heightened public and business sensitivities, has been for boards of directors to be comprised of more people who are independent of management, and who are much less protective of employees implicated in possible wrongdoing, than was the case in the *Upjohn* era. They are more prone to terminate such employees or turn them in. This is one of the purposes of the "up the ladder" reporting requirement: to produce "transparency" and "house cleaning", as it is called.

provisions?[9] Unlikely, since they would have expected top management to learn of their reports, and they spoke in an environment where it was unclear whether they, as lower-echelon employees, were covered by the privilege at all. But there were special circumstances of trust between Thomas and the employees, and most of them did not think they were doing anything wrong.[10] It seems likely that at least in some circumstances today, some employees might be more hesitant to disclose self-damaging material they thought might expose them to civil or criminal liability, or to embarrassment or job reprisals, if they thought material could be revealed under these new provisions.[11] The objective of *Upjohn*, to encourage disclosure by employees, to the corporation's lawyer, is undermined to that extent.

(2) *The Spread and Enhancement of Sporkin's Voluntary Co-operation Policy.* The program of leniency started by SEC enforcement head Stanley Sporkin, that treats more leniently those who come forward and cooperate with an investigation, is now increasingly found in a wide array of regulatory and law enforcement agencies and the Department of Justice. In addition, the U.S. Sentencing Guidelines for crimes, including corporate crimes, now give credit that lowers the sentence for co-operation with the prosecuting authority.

Under most of these programs, there is an accelerating tendency today, which did not exist then, to treat those persons and entities who will not waive their attorney-client privilege or work-product protection, as failing to co-operate and therefore disentitled to leniency.[12] Many lawyers believe this is a "gun to the head" requiring waiver. The greater the potential penalty, the greater the incentive to waive and get leniency. With today's corporations, the penalties can be huge. What makes things worse for the waiving party, is the fact that a waiver as to one agency waives as to the whole world, regarding the same (and sometimes related) material, unless a court subscribes to the "selective waiver" doctrine, which few do.[13]

---

[9] Thomas would probably have had an ethical duty to warn them of this, but they might have been aware anyway.

[10] They might have thought twice about revealing to a post-Enron board of directors, though. See note 8, *supra*.

[11] Since under the majority view in courts today, there is no notion of "selective waiver" of privilege, it may well be that the disclosure, once made to the SEC, could not be confined to the SEC. This would make the risks of talking even greater for the employees. A lawyer probably should warn of this too. With all these warnings, a frank discussion is exceedingly unlikely.

[12] The Justice Department's policy regarding waiver expressly emphasizes the desirability of waiver of a business entity's attorney-client and work-product protections, clearly evidencing an impatience with the *Upjohn* decision.

[13] The failure of most courts to recognize selective waiver, limiting the waiver to the agency receiving the disclosure, can, on occasion, reduce the incentive to waive by increasing the prospect of civil liability asserted by private plaintiffs.

The Upjohn employees knew when they were speaking with Thomas that he was not their personal attorney, and therefore the privilege was not theirs, but rather the corporation's, to raise or waive.[14] Again we may ask, would they have confided so readily to Thomas if they thought there might later be these incentives on the part of the company itself to broadly waive its privilege? Maybe they would have because of the special circumstances of trust and their belief they were doing nothing wrong. But today it seems likely that some corporate employees would be reluctant to confide potentially self-damaging or self-incriminating information, in view of the waiver incentives operating on the company.[15] Would employees necessarily know about these incentives when confiding in a corporate counsel? In view of the frequency of waiver today, probably yes. Anyway, a lawyer in today's regulatory environment probably would have an ethical duty to alert them to the potential for disclosure, especially if they risked bearing personally civil or criminal liability. To this extent, too, then, *Upjohn* is weakened.[16]

(3) *The Changing Allegiances of Corporations Today.* Thomas got the information he needed in considerable measure because the employees knew and trusted the company and its management and felt they would be protected if push came to shove, as in fact happened. But a look

---

[14] Thomas on the *Upjohn* facts probably could not ethically have represented both, even if he wanted to because of the potential for severe (and probably unwaivable) conflicts of interest.

[15] Additional waiver incentives for the corporation arise because, in this post-Enron era, independent auditors and audit committees, having been burned by liability for Enron-type derelictions, will often refuse to certify the accuracy of a company's financials, as required for the company to do business, unless the company allows full examination by the auditors even of attorney-client privileged or work-product protected material which, as indicated herein, usually means there is a waiver of privilege or protection regarding anyone who thereafter seeks this or related information. Worse still, from the corporation's and employees' standpoint, merely furnishing a report of an internal investigation to auditors or government agencies, has been held by some courts today to waive attorney-client and work-product protections covering underlying materials and conversations, especially if the furnishing was to obtain a certification or leniency. In part, this represents a post-Enron extension of the older principle that a party can use a privilege as a "shield but not a sword"—that is, if one affirmatively uses material, one cannot prevent the exploration of its bone-fides by asserting privilege.

Additional far-reaching waiver incentives to the corporation, are presented by the fact that, post-Enron, the stock exchanges (NYSE and NASDAQ) conduct vigorous investigations and have adopted policies requiring co-operation and (sometimes) waiver similar to those described here for government agencies.

[16] Further deterring employees from making statements to the corporate lawyer, is the fact that there have been cases in which the Justice Department has regarded statements made by employees to corporate lawyers in a corporation's own internal investigation as obstruction-of-justice, which is a crime if the Department feels the statements are purposely inaccurate. The theory is that corporate internal investigations now play a role in law enforcement under the new cooperation policies.

at the business section of newspapers today reveals a much higher rate of corporate turnover. Companies are bought, sold, merged, or taken over, and new management comes in that doesn't have the same stake in defending against wrongdoing that occurred under a previous management or predecessor corporation. Sometimes the public image and legal posture of the new management or entity is better served by taking their lumps and confessing that the old crowd were miscreants, but "we are different". In fact, recently, many years after *Upjohn,* the Upjohn Company itself was taken over by the Pharmacia Company, which in turn was taken over by the Pfizer Company, its current incarnation. Dr.William Erastus Upjohn's family company no longer exists.[17] Corporations also go bankrupt more frequently these days, and are taken over and managed by a trustee in bankruptcy who may have no special allegiance to the old employees.

Because the privilege belongs to the company and not to the employee who confides information, the privilege can be waived by the company, by a successor corporation or by a trustee in bankruptcy. This means that even a company's CEO cannot count on his confidential communications to the corporation's attorneys remaining forever private. Given an environment of changing companies and management, where personal trust and loyalty are muted, no employee can be sure that he will not be "hung out to dry" by existing or new management.[18] Employees at all levels may therefore be reluctant to talk candidly to corporate attorneys.

(4) *Expansion of the Privilege's Crime–Fraud Exception and Related Doctrines.* If the crime-fraud exception to the attorney-client privilege is determined by a court to apply, a privileged conversation can be stripped of its privilege. There is a marked modern tendency to expand the crime-fraud exception.[19] For example, traditionally the crime-fraud exception applied only where legal advice was sought or obtained by the client for the purpose of committing or facilitating an *on-going* or *future* crime or fraud, as opposed to seeking legal advice concerning past crimes. The latter kind of advice, e.g., advice directed at preparing defenses for a crime one has already committed, has been considered squarely within the professional functioning of a lawyer and is privileged.

---

[17] There is something sadly nostalgic about the passing of the company (Upjohn) that was responsible for such important drugs (whose names became household words) as Cheracol, Kaopectate, Methylprednisalone (the most commonly used low dose steroid for inflammation), and Orinase (the most widely used diabetes drug and the first capable of oral administration).

[18] Or the existing or new board of directors. See note 8.

[19] Some lawyers report a corresponding upsurge in instances where regulators and law enforcement authorities are formally charging lawyers with participation in their client's crime.

There is, however, an increasing tendency today for regulators, enforcement authorities, and courts, to blur the line between these temporal categories. They take the position that legal efforts related to past crimes are often really efforts to keep past crimes from coming to light, and therefore they amount to a conspiracy to cover-up or further deceive. This makes them a continuing crime, within the crime-fraud exception. The tendency is particularly marked in the corporate context, where there is an obligation to report to the SEC and investors any events (even past crimes and frauds) that may result in liabilities of the company. The failure to report is a continuing crime or fraud for as long as the initial wrongdoing is not reported or is reported incorrectly or insufficiently. The problem is escalated by the fact that in today's highly regulated business environment, things that did not seem to be crimes at the time of a communication may be regarded as crimes later by a court.

To the extent there are increased chances that the crime-fraud exception might apply, employees confiding to the corporate attorney will think twice about what they reveal, because a court may subsequently find that their revelations are not privileged, even if the company tries to protect the employee and asserts the privilege.

Further fueling the modern trends that increase the risk of the crime-fraud exception applying, is a progressive erosion of the quantum of proof required to show that the exception applies. Few courts require that it be proved by even a preponderance of evidence. Most require only a "prima facie case"—often defined in this area as a showing that would justify a reasonable person in thinking that a crime or fraud may be involved, without receiving counter-evidence or hearing, cross examination or impeachment of the witnesses who make out the prima facie case or any other appraisal of their credibility. Furthermore, the Supreme Court has held that a judge may hear or inspect *in camera* the allegedly privileged communication, on a lesser showing than needed to establish the crime-fraud exception, in order to determine the applicability of the crime-fraud exception, and may consider the contents of the communication in deciding whether the crime-fraud exception applies to the communication. The courts, while applying fairly constant word formulas describing these various burdens of proof, have been requiring less and less to satisfy them.

If this is not enough to erode the privilege, some courts are expanding the crime-fraud exception to include more wrongdoing than just crimes and fraud—for example, other torts. There is also a tendency for courts, when they find a crime or fraud, to broadly strip all communications between the client and lawyer of the privilege, even those communications that had nothing to do with the crime or fraud.

In view of these enlargements of the crime-fraud exception, employees communicating with corporate counsel today cannot have the confidence they once had that attorney-client privilege will be sacrosanct.[20] It is likely that some of their communications will be chilled.

Whether these four numbered "inroads" on the encouragement to communicate envisioned in *Upjohn* prove to be well-advised or ill-advised, most of them seem to stem from a somewhat more jaundiced view of the benefits of lawyer-client confidentiality than *Upjohn* expressed. While *Upjohn* did recognize that there must be qualifications on an unadulterated policy of confidentiality, and clearly allowed for the development of such qualifications, nevertheless, to most lawyers, *Upjohn* is a soaring endorsement of the lawyer-client privilege and the work lawyers do.

\* \* \*

In listening to Thomas talk about *Upjohn* today, you get a strong sense that he is most proud of the fact that he kept the faith with the employees. He is also very pleased that in the process he secured a decision that vindicates the role he always tried to play as corporate counsel, and that he believes most corporate counsel play—the role of helping the modern corporation do its work, which he believes generally is in the public interest. He believes corporate lawyers need to get information from employees at every level, in order to perform their role effectively. He is of the conviction that most corporations—by no means all—are good citizens and try to comply with the complex laws and regulations to which they are subject, and that fully informed corporate counsel play an indispensable part in that compliance. Next to his family, and perhaps his war experiences, you get the feeling that he regards *Upjohn* as a defining event in his life and the capstone of his career. He clearly enjoyed almost every minute of it, except perhaps when he was jailed in Egypt.

---

[20] There are also other attorney-client privilege doctrines that are being used to defeat a company's effort to assert attorney-client privilege to protect their employees communications. These include penetrating the privilege by dissident shareholders in certain instances; and the doctrine that the function the attorney was performing for the company when he garnered the communication was not a professional legal function but rather a business function—i.e., one that was predominantly motivated by business rather than legal concerns—and therefore it could have been done by someone who is not a lawyer. The risk of this last doctrine being used is highest when the attorney wears several "hats" in the company—that is, he is not only the company's lawyer, but is also on the board of or is an executive officer (other than legal officer) of the company, as Thomas was.

\*

# 8

# The Daubert Trilogy and the Law of Expert Testimony

## Paul Giannelli

Jason Daubert and Eric Schuller were born with serious limb reduction defects. During pregnancy, their mothers had taken Bendectin, a prescription antinausea drug that they would later claim was the cause of the defect. Because birth defects result even when Bendectin is not prescribed, the causal relationship between Bendectin and the boys' limb reductions would become the critical issue. From these tragic facts, the journey to one of the most important evidence cases ever decided, *Daubert v. Merrell Dow Pharm., Inc.*,[1] commenced. The Supreme Court followed with *General Elec. Co. v. Joiner*[2] and *Kumho Tire Co. v. Carmichael*[3] to make up what is now known as the *Daubert* trilogy. This is a story of the clash of science and law, or at least some views of science, and of the advent of scientific terms such as "falsifiability" in the legal lexicon. It is also the story of the triumph of the conservative political movement's tort "reform" efforts. This victory, however, left that movement in an embarrassing position—supporting higher admissibility standards in money-damage cases than in death penalty prosecutions.

## The Bendectin Litigation

The litigation over Bendectin's teratogenicity did not commence with Jason and Eric.[4] Instead, David Mekdeci, who was born with malformed and missing fingers, a shortened arm, and a concave chest,

---

[1] 509 U.S. 579 (1993).

[2] 522 U.S. 136 (1997).

[3] 526 U.S. 137 (1999).

[4] There are two excellent books on the Bendectin litigation. Michael D. Green, BENDECTIN AND BIRTH DEFECTS: THE CHALLENGES OF MASS TOXIC SUBSTANCES LITIGATION (1996); Joseph Sanders, BENDECTIN ON TRIAL: A STUDY OF MASS TORT LITIGATION (1998).

was the primary plaintiff in the first case, which was filed in 1977. It started when Betty Mekdeci, David's mother, asked the most human of questions: Why? Her relentless research eventually led her to suspect Bendectin, one of the drugs she had taken during the critical limb formation period of her pregnancy. Although Bendectin had been marketed since 1956, Betty Mekdeci learned that there was scant scientific data on the risks associated with the drug. A 1963 animal study on rabbits by one of Merrell's employees (Dr. Staples) had recommended more experimentation. The company, however, had not conducted further investigation and delayed sending the study to the Federal Drug Administration (FDA) for three years. "Most suspiciously, Dr. Staples' recommendations for further study were removed, and modifications were made in the data reported."[5] The one epidemiological study (Bunde & Bowles), conducted by Merrill researchers in 1963, suffered so many shortcomings that plaintiff attorneys used it effectively against Merrell in the subsequent litigation and the company's own experts eventually disavowed it. In addition, Merrill had attempted to persuade physicians reporting birth defects to classify their contact as only an "inquiry" rather than an adverse reaction report, thus avoiding a requirement to forward the acquired information to the FDA.

Betty Mekdeci also discovered Merrill's involvement in other drug cases, one of which was thalidomide. Developed by a German pharmaceutical company, Merrill had obtained the North American license to market the drug. With an extremely high teratogenicity effect, thalidomide became the nuclear bombshell of prescription drugs and birth defects. Pictures of deformed children with "flipper" arms filled the front pages of newspapers worldwide. Although the main fault lay with the German developer, Merrill had attempted to bully an FDA doctor into approving thalidomide and did not withdraw it from the market until after all the other overseas companies had. Moreover, "Merrell had abused the new drug investigation process by using it to premarket thalidomide, and Merrell had made false assertions about the safety of the drug."[6] The thalidomide debacle destroyed a widely held belief that the placenta was a protective barrier to drugs ingested by a mother during pregnancy. It also spurred the development of the science of teratology and resulted in amendments of the Food, Drug, and Cosmetic Act, giving the FDA more regulatory authority. But even under the amendments, the FDA must rely on company research to determine the safety and efficacy of new drugs.

More damning was Merrell's role in marketing MER 29 (triparanol), an anti-cholesterol drug, removed from the market in 1962 after thou-

---

[5] Michael D. Green, *supra* 4, at 129.

[6] *Id.* at 74.

sands of patients were harmed—most seriously with cataracts. A federal grand jury indicted Merrill and three employees, including the vice president in charge of research, for fraud in connection with its marketing of the drug. The defendants eventually pleaded "no contest," a plea equivalent to a guilty plea except that it is inadmissible as a party admission in subsequent civil cases. Nevertheless, the civil litigation on MER 29 resulted in one of the first punitive damage awards in a products liability case. A California appellate court upheld the award, commenting:

> Besides the falsification of test data under the direction of Dr. Van Maanen and the withholding from the FDA and the medical profession of vital information concerning blood changes and eye opacities in test animals, there was evidence that, after Dr. Fox reported eye opacities and blindness in her test animals, and after Merck, Sharp & Dohme had made a similar report, appellant continued to represent to the medical profession that MER/29 was a proven drug, remarkably free from side effects, virtually non-toxic having a specific and completely safe action. In light of appellant's knowledge, the jury could infer that these statements were recklessly made, with wanton disregard for the safety of all who might use the drug. Moreover, similar representations continued to be made even after the first report of cataracts in a human had been received and after appellant's later tests confirmed the presence of eye opacities in virtually all test animals. When respectable medical publications began to challenge the toxicity and efficacy of MER/29, appellant's salesmen were instructed to blame side effects on other drugs, or at least to suggest that as a good possibility. Even after a number of cases of cataracts in humans from use of MER/29 had been reported to appellant, and when its own tests had established blindness in its test animals, appellant continued to defend sale of its drug.... In December 1961 the FDA compelled appellant to issue a drastic warning letter notifying the medical profession of known cases of cataract in humans from use of the drug. Appellant nevertheless continued with plans vigorously to promote its sale.[7]

Merrell's track record and the paucity of research on Bendectin led Betty Mekdeci and her attorneys to sue. After prolonged deliberations, the jury awarded her and her husband only $20,000, the stipulated amount of medical expenses, but David received nothing. Because the verdict was legally self-contradictory, the court ordered a new trial, which Merrell won.[8] In a subsequent multidistrict litigation case, the trial court bifurcated the proceedings, submitting only the general causa-

---

[7] Toole v. Richardson–Merrell Inc., 60 Cal. Rptr. 398, 416 (Ct. App. 1967).

[8] Mekdeci v. Merrell Nat'l Labs., 711 F.2d 1510 (11th Cir. 1983).

tion issue to the jury in the first phase. Merrell won again, but independent lawsuits were not bound by this determination, and they continued. Jason Daubert and Eric Schuller's case was one of the later lawsuits filed in this litigation.

In the end, the epidemiological studies that were spurred by the litigation supported Merrell's position. Nevertheless, the litigation continued long afterwards. Approximately 2,000 cases were filed, and over thirty were tried, with verdicts nearly evenly split between the plaintiffs and Merrill. Merrill prevailed, however, in the one major consolidated law suit. Moreover, once courts learned of the mounting epidemiological evidence supporting Merrell, they began to take the issue away from juries, even overturning some verdicts on appeal. Apparently, no plaintiff ever collected damages.

### Toxic Torts

Bendectin was part of a wave of toxic tort litigation, which included substances such as asbestos, tobacco, DES, the Dalkon Shield IUD, Agent Orange, and later silicone breast implants. They are a subspecies of product liability cases, which may be based on faulty manufacturing, defective design, or failure to warn. *Kumho Tire*, a tire blow out case, is a typical products liability case.

The toxic tort lawsuits raise both general and specific causation issues. The former involves whether a substance causes a certain harm and the latter whether the substance caused that harm in the particular case. *Joiner* raised both issues: (1) whether exposure to polychlorinated biphenyls (PCBs) causes small-cell lung cancer and (2) whether Robert Joiner had sufficient exposure to PCBs at his place of work. In assessing general causation, scientists use, inter alia, epidemiological, animal (in vivo), and in vitro (cell) studies, as well as chemical structure analysis. Epidemiological studies, if done well, are the most persuasive, but they are expensive to conduct and have a number of limitations. The Bendectin litigation was unusual because of the large number of available epidemiological studies, which were sparked by the controversy surrounding the litigation. Asbestos and tobacco are other examples where there is a wealth of epidemiological studies. Often, however, such studies are unavailable or suffer methodological shortcomings. In addition, animal studies can provide important information about toxicity and teratogenicity, and are used extensively in the regulatory area. Long latency periods, sometimes years or decades, also make establishing causation difficult. Here, again, Bendectin is unusual due to the nine-month pregnancy period. Despite the problems inherent in this type of litigation, courts are nevertheless required to make decisions, no matter the level of uncertainty. The law, as the *Daubert* Court wrote, "must resolve disputes finally and quickly."

## Frye v. United States

The story of how we arrived at our current treatment of scientific evidence does not begin with Bendectin but rather with a precursor of the modern polygraph and a 1923 decision, *Frye v. United States.*[9] *Daubert*, in establishing a new approach to the admissibility of expert testimony under Federal Rule 702, rejected the D.C. Circuit Court's long-established holding in *Frye,* one of the rare lower court decisions with influence like that of a Supreme Court holding. In that case, the D.C. Court faced the problem of defining the point at which a "scientific principle or discovery crosses the line between the experimental [or inadmissible] and demonstrable [or admissible] stages." The court held that, when a scientific technique attains "general acceptance in the particular field in which it belongs," trial courts may admit heretofore novel scientific evidence. The court went on to hold that the polygraph had "not yet gained such standing and scientific recognition among physiological and psychological authorities," and so refused to admit the evidence.

The *Frye* court, in its brief two-page opinion, neither cited authority nor offered an explanation for adopting the general acceptance test. Later cases would supply that rationale: "The requirement of general acceptance in the scientific community assures that those most qualified to assess the general validity of a scientific method will have the determinative voice."[10] By the time *Daubert* came before the Supreme Court in 1993, the general-acceptance standard was the majority rule in both federal and state courts. In addition to polygraph evidence, the *Frye* test had been used to determine the admissibility of evidence derived from voice prints, neutron activation analysis, gunshot residue tests, bite mark comparisons, psycholinguistics, truth serum, hypnosis, blood analyses, microscopic hair examinations, intoxication testing, DNA, and numerous other forensic techniques. In addition, the general acceptance test had been employed in determining the admissibility of social science testimony on such matters as battered woman syndrome, rape trauma syndrome, child abuse accommodation syndrome, profile evidence, eyewitness testimony, and the like.

## Federal Rules of Evidence

The Federal Rules of Evidence were enacted in 1975, after ten years of preparation and several much commented on drafts. Yet, neither the viability of *Frye* nor the admissibility of novel scientific evidence was addressed in the advisory committee's notes, the congressional commit-

---

[9] 293 F. 1013 (D.C. Cir. 1923).

[10] United States v. Addison, 498 F.3d 741, 743–44 (D.C. Cir. 1974).

tee reports, or the extensive two-year hearings on the Federal Rules. As originally adopted, Rule 702 was deceptively simple:

> If scientific, technical, or other specialized knowledge will assist the trier of fact to understand the evidence or to determine a fact in issue, a witness qualified as an expert by knowledge, skill, experience, training, or education, may testify thereto in the form of an opinion or otherwise.

Expert testimony, however, is bounded on two sides—(1) the novel and (2) the commonplace—and Rule 702 addressed only the latter boundary. A respected judge, Edward Becker of the Third Circuit, would later observe that the failure to address the first boundary was "the greatest single oversight in the Rules."[11] This congressional omission turned out to be the foundation on which the *Daubert* opinion would be constructed. Meanwhile, federal courts battled over the issue, and legal commentators vigorously disagreed about the proper standard for admitting scientific evidence.

Here, we need to pause our story and consider how this "oversight," so vibrant in hindsight, came to be. The answer is rather straightforward. For most of the period between 1923 and 1970, the scientific techniques confronting the courts did not raise significant *Frye* issues— the admissibility of *novel* scientific evidence. A 1966 amendment to Federal Criminal Rule 16, which governs the pretrial disclosure of scientific reports in criminal litigation, provides some insight into the types of expert testimony used during this period. The accompanying committee note mentioned reports of "fingerprint and handwriting comparisons." Ballistics, blood, paint, fiber, and autopsy reports could be added to this list. None of these techniques presented *Frye* issues; they were traditional techniques, long accepted by the courts. Indeed, *Frye* was cited only five times in published opinions before World War II, mostly in polygraph cases. After the War, it was cited six times before 1950, 20 times during the 1950s and 21 times in the 1960s.

*Frye* became significant only toward the end of the 1960s as new forensic science techniques emerged and courts found themselves having to rule on the admissibility of such techniques as voice print identifications, bite mark comparisons, neutron activation analysis, and hypnotically-refreshed testimony. As late as 1972, a federal district court correctly observed that "[t]here is notably an absence of any discussion of the 'general acceptance' standard in federal decisions."[12] In civil cases,

---

[11] Edward R. Becker & Aviva Orenstein, *The Federal Rules of Evidence After Sixteen Years—The Effect of "Plain Meaning" Jurisprudence, The Need for an Advisory Committee on the Rules of Evidence, and Suggestions for Selective Revision of the Rules*, 60 Geo. Wash. L. Rev. 857, 877 (1992).

[12] United States v. Zeiger, 350 F. Supp. 685, 687 n. 6 (D.D.C.), *rev'd*, 475 F.2d 1280 (D.C. Cir. 1972) (polygraph evidence).

proffered scientific evidence was mostly long-received physician testimony about the medical condition of particular plaintiffs and economic analyses pertaining to antitrust and regulatory actions or damages. Thus, at the time the Federal Rules were enacted, *Frye* and the cases citing it were overwhelmingly criminal actions.

## The "Junk Science" Controversy

A central theme of the Federal Rules is the liberal admission of evidence. Exclusionary rules were either jettisoned or watered down. The drafters believed that juries would be better served with more, not less, information, a philosophy reflected in the rules governing expert testimony and the hearsay rule, among others. Indeed, scholars noted that the Rules "revolutionized"[13] the role of experts by "sweep[ing] away the restrictive dogma that curtailed expert proof."[14]

By 1986, however, a backlash against the expanded role of experts had developed. Articles like those entitled "Experts up to here" and "The Case Against Expert Witnesses" appeared in *Forbes* and *Fortune*. Terms such as "litigation medicine," "fringe science," and "frontier science" were in vogue, and physicians complained that "[l]egal cases can now be decided on the type of evidence that the scientific community rejected decades ago."

The criticism reached its zenith with the publication by Peter Huber, a prominent conservative polemicist, of *Galileo's Revenge: Junk Science in the Courtroom*. In two words, "junk science", he captured the sense that many citizens had acquired of the quality of the science offered in civil cases, a sense attributable not only to the evidence offered by plaintiffs in some cases but also to a decade of advertising by insurance companies and to the publicity efforts of large, repeat player tort defendants. Huber's most sensational example involved a "soothsayer" who "with the backing of expert testimony from a doctor and several police department officials" won a million dollar jury award due to the loss of her "psychic powers following a CAT scan." Huber advocated the *Frye* test as the way to curtail the use of junk science. His attack, however, was not limited to dubious expert testimony; he had bigger fish to fry—the tort system. As one journal noted, "[I]t is imperative to disentangle Huber's two criticisms: one evidentiary, against junk science; the other policy-oriented, against modern substantive tort law."[15]

---

[13] Michael H. Graham, *Expert Witness Testimony and the Federal Rules of Evidence: Insuring Adequate Assurance of Trustworthiness*, 1986 U. Ill. L. Rev. 43.

[14] Margaret A. Berger, *United States v. Scop: The Common–Law Approach to an Expert's Opinion About a Witness's Credibility Still Does Not Work*, 55 Brook. L. Rev. 559, 559 (1989).

[15] Book Note, *Rebel Without A Cause: Galileo's Revenge: Junk Science in the Courtroom*, 105 Harv. L. Rev. 935, 940 (1992).

Judicial opinions reflected similar concerns. Judge Higginbotham of the Fifth Circuit wrote that it "is time to take hold of expert testimony in federal trials."[16] There were two aspects to his criticism: First, "experts whose opinions are available to the highest bidder have no place testifying in a court of law." Second, courts should reject "opinions of experts not based upon a generally accepted scientific principle."[17] Some judges even felt compelled to justify their decisions to admit expert testimony by asserting that the evidence was "not 'junk science' " and that the expert was "no quack." By 1991, the Fifth Circuit, sitting *en banc*, was prepared to apply the restrictive *Frye* test to civil cases, a significant departure from prior practice.

Momentum for "reform" also came from the Civil Rules Committee, which in 1991 proposed an amendment to Rule 702. The proposal would have required expert testimony to "substantially" assist, rather than merely "assist," the trier of fact, and then only if the testimony were based on "reasonably reliable" information. The last provision apparently embodied a modified *Frye* rule.

Next, the President's Council on Competitiveness, chaired by Vice President Dan Quayle, jumped into the fray. A Civil Justice Reform Task Force once again targeted expert testimony. The Vice President declared: "We think it is time to reject the notion that 'junk science' is truly relevant evidence." The Task Force offered its own amendment to Federal Rule 702. That group's proposal tracked the Civil Rules Committee's proposal requiring expert testimony to provide "substantial" assistance to the trier of fact, but then added that expert testimony must be "based on a widely accepted explanatory theory," echoing *Frye*. Not waiting for the amendment process, the first President Bush imposed these requirements on government attorneys in civil cases by executive order. Under this order, a theory was considered "widely accepted" if it was propounded by at least a substantial minority of experts in the relevant field.

Somewhat surprisingly, the "junk science" debate all but ignored criminal prosecutions. With one exception, Huber's book focused only on civil litigation. Similarly, the Civil Rules Committee proposed an amendment to Rule 702 to combat perceived abuses in civil trials. The Committee wrote: "Particularly in civil litigation with high financial stakes, large expenditures for marginally useful expert testimony has become commonplace. Procurement of expert testimony is occasionally used as a trial technique to wear down adversaries." The Quayle proposals were

---

[16] In re Air Crash Disaster at New Orleans, 795 F.2d 1230, 1234 (5th Cir. 1986).

[17] Brock v. Merrell Dow Pharm., Inc., 884 F.2d 167, 168 (5th Cir. 1989) (dissenting from denial of *en banc* review).

also limited to civil litigation. Indeed, the Supreme Court passed over a DNA case and chose *Daubert*, a civil case, to address the *Frye* issue.

The failure to take account of criminal litigation led to some intriguing results. While the Bush executive order required U.S. Attorneys in civil cases to meet a heightened admissibility standard ("wide acceptance") when introducing scientific evidence, federal prosecutors were left free in DNA cases to argue for a lower standard, "urging that Rule 702 creates a liberal rule of admissibility which now supersedes *Frye*."[18]

## Daubert v. Merrell Dow Pharmaceuticals, Inc.

When Daubert and Schuller sued Merrell Dow, the company removed the case from state to federal court and filed a motion for summary judgment. By this time, the epidemiological record, as noted above, had developed, and the drug company proffered the affidavit of an expert who had reviewed the over 30 epidemiological studies involving 130,000 patients and concluded that no published study had demonstrated a statistically significant association between Bendectin and birth defects. The plaintiffs did not contest this precise conclusion; instead, they offered eight experts who "concluded that Bendectin can cause birth defects" based on in vitro and in vivo animal tests, chemical structure analyses, and a reanalysis of the epidemiological studies. The trial court granted the defense motion for summary judgment. Citing the general acceptance test, which it had applied in a 1985 criminal case involving truth serum, the Ninth Circuit affirmed.[19] The court also quoted from Huber's book.

## The Amici Briefs

When the Supreme Court took certiorari in 1992, *Daubert* was immediately dubbed the "junk science" case. Twenty-two amici briefs were filed. These briefs, in themselves, tell an interesting story. As would be expected, a number of trade organizations supported Merrell Dow. Big business wanted higher admissibility standards to thwart products liability and toxic tort suits, and for similar reasons, the medical profession desired demanding standards in malpractice litigation. These groups supported the *Frye* test as the way to achieve this result and found themselves with strange bedfellows—the criminal defense bar. Prosecutors, like civil plaintiffs, have the burden of proof and rely on expert testimony far more often than criminal defendants.

---

[18] United States v. Two Bulls, 918 F.2d 56, 59 (8th Cir. 1990), vacated after death of defendant, 925 F.2d 1127 (8th Cir. 1991) (*en banc*).

[19] 951 F.2d 1128, 1129 (9th Cir. 1991).

Perhaps criminal and civil defense attorneys were not such strange bedfellows—merely uncomfortable ones.

The most interesting amici briefs came from scientists, who were not of one mind. The *New England Journal of Medicine* and other medical journals filed an amici brief in support of Merrell Dow. The brief stated:

> "Good science" is a commonly accepted term used to describe the scientific community's system of quality control which protects the community and those who rely upon it from unsubstantiated scientific analysis. It mandates that each proposition undergo a rigorous trilogy of publication, replication and verification before it is relied upon.[20]

These scientists assumed that the phrase "general acceptance" in *Frye* reflected this view. It did not. *Frye* had developed in criminal cases, and many common techniques never excluded under *Frye,* such as fingerprint, ballistics, and handwriting comparisons, had scant empirical support—no publication, no replication, and no verification.

In contrast, a group of physicians, scientists, and historians of science filed a brief in support of Jason Daubert. They challenged the "consensus" view of science: "The conventional scientific wisdom is as often a stumbling-block as a stepping-stone to better understanding", and the "respondents cling nevertheless to a strangely idealized notion of scientific inquiry, arguing that the testimony of plaintiff's experts be ruled inadmissible because it contradicts a huge body of evidence and is therefore nothing less than 'heresy.' " Thomas Kuhn,[21] who questioned the view that scientific knowledge develops through a slow step-by-step accretion of knowledge, figured prominently in their analysis, as did Ortega y Gasset: "The man who discovers a new scientific truth has previously had to smash to atoms almost everything he had learnt, and arrives at the new truth with hands bloodstained from the slaughter of a thousand platitudes."[22]

These scholars also painted the peer review system in a different light. Their brief quotes a former editor of the *Journal of the American Medical Association*: "[p]eer review is far from being a 'perfect sausage

---

[20] Brief of the New England Journal of Medicine, Journal of the American Medical Association, and Annals of Internal Medicine as Amici Curiae in Support of Respondent at 2, Daubert v. Merrell Dow Pharmaceuticals, Inc., 509 U.S. 579 (1993). Other scientists filed amici briefs agreeing with the Journal's position.

[21] *See* Thomas Kuhn, THE STRUCTURE OF SCIENTIFIC REVOLUTIONS 7 (2d ed. 1970) ("[A] new theory, however special its range of application, is seldom or never just an increment to what is already known. Its assimilation requires the reconstruction of prior theory and the re-evaluation of prior fact, an intrinsically revolutionary process...").

[22] Josie Ortega y Gasset, THE REVOLT OF THE MASSES ch. XIV (1930).

machine for grinding out the truth.' ... 'Just because peer review is about a review of scientific data doesn't mean that it is itself a scientific process.' " In another amicus brief, different scientists also questioned the peer review system, going so far as arguing that cross-examination is as reliable a method of truth-determination as peer review. According to them, the peer review system is not intended to yield "the truth", and publication does not mean that an article's content is "generally accepted" or represents a "consensus" position of the relevant academic community. In addition, they noted that peer review journals do not replicate and verify experiments and do not warrant that the information contained in an article is valid or otherwise amounts to "good science." They pointed out that often only two reviewers are selected and that these individuals spend on average "2.4 hours" reviewing each manuscript.

### *Frye* Rejected

Writing for the Court in *Daubert*, Justice Blackmun quickly dispatched the *Frye* test. His rejection of *Frye* was based on the language of Rule 702, which addressed expert testimony but did not mention *Frye* either in the text of the rule or in its legislative history. Blackmun then turned to the more difficult issue—what, if anything, would replace *Frye* as the standard of admissibility.

Professor McCormick had advocated an alternative to *Frye* in his 1954 text. He believed that "general scientific acceptance" was a proper standard for taking judicial notice of scientific facts but not for the admissibility of scientific evidence: "Any relevant conclusions which are supported by a qualified expert witness should be received unless there are other reasons for exclusion. Particularly, its probative value may be overborne by the familiar dangers of prejudicing or misleading the jury, unfair surprise and undue consumption of time."[23] Under this relevancy approach, qualifying an expert generally qualifies the technique employed by that expert. This approach is consistent with the helpfulness language of Rule 702 and can be viewed as rejecting any separate reliability assessment for scientific proof. Indeed, although *Frye* was still the predominant test for the admissibility of novel scientific evidence at the time *Daubert* was decided, a number of jurisdictions had already rejected *Frye* and adopted either McCormick's relevancy approach or a variant that included some reliability component.

Justice Blackmun implicitly rejected a pure relevancy approach, saying expert evidence must be reliable in addition to being relevant. Perhaps he recalled *Barefoot v. Estelle*,[24] a capital murder case decided by

---

[23] Charles T. McCormick, Evidence 363–64 (1954).

[24] 463 U.S. 880 (1983).

the Supreme Court a decade earlier. In the penalty phase of that case, the prosecution offered psychiatric testimony concerning Barefoot's future dangerousness, a qualifying factor under the Texas death penalty statute. One psychiatrist, Dr. James Grigson, without ever examining Barefoot, testified that there was a " *'one hundred percent and absolute'* chance that Barefoot would commit future acts of criminal violence." Barefoot challenged this testimony on constitutional grounds due to its unreliability.

In an amicus brief, the American Psychiatric Association (APA) stated that the "large body of research in this area indicates that, even under the best of conditions, psychiatric predictions of long-term dangerousness are wrong in at least two out of every three cases." In a later passage, the brief remarked that the "unreliability of [these] predictions is by now an established fact within the profession." A substantial body of research supported the APA position.

Nevertheless, the Court rejected Barefoot's argument. According to the Court, "[n]either petitioner nor the [APA] suggests that psychiatrists are always wrong with respect to future dangerousness, only most of the time." The Court also noted that it was "not persuaded that such testimony is almost entirely unreliable and that the factfinder and the adversary system will not be competent to uncover, recognize, and take due account of its shortcomings." If this is a standard at all, it is an incredibly low one. It permitted the admission of evidence in a death penalty case, as one commentator observed, "at the brink of quackery."[25] Justice Blackmun dissented:

> In the present state of psychiatric knowledge, this is too much for me. One may accept this in a routine lawsuit for money damages, but when a person's life is at stake ... a requirement of greater reliability should prevail. In a capital case, the specious testimony of a psychiatrist, colored in the eyes of an impressionable jury by the inevitable untouchability of a medical specialist's words, equates with death itself.

As it turned out, the *Daubert* trilogy would demand a far higher standard of admissibility for money-damages than *Barefoot* required for the death penalty. Nor can *Barefoot* be readily distinguished from *Daubert* as a constitutional, rather than an evidentiary, decision. The Court's Eighth Amendment jurisprudence has long proclaimed that "death is different" and so has imposed higher reliability standards.

## The New Reliability Approach

Having rejected *Frye* on statutory interpretation grounds, Justice Blackmun had to anchor whatever standard he constructed on the

---

[25] George E. Dix, *The Death Penalty, "Dangerousness," Psychiatric Testimony, and Professional Ethics*, 5 Am. J. Crim. L. 151, 172 (1977).

language of the Federal Rules. In a tour de force, he created a new test based on the words "scientific" and "knowledge" in Rule 702: "[I]n order to qualify as 'scientific knowledge,' an inference or assertion must be derived by the scientific method. Proposed testimony must be supported by appropriate validation—*i.e.*, 'good grounds,' based on what is known. In short, the requirement that an expert's testimony pertain to 'scientific knowledge' establishes a standard of evidentiary reliability."

This approach assigned a "gatekeeping" role to the trial court, which may consider a number of factors. The Court then identified the now famous *Daubert* factors: (1) testability, (2) peer review and publication, (3) error rate, (4) maintenance of standards, and (5) general acceptance. The Court cautioned, however, that these factors were neither dispositive nor exhaustive and that the Rule 702 standard was "a flexible one." The first and the most important *Daubert* factor is testability. Citing scientific authorities, the Court noted that a hallmark of science is empirical testing. The Court quoted Hempel: "[T]he statements constituting a scientific explanation must be capable of empirical test"[26], and then Popper: "[T]he criterion of the scientific status of a theory is its falsifiability, or refutability, or testability."[27] The second factor, peer review and publication, tends to verify the results of the testing cited in the first factor and suggests acceptance of the methods and results within the broader scientific community. Similarly, an error rate is derived from testing.

## The Transformation of *Daubert*

*Daubert* was difficult to interpret even at the time it was handed down. As one commentary observed, "Astonishingly, all parties expressed satisfaction with the *Daubert* decision—the lawyers for the plaintiff and defense, and scientists who wrote amicus briefs."[28] "The catch," another reviewer remarked, "is that no one is exactly sure what the new standard is."[29]

A central question was whether the Supreme Court intended its new reliability standard to be more permissive than the *Frye* general acceptance test that it had rejected. The Court's disposition of the case,

---

[26] Carl G. Hempel, PHILOSOPHY OF NATURAL SCIENCE 49 (1966).

[27] Karl R. Popper, CONJECTURES AND REFUTATIONS: THE GROWTH OF SCIENTIFIC KNOWLEDGE 37 (5th ed. 1989). Interestingly, the Court seemed unaware that Hempel and Popper espoused opposing views of science. *See* Susan Haack, *An Epistemologist In the Bramble–Bush: At the Supreme Court with Mr. Joiner*, 26 J. Health Pol. Pol'y & L. 217, 232 (2001).

[28] Kenneth R. Foster et al., *Policy Forum: Science and the Toxic Tort*, 261 Science 1509, 1614 (Sept. 17, 1993).

[29] *See* David O. Stewart, *A New Test: Decision Creates Uncertain Future for Admissibility of Expert Testimony*, 79 A.B.A. J. 48 (Nov. 1993).

reversing the lower court's decision excluding the evidence, suggested a more lenient standard.[30] More importantly, the Court commented on the "permissive backdrop" of the Federal Rules, and *Frye* was labeled an "austere standard." Other passages noted that the Rule's basic standard of relevance "is a liberal one" and "a rigid 'general acceptance' requirement would be at odds with the 'liberal thrust' of the Federal Rules and their general approach of relaxing the traditional barriers to 'opinion' testimony." Further, *Daubert* recognized a methodology-conclusion distinction that further supported a lax standard of admissibility. The Supreme Court wrote: "The focus, of course, must be solely on principles and methodology, not on the conclusions that they generate." In short, trial judge review was limited.

A number of courts and commentators, noting this language and the reversal of the decision below, construed *Daubert* as lowering the admissibility bar. In *United States v. Bonds*,[31] for instance, the trial court had rendered its decision before *Daubert* was decided, admitting DNA evidence under *Frye*. On appeal, the Sixth Circuit explained that "DNA testimony easily meets the more liberal test set out by the Supreme Court in *Daubert*." Similarly, in *Borawick v. Shay*,[32] the Second Circuit wrote that "by loosening the strictures on scientific evidence set by *Frye*, *Daubert* reinforces the idea that there should be a presumption of admissibility of evidence." Several polygraph cases also underscored this view. In *United States v. Posado*,[33] the Fifth Circuit stated that "the rationale underlying this circuit's per se rule against admitting polygraph evidence did not survive *Daubert*."

There was, however, language in *Daubert* that pointed toward a more demanding standard. The Court did establish a reliability test and instructed trial courts to act as "gatekeepers." But these passages were often overlooked or minimized until the lower courts began to take up actively the Court's invitation to act as gatekeepers.

### General Electric Co. v. Joiner

This lower court gatekeeping led to the second case, *General Elec. Co. v. Joiner*. On first reading, *Joiner* also seems to support the theme of liberal admissibility. The Court ruled that the proper standard for

---

[30] On remand, however, the Ninth Circuit again excluded the evidence. That court noted that plaintiffs' experts had not submitted their analysis to the peer review process and that their analysis had not derived from their professional research but had been conducted in response to the litigation. Daubert v. Merrell Dow Pharm., Inc., 43 F.3d 1311 (9th Cir. 1995).

[31] 12 F.3d 540, 568 (6th Cir. 1993).

[32] 68 F.3d 597, 610 (2d Cir. 1995) (repressed memory).

[33] 57 F.3d 428, 429 (5th Cir. 1995).

reviewing a trial court's admissibility decision under *Daubert* was abuse-of-discretion, a standard adopted without even considering the principal alternative standard: de novo review. The Court's position suggested that admissibility decisions would not be second guessed on appeal and thus trial courts gained more leeway in admitting evidence. In contrast, a de novo review standard would have given appellate courts more authority to control junk science. But *Joiner* was a case in which the trial court had excluded evidence offered by the plaintiff and then, finding the plaintiff had offered insufficient admissible evidence to make out a *prima facie* case, dismissed the suit on motion of the defendant. So the Court's decision in *Joiner,* unlike *Daubert,* approved the exclusion of scientific evidence.

In reaching its decision in *Joiner,* the Court rejected the appellate court's conclusion that appellate review should be more stringent when expert testimony was *excluded* than when it was admitted. Moreover, the Supreme Court then applied the *Daubert* standard to the evidence offered below and held conclusively against the plaintiff Joiner without remand to the lower court. The Chief Justice, the author of *Joiner,* had voiced considerable discomfort in his *Daubert* concurrence with the capability of federal judges to understand scientific concepts such as "falsifiability" and was concerned that judges would be turned into amateur scientists. By the time of *Joiner,* he had apparently overcome these fears and revealed no hesitation in closely scrutinizing epidemiological and animal studies in that case. While many scientists would have viewed them in toto, the Chief Justice picked apart each study separately.

In addition, the "methodology-conclusion" dichotomy, so prominent in *Daubert,* was drawn into question. The *Joiner* Court remarked that nothing in *Daubert* "requires a district court to admit opinion evidence that is connected to existing data only by the *ipse dixit* of the expert. A court may conclude that there is simply too great an analytical gap between the data and the opinion proffered." Finally, the Court commented that, "while the Federal Rules of Evidence allow district courts to admit a somewhat broader range of scientific testimony than would have been admissible under *Frye,* they leave in place the 'gatekeeper' role of the trial judge in screening such evidence." The term "somewhat" is riveting. The *Daubert* language had presaged that a great deal more evidence would be admissible under *Daubert* than under *Frye.* In hindsight, *Joiner* was a transitional case, moving from the liberal standard of admissibility suggested by much of the language in *Daubert* to an exacting one.

## Kumho Tire Co. v. Carmichael

*Kumho Tire Co. v. Carmichael,* the third case in the *Daubert* trilogy, removed any doubts about the Court's intended direction. In the aftermath of *Daubert*, litigators thought that they might avoid the *Daubert* reliability requirement by calling their expert evidence "technical" or "experiential" rather than "scientific." The Court had to shut this door, or *Daubert's* impact would have been restricted to a narrow category of cases. *Kumho Tire*, which involved a tire expert opining on the cause of a blow out, was the court's vehicle for doing this. In upholding the trial court's decision to exclude the plaintiff's expert's testimony, the Court made clear that *Daubert's* reliability requirement extended to non-scientific testimony under Rule 702.

Further, the Court acknowledged the relevance of the *Daubert* factors in determining reliability in this context. The use of these factors and other tests of reliability was not limited to "scientific" evidence; they were potentially relevant in evaluating any expert testimony. This holding may turn out to be the more critical aspect of the case. Other courts had concluded that the reliability requirement applied to non-scientific expert testimony but had adopted extremely lenient standards for such evidence. For example, one court had written that, "although technical knowledge, like all expert testimony, must be both relevant and reliable, its reliability may be presumed."[34] In rejecting this position, the Court toned down the emphasis on "science" that was so prominent in *Daubert*. The issue now is whether empirical testing is possible, not whether a technique is "scientific."

In one respect, however, *Kumho* was disturbing. Unlike *Daubert* and *Joiner*, it did not involve the difficult causation issues associated with toxic torts, and the defense expert had a master's degree in mechanical engineering and ten years experience working for a leading tire manufacturer. Justice Breyer's dissection of that expert's testimony, replete with a diagram of a tire, was something one would expect during cross-examination at trial, not in a Supreme Court opinion. *Daubert* had pointed out that "[v]igorous cross-examination, presentation of contrary evidence, and careful instruction on the burden of proof are the traditional and appropriate means of attacking shaky but admissible evidence." It is not clear why the adversary system could not be trusted to handle this case, thereby preserving the plaintiff's right to a jury trial.

Most evidence of questionable admissibility is but a small piece of the case a party wishes to make and, while its exclusion will weaken that case, it seldom means there is no case to go to the jury. Expert testimony is, however, often essential in torts and other civil actions. If it is excluded, the plaintiff fails to carry her burden of production, and a directed verdict will follow. Thus, questions about evaluating evidence that the Constitution's framers intended to entrust to juries (unless crediting the evidence would be unreasonable) are after *Kumho* ques-

---

[34] State v. Fukusaku, 946 P.2d 32, 43 (Haw. 1997) (hair and fiber evidence).

tions for judges to first decide. Not only is the jury denied the opportunity to review evidence it might reasonably believe, but its role in checking possible judicial biases is undercut. In addition, if the decision to exclude outcome determinative expert testimony comes during a motion for summary judgment, it is made on a paper record, possibility based only on affidavits.

## Weisgram v. Marley Co.

In 2000, the Supreme Court confirmed a strict scrutiny approach in *Weisgram v. Marley Co.*[35] while reviewing a summary judgment in a wrongful death action against a manufacturer of an allegedly defective baseboard heater. Although expert testimony was involved, the Court was not required to elaborate further on the *Daubert–Kumho* standard. Nevertheless, the Court did remark: "Since *Daubert* ..., parties relying on expert evidence have had notice of the exacting standards of reliability such evidence must meet." So much for the "liberal" standard of the Federal Rules! In the same year, Rule 702 was amended to codify *Daubert–Kumho.*

## Metamorphosis Complete

The metamorphosis of *Daubert* explains some of the confusion in the cases and literature. Some jurisdictions have retained *Frye* on the belief that it provides greater protection for criminal defendants than *Daubert.* At the same time, commentators expressed concern about the stringency of *Daubert* in comparison with *Frye*—in both criminal and civil litigation. *Daubert's* evolution was predicted by some, but it was not foreordained. The *Daubert* doctrine today is quite different from what the language of the case might have suggested.

## The Aftermath

Tracing the effect of *Daubert* in the states is somewhat complex. First, although many states rejected *Frye* in favor of *Daubert,* they did not necessarily adopt *Joiner* or *Kumho.* Second, *Daubert's* impact on the *Frye* test has clouded the distinction between the two standards. Terms such as "gatekeeper", "testability", and "peer review" have crept into the *Frye* lexicon. Indeed, some *Frye* cases look like *Daubert* in disguise. For instance, in *Ramirez v. State,*[36] the Florida Supreme Court rejected the testimony of five experts who claimed general acceptance for a process of matching a knife with a cartilage wound in a murder victim— a type of "tool mark" comparison. Although the court applied *Frye,* it emphasized the lack of testing, the paucity of "meaningful peer review",

---

[35] 528 U.S. 440, 455 (2000).

[36] Ramirez v. State, 810 So. 2d 836, 844 (Fla. 2001).

the absence of a quantified error rate, and the failure to develop objective standards. Third, *Frye*, which had been limited to criminal cases, has been extended to toxic tort litigation, and a recent study "found no evidence that *Frye* or *Daubert* makes a difference" in this type of litigation.[37] Fourth, *Daubert's* effect on the third approach to scientific evidence, the relevancy approach, may have been the most profound development—and yet the least noticed. A number of courts had rejected *Frye* before *Daubert* was decided. Many of these courts now claim that *Daubert* is consistent with their former approach, a fair assessment in some instances but not in others. Many of these jurisdictions had, in practice, adopted the relevancy approach, and their movement toward *Daubert* raises their standard of admissibility. Finally, there have always been strict *Frye* jurisdictions and lax ones. Well-reasoned *Frye* decisions evidence far more than a superficial "nose-counting"—these courts demonstrate an understanding of the underlying science. In contrast, an Illinois court admitted "lip print" comparisons, somehow finding them generally accepted.[38] The same dichotomy can now be observed with *Daubert*. As a British scholar commented, "The choice is not between easy *Frye* and difficult *Daubert*; it is between strict and lax scrutiny."[39]

## Civil and Criminal Cases

Several further developments are clear. Some federal courts have demanded epidemiological studies in toxic tort cases. Many cases do not even survive summary judgment. Indeed, some commentators have argued that the standards are too strict. A Rand Institute study of civil cases concluded that "since *Daubert*, judges have examined the reliability of expert evidence more closely and have found more evidence unreliable as a result."[40] Federal Judicial Center studies mirror this finding.[41] In short, the conservative movement has won, at least for the moment. Of

---

[37] Edward K. Cheng & Albert H. Yoon, *Does* Frye *or* Daubert *Matter? A Study of Scientific Admissibility Standards*, 91 Va. L. Rev. 471, 511 (2005) (using removal rates).

[38] People v. Davis, 710 N.E.2d 1251 (Ill. App. Ct. 1999).

[39] Mike Redmayne, EXPERT EVIDENCE AND CRIMINAL JUSTICE 113 (2001).

[40] Lloyd Dixon & Brian Gill, *Changes in the Standards of Admitting Expert Evidence in Federal Civil Cases Since the* Daubert *Decision*, 8 Psychol., Pub. Pol'y & L. 251, 269 (2002).

[41] *See* Margaret A. Berger, *Upsetting the Balance Between Adverse Interests: The Impact of the Supreme Court's Trilogy on Expert Testimony in Toxic Tort Litigation*, 64 Law & Contemp. Probs. 289, 290 (2001) ("The Federal Judicial Center conducted surveys in 1991 and 1998 asking federal judges and attorneys about expert testimony. In the 1991 survey, seventy-five percent of the judges reported admitting all proffered expert testimony. By 1998, only fifty-nine percent indicated that they admitted all proffered expert testimony without limitation. Furthermore, sixty-five percent of plaintiff and defendant counsel stated that judges are less likely to admit some types of expert testimony since *Daubert*.").

course, *Daubert* may not be the culprit. "The increasing presence of perhaps more-conservative judges through appointments made by President Reagan and President Bush might have changed how courts handle evidence regardless of whether the *Daubert* decision was issued."[42] Yet, unlike federal civil litigation, admissibility standards in criminal litigation appear largely unchanged. An extensive study of reported criminal cases found that "the *Daubert* decision did not impact on the admission rates of expert testimony at either the trial or appellate court levels."[43]

Expert testimony in criminal and civil cases raises different issues. Instead of worrying about the "hired gun" phenomenon, as in civil litigation, the criminal defense lawyer often lacks money for any "gun." Moreover, the causation issues that loom so large in toxic tort cases are seldom an issue in criminal prosecutions, and the termination of the litigation before trial through summary judgment is also not a concern. These points, however, do not explain why the admissibility standard would be applied differently. As demonstrated by Barefoot's execution, the stakes can be far higher on the criminal side of the docket.

One might question whether a federal court in a toxic tort case would allow a plaintiff's attorney to get away with what passed for "science" in a criminal fingerprint case. In *United States v. Havvard*,[44] the court accepted testimony by a FBI expert (1) that there is a "zero error" rate in fingerprint examinations, (2) that "peer review" under *Daubert* means a second examiner looks at the prints, and (3) that adversarial testing is the equivalent of scientific testing. Particularly instructive is Judge Pollak's decision in *United States v. Llera Plaza*.[45] Here, Judge Pollak applied *Daubert* in all its rigor to fingerprint testimony, and, finding that *Daubert's* strictures were not met, he excluded it. The uproar that followed the exclusion of what to date had been untested expert evidence was as great as the earlier uproar against "junk science." On a motion for reconsideration, Judge Pollack changed his mind and admitted the evidence despite the absence of empirical research on the reliability of fingerprint identifications. His first decision was more faithful to *Daubert* than his second.

---

[42] Dixon & Gill, *supra* note 40, at 267.

[43] Jennifer L. Groscup et al., *The Effects of* Daubert *on the Admissibility of Expert Testimony in State and Federal Criminal Cases*, 8 Pyschol., Pub. Pol'y & L. 339, 364 (2002).

[44] 117 F. Supp. 2d 848 (S.D. Ind. 2000) (stating the fingerprint expertise is "the very archetype of reliable expert testimony under [the *Daubert–Kumho*] standards"), *aff'd*, 260 F.3d 597 (7th Cir. 2001).

[45] 188 F. Supp. 2d 549, 558 (E.D. Pa. 2002) (excluding and then admitting fingerprint evidence).

This is not to say that *Daubert* has had no effect in criminal cases. Some federal courts have read the *Daubert* trilogy as inviting a "reexamination even of 'generally accepted' venerable, technical fields." *Kumho* has been particularly important here, for it undercut an argument by prosecutors that had been adopted by some courts; namely, that most forensic science was of a technical or experiential nature and so unaffected by *Daubert*. Attacks have thus been launched against handwriting evidence, hair comparisons, fingerprint examinations, firearms identifications, bite mark analyses, and intoxication testing. While most of these challenges have not led to the exclusion of evidence, they have exposed the lack of empirical support for many commonly employed forensic techniques. Such challenges would not have occurred under *Frye*. In addition, there have been more legal articles on these subjects in the last few years than in the prior quarter century, which should mean closer scrutiny of this type of expert testimony for the foreseeable future. The forensic science community views these attacks as serious, noting that defense lawyers have "become more critical and aggressive in challenging forensic evidence and are more willing to hire qualified forensic experts to assist them."[46]

## The Jury System

In *Daubert*, the Court rejected the argument that discarding *Frye* would lead to cases in which "befuddled juries are confounded by absurd and irrational pseudoscientific assertions." According to the Court, this argument represents an "overly pessimistic" view of the "capabilities of the jury, and of the adversary system." Nevertheless, the petitioners in *Kumho* stressed the jury's deficiencies in their briefs. However, an amicus brief, filed by experts in jury research, attempted to educate the Court on this issue, advising that it should not decide the case "based on the Petitioners' unsupported or flawed assertions that juries fail to critically evaluate expert testimony, that they are overawed by experts, that they have a 'natural tendency' to defer to experts, and that they have pro-plaintiff and anti-business biases. The heavy preponderance of data from more than a quarter century of empirical jury research points to just the opposite view of jury behavior."[47] Similarly, although some courts and commentators have expressed concern about the risk of jurors overvaluing statistical estimates, the research on the subject suggests the exact opposite may be true. The 1996 National Academy DNA Report recommended further research on jury understanding, and

---

[46] Graham R. Jones, *President's Editorial—The Changing Practice of Forensic Science,* 47 J. Forensic Sci. 437, 437 (2002).

[47] Brief Amici Curiae of Neil Vidmar et al., Kumho Tire Co. v. Carmichael, 526 U.S. 137 (1999).

several studies conducted since the Report was issued confirm that jurors undervalue this evidence.

If strict standards for the admissibility of scientific evidence are based on jury inadequacy, a far more "scientific" record of those defects is required to justify erosion of Seventh Amendment rights. Moreover, the use of bifurcated trials, as in the multidistrict litigation in the Bendectin lawsuits, and the employment of court-appointed experts, as in the silicone breast implant litigation, although not without problems, offer ways to preserve the jury trial system. Perhaps, if the massive Firestone tire recall had occurred before *Kumho* was decided, the Court might have adopted a less intrusive role for judges.

## The Adversary System

The *Daubert* Court also commented that "[v]igorous cross-examination, presentation of contrary evidence, and careful instruction on the burden of proof are the traditional and appropriate means of attacking shaky but admissible evidence." The same refrain echoed in *Barefoot*, where the Court wrote that the "jurors should not be barred from hearing the views of the State's psychiatrists along with opposing views of the defendant's doctors." In a footnote, the Court noted in passing that there was no "contention that, despite petitioner's claim of indigence, the court refused to provide an expert for petitioner." The Court, however, failed to mention that only $500 was available for an expert under the extant Texas statute. Similarly, before the reforms triggered by the Illinois death penalty moratorium, that state provided a meager $250 for defense experts. Although there is a constitutional right to experts for indigent defendants, most studies indicate that lack of resources remains a substantial impediment.[48] One request for a DNA expert was rejected due to a lack of county funds and another because defense lawyers had access to "CLE" materials on DNA.

Perhaps this is not surprising, since there is a widespread belief that the basic right to counsel under *Gideon v. Wainwright*[49] has not been fully implemented, especially in capital cases. Texas executed over 300 prisoners before a state-wide defender system was enacted. Civil cases have their own inequities. Without addressing such inequities, juries—no matter how competent—are handicapped in their work by the resulting skewing of the information they receive.

## Science & Law

James Watson, one of the discoverers of the double helix structure of DNA, recently wrote that "[t]he law has always had difficulty assimilat-

---

[48] *See* Paul C. Giannelli, Ake v. Oklahoma: *The Right to Expert Assistance in a Post–Daubert, Post–DNA World*, 89 Cornell L. Rev. 1305 (2004).

[49] 372 U.S. 335 (1963).

ing the implications, if not the very idea, of scientific evidence."[50] In *Daubert*, the Court addressed the overarching issue of the relationship between law and science, an issue raised in the numerous amici briefs.

If there is a clash between science and law, it is not because of any inherent incompatibility. The law simply cannot ignore scientific information. No one wants to go back to the days of the Charlie Chaplin paternity trial in the 1940s, where the court held that blood tests conclusively excluding Chaplin as the father were not binding on the jury,[51] while permitting the use of "Madonna evidence"—i.e., requiring Chaplin, mother and child to stand before the jury, so that the jury could make a visual comparison. Similarly, few would ignore the power of DNA profiling to convict the guilty and exonerate the innocent (175 convicts have been exonerated so far).

The critical question is not whether to apply *Daubert*, *Frye*, or some other reliability test, but the quality of the information before the court. This, in turn, requires confronting a larger policy issue: Who should be responsible for producing that information? Typically, the proponent of evidence has the burden of persuasion, but another well-recognized principle allocates the burden to the party with the greatest access to the evidence. The latter principle is generally ignored in determining whether scientific evidence should be admitted and when summary judgment should be granted.

The courts, of course, would be better off if sufficient scientific information existed before a legal controversy erupted, but life is rarely so simple. Sometimes the litigation itself triggers the research, as illustrated by the Bendectin litigation. Similarly, the DNA "wars" led to a searching critique of DNA evidence. Some experts in those battles later concluded that "most would now agree that this extended debate has been good for the science."[52]

Further research, however, is not the only response to a legal challenge. The first post-*Daubert* attack on fingerprint evidence came in *United States v. Mitchell*.[53] After the trial, the defense attorney learned that a National Institute of Justice (NIJ) solicitation for research on fingerprints had been postponed, arguably so that it could not be used in

---

[50] James D. Watson & Andrew Berry, DNA: THE SECRET OF LIFE 266 (2004).

[51] Berry v. Chaplin, 169 P.2d 442 (Cal. 1946).

[52] Ian W. Evett & Bruce S. Weir, *Interpreting DNA Evidence: Statistical Genetics for Forensic Scientists* xiv (1998). *See also* Richard Lempert, *Comment: Theory and Practice in DNA Fingerprinting*, 9 Statistical Sci. 255, 258 (1994) ("[I]n this instance the importation of legal adversariness into the scientific world has spurred both valuable research and practical improvements in the way DNA is analyzed and presented.").

[53] 365 F.3d 215 (3d Cir. 2004).

*Mitchell* to support the defense challenge. The Third Circuit felt compelled to comment: "We are deeply discomforted by Mitchell's contention—supported by Dr. Rau's account of events, though contradicted by other witnesses—that a conspiracy within the Department of Justice intentionally delayed the release of the solicitation until after Mitchell's jury reached a verdict. Dr. Rau's story, if true, would be a damning indictment of the ethics of those involved."[54] Dr. Rau was the NIJ official who coordinated the drafting of the solicitation for the Department of Justice.

A subsequent attempt to establish an empirical basis for fingerprint comparison was also thwarted. An editorial in the prestigious scientific journal, *Science*, entitled "Forensic Science: Oxymoron?" and written by the editor-in-chief, discussed the cancellation of a National Academy of Sciences project designed to examine various forensic science techniques, including fingerprints, because the Departments of Justice and Defense insisted on a right of review that the Academy had refused to other grant sponsors.[55] Only after the embarrassment resulting from the Madrid train bombing fiasco, in which the FBI misidentified fingerprints, was further research reconsidered. With DNA evidence, by contrast, there was not one but two National Academy of Science reports sponsored by the FBI and other agencies, which evaluated both DNA technologies and the scientific principles that supported DNA identifications.

*Criminal cases.* In criminal cases, both policy and the availability of resources require that the government should shoulder the burden of conducting empirical validation studies: "To put the point more bluntly: if the state does not test the scientific evidence with which it seeks to convict defendants, it should forfeit the right to use it."[56]

*Civil cases.* While not as compelling as criminal cases, the stakes in civil litigation are no small matter. In his concurring opinion in *Joiner*, Justice Breyer wrote:

> [M]odern life, including good health as well as economic well-being, depends upon the use of artificial or manufactured substances, such as chemicals. And it may, therefore, prove particularly important to see that judges fulfill their *Daubert* gatekeeping function, so that they help assure that the powerful engine of tort liability, which can generate strong financial incentives to reduce, or to eliminate, production, points toward the right substances and does not destroy the wrong ones.[57]

---

54 *Mitchell*, 365 F.3d at 255.

55 Donald Kennedy, Editorial, *Forensic Science: Oxymoron?*, 302 Science 1625 (2003).

56 Mike Redmayne, *supra* note 39, at 139.

57 522 U.S. at 149–50.

Bendectin is a prime illustration; it was driven off the market. But this example merely highlights the problem. It does not provide the answer. Allocating the burden to the person offering expert testimony and then demanding epidemiological studies impacts plaintiffs harshly; they simply cannot afford to sponsor this type of research.

The larger questions are: (1) "On whom should the burden of showing product safety or lack of safety be placed?" (2) "If a toxic tort or a product defect plaintiff is given the initial burden of showing lack of safety, how much evidence must he present before the defendant is required to come forth with evidence suggesting safety?" Arguably, the standard for triggering such burden shifting should be light because the manufacturer who markets a drug or product has an obligation to ensure that sufficient research suggesting safety has been conducted before placing a product on the market. After reviewing case studies of Agent Orange, asbestos, Bendectin, breast implants, tobacco, and other substances, one prominent scholar wrote: "All report that the corporation in question did not test its product adequately initially, failed to impart information when potential problems emerged, and did not undertake further research in response to adverse information. It appears that the corporations took virtually no steps to determine or minimize the possibility of harm until their hands were forced, usually by litigation."[58] The Vioxx litigation may add another chapter to this sordid record.

It was not until 2001 that prominent medical journals adopted conflict of interest policies—long after Merrell had "ghost written" favorable articles on thalidomide and Bendectin. These journals have announced that they will not publish studies done under contracts that give sponsors the right to preclude publication of unfavorable results. Not until 2004 did these journals require that articles reporting the results of clinical trials would not be published unless the trials had been publicly registered before they commence, a requirement designed to preclude companies from hiding unwelcome clinical trial results.

Importing *Daubert* into administrative law, as some have suggested, without addressing the policy issues may be dangerous. The objectives of regulatory schemes differ from those of tort litigation. Indeed, some public health advocates trace the "junk science" movement back to the lead, tobacco, and asbestos industries' marketing campaigns that attempted to "institutionalize uncertainty" in an effort to avoid liability and preclude regulatory control.[59] As a tobacco executive once famously

---

[58] Margaret A. Berger, *Eliminating General Causation: Notes Towards A New Theory of Justice and Toxic Torts*, 97 Colum. L. Rev. 2117, 2135 (1997).

[59] David Michaels & Celeste Monforton, *Manufacturing Uncertainty: Contested Science and the Protection of the Public's Health and Environment*, 95 Am. J. Pub. Health S39 (2005).

announced, "Doubt is our product."[60]

## Conclusion

Over a 100 years ago, Learned Hand posed the question addressed by *Daubert*: "No one will deny the law should in some way effectively use expert knowledge wherever it will aid in settling disputes. The only question is as to how it can do so best."[61] As a matter of evidence law, *Daubert* is superior to *Frye* because it asks the right question directly—is the evidence reliable—and asking the right question is the first step toward getting the right answer. Nevertheless, the application of either standard often requires courts to digest a lot of scientific information. Under any approach, however, stricter admissibility standards in civil cases than in criminal prosecutions is unjustified, if not shameful.

Moreover, an evidentiary standard cannot be viewed without context, without understanding the substantive and procedural rules that frame the issue. In short, many of the most important questions surrounding the admissibility of scientific evidence in courts and other fora involve neither science nor evidence issues. They are policy issues, pure and simple.

But the implications of legal policies are, as the story of *Daubert* and its aftermath reveals, not always simple. Nor are they abstract, for they affect the lives of real human beings. Jason Daubert's mother reports that it was "a blow to her family" when the Ninth Circuit, on remand from the Supreme Court, decided the case in favor of Merrell Dow.[62] "We wanted," she said, "to go to court—have our day in court." They won in the Supreme Court but did not win the policy that they and others thought they had gained that day: the freer admissibility of expert evidence and trial by jury. The decision on remand made that clear. Whether justice won is a different question. Given the number of epidemiological studies that had been done and the fact they pointed in one direction, it is easy to argue that justice prevailed in both the Supreme Court and the Ninth Circuit on remand, but other plaintiffs have lost in situations where the justice of *Daubert* exclusions has not been as clear. Also, as we have seen, on the criminal side, the failure of judges to scrutinize forensic science evidence with the rigor *Daubert* allows may have led to serious, even fatal, injustice. As for the person at the heart of the litigation, Jason Daubert, he is now 32. He has graduated from college and is happily married. Whatever else the case meant, it has not ruined his life.

---

[60] *See* David Michaels, *DOUBT Is Their Product*, 292 Sci. Am. 96 (Jun. 2005).

[61] Learned Hand, *Historical and Practical Considerations Regarding Expert Testimony*, 15 Harv. L. Rev. 40, 40 (1901).

[62] Telephone conversation with Joyce Daubert, Nov. 8, 2005.

## SUGGESTED READINGS

David E. Bernstein & Jeffrey D. Jackson, *The* Daubert *Trilogy in the States*, 44 Jurimetrics J. 351 (2004).

David E. Bernstein, Frye, Frye, *Again: The Past, Present, and Future of the General Acceptance Test*, 41 Jurimetrics J. 385 (2001).

Bert Black et al., *Science and the Law in the Wake of Daubert: A New Search for Scientific Knowledge*, 72 Tex. L. Rev. 715 (1994).

Paul C. Giannelli, *The Admissibility of Novel Scientific Evidence:* Frye v. United States, *a Half–Century Later*, 80 Colum. L. Rev. 1197 (1980).

Paul C. Giannelli, Daubert: *Interpreting the Federal Rules of Evidence*, 15 Cardozo L. Rev. 1999 (1994).

Susan Haack, *An Epistemologist in the Bramble–Bush: At the Supreme Court with Mr. Joiner*, 26 J. Health Pol., Pol'y & L. 217 (2001).

David H. Kaye et al., The New Wigmore: Expert Evidence § 6.2 (2004).

Dale A Nance, *Reliability and the Admissibility of Experts*, 34 Seton Hall L. Rev. 191 (2003).

D. Michael Risinger, *Navigating Expert Reliability: Are Criminal Standards of Certainty Being Left on the Dock?*, 64 Albany L. Rev. 99 (2000).

Wendy E. Wagner, *Importing Daubert to Administrative Agencies Through the Information Quality Act*, 12 J.L. & Policy 589 (2004).

# 9

## *People v. Castro*: Challenging the Forensic Use of DNA Evidence

### Jennifer L. Mnookin

In a well-told murder mystery, the reader is left hanging until the very end. Figuring out what actually happened is part of the reader's job, as the author metes out clues and false leads, hints and distractions, bit by bit until it all fits together in a denouement that, ideally, is both surprising and satisfying.

Looking back on *People v. Castro*, there is no particular mystery about what happened. There is no reason to doubt that the defendant, Joseph Castro, a handyman, did in fact commit the murders with which he was charged, the fatal stabbings of Vilma Ponce and her two-year old daughter. In fact, in *People v. Castro*, there was no trial, for the defendant ended up pleading guilty to second degree murder before the trial began. The case we now call *People v. Castro* was nothing more than a preliminary hearing about the admissibility of evidence at trial. Nor did *People v. Castro* lead to any change in legal rules or to a formal, explicit shift in any evidentiary doctrine.

Why then, should we tell the story of *People v. Castro*? What is it about a preliminary hearing in New York City in 1989 that adduced no new legal standard that has led to the case being cited more than 130 times by later courts and equally often in law review articles? And why is it worth retelling in detail more than 15 years later?

*People v. Castro* was a preliminary hearing about the admissibility of DNA evidence in the courtroom. It was by no means the first such case—more than a handful of trial courts had already permitted DNA evidence when the preliminary hearing in *Castro*, that would last 14 weeks and take up more than 5000 transcript pages, began in February, 1989. But *People v. Castro* was, in its own way, an extraordinary drama: the *dramatis personae* were not the defendant or eyewitnesses or the relatives of the victim, but instead, leading research scientists, including winners of Macarthur genius grants and future Nobel Prize winners; forensic biologists who had developed the use of DNA identification for courtroom use, and some determined attorneys who, with both grit and luck, managed to put together a set of arguments about the inadequacy of the state's DNA evidence that the judge simply could not ignore. At the preliminary hearing, it was not Joseph Castro who was on trial so much as it was forensic DNA. Much to the surprise of the public, not to mention significant swaths of the legal and scientific community, the verdict on the new technology that emerged from *Castro* was the Scottish verdict of "not proven."

Although the hearing in *Castro* may not have ultimately made much difference to Joseph Castro, beyond likely reducing the sentence that he was offered in a plea bargain, its broader consequences were significant indeed. *Castro* arguably inaugurated a radical, though perhaps in the end, temporary, shift in the evaluation of DNA evidence. Prior to *Castro*, no court had even come close to rejecting DNA evidence. But *Castro* made it clear that DNA evidence was vulnerable, and enterprising defense attorneys poked and prodded those vulnerabilities in numerous subsequent cases across the country over the next several years, leading a number of courts to reject DNA evidence altogether, something that would have been nearly unthinkable prior to *Castro*.

*Castro* directly and indirectly affected not only attorneys but scientists too. *Castro* led to a host of changes of standards in forensic DNA laboratories, and contributed to a set of controversies, that motivated additional research, among scientists themselves. Forensic DNA, although no one quite realized it at the time, existed in a tinderbox. *Castro* was the spark that set off a firestorm over the reliability of forensic DNA, a flare-up that grew so heated and intense that press accounts referred to what ensued as "the DNA wars." These battles played out not only in the courtroom but in the pages of leading scientific journals, like *Nature* and *Science*. It took a number of years, additional court disputes, continued scientific research, and the weighing-in of two distinguished commissions created by the National Research Council, to reach stability and closure in both the legal arena and the scientific one.

*People v. Castro* is also useful for the insight it provides into the complex intersection of science and law. We can see, on the one hand, how unnatural the adversarial system and its dictates can seem to scientists. We will even see how productive it was, in *Castro*, for the scientists to make an end-run around the adversary system and behave in ways that were both irregular and, in the end, enormously helpful for the production of consensus in the case. *Castro* could therefore be Exhibit A in a sharp critique of the adversarial method of proof, at least with respect to the evaluation of novel scientific techniques. But at the same time, *Castro* also shows how the adversarial system—at least in those instances when parties have equal access to highly qualified experts—may be especially well-suited for revealing limitations and weaknesses in evidence that other evaluative methods, including scientific peer review, reputation, and publication, may not necessarily uncover. *Castro* therefore illustrates how the adversarial testing of expert evidence may be *both* truth-obscuring and truth-producing, depending on the circumstances.

Finally, in addition to being an object lesson in the inevitably awkward relationship between legal ways of doing things and scientific ones, *Castro* may perhaps be a beacon. There are significant debates going on right now about many other kinds of forensic evidence, and precisely what and how much evidence of reliability the courts ought to require from them. The substance of the preliminary hearing in *Castro* stands for the idea that the standards of *research scientists* ought to be the standards of *forensic science*—an idea that, if taken to its logical extreme, could make many kinds of commonly-used forensic evidence, from fingerprint identifications to expert document examination to ballistics analysis inadmissible in court until additional research is done to establish the validity of the claims to which forensic experts routinely testify.

In addition to raising these significant questions about science and law, *People v. Castro* is an interesting story, and it is with the story of the case that we shall begin. After laying out the background facts, I will present an abbreviated history of DNA evidence and its legal use prior to *Castro*, and then describe in some detail the preliminary hearing that made *Castro* special. Then we shall explore the aftermath of *Castro*, concluding with broader ruminations about *Castro*, the use of science in the adversarial system, and forensic science.

**Facts of the case:**

David Rivera returned to the Bronx apartment he shared with his common-law wife, 20–year old Vilma Ponce, late in the afternoon on February 5, 1987. He unlocked both of the two locks on the door, but could not enter because the chain locking the door was attached from the inside. He called out the name of his wife and daughter, but was answered only by silence. Concerned and somewhat anxious, he attempted to phone his wife, thinking that perhaps she was sleeping. When no one answered, he called his mother, who lived nearby, to see if she had any possible explanation, but she hadn't spoken to his wife since earlier that afternoon. Growing increasingly concerned, Rivera asked his mother to call the police. He stood outside his building, and attempted to whistle up to his apartment, thinking that maybe his wife or daughter would hear him. Just then he saw a ghastly sight: a man leaving the building, his face, arms and shoes smeared with blood. Moments later, the police arrived. When they entered Rivera and Ponce's apartment, they discovered that Ponce, six months pregnant at the time, and Natasha, the couple's two-year old daughter, both lay dead, victims of a brutal stabbing. Ponce, found nude from the waist down, had been perforated nearly 60 times, and her small daughter's body had been stabbed at least 16 times While Rivera initially failed to pick Castro out of an array of photographs, he subsequently identified Joseph Castro as the man he saw leaving the building with bloody hands that afternoon. Castro lived nearby, and did odd jobs in various buildings in the neighborhood, including, on occasion, Vilma Ponce's.[1]

Police investigation found further evidence to buttress Rivera's identification of Castro and to support a circumstantial case that Castro was indeed the murderer. According to one of Vilma Ponce's friends, Ponce had pointed Castro out to her on the street just a week before the murder, complaining that he frequently made suggestive remarks to her. Her friend urged her to tell her husband, but Ponce said she didn't want to provoke a possibly violent confrontation between the two men. The police found that one of the locks on Ponce and Rivera's door was improperly installed, and therefore didn't work—and they discovered that Joseph Castro himself, assisting the building superintendent's nephew, had helped to install the malfunctioning lock just two weeks earlier. In addition, because the police found Ponce's just-bought groceries, including meat and chicken, still sitting in a bag on the living room sofa rather than in the refrigerator, they speculated that Ponce had been surprised by her attacker just after getting home—perhaps before she had a chance to latch the second, actually-functioning lock on her door.

All of this was suggestive: it provided the outlines for a story that fingered Castro as a possible suspect and gave tantalizing hints of both motive and opportunity. But the police still might not have had a persuasive case had they not, when they questioned Castro, seized a watch he was wearing, stained with what looked like dried blood. If it *was* blood and if it could be persuasively linked to Vilma or Natasha, that would transform a circumstantial case into a slam-dunk story of Castro's guilt.

The prosecution sent Joseph Castro's watch for DNA testing in the summer of 1987. A few weeks later, Lifecodes, the company that conducted the test, reported that the DNA found on the watch matched

---

[1] This description of the facts draws extensively on the detailed account in Harlan Levy, AND THE BLOOD CRIED OUT: A PROSECUTOR'S SPELLBINDING ACCOUNT OF THE POWER OF DNA (1996). It is based as well on Roger Parloff, *How Barry Scheck and Peter Neufeld Tripped up the DNA Experts*, American Lawyer, 50 (1989); Edward Humes, *The DNA Wars; Touted as an Infallible Method to Identify Criminals, DNA Matching has Mired Courts in a Vicious Battle of Expert Witnesses*, L.A. Times, (Magazine, p. 20, Nov. 29, 1992), and Howard Coleman & Eric Swenson, DNA IN THE COURTROOM: A TRIAL WATCHER'S GUIDE (1994).

Vilma Ponce's DNA profile. Lifecodes claimed that the chance that a person selected at random from the population would match the blood found on that watch was a minuscule 1 in 189,200,000.

## The Rise of DNA Evidence

Testing blood for blood types goes back many decades, and over the years ever-more sophisticated tests had been developed. Nonetheless, just a few years earlier, no such definitive identification would have been possible Although blood testing had grown increasingly sensitive, and had long been able to reliably determine that an individual was *not* the source of a particular blood sample, it could not do any more than show that an individual was a possible source of a blood sample, one among a significant number of people that had the same blood type or the same blood proteins.

Then in 1984, a British scientist named Alec Jeffreys, a DNA researcher at the University of Leicester, made an astounding and surprising discovery. He was studying myoglobin, a protein that stores oxygen, and quite by accident, while working on a problem related to gene mapping, not individual identification, Jeffreys and his colleagues realized that they had found a way to examine a region of DNA that was both inherited in Mendelian fashion (that is, passed along through the generations, half from each parent) and highly variable across individuals. Jeffreys first published the news of his invention in March of 1985, and by July, he and his co-authors were claiming in the prestigious scientific journal *Nature*, that the new technology was a reliable and "unambiguous" way to identify individuals. Quite self-consciously, Jeffreys gave this new technique a name that would resonate: DNA fingerprinting.

Drawing on the widespread belief in the uniqueness and power of fingerprinting was a masterful PR move—it both suggested that DNA evidence shared in the cultural authority of its predecessor, the fingerprint, and it provided for the non-scientific, for those who knew nothing about DNA at all, a mental image of what it was that this new technique could do. As Jeffreys reported in an interview,

> One of the reasons we called this DNA fingerprinting was absolutely deliberate. If we had called this "idiosyncratic Southern blot profiling," nobody would have taken a blind bit of notice. Call it "DNA fingerprinting" and the penny dropped.[2]

---

[2] Alec Jeffreys, interview with Michael Lynch, 6 August 1996, cited in Jay Aronson, The Introduction, Contestation and Regulation of Forensic DNA Analysis in the American Legal System (1984–1995), 56 (Ph.D. Dissertation, Univ. of Minnesota, 2004). Aronson's dissertation, a detailed and insightful account of the rise of DNA as a form of legal evidence, and, apart from the *Castro* trial transcript, the most important source for this

Sure enough, the penny *did* drop; the technique quickly got world-wide attention. It was used for the first time in a legal setting that very year, in an immigration dispute in England over whether a teenage boy was in fact a legitimate British citizen returning to be reunited with his British mother, or somebody else, a mere faker who had tampered with a passport. The family's lawyer persuaded Jeffreys to use the new technique to analyze the boy's DNA, and the test's results identified the boy as the mother's biological son. In the face of this DNA evidence and under pressure from the appellate tribunal, the British Home office ended up withdrawing their case. This saved the tribunal from having to decide about the admissibility and validity of a powerful but untested brand new technology. Press accounts nonetheless celebrated both the result and the new technique.[3]

Shortly thereafter, in 1986, the technique was put to use for the first time in a criminal investigation.[4] A teenage girl had been raped and murdered in rural England in 1983, and then in 1986, another girl was found dead nearby. A kitchen worker with a low IQ was fingered as a possible suspect. The DNA evidence from both murders was tested against the suspect's, and it turned out that the two criminal samples matched each other, strongly suggesting that the same person committed both crimes. But much to the disappointment of police investigators, neither sample matched the original suspect. The kitchen porter was freed, the first criminal suspect in history to be exonerated by his own DNA. Frustrated and desperate for new leads, police eventually decided to take on a genetic manhunt: every man in the appropriate age range in the vicinity was asked voluntarily to submit blood for testing. Although thousands of samples were tested, none matched the DNA evidence extracted from the semen found at the murder sites. An enormous and controversial effort seemed to have produced nothing useful. Then the police got a much-needed lead: it turned out that a young man who worked at a bakery let slip that he had been coaxed into giving blood in place of one of his co-workers. Police unraveled the story and confronted the co-worker, who promptly confessed to the murders. The DNA evidence confirmed the confession: this time, the police had found the killer.

---

essay, will be published in book form as THE DEVELOPMENT OF DNA PROFILING: SCIENCE, LAW AND CONTROVERSY IN THE AMERICAN JUSTICE SYSTEM (Rutgers University Press, forthcoming 2007).

[3] This account of the first legal use forensic DNA is drawn from Aronson, supra note 2 at as well as contemporaneous newspaper articles.

[4] For a detailed and novelistic book-length account of this case, upon which this short summary is based, see Joseph Wambaugh, THE BLOODING (1989).

By 1987, Jeffreys and his research institute had sold their rights in their DNA technique to ICI, a private company that would further develop and commercialize their new technique. That same year, ICI opened up Cellmark Diagnostics USA, and began to offer the technique for paternity testing and forensic matters in the United States. Around the same time, another company, Lifecodes, began offering its services for forensic analysis—based on somewhat different techniques for analyzing DNA, but also designed to provide reliable information about whether two biological samples were likely to have come from the same source.[5]

The DNA techniques used by both companies measured the length of particular genes. DNA profiling looks at specific parts of the human DNA with no known function (therefore sometimes called "junk DNA"). At these places, or *loci*, on the genome, short sequences of DNA are repeated, but the number of repetitions is highly variable across the population. (These are known as VNTRs, or "variable number tandem repeats.") Each possible variant is called an *allele*. Every person inherits DNA from both parents, so an individual will typically have two alleles at each locus. At any one locus, two people could easily have the same allele, but if you examined their alleles at several different loci, the chance that all their alleles would match decreases exponentially.

To examine DNA with these methods, it is first chopped into small pieces using special enzymes that break it apart whenever certain patterns of base pairs within the DNA are found. This broken-up DNA is next divided up using a technique called "electrophoresis," in which the DNA is loaded into a lane in a gelatin slab. In the forensic context, the DNA found at the crime scene is loaded into one lane, while the DNA known to come from, say, the victim and the suspect are each loaded into their own lanes. All the lanes are then subjected to an electrical current, and because they are different sizes, they travel at different speeds down the gel. Then the DNA is converted from double-stranded to single stranded, transferred and affixed to a membrane, and exposed to a radioactive "probe" that latches onto it and can be visualized by exposing x-ray film to the membrane. This produces an "autoradiogram," or autorad, which visually displays the bands attributable to each allele at

---

[5] Although a detailed explanation of the differences between Lifecodes and Cellmark's early techniques is beyond the scope of this essay, here is a quick explanation: Jeffreys' and Cellmark's technique originally used a "multi-locus probe" (MLP) that bound to many loci in a person's DNA and produced an image that looked like a complex pattern, while Lifecodes' approach was to use "single locus probes." Individually, these single locus probes could not provide as much information as an MLP, but they could be aggregated to build up information about an individual's genetic profile, and they could be used on smaller amounts of blood and were easier to interpret than MLPs. Over time, SLPs came to be the dominant approach.

each locus. If two DNA samples came from the same person, the bands displayed on the autorad would line up and show a "match."

Both companies advertised their new techniques in very strong terms. One advertisement in Trial magazine proclaimed "Only DNA Fingerprinting Determines Paternity in Just Two Words: Yes/No. Thirty billion to one accuracy in one conclusive test." "NO ifs, NO maybes," announced another advertisement. In Criminal Justice magazine, around the time of the *Castro* case itself, one of Cellmark's advertisements showed two cuffed hands linked by a chain in the shape of the DNA double helix, explaining that DNA fingerprinting "positively identifies suspects . . . by examining a suspect's one-of-a-kind genetic material.".

## The Early Legal Reception of DNA Evidence

These advertisements—making strong claims for the technology and broadcasting total confidence in its results—illuminate not only how DNA analysis was portrayed by its developers, but also the context in which the first judges in American courtrooms received the exciting new technique. It was presented—not only in these advertisements, but to some extent in the early court cases as well, as a kind of "magic bullet"—powerful, infallible, almost miraculous.

In a number of the earliest court cases involving DNA, scrambling defense lawyers were unable to find any expert witnesses of their own. For example, in *Andrews v. State*, the first criminal case in the United States in which DNA evidence was deployed, the prosecution hired as a consultant and expert witness David Housman, a prominent biologist from MIT. The defense, by contrast, had no expert witnesses.[6] Later, the defense attorney in the case explained that although he had made calls to many biology departments, he was unable to find anyone interested in getting involved—and many scientists had told him that if Housman was standing behind the evidence, than it was almost certainly valid.

According to historian of science Jay Aronson, this problem grew even more acute over the next year. In addition to the impressively-credentialed molecular biologists who worked for the DNA testing companies, prosecutors soon had at their disposal a growing list of highly respected academic researchers who were prepared to testify in favor of the new technology. Very prominent scientists—geneticist Kenneth Kidd from Yale, molecular biologist Richard Roberts (who would go on to win the Nobel prize in biology in 1993), and many others of equally high repute—testified about the principles of molecular biology and population genetics, and affirmed the legitimacy and validity of the DNA identification techniques. The early defense witnesses—when there were any at all—were not nearly as prominent. Aronson writes, "These early

---

[6] Andrews v. State, 533 So. 2d 841 (Fla. App. 1988).

endorsements may have served to inhibit other scientists ... from really examining the forensic uses of the technique closely.''[7] Interestingly, the prominent scientists testifying for the prosecution, while leading experts in DNA techniques in general, had very little knowledge about the *forensic* use of DNA or what distinctive problems might arise in the forensic identification context. Questions of *technology transfer*—the special problems that might arise in translating DNA testing from the research laboratory or clinical setting into the forensic science context— did not strike these experts as either salient or problematic. Nor had they examined in detail the specific probes and validation techniques used by the DNA profiling companies, nor the data underlying their population genetics. In fact, both the probes that the companies were using and their population databases were deemed by the companies to be proprietary knowledge, trade secrets.

Given this state of affairs, it is not all that surprising that the early judicial opinions about DNA evidence not only deemed the technique admissible, but sometimes engaged in rhetoric that borders on the reverential. For example, in *People v. Wesley*, the first trial judge in New York State to consider the admissibility of DNA evidence wrote:

> The immediate advantage of DNA fingerprinting ... is the claimed certainty of identification. Blood-grouping identification tests often can narrow down the number of suspects to from 30 to 40% of the population. The laboratory the People propose to utilize claims a mean power of certainty of identification for American Whites of 1 in 840,000,000; for American Blacks, 1 in 1.4 billion. There are approximately only five billion people in the entire world.
>
> The overwhelming enormity of these figures, if DNA fingerprinting proves acceptable in criminal courts, will revolutionize the administration of criminal justice. Where applicable, it would reduce to insignificance the standard alibi defense. In the area of eyewitness testimony, which has been claimed to be responsible for more miscarriages of justice than any other type of evidence, again, where applicable, DNA fingerprinting would tend to reduce the importance of eyewitness testimony. And in the area of clogged calendars and the conservation of judicial resources, DNA fingerprinting, if accepted, will revolutionize the disposition of criminal cases. In short, if DNA fingerprinting works and receives evidentiary acceptance, it can constitute the single greatest advance in the "search for truth", and the goal of convicting the guilty and acquitting the innocent, since the advent of cross-examination.[8]

---

[7] Aronson, supra note 2 at 128.

[8] 140 Misc.2d 306, 308–09 (N.Y. County Ct. 1988).

New York, like most states at that time, evaluated novel forms of scientific evidence under the *Frye* standard, named for a 1923 case in which a systolic blood pressure test, an early and crude attempt at a lie detector, was excluded from evidence.[9] Admissibility under this test depended on whether the new form of science was "generally accepted" by the relevant scientific communities. Sure enough, after a detailed review of both the substance of the testimony and the glowing credentials of the prosecution experts, the trial judge in *Wesley* found that DNA fingerprinting was "reliable and has gained general acceptance in the scientific community," and hence, was admissible in court.[10]

The judge in *Wesley* was especially reassured by his belief that DNA evidence could not give an erroneous result. He wrote:

> A matter of extreme significance testified to by Dr. Roberts, and confirmed by [the other prosecution experts] and unrefuted by the defense experts, is that it is impossible under the scientific principles, technology and procedures of DNA fingerprinting (outside of an identical twin), to get a "false positive"—i.e., to identify the wrong individual as the contributor of the DNA being tested. If there were insufficient DNA for the test, or if the test, or any of its steps, were performed improperly, no result at all would be registered—in other words, the autoradiograph would be blank. Thus the dichotomy can never be between an accurate answer and a false answer, but only between an accurate answer and "no answer." Under the undisputed testimony received at the hearing, no "wrong" person, within the established powers of identity for the test, can be identified by the DNA fingerprinting test.

This belief, that interpreting a DNA test was a straightforward process that would inevitably provide either the right answer or no answer at all, was shared by many of the early courts that considered the admissibility of DNA evidence. As we shall see, this confident belief that DNA tests could never declare an erroneous match was thrown into doubt in *Castro*.

Meanwhile, at the end of November, 1988, an academic conference was taking place that would turn out to have significant consequences for the *Castro* case. Some molecular biologists and forensic scientists had decided to organize a meeting at the renowned Banbury Center to create the opportunity for a wide variety of participants in DNA typing—

---

[9] Frye v. United States, 293 F. 1013 (D.C. App. 1923).

[10] Id. The court did give a certain grudging credence to arguments the defense had made about the inadequate database-size used for the population genetics, and thus required the prosecution to reduce their stated probabilities by a factor of 10, permitting them at trial to claim identification ability at the level of 1 in 84,000,000 for American Caucasians and 1 in 140,000,000 for American Blacks.

including molecular biologists, forensic scientists, population geneticists, lawyers and judges, to discuss DNA techniques, their power and their limits. This meeting was the first structured occasion for discussion between university-based academic molecular biologists and commercially employed forensic scientists, and by all accounts, the conversations were both lively and contentious.

One of the participants at the Banbury Conference was Eric Lander, a brilliant MIT scientist who had received a Macarthur "genius" grant one year earlier for his work on techniques to help decipher the human genome. At the Banbury conference, he presented a paper suggesting that the population genetics and statistical issues surrounding the interpretation of DNA profiling—essentially, the knowledge necessary for making the claim of a 1–in–something chance that a random person would have matched the biological material in question—were significantly more complicated than the private companies had acknowledged. Over the course of the meeting, his probing remarks combined with his critical perspective caught the attention of two defense attorneys participating in the conference, Barry Scheck and Peter Neufeld. Both were members of a New York State panel commissioned to study the forensic use of DNA, and they had also recently taken over Joseph Castro's defense from a court-appointed lawyer who felt overwhelmed by the DNA evidence. Scheck and Neufeld are now very well known, both for their creation of the Innocence Project, which uses post-conviction DNA evidence to exonerate the wrongly convicted, and for their role as members of O.J. Simpson's defense team. At the time of the Banbury conference, Scheck was a clinical law professor at the Cardozo Law School and Neufeld a sole practitioner, and they were beginning to look for experts who might be able to help them challenge the DNA evidence in the case.

Toward the end of the conference, Peter Neufeld approached Eric Lander and asked him to take a look at the DNA evidence in the *Castro* case. As Neufeld told the story to the press after the *Castro* case was over, Lander took a look at the autorad and said,

> "Let me show you how we do things in science." Lander then called over several colleagues, slapped the autorad up against a window, and said, "Match, or no match?"
>
> "Garbage," one responded.
>
> "Do it again," said another.
>
> "Garbage," said a third.[11]

Neufeld asked Lander if he would testify for the defense in the *Castro* case. He declined. He had plenty on his plate already, and besides, at

---

[11] Parloff, supra note 1.

some level, he doubted that there were serious problems with Lifecodes' methods or their implementation. But he did agree to help educate Scheck and Neufeld about DNA evidence and to assist them in making effective discovery requests in the case.

The more Lander learned about Lifecodes' practices in this case, the more disturbed he became. By the time the *Castro* case was over, Landers had agreed to testify after all, had written a 50–page report for the defense, and had devoted more than 350 hours of his time, all of it pro bono, to the case.

## People v. Castro: the Preliminary Hearing[12]

By the time the *Castro* hearing began in February 1989, DNA had been used in quite a few cases throughout the country; some knowledgeable participants estimated that it might already have been used in as many as 80 proceedings nationwide. In many more cases defendants had accepted plea bargains in the face of DNA evidence. Up until *Castro*, every judge confronted with DNA evidence had deemed it admissible. However, these cases had resulted in only a handful of written opinions and even fewer appellate opinions. In New York, the only written opinion was that issued by Judge Harris in *People v. Wesley*, discussed earlier.

The *Castro* hearing—which lasted more than three months—was presided over by Judge Gerald Sheindlin, who would thereafter retain an abiding interest in DNA. He later wrote two books relating to DNA: *Blood Trail: True Crime Mysteries Solved by DNA Detectives*, and *Genetic Fingerprinting: The Law and Science of DNA Evidence*, both published in 1996, as well as a never-produced screenplay about a murder case in which DNA evidence played a role. Sheindlin also did a stint from 1999–2001 as a television jurist on The People's Court. (Sheindlin's wife Judy, at the time of the *Castro* hearing, was a Supervising Judge on the Manhattan Family Court—but she is much better known today as television's Judge Judy.)

The prosecution, led by Risa Sugarman, the homicide bureau chief for the Bronx district attorney's office, began its case by offering the testimony of geneticist Richard Roberts, who explained DNA typing and told the court that it was generally accepted in the scientific community. The next witness was Michael Baird, Lifecodes corporation's chief scientist, who described the techniques and methods Lifecodes used to get

---

[12] My most important two sources for the hearing are the transcript itself, a copy of which was obtained from the O.J. Simpson Archive at Cornell University, and the extensive and thoughtful account in Aronson, supra note 2. Other important sources include Parloff, supra note 1, and newspaper accounts written during and after the hearing. Quotations in this section come from the trial transcript unless otherwise noted.

results. Up to this point, the preliminary hearing seemed to be business as usual, not particularly different from, say, the prosecution's evidence presented in the *Wesley* case a year earlier.

But then Eric Lander entered the picture. Michael Baird later told an interviewer,

> "Things were going pretty routinely in terms of presenting the background, presenting the data, presenting the information. Suddenly Eric Lander shows up for the defense and has a booklet that is numerous pages thick that has what he critiques as all kinds of problems with the case. The prosecutor in that case is like, 'who is this guy? Where did he come from?' ... You know Scheck and Neufeld spent half a day just on his credentials to show that this guy walks on water before the judge."[13]

Indeed, Lander's participation in *Castro* marked the first time that the defense counsel had an expert witness every bit as illustrious as those offered by the prosecution.

But well beyond Lander's sterling credentials, Scheck and Neufeld were able to present, a number of extremely significant challenges to Lifecodes' DNA evidence. In brief, the defense arguments can be fit into three categories: (1) that Lifecodes had failed to follow their own protocols both for declaring a match and for interpreting its probability; (2) that forensic analysis posed challenges different from DNA analysis in the research setting, and that these technically demanding challenges posed by "technology transfer" had not yet been fully met by Lifecodes, as indicated by some of their analysis and their interpretation of the blood evidence in this case, and (3) that there were additional problems with the population genetics databases that Lifecodes was using to determine the probability of a "match."

## Sloppiness in Declaring a Match:

In Lifecodes' report of their test of the DNA found on Castro's watch, they stated that they were able to test the blood at three loci. At each of these loci, they reported a precise match between Vilma Ponce's blood and the stain found on Castro's watch. At one of the loci, the D2S44 locus, they reported that both samples were homozygous (in other words, had two identical alleles, or just one band on the autorad) and had a band sized at 10.25 kb (Kb stands for kilobase, a unit of size measuring 1000 base pairs on the DNA ladder). But when Lander and the attorneys looked over the materials they had received through

---

[13] Michael Baird, interview with Saul Halfon and Arthur Daemmerich, 14 July, 1994 (O.J. Simpson Murder Trial and DNA Typing Archive, Cornell University, #53/12/3037, Box 2, Division of Rare and Manuscripts Collections, Cornell University Library), quoted in Aronson, supra note 2 at 221.

discovery, they learned that in fact, the band in Ponce's blood was actually 10.35 kb, and the band from the bloody watch measured 10.16 kb. (The reported 10.25 was in fact the average of the two measurements.) Small variations in measurement were nothing uncommon—the hard question was how much discrepancy in measured size could still support the claim that the two bands really did "match."

In published papers, Lifecodes had maintained that technicians first made matches "visually"—in other words, they "eyeballed" the autorads to see if they looked the same. But they also claimed that visual matches were confirmed through computerized comparison, and their own protocols required that the bands size be within three standard deviations of each other in order to call it a match. But Lander found that 10.16 and 10.35 differed from each other by more than three standard deviations! And this wasn't the only example of overreaching. Similarly, he found that one of the bands on another of Ponce's loci differed from the "matching" band on the bloodstain by more than 3 standard deviations. In other words, if Lifecodes had followed their own published standards about when to declare a match, they should have concluded that the blood from the watch and Vilma Ponce's blood did *not* definitively match.

On cross-examination, Michael Baird was forced to acknowledge that, no matter what the published papers said, in fact, Lifecodes technicians often just identified a match solely through visual observation, rather than using any predetermined objective standards. Scheck was pleased by this damaging concession, and lifted his arms "in a touchdown-like motion," to the irritation of the district attorney. On redirect, Baird pointed out that all of the measured bands were within three standard deviations of the *average* measurement. When Lander testified later in the hearing, he mocked Baird's effort to recover: "That's similar to saying New York and Boston are both within one hundred and twenty-five miles [of] each other because they're each within one hundred and twenty-five miles of Hartford. I found it somewhat difficult to take seriously."

Even more disturbing, while Lifecodes was clearly a little loose about what measurements were required for declaring a match, when it came time to determine the probability of a match, they used a different matching rule, one much stricter than 3 standard deviations. In essence, it was as if they were using one set of rules for deciding whether a match existed, and then a much stricter rule for determining the statistical likelihood that two samples matched. To illustrate, suppose that I wanted to know how many law students at a particular school were both 24 years old and had summer birthdays. In order to decide who counted, suppose I defined "summer" broadly and counted all 24 year olds with birthdays anytime between March and October, inclusive. But then in order to decide how likely it was that someone I picked at random from the law school community would "match" my criteria—that is, be 24 and have a summer birthday—suppose I now only counted those people with birthdays between June and August. Using these narrower criteria, I might find that only 1 in 25 people picked at random matched. But using the broader criteria, I might find instead that 1 in 10 matched. The misleading aspect is to use *one* criterion for determining what counts as a match and a *different* one for interpreting the probability of a match—and yet that is exactly what Lifecodes seemed to have done. As Lander put it in his testimony:

> Whatever choice you make for your matching rule, when you go and tell a court what is the chance this would have arisen at random in the population, you had better be using the same matching rule. To do otherwise is to report a probability that is simply not true. If I go out and I catch matches with a ten-foot wide butterfly net and I say I caught a match, and then I come to court and I say, and it was so rare that I caught this match, and I will prove it to you by showing that when I go out with a six inch butterfly net, I never catch matches in the population, that would be absurd.

The defense, by looking closely at the actual data on which Lifecodes' claims were made, was therefore able to show significant problems with Lifecodes' implementations of their own procedures.

## The Special Problems of Forensic Science

In the research and diagnostic setting, and with paternity testing as well, the issues involved with using DNA are more straightforward. Blood is plentiful. It can be taken under sterile conditions, and kept uncontaminated. If something isn't quite right with one testing procedure, the scientist can run another sample just to make sure. If the scientist runs out of blood, she can go back to the source and get more. By contrast, in the forensic setting, scientists often have only minute samples of blood, perhaps quite old, possibly contaminated with bacteria or other materials from the crime scene—and some of these contaminants might themselves contain other DNA. Depending on the sample size and the techniques used, running one sample might use up all of the available blood—in which case, if anything goes wrong, the examiner would be out of luck. As Judge Sheindlin put it in his opinion in *Castro*, "for forensic purposes, there is only one bite at the apple."[14]

One of the ways that scientists using the new technology made sure that everything was working properly was by having a "control lane," in which they tested DNA from a known source, to make certain that all of

---

[14] People v. Castro, 144 Misc. 2d 956, 970 (N.Y. 1989). DNA technology has, however, changed since *Castro*. Techniques for multiplying minute quantities of DNA now allow DNA comparisons that were impossible in 1989.

the probes were working properly. In *Castro*, Lifecodes had properly used a control lane—but figuring out whose DNA had been used in the control lane became a comedy of errors. At first, Baird testified that the blood used in the control lane came from the HeLa cell line, a commercially available cell line widely-used in research and experimentation. But another Lifecodes employee testified that the blood probably came from a male scientist who worked at Lifecodes, and Baird subsequently agreed with this assessment. However, the control DNA had not reacted with a probe that targeted parts of the Y-chromosome—which, if the control DNA were male, it should have done. Baird explained that this Lifecodes employee must have an unusual genetic condition in which his Y chromosome was "short," and thus happened not to react with this probe.

Lander was skeptical. A genetic condition like the one Baird described would be extremely rare—and it would be both odd and extremely poor judgment to use for control purposes the DNA of an employee who was so genetically atypical. Upon further investigation, Lifecodes established that sure enough, the "control" DNA belonged to a *different* Lifecodes employee, this time a female.

The defense suggested that the dreadful recordkeeping and sloppiness illustrated by Lifecodes' inability accurately to identify the source of the control DNA was both inexcusable and illustrative of a more general pattern of unjustifiably poor quality control that made their results uncertain and untrustworthy. Lander detailed many other problems with the laboratory's records: failures to note experiments that had been run, failure to note dates accurately, failure to label autorads correctly. While granting that "no one of these things is fatal," Lander opined that "so many of them are questionable here that it makes me worry a great deal about whether a recognized procedure was in place for doing [these experiments]." In addition, it appeared that Lifecodes had continued to use a probe even after they realized it was contaminated. At one point on the autorad, there was an extra band on Ponce's DNA not visible on the blood from the watch. Lifecodes went to great length, and performed several experiments, to establish that this extra band was bacterial in origin—the result of a contaminated probe, rather than the result of an actual difference between Ponce's DNA and the bloodstain from the watch. The defense suggested that to continue to use the contaminated probe was scientifically unacceptable. While Baird explained that they had no choice, because making a new probe would have entailed significant delays, the defense claimed this was another example of sloppiness, and an example of how commercial interests had gotten in the way of doing science properly.

At another locus, DSXY14, the DNA sample on the watch bloodstain revealed two bands that were not present in Ponce's blood. Baird testified that these "extra" bands were of unknown, non-human origin, and were simply the result of some kind of contamination of the watch stain. But how he could be certain that these bands were the result of contamination was far from clear. Though he claimed that they did not have the proper intensity for their length, which convinced him of their non-human origin, other credible witnesses—including Howard Cooke, the man who invented the very probe that Lifecodes was using at this locus—testified that there was no necessary correlation between band size and intensity.

The defense made much of the fact that Lifecodes did not do further experiments to establish whether or not these extra bands were the result of contamination. Nor did they endeavor to rule "in" these bands as genuine, even though there were experiments that could have given them more information on this score. By contrast, they put far greater energy into ruling "out" the extra band on Ponce's DNA. This difference in emphasis troubled Lander: if a laboratory "pursues all of the lines saying 'rule out possible differences' and does not chase down the path saying 'rule in possible differences,' one is putting oneself in the position of—well, one is running the risk of making mismatches." According to Lander, based on Lifecodes' analysis and the tests that they had actually conducted, "There's no reason those bands don't count."

Lander also emphasized the danger of examiner bias: the danger that people—even scientists—tend to see what they are looking for when they interpret an autorad. He said that in his lab at MIT, they sometimes joked about the risk that a scientist might "hallucinate a band" when they expected to see one, and "just as one hallucinates bands where one expects to see them, one tends to discount things where one does not expect to see them." Therefore conducting follow-up tests to check any interpretations that might have been colored by prior expectations was absolutely critical. In his opinion, Lifecodes had routinely failed to do that.

Lander also suggested that the Lifecodes had failed adequately to test to ensure that the DNA taken from the watch was not degraded. The most common alleles among the Hispanic population at one of the loci Lifecodes tested are above 10.25 kb, and if there had been degradation of the blood from the watch, it was possible that these alleles might not have shown up in the test. Lander outlined a simple test that would have offered assurances on this score, and criticized Lifecodes for not performing it.

Baird, in retrospect, thought that the problem was in part the daily reality of forensic science being evaluated from the lofty perspective of research scientists. He said in a 1994 interview, "the reality is that when you do a test on a forensic sample, it is what it is, and you have to interpret it. It isn't my fault if the sample is contaminated or mixed or shitty.... I'm just trying to interpret what's there."[15]

All in all, the defense was able to show persuasively that Lifecodes had exercised poor judgment, engaged in shoddy quality control practices, and that their conclusions could not simply be presumed accurate. As Judge Sheindlin wrote in his opinion, "In a piercing attack upon each molecule of evidence presented, the defense was successful in demonstrating to this court that the testing laboratory failed in its responsibility to perform the accepted scientific techniques and experiments in several major respects."

## Population Genetics

The defense also raised important issues in *Castro* about the way that Lifecodes had conducted its population genetics in the case; that is, the methods by which it determined not the fact of a match but its statistical meaning. To figure out how often one would expect to find two DNA samples that matched at a given set of loci, a scientist must have information about how frequently each allele is found in the population, and must also know to combine the likelihood of each particular allele into one combined frequency statistic.

If alleles at a particular locus are inherited at random within a given population, then that population is in what scientists call "Hardy–Weinberg equilibrium." If, within a given a population, the chance of inheriting a particular allele at one chromosomal location is unrelated to the chance of inheriting a particular allele at another locus, then the population is said to be in "linkage equilibrium."

If a population is in both Hardy–Weinberg equilibrium and linkage equilibrium, then determining the statistical meaning of a match is straightforward. As long as the inheritance within a locus and the chance of an association across loci is random, the frequency of an overall match can be determined using the product rule, a simple statistical calculation in which the probabilities of the chance of each genetic combination at a given allele are multiplied together. (For example, if the chances of the various allele combinations in a given population, found in a blood sample tested at four loci, were 1/1000, 1/80, 1/500 and 1/40, the combined chance of a randomly selected person from this population having all four allele combinations would be 1/1000 x 1/80 x 1/50 x 1/40, or 1/1,600,000).

If people chose their mates entirely at random, then the American population would be in Hardy–Weinberg equilibrium, and using the product rule would be an appropriate way to calculate the statistical

---

[15] Michael Baird interview, supra note 13, cited in Aronson supra note 2 at 243.

meaning of a match. However, in the real world, people do not choose their sexual partners at random; they are likely, statistically speaking, to choose partners similar to themselves in terms of ethnicity, race, and so forth. This creates the possibility of population "substructures" that makes calculating the statistical meaning of a match more complicated. For example, if Norwegians or Native Americans or New Englanders had a tendency to intermarry rather than choosing their spouses at random, a homozygous allele combination could possibly be far more common in one population group than it was in another. If scientists used only overall population statistics to measure the frequency of allele distributions, their calculations of the statistical probability of a match could depart dramatically from the true frequency. Perhaps the overall Caucasian population was homozygous at a particular locus only .01 percent of the time, but Norwegians were homozygous there 10 percent of the time. If a scientist used the overall Caucasian frequency in a case where the perpetrator was likely to be Norwegian, he would be overstating the statistical meaning of a match by a factor of 1000.

At the time of the *Castro* case, the usual forensic science approach to the problem of possible population substructure was to create population genetics databases for major racial categories: Caucasian, Black, Hispanic and, somewhat later, Asian. This approach rests on the assumptions that within these categories, people tend to choose mates at random (genetically speaking), and that the people who are the sources of the forensic science databases are a sufficiently representative sample of a given race.

In *Castro*, Lander challenged these assumptions. He examined the proportion of homozygotes in the aggregate raw data that Lifecodes had used for its Hispanic population database, and compared it to the proportion that he would have expected to be homozygous if the population were in equilibrium. For Ds244, for example, he would have expected, based on Lifecodes' published papers and data, that 4.7 percent of the population would be homozygous; instead, he found that the proportion in their sample was 17 percent. He concluded that this "surprisingly large number, statistically significant excess of homozygotes" made it "unacceptable" to conclude that the population was in Hardy–Weinberg equilibrium. In Lander's view, more study was needed regarding the real extent of population substructure, so that scientists would know enough to be able to make appropriate "corrections" to their probability calculations when needed.

**An Extraordinary Meeting**

Shortly after Eric Lander had finished testifying for the defense, he and Richard Roberts, one of the key witnesses for the prosecution in the case, ran into each other at a scientific meeting on genome mapping in

Cold Spring Harbor. Lander gave Roberts a copy of his written report about Lifecodes' DNA evidence in the case and suggested that Roberts would likely find it to be interesting reading. Roberts was certainly troubled by what he read. In fact, he was so troubled that he proposed that all of the expert witnesses in the case—both prosecution and defense witnesses—should gather to talk about the issues, scientist to scientist, no lawyers allowed. Although eight of the ten witnesses who were contacted liked the idea of meeting, only four were able to fit the meeting into their schedules. On May 11, 1989—before the conclusion of the preliminary hearing—Lander, Roberts, and two other witnesses (one from the defense, one from the prosecution) convened a mini-conference to see what they all thought about the evidence in *Castro*. They found that there was indeed much upon which they could agree.

After the meeting the attendees issued a joint statement that left the prosecutors in *Castro* almost helpless: "Overall, the DNA data in this case are not scientifically reliable enough to support the assertion that the samples ... do or do not match," they concluded. "If this data were submitted to a peer reviewed journal in support of a conclusion, it would not be accepted." The consensus of the experts on both sides that the evidence was invalid made it very difficult to imagine that the court would find it nonetheless to be "generally accepted" by the scientific community. All of the experts in the case, except for Michael Baird from Lifecodes, eventually endorsed the conclusions reached in this meeting.

The prosecution successfully kept the joint statement itself from being introduced in the hearing, on the grounds that it was hearsay. But the defense responded by calling several prosecution expert witnesses and getting them to repeat on the stand the conclusions that they had reached about the inadequacy of the particular DNA evidence in the case. In a way, the joint meeting and its consequences made Sheindlin's job in the *Castro* case a good deal easier: when the standard is "general acceptance" and the enormously-credentialed, hand-picked experts on both sides actually reach a *consensus*, who is the judge to second guess these shared conclusions of the experts?

Such a gathering of witnesses on both sides, *ex parte*, was of course highly irregular; with a flair for the dramatic, Peter Neufeld later called it "unprecedented in the annals of law." "We wanted to be able to settle the scientific issues through reasoned argument, to look at the evidence as scientists, not as adversaries," Richard Roberts explained afterwards to the press. "We all did so much better when we sat down without the lawyers, and had a reasoned scientific discussion. Perhaps it's time the system changed." Indeed, the scientists' joint statement criticized the use of the courtroom as a venue for reaching scientific consensus:

> All experts have agreed that the Frye test and the setting of the adversary system may not [be] the most appropriate method for reaching scientific consensus. The Frye hearing is not the appropriate time to begin the process of peer review of the data.... The setting also discourages many experts from agreeing to participate in the careful review of the data.[16]

The joint statement also called on the National Academy of Sciences to organize a committee to study the questions surrounding the use of forensic DNA.

Roberts, in particular, had harsh words for the adversarial process in his comments to the press. "Lawyers are more interested in getting certain words down on the written record than in arriving at the truth. Lawyers hope or want witnesses to say slightly more than they feel comfortable saying.... I do not find that the best way to reach the truth." While the scientists' discomfort with adversarial processes is understandable, it is also undoubtedly the case that *Castro*—the hearing itself, the ruling, and the significant publicity—revealed far more about how Lifecodes was conducting its DNA tests than any non-adversarial process had yet done. Outside of the setting of the courtroom, it is very difficult to imagine a research scientist of Eric Lander's caliber spending as much time and effort analyzing in detail the work product of a commercial forensic laboratory. The adversarial process has both flaws and excesses, but it also is a setting in which participants can drill down, analyze, and unpack weaknesses in evidence in ways that may sometimes risk being unfair—but that also can be very revealing. Lander, for example, was able to work with Lifecodes' data and examine their protocols because courts can force the disclosure of material that in other settings could be kept confidential as trade secrets and proprietary information.

Roberts himself had testified in a number of earlier cases for Lifecodes, without ever having seen the kinds of data that Lander, Scheck and Neufeld had insisted upon in *Castro*. He simply assumed that the prosecutor and Lifecodes were showing him all of the relevant information. He had seen his role primarily as providing background information about DNA in general, but of course, both his presence and the substance of his testimony served to shore up the legitimacy of the forensic use of DNA in particular. While his criticisms of the adversarial system should be taken seriously, it is also important to recognize, as sociologist of science Jay Aronson points out, "until [Roberts] was confronted with information presented by a witness who only emerged because of the adversarial legal process (Lander), he was unaware of the

---

[16] "Statement of the Independent Expert Scientists Having Testified in the Frye Hearing in People v. Castro," 11 May 1989, quoted in Aronson, supra note 2 at 250.

problems associated with the technique and had almost complete faith in the work of a company that he knew very little about." There is certainly the risk that the adversary process encourages expert participants to make stronger statements than they would in other settings, to become partisans rather than fair-minded evaluators, or to overstate minor errors or mistakes that may be an inevitable part of any human endeavor. And yet, the adversary process can have a productive dimension as well: until the hearing in *Castro*, no one had any idea that Lifecodes was not following its own procedures and protocols in a variety of meaningful ways. Up to that point, neither scientific conferences, nor publication, nor peer review, nor internal laboratory checks nor audits had brought to light what the adversary process made quite visible: both the significant deficiencies in how Lifecodes had handled the DNA in the Castro case, and more generally, that there were a number of important, not fully resolved problems relating to the transfer of DNA technology into the forensic setting.

### The Ruling

At the end of the preliminary hearing, Judge Sheindlin had presided over the longest, most in-depth legal examination of DNA profiling that had ever taken place. He had listened to days on end of testimony at the cutting edge of science, no doubt often far outside of his comfort zone. As he told the defense counsel at one point during Lander's cross-examination, "I am still not comfortable with some of the testimony presented by this witness, in terms of, not his credibility, but in terms of its understanding ... I know approximately what it is that this witness is testifying to. I understand the two-thirds deviation and the gaucian [sic] curve and adding the bins and not adding the bins.... I am not comfortable, as I told you, with some of the other explanations.... although I don't have the support staff which can give me input, I don't have any scientists who I can ask about these things; therefore, I stand up here—sit up here alone attempting, as best as I can struggle. I work on [these issues] after Court session until late in the evening so that I can understand it."

In his ruling, Judge Sheindlin explained that he would be guided by a three-prong test for examining whether the prosecution's DNA evidence met the *Frye* standard of general acceptance:

> Prong 1. Is there a theory, which is generally accepted in the scientific community, which supports the conclusion that DNA forensic testing can produce reliable results?

> Prong II. Are there techniques or experiments that currently exist that are capable of producing reliable results in DNA identification and which are generally accepted in the scientific community?

Prong III. Did the testing laboratory perform the accepted scientific techniques in analyzing the forensic sample in this particular case?[17]

Sheindlin recognized that courts often viewed the *Frye* test as encompassing only the first two prongs, figuring that the third prong—the case-specific implementation of the general tests—went to the weight of the evidence rather than its admissibility. Whether or not the third prong was appropriately defined as part of the *Frye* test or as something separate from it, Sheindlin thought that it was a crucial focus for pre-trial assessment of DNA. "[G]iven the complexity of the DNA multistem identification tests and the powerful impact that they may have on the jury, passing muster under *Frye* alone is insufficient to place this type of evidence before a jury without a preliminary, critical examination of the actual testing procedures performed in a particular case," he explained.[18]

That he took this approach in his ruling would have come as no surprise to the participants, for in conversations with them, as well as on the record in the pre-trial hearing, Sheindlin had laid out his intention to follow precisely this approach. In an extensive colloquy, Sheindlin explained to the attorneys his discomfort with the failure of earlier DNA rulings to focus on the *particular* techniques and any possible shortcomings in the way the DNA had been tested in that specific case, and expressed his intention to examine each of these three prongs, though he also made clear that if the evidence or the attorneys persuaded him that this approach was unsuitable, he would reconsider his approach. Scheck was uncomfortable with his three prongs, and in particular tried to emphasize to the judge that there was substantial overlap between Prongs II and III. While Sheindlin granted that there was "an overspill," and "a gray area" between these two prongs, he nonetheless reiterated that his working plan was to consider each prong separately.

And that is precisely what Sheindlin did in his ruling. Going through the prongs one by one, he provided an introductory primer to both DNA identification in general (prong I), and the forensic use of DNA for determining identification (prong II). Prong I was, he thought, quite unproblematic: "The evidence in this case clearly establishes unanimity among all the scientists and lawyers as well that DNA identification is capable of producing reliable results." Sheindlin also answered Prong II, the question of whether there were presently techniques for reliably making DNA identifications in the *forensic* context, in the affirmative.

But when it came to the third prong, whether the specific tests in this case were adequately performed by the laboratory in analyzing the

---

[17] People v. Castro, 144 Misc. 2d 956, 960 (N.Y.1989).

[18] Castro, 144 Misc.2d 956.

DNA sample, Sheindlin's answer was a resounding "no." He spent several pages describing the "major respects" in which Lifecodes "failed to conduct the necessary and scientifically accepted tests," such as their unacceptable use of an apparently contaminated probe, their failure to use adequate controls for sex typing, their failure to do further tests to assess the two extra bands seemingly visible in the watch sample, and their failure to use the same standards for measuring the existence of a match and assessing its statistical probability. As a result of these many lapses, Sheindlin concluded that he would permit at trial any evidence of exclusion—that is, that two samples did not match—but he would exclude the evidence suggesting a match between the watch sample and Vilma Ponce's DNA. In other words, the prosecution would be able to offer evidence that the blood found on the watch did not belong to Castro, but they would not be permitted to say that it was almost certainly Ponce's.

Because Sheindlin decided that the evidence of a DNA match would not be permitted at trial, he deemed it unnecessary to delve into the questions of population genetics and frequency estimations. At the conclusion of his ruling, Sheindlin also provided some "suggested procedures" for future Prong III hearings, mostly detailing what should appropriately be included in discovery.

This marked the conclusion of what "some have referred to as the most comprehensive and extensive legal examination of DNA forensic identification tests held to date in the United States."[19] Sheindlin's decision marked the very first time that any American judge had restricted the use of DNA evidence in court. In addition, his opinion made clear that, when scrutinized carefully, DNA tests in actual practice might turn out to have serious flaws.

And yet, without a doubt, Sheindlin's framework cabined the defense victory by making the emphasis quite particularistic and local, emphasizing Lifecodes' sloppy examination of *this* DNA comparison rather than recognizing problems with forensic DNA analysis more generally. Given the many embarrassing revelations that had emerged at trial, and considering the consensus view by the end of the hearing of nearly all of both sides' experts, that this particular DNA test could not be validly interpreted, an opinion that rejected the DNA evidence in this case without formally casting any doubt on the forensic use of DNA more generally was about the best outcome that the prosecution could have reasonably hoped for. In fact, in their final brief, the prosecution acknowledged that the DNA evidence in this case was insufficiently reliable: "Here, the People believe that we have not met our burden of demonstrating by a preponderance of the evidence that the accepted

---

[19] Castro, 144 Misc. 2d at 960.

scientific techniques were utilized in this case. The scientific evidence generated in this case, as a whole, is too ambiguous to be admissible in a criminal case."[20]

By the time the hearing was over, the prosecution was thus granting that this particular DNA match was unreliable, and was hoping that Sheindlin would nonetheless recognize the general validity of forensic DNA typing. In this sense, although they of course had been forced by the defense over the course of the hearing to back-pedal considerably, the prosecution got exactly what it had hoped for from Judge Sheindlin's ruling. By contrast, Scheck and Neufeld were sorely disappointed: from their point of view, there was little reason to believe that Lifecodes had been unusually careless or sloppy in their testing of the evidence in *Castro*. It seemed clear to them that the problems with Lifecodes' protocols and quality control were both systemic and widespread, rather than the result of atypical lapses in this particular case alone. They would no doubt have preferred it had Sheindlin reached a more general conclusion, clearly signaling that forensic DNA, while highly promising, was not ready for prime time. They would have liked him to have recognized that the problems with Lifecodes' analysis were so serious as to implicate his second as well as his third prong.

Though Sheindlin's unwillingness to make his criticisms in a more generalized way greatly frustrated Scheck and Neufeld, Sheindlin's analysis under Prong II was not a complete whitewash of Lifecodes in particular or forensic DNA more generally. The opinion did recognize the importance of inquiring into technology *transfer*. Unlike several of the earlier judges who had assessed the admissibility of DNA evidence, Sheindlin well understood that the validity of DNA identification techniques in other contexts did not necessarily translate into reliability in the forensic context, where there might be particular problems arising from the sometimes miniscule amounts of available biological material, from possible contamination or deterioration of the sample, and from more difficult problems of measurement and interpretation. Even though Sheindlin did rule that presently available techniques were adequate for dealing with these special difficulties of forensic DNA testing, the opinion was significant for at least recognizing them as difficulties that had to be dealt with.

Moreover, Sheindlin explicitly took issue with the widespread assumption, captured, for example by the court's ruling in *People v. Wesley*, that DNA testing would automatically produce either the right answer or no answer at all. Sheindlin explained that while several earlier cases had suggested that "improper procedures and experiments will

---

[20] Timothy Clifford, *DNA–Test Errors Conceded*, Newsday (July 4, 1989 at 7) (quoting from memorandum submitted by the prosecution in *People v. Castro*).

automatically and clearly be revealed, this court, on the contrary, advises caution in reviewing the procedures. For example, contaminated samples, probes or controls, may produce extra bands on the autorads which can cause differing scientific opinions in the interpretation of the autorads. On the other hand, degradation of a sample may fail to produce a band, again resulting in interpretation problems." Any court that took *Castro* seriously could no longer repeat the oft-made, comforting claim that there was no such thing as a false positive when DNA was examined, nor buy into the implicit corollary that a DNA test was virtually self-interpreting.

Thus the case was quite a mixed result. Certainly it was a partial and significant victory for the defense, but at the same time, because it was so narrowly drawn, the Bronx district attorney's office could simultaneously call it a "victory of national importance" that reaffirmed the general validity and admissibility of DNA evidence. Interestingly, the opinion itself makes only a passing and opaque reference to the important fact that by the time the hearing had concluded, almost all of the experts for both sides (and even the prosecution itself) had conceded that the DNA test in this case was inconclusive. The savvy reader can find, in footnote 12, an aside mention that two of the prosecution's experts were recalled by the defense and, having earlier testified to the reliability of DNA identification, now allowed that the laboratory's lapses made this particular result inconclusive.

When Joseph Castro pleaded guilty to second degree murder on September 15, 1989, he admitted that the blood on the watch was likely that of Vilma Ponce after all. With that, the *Castro* case officially came to an end, but the controversies over DNA most certainly did not.

## The Aftermath and the Broader Consequences of *Castro*

In the wake of *Castro*, Lifecodes made several significant changes to their internal procedures. For example, they began to use a computer-based matching system instead of relying only on visual comparison to declare a match, and they modified the way that they determined the frequency of alleles in their population databases: essentially, they took a number of Eric Lander's suggestions. (Lander himself was invited to testify in 57 DNA cases in the six months after *Castro*. Though he provided some technical assistance in a handful of select cases, he turned down all 57 of the offers to testify.)

In addition, the *Castro* hearing, along with the joint statement signed by the experts from both sides, fueled a growing belief that forensic DNA needed to be examined and studied by an authoritative, neutral group of scientists and other experts. In December 1989, the National Academy of Sciences appointed a committee to investigate and, if possible, forge a consensus, about the scientific resolution of the many technical and procedural issues surrounding the forensic use of DNA that the *Castro* hearing had highlighted.

Considering the many revelations of the pre-trial hearing, Sheindlin's opinion was about as narrowly-drawn as possible, but it was still a watershed moment for the forensic use of DNA. Along the way, the case had received a good deal of publicity, and newspapers in the months after *Castro* wrote about DNA quite differently than they had before. Doubt and uncertainty replaced the earlier tendency toward breathless enthusiasm. "DNA fingerprinting doesn't live up to initial promise," read one headline in the fall of 1989; "DNA 'Fingerprinting' Questioned; Geneticist Says Test May Be Less Reliable Than First Believed," said another. "Caution Urged on DNA Fingerprinting," warned *Science* magazine. "DNA Tests Unravel?" asked the *National Law Journal*. After *Castro*, journalists, the public, judges, and jurors all became more willing to question DNA: it no longer seemed like an infallible magic bullet.

*Castro* affected the scientific landscape as well. In June, 1989, Eric Lander published an article in *Nature* concluding that the courts had been "too hasty" to accept DNA. He described in detail why forensic DNA fingerprinting is far more technically challenging than the diagnostic use of DNA. He also laid out a challenge to the scientific community: "It is my belief that we, the scientific community, have failed to set rigorous standards to which courts, attorneys, and forensic-testing laboratories can look for guidance—with the result that some of the conclusions presented to courts are quite unreliable." He described the many problems with Lifecodes' evidence in the *Castro* case and in other cases, and called in strong terms for both additional scientific study and greater regulation and oversight.[21] The case thus spurred greater scientific interest in the actual practices of forensic DNA testing and led to increased attention to questions of quality control, autorad interpretation, and population genetics.

In this changed climate, defense attorneys became both more aggressive about challenging DNA and better able to locate the people and resources to mount effective challenges. In addition, more scientists began to evince a professional interest in the issues raised by forensic DNA evidence, especially in the questions surrounding population genetics and the statistical meaning of a match. After *Castro*, there is no doubt that DNA evidence in court received substantially more scrutiny—and a number of courts, including several state supreme courts, decided

---

[21] Lander noted that "at present, forensic science is virtually unregulated—with the paradoxical result that clinical laboratories must meet higher standards to be allowed to diagnose strep throat than forensic labs must meet to put a defendant on death row." Rorie Sherman, National Law Journal (December 18, 1989, at 1).

that problems with the DNA evidence made either restriction or exclusion necessary.

Indeed, over the next few years, the legal controversies over DNA increased in intensity and vociferousness. A *Los Angeles Times Magazine* article could write, in 1992, that "the battle over DNA fingerprinting has become the most entertaining and bewildering legal spectacle around." While quality control issues remained significant, and questions of autorad interpretation received increased focus and attention, the most significant issue of all—both in the courtroom and in the pages of prestigious scientific journals—came to be the question of population genetics and the extent of substructure within a given population. In the courtroom, these issues came to a head in cases like *United States v. Yee*[22]—in which the defendant was represented by none other than Barry Scheck and Peter Neufeld. The case was fought aggressively by both sides—so aggressively that each viewed the other as going beyond all reasonable limits in their efforts to win the case. Moreover, the politics of the court cases affected the doings of science: in a highly unusual move, the authors of an article on population genetics issues in the prestigious journal *Science* were asked by the editor to "tone down" their article, and the magazine—in part because of a recommendation by a member of their board of reviewing directors who also had a licensing relationship with Cellmark, one of the forensic DNA companies—decided to publish a simultaneous "rebuttal" alongside the original article. While in the end, the presiding magistrate judge in *Yee* decided to permit the DNA evidence, the legal decision only fanned the flames of the ongoing scientific controversies over population substructure.

In the meantime, the National Research Council (the research arm of the National Academy of Sciences) issued its long-awaited report in 1992. But instead of resolving disputes, the report generated new ones. It had proposed a compromise approach to the issue of population genetics that critics deemed scientifically unjustifiable, viewing it as an overtly political attempt at a compromise without scientific foundation. While the NRC report was being debated, scientific research proceeded, and some of the issues that had divided scientists or been insufficiently explored in 1989 were more or less resolved. In 1994 (and, not accidentally, just before the O.J. trial was beginning), the growing scientific consensus on these issues led Eric Lander and FBI DNA expert Bruce Budowle to publish a joint article in Nature entitled "DNA Fingerprinting Laid to Rest." While the O.J. Simpson case revealed starkly that DNA evidence was still controversial, the intense disputes over admissibility of the technique itself largely came to an end. When the NRC

---

[22] United States v. Yee, 134 F.R.D. 161 (N.D. Ohio 1991), aff'd sub nom. United States v. Bonds, 12 F. 3d 540 (6th Cir. 1993).

issued a follow-up report in 1996, its recommendations were received with far less controversy.

## A Precursor to *Daubert*

The significance of the *Castro* case goes beyond DNA itself in two important respects. First, the sheer detail and length of the hearing, and the tremendous focus on reliability—both of the technique in general and its particular application in the case—revealed a quite different approach to the evaluation of science in court than was typically seen under the *Frye* standard of general acceptance. *Castro* was an example of a growing trend by the courts to engage in the substantive assessment of the reliability of expert evidence, a trend that has only grown over the years since *Castro* was decided. In 1993, the Supreme Court decided in *Daubert v. Merrell Dow* that the Federal Rules of Evidence did not incorporate the *Frye* test of general acceptance, but that trial courts nonetheless had an obligation to serve as gatekeepers with respect to expert evidence to ensure that it was sufficiently valid and reliable.[23] Although many states (including New York) have continued to use the *Frye* test, there has been an undeniable, though uneven, trend to examine expert evidence with increased scrutiny. Whether courts should be in the business of assessing the substance of scientific evidence— whether they have the know-how or the institutional competence—are certainly fair questions. But *Castro* is of a piece with this more general trend over the last several decades to examine scientific evidence proffered in court with increasing detail and care.

## *Castro* as a Beacon: The Forensic Science Issue

If *Castro* stands for anything, it stands for the idea that the standards of research science are highly relevant for evaluating forensic science. Eric Lander's critique could be boiled down, in significant part, to the concern that Lifecodes was not taking issues of quality control, interpretation, and population genetics as seriously as an academic research laboratory would, and that given the stakes involved, this failure was unjustifiable and inexcusable. To meet the standards of academic scientific laboratories does not require perfection—time and time again, in his testimony, Lander emphasized that no laboratory operates completely without errors. But he saw no reason why commercially-run forensic science laboratories should be given anything approaching a free pass.

The DNA cases like *Castro*, along with *Daubert*'s increasing focus on judicial gatekeeping, have in recent years given ammunition to critics of many other forms of forensic science. Although some forensic science

---

[23] 509 U.S. 579 (1993).

techniques have been in use for a century or more, many approaches to identification science, including handwriting identification evidence and fingerprinting, simply do not have the kind of empirical basis for their claims to validity that one would ordinarily associate with research science. These and similar forensic "sciences" may usually provide "right" answers, but because they have been subject to little rigorous validity testing, it is difficult to assess the real-world frequency of error. Of course, in *Castro* itself, notwithstanding the significant problems with Lifecodes' procedures, the laboratory's bottom-line conclusion that the watch stain matched Ponce's blood was, it seems, correct—but Sheindlin's decision to exclude the evidence was nonetheless indisputably the right answer based on the record before him. Other kinds of forensic science evidence raise problems analogous to those faced in the *Castro* case. Although fingerprint experts testify that they can identify a match with 100 percent certainty and to the exclusion of all other fingerprints in the world, fingerprinting lacks any kind of statistical foundation. Just as Lifecodes' technicians eyeballed an autorad to determine whether there was a match, fingerprint experts do not have formal standards or protocols for deciding when to declare a match. Nor do we have any real idea of how often, in the real world, fingerprint experts or handwriting identification experts make honest mistakes in their evaluations. Fingerprint experts' frequent insistence that their technique is error free is reminiscent of the early—and erroneous—claims with DNA that there was no such thing as a false positive.[24]

The DNA cases, combined with *Daubert*, have led a set of defense lawyers to mount in recent years a number of challenges to other forms of forensic science. Some of the challenges to handwriting have been successful; the challenges to fingerprinting largely have not. But *Castro* invites the questions: should we evaluate forensic science differently from other kinds of scientific enterprises, and, if so, upon what justification? If not, then should these kinds of evidence be excluded or limited until further research and study validates both the proficiency of the examiners and the scientific bases for their claims? And so, we end with an irony: the technique that drew its earliest authority from a metaphoric association with "fingerprinting" may, in the end, help to reveal the weaknesses of fingerprinting and other forms of forensic science.

## SUGGESTED READINGS

Howard Coleman & Eric Swenson, DNA in the Courtroom: A Trial Watcher's Guide (Genelex, 1994).

---

[24] An historian of fingerprinting has recently documented 22 publicly-known instances of fingerprinting identification error, and argues persuasively that these known misattributions probably account for only a small fraction of the mistakes that have actually been made. See Simon Cole, *More Than Zero. Accounting for Error in Latent Fingerprint Identification*, 95 J. Crim. L. & Criminology 985 (2005).

David H. Kaye, DNA Evidence: Probability, Population Genetics, and the Courts, 7 Harv. J. Law and Tech. 101 (1993).

Jonathan J. Koehler, On Conveying the Probative Value of DNA Evidence: Frequencies, Likelihood Ratios and Error Rates. 67 University of Colorado Law Review 859 (1996).

Richard Lempert, After the DNA Wars: Skirmishing with NRC II, 37 Jurimetrics J. 439 (1997).

Michael Lynch and Sheila Jasanoff, eds., special issue on Contested Identities: Science, Law and Forensic Practice, 28 Social Studies of Science (1998).

Jennifer L. Mnookin, Fingerprint Evidence in an Age of DNA Profiling, 67 Brooklyn L. Rev. 13 (2001).

David Lazer, ed., DNA and the Criminal Justice System : The Technology of Justice (MIT Press, 2004).

National Research Council, DNA Technology in Forensic Science 51–52 (National Acad. Press 1992).

National Research Council, The Evaluation of Forensic DNA Evidence (National Acad. Press 1996).

Barry Scheck, DNA and Daubert, 15 Cardozo L. Rev. 1959 (1994).

William C. Thompson, Evaluating the Admissibility of New Genetic Identification Tests: Lessons from the "DNA War", 84 J. Crim L. & Criminology 22 (1993).

William C. Thompson & Simon Ford, DNA Typing: Acceptance and Weight of the New Genetic Identification Tests, 75 Va L. Rev. 45 (1989).

\*

# 10

## The Story of *Mahlandt v. Wild Canid Survival & Research Center, Inc.*: Encounters of Three Different Kinds

### Professor Eleanor Swift[*]

Whether or not it is true that "every dog gets one bite," it is not true for wolves. A pet wolf's *first* injurious bite will subject the owner to liability. For owners (and keepers) of wolves, liability for the wolf's injurious behavior is not based on knowledge, negligence or fault; the wolf need not ever have bitten anyone or ever have behaved in a vicious or dangerous manner. A wolf is a wild animal, *ferae naturae* as referred to at common law, and as such is presumed to be dangerous. As Professor Prosser put it, liability here is "an instance of the strict responsibility placed upon those who, even with proper care, expose the community to the risk of a very dangerous thing."[1]

It still must be shown in a wolf bite case, of course, that the wolf did bite or otherwise attack a person, causing injury. In the case of *Mahlandt v. Wild Canid Survival & Research Center, Inc.,*[2] this was the only disputed issue. On March 23, 1973, a little boy was found injured, inside a backyard enclosure in St. Louis where Sophie the wolf was kept. The boy's parents sued both the owner and the keeper of the wolf. No one had seen what happened except Sophie and the boy, who was found not competent to testify about the incident in court. But after the incident

---

[*] School of Law (Boalt Hall), University of California at Berkeley.

[1] Prosser, Law of Torts, § 75, Animals, p. 513. This principle of absolute liability was accepted in the vast majority of jurisdictions at the time of the *Mahlandt* case and was referenced in Missouri case law.

*See* Restatement of the Law of Torts §§ 507, 510; Anno., 21 A.L.R.3d pp. 608, 618; 4 Am.Jur.2d, Animals, § 80 et seq.; Merritt v. Matchett, 115 S.W. 1066 (Mo.App. 1909).

[2] 588 F.2d 626 (8th Cir. 1978).

Sophie's keeper several times said, "Sophie bit a child." These statements were hearsay because the parents wanted to use them to prove the truth of the matter asserted. In addition, they were not based on the keeper's personal knowledge of the incident.

The plaintiffs sought admission of these hearsay statements at trial as "party admissions," made by the keeper of the wolf and offered against him and against his employer, the Wild Canid Survival & Research Center, which owned the wolf. The federal district judge excluded these statements, and the jury found for the defense. On appeal, the Eighth Circuit Court of Appeals reversed and remanded for a new trial, holding that the Federal Rules of Evidence, specifically Rule 801(d)(2), required admission of the statements. On remand the parties settled out of court.

This abbreviated sketch of the *Mahlandt* litigation masks the human drama behind this traumatic incident and ensuing trial. Drawing on the trial transcript and the companion court papers, Part One of this essay tells the story of the injured child, Danny Mahlandt, and his encounter with the wolf, Sophie. Part Two explains why U.S. District Court Judge H. Kenneth Wangelin, in his encounter with the then recently enacted Federal Rules of Evidence, decided to exclude the crucial hearsay statements. It suggests that Judge Wangelin perceived a conflict between the literal application of the Rules in this case and the search for truth. It further suggests that Judge Wangelin assumed that he had the authority to decide how the value of truth would best be served. The Eighth Circuit opinion stands for the proposition that the trial judge does not have this authority, at least not under the categorical language of the hearsay exemptions for party and vicarious admissions. Part Three of this essay examines the justifications for this holding, revealing tension between the Federal Rules and the values of our adversary system of justice. It asks whether trial judge discretion to exclude seemingly unreliable admissions would resolve that tension.

### Part One

### The Mahlandts' Case: An Encounter Between a Boy and a Wolf

The story begins in 1973, in University City, Missouri, an academic and professional community close to Washington University in St. Louis.[3] Its main characters are members of two families who lived across

---

[3] All of the facts stated in the narrative are undisputed unless specifically stated otherwise. This account is based on records stored in the National Archives and Records Administration: The Docket Sheet in Case Number 76–606C; Complaint; Separate Answer of Defendant Wild Canid Survival & Research Center, Inc.; Joint Answer of Defendants Kenneth Poos and Jean Poos; Suggestions of Plaintiffs in Opposition to Motion of Defendant to Dismiss; Plaintiffs' Pre-trial Compliance and Memorandum; Compliance of Defendant with Pre-trial Order; Objections to Plaintiffs' Exhibits; Plaintiffs' Motion for

the street from each other. Donald and Dorcas Eugenia (Jean) Mahlandt and their five children lived in a corner house on the north side of Pershing street. Kenneth and Jean Poos and their four children lived on the south side of Pershing, one house to the west of the Mahlandt home. The neighborhood was close-knit, children often playing in each other's homes and yards.

Around mid-day on March 23, 1973, Jean Mahlandt told her youngest child Danny, who was three years and ten months old at the time, to find his brother at the Thompson house, located directly behind the Pooses' property, and to bring him home. She watched Danny cross Pershing and start walking down a narrow walkway between the Pooses' yard and the side wall of the neighboring house to the east in order to get to the Thompsons' home.

Danny never reached the Thompsons' house. Instead, within minutes, he was found lying inside the chain link fence which surrounded the Pooses' back yard, crying hysterically and bleeding profusely from lacerations on his face and legs. Sophie the wolf was chained to the inside of the fence, and she was wailing. Clarke Poos, at sixteen the Pooses' oldest child, heard Danny's cries as he left a neighbor's home. From his own front yard, he saw Danny and Sophie inside the fence. Running to his back gate, Clarke entered the back yard, picked up Danny and brought him into the Pooses' back porch. Clarke's sister Dee Dee ran across the street to get Jean Mahlandt, who, arriving at the Poos home, found Danny lying on the floor of the porch, still bleeding. Soon police arrived on the scene, and Danny and his mother left for the hospital in an ambulance. Danny was treated by a plastic surgeon, receiving more than 200 stitches to close his facial lacerations, stitches inside his mouth to repair the avulsion of his lower lip from his jawbone, and stitches for puncture wounds and lacerations on his legs. He stayed in the hospital for three days, and then received rabies shots, medical monitoring and psychological counseling.

Just before Danny and his mother left for the hospital, Kenneth Poos, the father of Clarke and Dee Dee, arrived home from his work as Director of Education for the Wild Canid Survival & Research Center. Sophie belonged to the Center. Poos was Sophie's keeper. Sophie had lived with the Poos family for five months since leaving her home at the

---

New Trial and Memorandum; Plaintiffs' Notice of Appeal; Appellants' Brief in the United States Court of Appeals for the Eighth Circuit; Brief of Appellee Wild Canid Survival & Research Center, Inc.; and Petition of Appellee Wild Canid Survival & Research Center, Inc., for Rehearing.

The story of the Mahlandt case has been told once before. See Bein, *Parties' Admissions, Agents' Admissions: Hearsay Wolves in Sheep's Clothing*, 12 Hofstra L.Rev. 393 (1984). In that article, Professor Bein summarized some of the facts of the case, some of the trial testimony, and developed her own analysis of the hearsay issues.

St. Louis Children's Zoo. Kenneth Poos learned that no eyewitness had seen how Danny crossed the fence and got into the Pooses' yard, or how he was injured. But Poos's suspicions fell on Sophie as the cause of the injuries, and he later made the statements, "Sophie bit a child," that were crucial to the Mahlandts' case.

***The Lawsuit.*** On July 7, 1976, more than three years after this distressing event, the Mahlandts filed a lawsuit in the United States District Court in St. Louis. Named as a plaintiff was Daniel Mahlandt, a minor, by and through his parents Donald Mahlandt and Dorcas Eugenia (Jean) Curry[4] who were appointed by the court to be Danny's representatives for purposes of this suit. The complaint named the Wild Canid Survival & Research Center, Inc. as a corporate defendant, and Kenneth and Jean Poos as individual defendants. Subject matter jurisdiction was based on diversity of citizenship pursuant to 28 U.S.C. § 1332. Donald Mahlandt was alleged to now be a resident of Pennsylvania; Jean Curry, a resident of Nevada; Daniel, a resident of either Pennsylvania or Nevada; and all defendants were alleged to be residents of Missouri.

Count I of the complaint pleaded a theory of strict liability for injuries arising out of an attack by a domestically held wild animal. Count II pleaded negligence on a "dog bite" theory—that the Center and the Pooses knew or should have known that the wolf Sophie possessed dangerous and vicious characteristics. Damages of $250,000 were sought for Danny's medical and emotional trauma and the cost of his future treatment. Donald Mahlandt and Jean Curry, suing individually as plaintiffs, sought $25,000 for the medical expenses they had paid for Danny's treatment.

The defendants filed separate answers, denying all allegations except their own residency in Missouri.

***The Wolf.*** What makes this legally rather ordinary case extraordinarily interesting is, of course, Sophie. What was a wolf doing in the Pooses' yard in the middle of a neighborhood full of children? Did Sophie attack Danny after he got into the back yard on his own? Or, as was argued later, did she pull him under the fence by the foot, lacerating his face and legs on the sharp barbs at the bottom of the chain links? Or, did she do nothing to injure the child? How Danny was injured was the focus of most of the evidence at the trial. Sophie's story was also told at trial, but at this point she needs her own separate introduction as a member of the cast of characters.

Sophie was born in May of 1972 at the St. Louis Zoo. She was hand raised, meaning that from the moment she opened her eyes, she was

---

[4] Donald and Jean Mahlandt had been divorced, and Jean had married Jerome Curry, shortly after Danny was injured.

nurtured by human beings toward whom she, in the words of an expert who testified at trial, transferred her "whole allegiance" as her foster parents—"in a way the human being becomes a surrogate wolf." Sophie soon joined the Children's Zoo and she was raised there until the age of five months. She was a "contact animal," meaning that she was used for display and close contact by the thousands of children who visited the Children's Zoo on a daily basis.

Zoo policy required that Sophie leave the Children's Zoo as she approached six months in age, primarily due to constraints of space and supervision. Some concern about injuring children was obviously part of this policy, but there was no concern about Sophie in particular. She was described by both experts who knew her as "a very gentle wolf."

**The Center.** So, in September of 1972 the Zoo was looking for a home for Sophie. At the same time, the Wild Canid Survival and Research Center was looking for a wolf. The Center had been formed as a non-profit corporation several years before by a group of about twenty St. Louis residents who were interested in the conservation of wild canids (dogs, wolves, coyotes, jackals and foxes). Among the organizers of the Center were Dr. Marlin Perkins, the former Director of the St. Louis Zoo, famous for his pioneering 1950s television program called "Zoo Parade;" Dr. Owen Sexton, a Professor of Biology at Washington University; and Richard Grossenheider, a prominent wildlife artist and zoologist.

The Center planned to establish a preserve, the Tyson Research Center, where the canids owned by Grossenheider, and others as well, could be kept, conserved, studied, and used for educating the public. This preserve was in fact opened in September of 1973, six months after Danny was injured.

**The Wolf At Home.** Until the preserve was ready to receive animals, Sophie was the responsibility of Kenneth Poos, the Center's Director of Education, who had been hired by the Center in 1972. The care and handling of Sophie was an important part of Poos's job. She slept in a holding cage in the basement of the Poos home, and roamed at liberty in the Poos yard, surrounded by a chain link fence with gates which were kept locked. Most days, Sophie accompanied Poos on visits to schools and other groups as part of a program on wolves and other wild canids and the ecological roles they filled. Sophie, as might be expected, "was a focal point of interest for the young people." Children were allowed to pet her and at times "literally hundreds of students would crowd around her."

**Sophie's Companions.** Two other animals were living at the Poos home as family pets with Sophie. These were hybrid "sled dogs," crosses between a wolf and a husky-malamute, also known as "moofs." Although they, like Sophie, roamed free in the fenced-in Poos yard, their possible role in Danny's injuries was not explored. As plaintiffs' counsel stated in open court, "I'm just going Sophie."

***What the Other Neighbors Saw.*** Two neighbors of the Poos and Mahlandt families on Pershing played supporting roles in this story. John Gillis, an attorney who lived in St. Louis, was ill and home in bed on the day of the incident. Hearing a child screaming, Gillis looked out of his second story bedroom window and saw a small child lying prone in the Poos yard, straddled by Sophie the wolf. The wolf's face was near the child's, but Gillis was sufficiently far away that he "could not see what the wolf was doing with its jaws."

James Burgess, a physics professor at Washington University, lived next door to the Poos family. His family had a pet dog, a beagle, that would run along the west side of the Poos fence "yapping" at Sophie and the two moofs. On the west side, the fence was four feet high. On the day before Danny was injured, Sophie had jumped the four foot fence and made a four inch gash in the beagle's abdomen before Burgess's son separated them. Sophie had never jumped the fence before, and it was on account of this incident that Sophie was chained to the five foot fence on the east side of the Poos yard on March 23rd.

None of the Pooses' neighbors had ever expressed any serious concerns about the presence of a wolf in their neighborhood. Their children had been introduced to Sophie and had been inside her enclosure. There had been some complaints about Sophie and the moofs howling at night, and some of the older residents had expressed general concern. But the neighborhood was, in fact, very tolerant.

***Pre-Trial Proceedings.*** The trial of the Mahlandts' case against the Center and Kenneth and Jean Poos took place on November 9–11, 1977, fifteen months after the Complaint was filed. Pre-trial proceedings were minimal. The Center had filed a Motion to Dismiss based on the fact that the plaintiffs had also brought a suit against it in Missouri state court. The plaintiffs responded by taking a voluntary nonsuit in state court. Plaintiffs' counsels' reasons for preferring a trial in federal court are unknown. What can be known, and will be shown below, is that this case probably did not belong in federal court at all.

On March 11, 1977, the parties exchanged witness and exhibit lists. These documents reveal the simplicity of each party's theory of the case. The plaintiffs wanted the jury to hear all of the statements made after the incident that suggested or assumed that Sophie had bitten Danny. These included not just Kenneth Poos's statements, but also statements made (probably by Danny's mother) to Danny's treating physician, statements incorporated into the police report, written statements between members of the Board of Directors of the Center, statements made by Board members to the Center's insurance carrier, and statements incorporated into the minutes of the Board's meetings. In response to defendants' hearsay objections, the plaintiffs ultimately offered into evidence only three statements made by Kenneth Poos and one statement in the minutes of the Center's Board. The Center's witness list included those Board members (among them its expert Dr. Fox) who knew Sophie and were knowledgeable about wolf behavior in general. Their testimony would be akin to "character" evidence to show that Sophie would not attack a child. The plaintiffs prevailed in a legal dispute over whether Sophie was a wild or a domesticated animal, and the court later instructed the jury only on the theory of strict liability applicable to wild animals.

*The Lawyers.*[5] Counsel for the plaintiff Donald Mahlandt was Terence Crebs from a St. Louis law firm. Crebs took the lead at trial, assisted by Frank Susman who represented Mrs. Mahlandt and Danny separately due to the Mahlandts' divorce. The defense was conducted on behalf of all defendants by Eugene Buckley, a well-known and highly respected insurance defense attorney who actually represented the Center. The Pooses were represented by another firm, Richard Bender appearing for them at trial. The insurance company that carried the Pooses' homeowners' insurance had refused coverage for this incident. Thus the Pooses had to pay for their own legal representation, and had they been found liable, would have had to pay out of their own pocket. Since they had no significant assets, it was the view of one of the defense lawyers that Kenneth Poos was joined in the suit against the Center solely to secure the admission into evidence of his hearsay statements as party admissions.

*The Judge.* Presiding over the trial was District Court Judge H. Kenneth Wangelin, a former "country lawyer" and a past chair of the Missouri Republican Party, who had maintained a general practice in Poplar Bluff, Missouri, for many years before being appointed to the federal bench by President Nixon. Judge Wangelin had considerable trial experience and, like many country lawyers, had represented both plaintiffs and defendants. He is described as a colorful, humorous and interesting man, not a legal scholar but "an excellent listener who could get right to the heart of a case." Behind his bench he is said to have kept a shotgun (due to minimal courthouse security at the time) and in his office were deer and bear trophies.

---

[5] Telephone interviews were conducted with the two lawyers who represented the defendants in this case, Eugene Buckley and Richard Bender. Thomas Jayne, law clerk to Judge H. Kenneth Wangelin in 1976–78, when the *Mahlandt* case was heard, was also interviewed. Terence Crebs, lead counsel for the plaintiffs, is deceased. Judge Wangelin died in the mid–1980s.

It appears that Judge Wangelin listened very attentively at trial to the testimony given before him. He interjected questions of his own primarily to clarify locations and words used by the witnesses. For example, as the "barbs" at the top and bottom of the Pooses' chain link fence were mentioned during the testimony of Donald Mahlandt, Judge Wangelin clarified the meaning of that term:

> I don't know whether any of the Jury is from the country, knows what barbed wire is. The Court happens to know. . . . It's not your contention, anybody elses, that there was strands of barbed wire at the bottom of this fence?

He similarly tried to clarify the issues and move things forward during sidebar conferences with the lawyers. For example, concerned about whether the plaintiffs might claim that the moofs played a role in Danny's injuries, he asked:

> As I understand it, Counsel are all in agreement that the actor involved in this proceeding was Sophie to the exclusion of any other dog or varmint that was in that back yard, is that right or wrong?

Throughout the trial, Judge Wangelin displayed an old-fashioned and somewhat folksy style while insisting on courtroom decorum.

***Snapshot of the Trial.*** The trial of this case took barely three days. There were ten live witnesses, including one expert. Clarke Poos's deposition was read into evidence. The exhibits consisted of two documents (the Center's wildlife breeder's permit and St. Louis Zoo records relating to Sophie the wolf); twenty-two photographs (twelve photos of Danny's injuries, three photos of Sophie at work with Kenneth Poos and school children, and seven photos of portions of the Pooses' chain link fence); and one map of the neighborhood. Both sides rested in the morning of the third day; then at 2:30 p.m. of the same day, closing arguments (strictly limited by the court to 30 minutes per side) and instructions to the jury began; the six-person jury returned its verdict for the defendants that same afternoon.

How was the jury able to decide the case so quickly? This trial presented two sharply drawn questions of fact: How did Danny get into the Pooses' yard? Did Sophie the wolf bite or attack him? There was no normative legal standard for the jury to apply. If Sophie injured Danny, the defendants were liable. Most of the witnesses—John Gillis, James Burgess, Dr. Owen Sexton (President of the Wild Canid Survival & Research Center), Danny's treating physician, the policeman who arrived at the Poos home, the Curator of the St. Louis Zoo, and Danny's father Donald Mahlandt—were not impeached in any serious way. Even the defense expert on the behavior of wolves and other canids, the aptly named Dr. Fox, was not impeached or contradicted. In short, the underlying facts were largely not in dispute. What was in dispute were the inferences to be drawn from those facts.

The testimony of John Gillis, who saw Danny, Sophie and Clarke Poos in the yard, has already been described, but four other aspects of the trial are of note.

### What Did Clarke Poos See and What Did He Say About It?

Clarke Poos testified in his deposition, and Gillis confirmed, that he did not see Danny being injured, but arrived soon after the injury. Clarke's testimony diverged from Gillis, however, in that Gillis testified that when Clarke arrived, Sophie was straddling Danny and that Clarke pushed Sophie away as he picked Danny up. Clarke said that when he saw Sophie she was standing back from Danny, a chain's length away. He also said he looked at her and there was no blood around her mouth, body or paws.

Two prior statements, allegedly made by Clarke, conflicted with this deposition testimony. Jean Curry, Danny's mother, testified that while they were ministering to Danny on the Pooses' back porch, Clarke said to her:

> I looked out the window and I saw the boot—a boot laying in the back yard, a cowboy boot, and I ran out and picked it up and I saw the wolf—I saw Sophie on top of Daniel. She was eating his face.... So I ran over and pulled her off and got Daniel and brought him back in the house.

While this alleged statement would be hearsay if offered for its truth, once Clarke testified that he had found Sophie some distance from Danny, it could be offered to impeach him. Asked about this statement in his deposition, Clarke denied ever saying or ever hearing his sister Dee Dee say that Sophie was "eating Danny's face." He did say that he later found Danny's cowboy boot in the back yard, badly torn, and it was returned to the Mahlandts. Jean Curry testified that she had discarded it.

Jean Curry was forcefully cross-examined about this statement by defense counsel. In her deposition in 1975 she had testified that either Clarke or his sister had made the "eating Danny's face" comment but she couldn't remember who. Defense counsel sought to impeach her as "conveniently" remembering now that it was Clarke, since the comment could only be admitted if it was his prior inconsistent statement. In response, Jean claimed that her mind was muddled in 1975, that she had thought carefully about this event during the past two weeks, and that she was now sure it was Clarke.

Kenneth Poos's deposition was the source of the second prior inconsistent statement allegedly made by Clarke. In his deposition, Poos had testified as follows:

He [Clarke] said that when he went out he saw obviously that the boy needed help. He picked the child up and at the time he obviously had entered the radius where Sophie was chained and Sophie didn't want him to take this child away. He (sic) had been licking the child, she had been licking the child. He picked her (sic) up and Sophie indicated that she didn't want the child to leave. That's about it.

This deposition testimony, like the statement Jean Curry recalled, was admitted as Clarke's prior inconsistent statement for impeachment only. No instruction as to this limited use was requested as to either statement and none was given.

**Dr. Fox Talks About Wolves.** According to Dr. Michael Fox, defendants' expert witness on the subject of wolf behavior, the testimony in the case did not support an inference that Sophie had attacked or bitten the child. Highly credentialed in the fields of veterinary medicine, psychology, biology and animal behavior, Dr. Fox had been an Associate Professor of Psychology at Washington University for nine years. At the time of the trial, he was a Research Director for the Institute for the Study of Animal Problems, a Division of the Humane Society of the United States. Most of his professional career had been spent studying and writing about the behavior of wolves and other wild canids. He was on the Board of Directors of the defendant Wild Canid Survival & Research Center and knew Sophie, facts which were not used by the plaintiffs to impeach him.

Dr. Fox was a clear and compelling lecturer. He told the jury about the behavior of wolves in general, and about hand raised wolves like Sophie in particular. He also described the only time he had been bitten by a wolf and spoke about his own personal experiences with his own pet wolves. Finally, he examined the photographs of Danny's injuries and gave his expert opinion that the lacerations and puncture wounds were not inflicted by a wolf.

In brief, his testimony was that wolves in general are not aggressive toward human beings but are rather timid, unless threatened or attacked, and that they are fully aware of when they themselves are attacking or threatening to attack. They attack prey, but not other wolves. Hand raised wolves are socialized to human beings as their "family," are empathetic to injured persons, and highly protective of children. A wolf's bite is very powerful, would create apposite teeth marks on a limb, and would crush a child's bones.

Asked about the evidence in this case, Dr. Fox stated that if Sophie was straddling Danny, had her face close to his, or was licking him, this would be,

more likely an indication of friendly approach. Wolves are like dogs, they're very facially oriented. They like to kiss . . . the licking could be either greeting or care giving. . . . [when I] cut my own hand one day when I was cleaning the wolves . . . they came over and licked my wound. The smell of blood doesn't turn the animal on to attack, it was natural care giving behavior, which I've seen them do to each other.

If Sophie had been heard wailing, it was not the sign of attack. In an attack,

[t]he wolf is either silent or gives a growl before it lunges. . . . The wail can indicate that I want your attention or I want to give attention. It's an ambiguous signal to the human ear but the wolves are aware of the context in which it occurs, so they don't get confused.

The attack on the beagle, he said, did not indicate any tendency to attack a child, as wolves are very aware of who is irritating them and whom they are attacking; "the aggression or threat can be switched off immediately."

Finally, Dr. Fox testified that none of the photographed injuries indicated a wolf attack. There were no apposite bite marks; wolves do not slash with their claws; the lacerations did not conform to the type of sideways slashing wolves can do with one canine tooth; there were no marks on Danny's hands or arms which would be expected as a person instinctively tries to ward off an attack; and there were no teeth marks on Danny's foot or leg which necessarily would have been made had Sophie used sufficient force to pull Danny under the fence.

***Inspecting the Fence.*** Donald Mahlandt, Danny's father, testified that about one month after the incident he had his first opportunity to see Kenneth Poos. The two men, with Danny along, made a detailed investigation of the fence surrounding the Pooses' yard. Mahlandt stated that he and Poos found an area between the second and third fence posts where the fence was "loose" at the bottom. Nothing more was said about the issue on direct examination. In his own testimony, Kenneth Poos agreed that there was a loose area, but said that it was not loose enough for a child to crawl under.[6]

On cross-examination, defense counsel asked Mahlandt whether he went to look at the fence because Danny's lacerations did not look like bites. Mahlandt admitted that the long cut on the face did not look like a bite; he didn't know about the smaller ones. Mahlandt also testified,

---

[6] Perhaps more was not said about the looseness of the fence because, according to Poos's defense lawyer, the bottom of the fence was only a few inches off the ground and would have had to be bent severely by a very powerful pull for a child of Danny's size to fit under it.

after an objection, that he had not looked at the barbs on the fence until Danny had told him that he had "gone under" it.

During this joint inspection of the fence, Poos compared Danny's injuries to the barbs on the top and bottom of the fence. He found that the spacing of the puncture wounds on the inside of Danny's leg matched the distance between the barbs.

***How Was Danny Injured? Two Competing Theories***. In their closing arguments, opposing counsel put forward two competing theories about how Danny got into the Pooses' yard and was injured. Donald Mahlandt's attorney, Terence Crebs, blamed Sophie, suggesting that Sophie bit Danny's cowboy boot as he either stuck it under the fence or tried to get under the fence himself; that she pulled him under the fence; and that Danny scraped his face and legs on the sharp barbs at the bottom of the fence. The second plaintiffs' counsel, Frank Susman, argued that Sophie also attacked Danny once he was inside the yard, and he accused Clarke Poos of lying about Sophie "standing back" from Danny when Clarke arrived on the scene. Without objection, counsel used the out-of-court statements allegedly made by Clarke as substantive proof that Sophie had attacked Danny.

Defense counsel Gene Buckley used the photographs of Danny's injuries to support his argument that Danny was injured climbing over the fence, not under it.

> Picture in your mind's eye this: This chain link fence, a little boy goes up the fence, to climb the fence, an active little boy. He gets to the top, he puts his left thigh on top of the fence in order to go over. It gets cut on the barbs at the top. He falls to the right at the top of the fence and scrapes the right side of his face, falls over the fence, cuts his lip on the barbs on the top of that fence. That's exactly how those wounds occurred, and when he fell to the right, then he went over into the yard.

Buckley also emphasized that no one had seen Sophie bite Danny and that plaintiffs' circumstantial evidence of Sophie's behavior was explained by Dr. Fox as attentive rather than attacking.

Neither the "under" nor the "over" the fence theory seems wholly consistent with Danny's injuries as described at trial or with what an almost four year old boy, or a wolf, would do. Rather, this seems to be a case in which essential questions remain unresolved. In our legal system, Buckley argued forcefully, this means that the plaintiffs cannot win:

> Our law is concerned that people get fair trials, that nobody be required to pay any money damages unless the plaintiff has proved by the greater weight of the believable evidence the charges that are made ... the Court will tell you ... the plaintiffs have to prove to

you by a preponderance, not just some evidence, not just any evidence, not just a little evidence, but by the preponderance . . . of the believable evidence the charges they've made in this case . . . if the evidence is evenly balanced and you say, well, it could have been this or it could have been that, they're evenly balanced, the plaintiffs cannot recover in this case. . . . I think you'll find that that burden of proof has not been met, that we have in this case nothing other than guesswork, nothing other than speculation, and if . . . it's just as reasonable to believe . . . that that child sustained those wounds climbing over the fence [as being dragged under it], then your verdict must be for the defendants. . . .

The jury appears to have agreed with Buckley's argument, for it found for the defendants.

***Missing Voices.*** The voices of two central characters in this story were missing from the trial, both excluded by rulings of the district judge. First, Danny's voice was missing. Defense counsel had objected that Danny was not a competent witness at the time of the event, and had told three different versions of the incident. But under Missouri law, competence was to be determined at the time of testifying. Danny was individually examined by voir dire, with the jury absent, and stated that the wolf grabbed his cowboy boot which he was sticking under the fence and "threw it into the yard;" the "wolves" (meaning, evidently, the moofs as well) played with it, and then "they got me;" the wolf "grabbed my foot and pulled me under." But in response to a question from the judge, Danny said that it was "not Sophie," it was either "Jethroe or Wolf–Wolf."[7] The judge then refused to let Danny testify, adding that the testimony was damaging to Danny's own case.

The other missing voice was the out-of-court voice of Kenneth Poos, Sophie's constant companion and the person who knew her best. Poos made two statements to Dr. Owen Sexton on the day of the incident, and a third statement to Donald Mahlandt during their investigation of the fence. All three statements asserted that Sophie bit the child or was somehow involved in his injuries. In addition, plaintiffs offered the minutes of a meeting of the Board of Directors of the Wild Canid Survival & Research Center, held on April 4th, which mentioned the incident. These out-of-court statements were all excluded as inadmissible hearsay.

***Making a Federal Case of It.*** One further point deserves mention. It is questionable whether this case was properly in federal court at all, for Danny's and his mother's diversity of citizenship from the defendants appears contrived.

---

[7] Jethroe was a wolf that had visited the Pooses' home three times; Wolf–Wolf was the name of one of the moofs.

Before and after the suit was filed, Danny lived primarily with his mother and stepfather in Kirkwood, Missouri and attended school there. His alleged residence in Nevada was only for part of the summer of 1976, at which time the plaintiffs filed their suit. Danny's stepfather was in Nevada on a temporary assignment for the Associated Press; Danny and his mother (and probably stepfather) lived in a motel and a hotel; Jean Curry did not register to vote in Nevada and did not work there. The defense objected to the Court's subject matter jurisdiction at the close of plaintiff's case, and although the judge recognized the objection was proper at any time, he overruled it, and the defendants never raised the issue again, either at the close of trial or on appeal.

We can only speculate as to why plaintiffs' counsel preferred a trial in federal court, even to the extent of making specious jurisdictional allegations. One possibility is that they thought they would draw a more pro-plaintiff jury from the federal jury pool that included the urban area of St. Louis, rather than from the more rural area of St. Louis County where their state case had been filed. Another is that they thought they might gain an evidentiary advantage from the newly-enacted Federal Rules of Evidence.

### Part Two

### An Encounter Between the Trial Judge and Federal Rule of Evidence 801(d)(2)

The plaintiffs offered the three out-of-court statements made by Kenneth Poos, and the statement in the minutes of the Center's board meeting, to prove that Sophie had bitten Danny. The first Poos statement was a note written about one hour after the event when Poos was trying to contact his boss, Dr. Owen Sexton, the President of the Wild Canid Survival & Research Center. Not finding Sexton in his office, Poos left a note on the office door. The note read:

> Owen, would [you] call me at home, 727–5080? Sophie bit a child that came in our back yard. All has been taken care of. I need to convey what happened to you.

The second statement was made later that same afternoon, when Poos did find Sexton. Though it is not clear exactly what Poos said, the plaintiffs' offer of proof indicated that Dr. Sexton would testify that Poos had told him that Sophie had bitten a child. The third statement was allegedly made when Donald Mahlandt and Kenneth Poos were inspecting the Poos fence together about a month after the incident. Plaintiffs indicated that Mahlandt would testify that:

> Mr. Poos acknowledged to him at that time that the wolf indeed had been involved with the thing in the back yard. Whether we are talking about the biting or the pulling under the fence, you know, he

had no reason why, but he did, you know, acknowledge the wolf had done the damage.

The minutes of the Center's Board of Directors meeting held on April 4th, twelve days after the incident, stated that there was a "great deal of discussion . . . about the legal aspects of the incident of Sophie biting the child."

*Relevance.* To be admissible, the Poos statements and the Board minutes had to be relevant to the dispute; that is, under Federal Rules 401 and 402, their admission would have to make the probability of a fact of consequence to the litigation somewhat more or less likely. Because Kenneth Poos had not seen the incident himself, his statements expressed his opinion. Based on his knowledge of Sophie, his prior experience with wolves, and what he had heard about the incident, his opinion that Sophie attacked Danny was that of a knowledgeable layman, or a (pre-Daubert) expert, and would almost certainly have withstood a relevance challenge had he testified at trial.[8]

*Hearsay.* Kenneth Poos's statements and the Board minutes were in all but a technical sense hearsay.[9] Although party admissions are defined under Rule 801(d) to be "not hearsay," the statements fit the definition of hearsay in Rule 801(a)–(c): They were written and oral assertions ("Sophie bit a child"), made by a declarant (Poos or the Board) speaking out of court, and they were offered to prove the truth of the matters they assert—the "truth" being that Sophie did bite the child, whether around the face or on the foot while pulling him under the fence.

***Application of Rule 801(d)(2) to Poos's Statements.*** The question for the court was whether FRE 801(d)(2)(A) and (D) required the admission of these statements.[10] Plaintiffs offered them against Poos

---

[8] This analysis rejects that of Professor Bein in her discussion of the *Mahlandt* case. She asserts that Poos's statements would have been stricken as "irrelevant" had he testified as a witness because he was "incapable of explaining the degree to which it reflected or varied from the objective facts." Bein, supra note 3, 12 Hofstra L.Rev. at 417. However, had Mr. Poos really reflected on what he actually did know about the incident, he would have been able to explain his opinion and its relation to the objective facts. The distinction between Poos's statements and "speculation or conjecture" is discussed further at page 252 infra.

[9] It is well-accepted in evidence commentary that Rule 801(d)(2) *exempts* admissions from the ban on hearsay, but it does not change their functional status as hearsay when they are offered to prove the truth of what they assert. See, e.g., Blakey, *You Can Say That If You Want—The Redefinition of Hearsay in Rule 801 of the proposed Federal Rules of Evidence*, 35 Ohio St.L.J. 601, 616 (1974).

[10] The focus of this discussion is on Poos's statements because the district court treated the Board's minutes as wholly derived from those statements. There was no

under subsection (A) as statements made by a party opponent, and against the Center under subsection (D) as statements made by an agent or servant (hereinafter "employee") of a party (hereinafter "employer").

In the guise of defining what is not hearsay, these subsections of Rule 801(d)(2) function as the hearsay exceptions do—they establish categorical requirements within which a declarant's statements have to "fit" in order to be admitted. The burden is on the proponent of the statements to prove to the judge that the statements *do* fit. In this case, to be admissible against Poos as an individual defendant under (A), the plaintiffs had to prove that the statements (1) were made by Poos himself, the party opponent of the plaintiffs, and (2) were offered against him. To be admissible against the Center under (D), the plaintiffs had to prove that the statements (1) were made by Poos, an employee of the Center, (2) were made during the existence of the employment relationship between Poos and the Center, and (3) concerned a matter within the scope of Poos's employment by the Center.

**Defense Objections.** The defendants' objections to the admissibility of Poos's statements focused on *none* of these foundational requirements. To do so would have been futile, for the terms of Rules 801(d)(2)(A) and (D) were clearly satisfied. The Center's objections were instead that Poos lacked personal knowledge of the facts he stated; he was not present when this incident occurred; his statements were mere opinion; and, they were nothing but "hearsay, rumor, conjecture and speculation."

Some of these objections would have had merit if Poos had testified as a witness that "Sophie bit a child." Poos did not see what happened between Sophie and Danny, so defense counsel was correct in asserting that Poos *lacked personal knowledge* of the facts he asserted. Under Federal Rule of Evidence 602, a witness must have personal knowledge of the facts to which he testifies. Defense counsel was also correct that Poos' statements expressed his *opinion,* but they were not *speculation* or *conjecture,* given his experience with and knowledge about wolves in general and Sophie in particular. The fact that they were made with little reflection, following an anguishing event and serious injury to a little boy, relates to their weight and does not render them inadmissible as irrelevant speculation.

---

independent analysis of the minutes. The treatment of the minutes by the appellate court is discussed on page 260 infra. Rule 801(d)(2) provides in part:

(d) Statements which are not hearsay. A statement is not hearsay if—(2) Admission by party-opponent. The statement is offered against a party and is (A) the party's own statement, in either an individual or a representative capacity or ... (D) a statement by the party's agent or servant concerning a matter within the scope of the agency or employment, made during the existence of the relationship, . . . .

Poos was never qualified by the court to give an opinion as an expert witness, however, and his opinion as a lay witness would probably not have been allowed under Federal Rule 701. It may have required some specialized knowledge, and it was certainly based at least in part on the hearsay statements of others. Thus the question presented to Judge Wangelin was clear: If Poos could not testify that "Sophie bit a child" at trial, should his hearsay statement nevertheless be admitted?

***The District Court's Rulings.*** Judge Wangelin put off ruling on all of these defense objections until Kenneth Poos was on the stand. Then he questioned Poos out of the presence of the jury:

> THE COURT: Mr. Poos, did you at any time on the 23rd day of March, the day this incident occurred, ... see Danny inside the fence on that date?

> THE WITNESS: I did not see him inside the fence. I saw him only in the kitchen floor for a few brief minutes.

> THE COURT: Do you know—and I'm talking about eyeball knowledge or personal knowledge; do you know how he happened to get inside the fence?

> THE WITNESS: No, Your Honor, I do not.

> THE COURT: Do you know whether or not that child was bit, mauled, clawed or whatever by Sophie?

> THE WITNESS: I do not, no.

> THE COURT: Do you know whether he was bit or mauled or whatever by any other canine?

> THE WITNESS: No, sir.

The judge also asked Poos about the meaning of the note he left for Sexton:

> THE COURT: "All has been taken care of," is that what that language is?

> THE WITNESS: Yes, sir.

> THE COURT: What did you mean by that?

> THE WITNESS: I meant that the child had been taken to the hospital and that part was under control.

> THE COURT: "I need to convey to you what happened." Now, do you know what happened?

> THE WITNESS: I do not know what caused it, no.

Judge Wangelin then sustained the objections to the admissibility of all of Poos's statements.

***Understanding Judge Wangelin's Decision.*** Why did Judge
Wangelin exclude Poos's hearsay statements? Not, it appears, on the
basis of a careful analysis of Rule 801(d)(2). Judge Wangelin did not
discuss subsections (A) and (D) nor acknowledge the Advisory Committee Note to Rule 801(d)(2), which states that admissions are exempt from
the restrictions of the personal knowledge requirement and the opinion
rule. Yet, it is not clear that the judge disagreed with the Note. He did
not hold that a requirement of personal knowledge must apply to party
admissions, as it applies to traditional hearsay exceptions,[11] nor did he
state that party admissions in the form of "opinions" were inadmissible.

The judge did say, after rejecting the Poos statements, that "expertise" was not needed on the issue the jury had to decide:

> As far as the Court's concerned, this is a matter that reasonable
> people on the Jury as a result of common experience can conclude. It
> would not be the subject of expert testimony by someone. . . .

> I think we're not confronted with a situation where an expert needs
> to talk about the speed of a projectile or the speed of a vehicle or
> stopping distances or things like that. . . .

Not only was Poos's opinion not needed, it was also Judge Wangelin's
belief that it *invaded* the province of the jury:

> We are confronted with a situation where this statement made by
> this witness—I think clearly invades the province of the Jury since
> he does not, by his sworn statement, know, and it's obvious that he
> couldn't if he wasn't there and didn't see.

In speaking this way, the judge ignored the recently enacted Federal
Rule 704, which stated: "[T]estimony in the form of an opinion is not
objectionable because it embraces an ultimate issue to be decided by the
trier of fact."

---

[11] The Advisory Committee Note to Rule 803 states that a hearsay declarant is the
equivalent of a witness and thus must have personal knowledge of the matter asserted if
the declarant's statement is to be admitted under any hearsay exception. Plaintiffs argued
that Poos's note was admissible as a present sense impression (FRE 803(1)), an excited
utterance (FRE 803(2)), and a business record (FRE 803(6)). The judge rejected all three
grounds, but not on the record. Fatal to all three was, of course, the requirement that
hearsay admitted under Rule 803 exceptions had to be based on personal knowledge.

Even apart from the lack of personal knowledge, it is unlikely that any of the cited
hearsay exceptions would have applied. The note was written at least an hour after the
events. It is doubtful that it qualified as a statement made "immediately thereafter" the
incident. There was also no foundational testimony that Poos was "under the stress of
excitement cause by the event" when he wrote the note to Sexton. It is unlikely that a
handwritten note reporting such an untoward and unexpected event would qualify as a
record made as a "regular" business practice, and it would mostly likely have been held by
the judge to lack trustworthiness under Rule 803(6).

In short, Judge Wangelin's decision cannot be understood as a considered application of the Federal Rules of Evidence to Poos's statements. It is perhaps better understood as a judicial attempt to serve the goal of truth-seeking. No one knew for sure what had happened to Danny. The jurors had been educated by an expert, they had been presented with all of the available circumstantial evidence, and the lawyers were going to develop the competing inferences in their closing arguments. In Judge Wangelin's mind, it was the jury's job to decide whether the preponderance of the evidence favored the plaintiffs' version, and Poos's out-of-court opinion was unlikely to add to the case, particularly since he had told the judge under oath that he really did not know what had happened and thus could not have stated that opinion in court.

Judge Wangelin tried to persuade the plaintiffs' attorney of the justness of his ruling:

> But let's turn the coin over and assume that Mr. Poos, by some theorem or syllogism, major premise, minor premise and a conclusion, had concluded that something else happened. I think you would strenuously object if it was against your interest.

This comment suggests that Judge Wangelin thought not only that Poos's conclusion had little probative value, but also that it might exert undue influence on the jury.

If so, the judge was motivated by the concerns that underlie Federal Rule 403, which permits a trial judge to exclude relevant evidence if it presents a risk of prejudicing or misleading the jury and that risk substantially outweighs its probative value. Although Judge Wangelin did not mention this Rule, his finding that the jury could learn nothing valuable from Poos's hearsay and his implication that it might unduly defer to Poos's views reflect Rule 403 concerns for the jury's truth-finding capacity—low probative value and risk of being misled. The judge's ruling expressed his desire to "protect" the province of the jury—yet his use of Rule 403–type reasoning diminished the role of the jury as envisioned by the drafters of Rule 801(d)(2).

Judge Wangelin's ruling thus presented an important question for appellate review: Could federal district courts exercise their discretion to exclude party admissions that they believed were at best unnecessary and at worst downright harmful to the truth-seeking goals of trial? Put another way, are district courts required to admit party and employee admissions, when their probative value is drastically diminished because the declarant has no personal knowledge of the basic facts, has relied on hearsay sources, and has made inferences that might border on speculation and conjecture?

## Part Three

### An Encounter Between the Federal Rules
### and Adversary System Values

Plaintiff-appellants appealed the judgment entered against them to the Court of Appeals for the Eighth Circuit, alleging error only in the district court's exclusion of two of the Poos statements and of the minutes of the Center's Board of Directors meeting. They argued that the rulings below were clear violations of the terms of subsections (A) and (D) of Rule 801(d)(2) and that Judge Wangelin's misgivings about admitting statements of opinion lacking personal knowledge did not justify exclusion. The appellants cited the Advisory Committee Note to Rule 801(d)(2), leading evidence treatises, and Missouri case law to make the point that while lack of personal knowledge might affect the *weight* a jury gave to a party admission, it did not affect its admissibility.

Defendant-appellees struggled to justify Judge Wangelin's decision under the Federal Rules, and produced a variety of arguments aimed largely against the vicarious use of Poos's statements against his employer, the Wild Canid Center. They claimed that statements made by employees lacking first hand knowledge should be inadmissible against employers when based on "gossip or speculation," and they cited pre-Rules federal case law to show that an employee's statements to his principal were admissible against the principal *only* when the employee had personal knowledge of the facts. They also argued that Judge Wangelin's ruling should be seen as an exercise of discretion, to be reviewed under the deferential "abuse of discretion" standard. And they claimed that if there was an error in excluding Poos's statements it was harmless, because the principal issue was not whether Sophie bit Danny but whether the wolf pulled him under the fence.

As we shall see, the Eighth Circuit rejected the appellees' arguments and upheld the plaintiff-appellants claims of error. To better understand the contribution of the court's decision to the developing interpretation of the Federal Rules of Evidence, it is necessary to look first at the pre-existing law regarding both party and employee admissions. Prior to 1975, there was no general body of distinct, independent federal evidence law. Federal Rule of Civil Procedure 43 mandated that federal courts apply a mixture of federal statutory evidence law, federal "equity" evidence law, and the evidence law of the state in which the court was located. Missouri law was thus a significant part of what a federal district judge in Missouri would use to decide evidentiary disputes prior to 1975.[12]

---

[12] In describing the effect of Rule 43 on federal trial judges, Wright & Graham, FEDERAL PRACTICE & PROCEDURE, EVIDENCE § 5002, at 43 has this to say:

### Federal and State Evidence Law Prior to the Federal Rules of Evidence.

Well before 1975, under both state and federal law, admissibility of a party's own hearsay statements required proof only that the party had made the statement, and that it was offered against the party at trial. It did not require that the party have firsthand knowledge of the facts asserted, nor did the opinion rule apply, at least in most jurisdictions.[13]

However, several Missouri cases seemed to draw a line between party admissions which took the form of conclusions of law rather than statements of fact. Statements such as "it was my fault" or "plaintiff was covered by Workmen's Compensation" were excluded, whereas statements of "ultimate fact" were admissible. Judge Wangelin may have had this case law in mind when he excluded Poos's statements, since its rationale was to protect against invasions of the province of the jury, even though "Sophie bit a child" is not a legal conclusion.

Also prior to 1975, employee hearsay statements were admissible against their employers in federal courts, as well as in Missouri and most other states. These admissions were restricted, however, to employee statements made *within* the scope of their employment. In many states this meant that courts had to find that the employer had "authorized" the employee to speak of a matter as part of the employee's job.[14] In Missouri, a line of cases held that "official" reports made from an employee to the employer in the course of an authorized investigation, or directly in the line of duty, were "authorized" and therefore admissible, but it is not clear that any of Poos's statements would have so qualified.

As to a personal knowledge requirement, and the admissibility of employee statements of opinion, the pre-Federal Rules law is more ambiguous. The major evidence treatises that lawyers and judges turned to for guidance, Wigmore and McCormick, are silent on these two issues.

---

[T]he three bodies of law referred to in Rule 43(a) proved upon close inspection to be elusive, to some extent even illusory. There were very few federal statutes dealing with evidence. The most significant of these required conformity to state law.... [rules of evidence in equity cases] was a phantom body of law.... As a result of these weaknesses in the federal sources, the dominant effect of Rule 43(a) was to require conformity to state law.

[13] In 1923, Wigmore reported that "[t]he *Opinion Rule* ... does not limit the use of a party's admissions ... every case presented in the allegations of pleadings ... includes both facts and inferences; hence, the opponent's admissions will naturally range over both facts and inferences without distinction...." 2 Wigmore, EVIDENCE § 1053 at p. 513 (2d ed. 1923). The 1972 Chadbourn Revision of Wigmore and the McCormick hornbook agreed. McCormick, EVIDENCE § 26 at p. 632 (2d ed., Cleary Ed. 1972).

[14] This requirement was heavily criticized, as it excluded many relevant statements. It was liberalized in influential model codes of evidence prior to the Federal Rules, and finally in the Federal Rules themselves.

Case law is mixed, but there are at least some cases that treat employee admissions like a party's personal admissions with respect to these requirements.

Thus it appears that Rules 801(d)(2)(A) and (D), when they were enacted in 1975, were generally consistent with federal and state evidence law, apart from the expanded scope of subsection (D), drafted to admit employee statements that simply *concerned* a matter within the scope of employment. With this background in mind, the result of the appeal of the *Mahlandt* case to the Eighth Circuit is no surprise. What is of interest is that court's methodology.

***The Court of Appeals' Methodology.*** In its opinion, the Eighth Circuit rigorously applied the text of subsections (A) and (D) to determine the admissibility of the Poos statements; the Board of Directors' minutes were treated under subsection (C). For interpretive help, it used the Advisory Committee Note to Rule 801 (d)(2). The opinion made no reference to prior federal or state cases defining party admissions, and it did not rely on any of the classic treatises that had helped to shape preexisting law. It did cite for support, and in one important instance rejected, arguments from *Weinstein's Evidence*, at the time the sole treatise focused on the Federal Rules.

***Poos's Statements under Rule 801(d)(2)(A) and (D).*** The court held (in one short paragraph) that Poos's written and oral statements made to Dr. Owen Sexton on the afternoon of the incident were admissible against him as a party defendant. The court straightforwardly applied Rule 801(d)(2)(A) and rejected the contention that Poos's statements conveyed the hearsay statements of those to whom he had spoken: "It was his own statement, and as such was clearly different from the reported statement of another."

The court next found that these statements were admissible against the Center under the terms of Rule 801(d)(2)(D): "They were made by Mr. Poos when he was an agent or servant of the ... Center, and they concerned a matter within the scope of his ... employment, i.e., his custody of Sophie, and were made during the existence of that relationship." It also rejected the appellees' claim that the admissibility of statements made "in house" between employee and principal was more restricted. The court cited Weinstein's treatise and the Advisory Committee Note: "[C]ommunication to an outsider has not generally been thought to be an essential characteristic of an admission."

Defendant-appellees were equally unsuccessful in arguing that employee admissions required personal knowledge, although they had the following authority of Judge Weinstein's treatise behind them:

> [S]tatements not based on personal knowledge ... may often consist of no more than gossip or speculation about the matter in issue. The

mere fact that the agent heard it and repeated it does not remove any of the dangers against which the hearsay rule has traditionally guarded.... The danger is particularly apparent as regards intra-company reports. Certainly, even an employee well-disposed towards his employer may report rumors he has heard, not because of their truth, but because his employer may be interested in the fact that there are rumors....

Permitting the witness to testify to a statement of the declarant based on hearsay, which cannot be evaluated, is contra to the philosophy of Rule 403 as well as Rule 805 which allows hearsay within hearsay only if both statements conform to the requirements of a hearsay exception.... Rule 403 ... would have to exclude an agent's statements if their probative value was substantially out-weighed by the dangers of prejudice or confusion. Such a conclusion would seem warranted where the statements refer to a crucial issue and are based on nothing more than office rumor.[15]

The court rejected this argument with its straightforward reading of the Rules cited in the treatise. Rule 805, the court said, applies only where the declarant's out-of-court statement repeats the contents of a separate out-of-court hearsay statement. The Rule then provides that the repeated statement is admissible only if both statements fall under exceptions to the hearsay rule. But, the court found that "Sophie bit a child" did not repeat any other hearsay statement, so Rule 805 did not apply:

A statement based on the personal knowledge of the declarant of facts underlying his statement is not the repetition of the statement of another, thus not [a repetition of] hearsay. It is merely opinion testimony. Rule 805 cannot mandate the implied condition desired by Judge Weinstein.

The appellate court got it right. While "Sophie bit a child" was Poos's opinion, it was an opinion based on some "underlying facts" of which he did have personal knowledge: his experience with Sophie, Danny's injuries, as well as Clarke's hearsay statements to him. It was not "hearsay within hearsay."

The court also rejected the contention that Rule 403 *mandated* that employee admissions be based on personal knowledge, for the obvious reason that such a requirement was not found in the Rule. The court did recognize, however, that Rule 403 did provide "additional bases for excluding otherwise acceptable evidence ...," and it proceeded to deal with the Rule 403 issue.

---

[15] Jack B. Weinstein & Margaret M. Berger, WEINSTEIN'S EVIDENCE, ¶ 801.(d)(2)(C)[01], at pp. 801–132–801–133 (1977).

***Poos's Statements under Rule 403.*** Although Judge Wangelin had not cited Rule 403 in his rulings on the record, the appellate court read him as concerned that the Poos statements were not reliable, primarily because Poos lacked personal knowledge of the event. The appellate court acknowledged that there might be a "problem" here, but also found that the Advisory Committee, and by extension the Rule, presumed the contrary. The court cited with approval the Committee's statement that admissions have enjoyed freedom from the demands of searching for trustworthiness, and from "the restrictive influences of the opinion rule and the rule requiring first hand knowledge," and it agreed with the Committee's conclusion that the history of admissions "calls for generous treatment of this avenue to admissibility." Applying the Rule's generous spirit, the Eighth Circuit found no cause to exclude "Poos's statements as against himself or Wild Canid Survival & Research Center, Inc." The court did approve Judge Wangelin's exclusion of the Center's Board minutes on Rule 403 grounds. Because the minutes were not admissible against Poos, their use at trial might unfairly prejudice him even if introduced only against the Center. And once the appellate court found that Poos's statements would be admitted against the Center, it also found that the minutes would add almost nothing to the plaintiffs' case.

***The Aftermath of the Case—In Personal Terms.*** The distressing events of March 23rd, 1973, must have affected all of the characters in this story. Danny's injuries no doubt added to the domestic troubles of the Mahlandt family. Sophie lost her home, and the Poos family lost the "very gentle wolf," Sophie. After 10 days quarantine in the basement of the Poos house to check for rabies, she was sent to a genetic research center in Kankakee, Illinois, similar to a game reserve. Danny himself bore a long scar from the laceration on the right side of his face. His injuries seem not to have affected the motor capacity of his mouth and jaw, but the scar did cause some social embarrassment to the young boy. During his voir dire at the trial, when he was nine, Danny said that he was more used to it now and just told people "I was bitten by a wolf." Danny's mother testified that Danny had not lost his love of animals.

The *Mahlandt* lawsuit itself was remanded to Judge Wangelin, who dismissed the case without prejudice to re-file it, due to the absence of Danny and his mother on the day the case was set for re-trial. It appears, however, that the case was never refiled. Interviews with counsel indicate that it was instead settled for not very much money. The plaintiffs would have recovered more (and avoided litigation costs) had they accepted a settlement offer made by the Center's insurers prior to trial and held open until the case went to the jury. But apparently Donald Mahlandt and Jean Curry could not agree between themselves on settlement.

***The Impact of the Appellate Opinion—In Legal Terms.*** The opinion in *Mahlandt v. Wild Canid Survival & Research Center, Inc.* created no shock waves in the evidence law community, for its holding that party and employee admissions were not subject to the requirement of personal knowledge or the restriction of the opinion rule followed the text of the Advisory Committee Note. Although it was the first published appellate court opinion to make these definitive rulings, the holding was not surprising or controversial enough to make *Mahlandt* into a "landmark" opinion in the law of evidence. Indeed, since the Federal Rules were adopted, only Supreme Court decisions have been true landmarks.

Some commentators did disagree with its holding, however, and advocated a judicially-imposed personal knowledge requirement, at least under subsection (D).[16] The Weinstein treatise retained its above-quoted critique of the Rule until at least 1990. It also summarized the holding of the *Mahlandt* opinion and said "The case seems doubtful."[17]

The subsequent history of the *Mahlandt* opinion, however, demonstrates that courts were not in much doubt about the correctness of the Eighth Circuit's analysis. There have been twenty-eight citations to *Mahlandt* in federal courts, and three in state supreme courts, and no case disputes its holding. Moreover, the Weinstein treatise now states that under Rule 801(d)(2)(D) "there is no additional requirement that the proponent must show that the statement is trustworthy, or that the declarant had personal knowledge of the facts underlying the statement."[18] It goes on to add, however, that Rule 403 still applies: "[T]he statement must be evaluated in light of the requirements that its probative value outweigh any danger of unfair prejudice or confusion."[19] This is *not* a correct statement of the discretionary standard. Rather, the correct standard is the opposite—an item of relevant evidence can be excluded only when it is the danger of unfair prejudice or confusion that *substantially outweighs* the item's probative value. Perhaps the Weinstein treatise is still struggling with what, in retrospect, is the most significant contribution of the *Mahlandt* opinion. That is, that Rule 403, and hence trial court discretion, has only a very small role to play in the admission and exclusion of hearsay under a categorical system of exceptions and exemptions. Judge Weinstein has long been an advocate of

---

[16] See Lilly, An Introduction to the Law of Evidence, § 58, at n.3 (1978):"Since one basis of admitting another's declaration as an admission of a party is that the declarant probably knows the subject about which he speaks, it should be required that the representative have personal knowledge." Bein, supra note 3, 12 Hofstra L.Rev. at 451.

[17] Weinstein & Berger, Weinstein's Evidence, ¶ 801(d)(2)(D)[01] at p. 801–299 (1990).

[18] Weinstein & Berger, Weinstein's Federal Evidence § 801.33[1] at p. 801–70 (McLaughlin, ed., 2d ed. 2005).

[19] Id. at p. 801–70.

turning the hearsay rule into a rule of discretion, based largely upon the trial court's evaluation of the probative force of a proffered hearsay statement.[20] In the first published draft of the Federal Rules of Evidence, written by the Advisory Committee on which he served, this view prevailed but ultimately it lost out to the categorical system that admits or excludes hearsay depending mainly on whether a statement fits into the doctrinal boxes of Rules 801(d), 803, and 804.

The categorical treatment of hearsay in the Federal Rules, and interpretations of the Rules in cases like *Mahlandt,* do not, however, relieve an ongoing tension between two fundamental ideas about achieving accurate trial outcomes through the law of evidence—the idea that broader admissibility of relevant evidence will enable more accurate jury decision making and the idea that judges, through the exercise of discretion, can and should perform a gatekeeping function to ensure accurate outcomes.

Judge Wangelin encountered this tension and favored the discretionary approach, and so took the question whether Kenneth Poos's opinions should be credited away from the jury. The Eighth Circuit, and the Federal Rules of Evidence, gave it back. In doing so, the appellate court held, with regard to admissions at least, that the "spirit" of the Federal Rules favored the broad admissibility of relevant evidence and that district court judges had little "discretion" to use Rule 403 to exclude seemingly unreliable hearsay out of fear that the jury might rely on it.

**The Result in *Mahlandt* Encounters Adversary System Values.** Relying only on the Federal Rules and Advisory Committee Notes, the Eighth Circuit did not discuss whether the broad admissibility of admissions, and less judicial discretion, is the best approach to promoting accurate jury decision making. The court never asked whether the jury would get closer to the truth if Poos's hearsay statements were to be admitted. It thus avoided any encounter between the Federal Rules it was applying and the basic values of the adversary system. The remainder of this essay engages in this encounter and asks whether the broad admissibility of party admissions, and in particular employee admissions, is justified by adversary system values. First, the issue of accuracy is addressed, and then we find that the question must be broadened: Will the result in *Mahlandt* lead to cases being more "justly determined," to use the language of Federal Rule 102?[21] If not more accurate, will the result be more "fair"?

---

[20] See Weinstein, *Probative Force of Hearsay*, 46 Iowa L.Rev. 331 (1961).

[21] Federal Rule of Evidence 102 provides:

These rules shall be construed to secure fairness in administration, elimination of unjustifiable expense and delay, and promotion of growth and development of the law of evidence to the end that the truth may be ascertained and proceedings justly determined.

***Employee Admissions and the Value of Accuracy.*** The Advisory
Committee Note to Rule 801(d)(2) states: "No guarantee of trustworthiness is required in the case of an admission." But concern about "just
determinations" makes trustworthiness issues difficult to ignore, and
supporters of subsection (D) have argued that employee admissions *are*
likely to be trustworthy when they are made *during* the employment
relationship:

> Ordinarily employees do not jeopardize their jobs by making false
> statements which are costly to their employers. Indeed, so unlikely
> is it that one writer has proposed that statements made by agents
> and employees against the interest of their principals and employers
> be characterized as declarations against [their own] interest, the
> interest being their stake in the job....[22]

Moreover, if the employee is speaking about a matter *concerning the
scope of his employment*, he may be assumed to know something about
it.[23] There is, however, no requirement of an "against interest" element
for employee admissions; they can be blatantly self-serving when made
so long as they are offered *against* the party at trial.

In addition, any general assumption about trustworthiness runs
afoul of the problem that Judge Wangelin encountered with the Poos
statements—the trustworthiness of an employee's statements can be
gravely compromised by the employee's lack of personal knowledge and
mistakes of judgment. To insure some modicum of reliability, major
reform efforts prior to the Federal Rules had provided that the employee
must be speaking on the basis of personal knowledge and that the
statement be subject to the restrictions of the opinion rule.[24] Federal
Rule 801(d)(2) abandoned these safeguards.

Thus, it seems that the drafters of the Federal Rules did not even
try to justify Rule 801(d)(2)(D) on trustworthiness grounds, a standard
justification for hearsay exceptions. Rather, the Advisory Committee
Note states that this Rule "is the result of the adversary system rather
than satisfaction of the conditions of the hearsay rule." The sources
cited by the Advisory Committee for this proposition, however, discuss
only the admissibility of *a party's own statements*. Their justifications all
turn on the fact that the party who made the admission is himself

---

[22] Brooks, Report, New Jersey Supreme Court, Committee on Evidence 165–167 (1963)
(discussing Uniform Rule of Evidence 63(9)(a)).

[23] The McCormick treatise, edited by Professor Cleary in 1972, stated that an employee
"is well-informed about acts in the course of business." McCormick, supra note 13, § 267
at p. 641. This statement was adopted by Professor Lilly in his treatise, supra note 16, § 58
at p. 206.

[24] Model Code of Evidence rule 508 (1942) and Uniform Rule of Evidence 63(9)(a)
(1953).

*participating* in the adversary system. The same justifications do not apply in the same way to admissions made by a party's employees.

**Party Admissions, Accuracy and Fairness.** The Wigmore treatise, cited by the Advisory Committee as 4 Wigmore § 1048, offers two justifications.[25] First, a party's admission, offered *against* him at trial, has evidentiary value beyond the facts it asserts because it must in some way be inconsistent with that party's present claim. Impeaching inferences can drawn from this "conflict of claims" regardless of what the party knew first hand, and personal knowledge need not be required. But this rationale, which suggests that admitting the statement will allow the jury to better evaluate the party's legal case, seems strained when the admission is not the statement of the party but that of his employee. Employees are not the ones asserting claims or defenses when their employer sues or is sued, so there is no necessary added impeachment value to an employee's out-of-court statements simply because they contradict the employer's claim or defense.

Wigmore's second justification for making party admissions broadly admissible rests on fairness rather than accuracy. According to Wigmore, the basic purpose of the hearsay rule is to protect the opponent's opportunity to cross-examine the sources of all statements offered against him. Party admissions "pass the gauntlet" of the rule because when a party's prior statement is offered against him at trial, he can always take the stand to explain it. There is no unfairness to that party—he is not denied the opportunity to cross-examine himself, as he is when a third party's hearsay statement is offered against him.

Professor Morgan, also cited in the Advisory Committee Note, agreed that there is no unfairness in admitting a party's statements against that party:

> The admissibility of an admission by the party himself rests not upon any notion that the circumstances in which it was made furnish the trier means of evaluating it fairly, but upon the adversary theory of litigation. A party can hardly object that he had no opportunity to cross-examine himself or that he is unworthy of credence save when speaking under the sanction of an oath.[26]

From this perspective, the party has the same *fair* opportunity to explain even when his statements are opinions, or not based on personal knowledge, or self-serving when made.

Moreover, in one respect fairness and accuracy are arguably intertwined. It may not be possible for a party's opponent to call that party to

---

[25] This description of Wigmore's argument is drawn from 4 WIGMORE, EVIDENCE § 1048 (Chadbourne rev. 1972) and 5 WIGMORE, EVIDENCE § 1371 (Chadbourne rev. 1974).

[26] Morgan, BASIC PROBLEMS OF EVIDENCE 266 (1962).

the witness stand. Criminal defendants are privileged not to testify, and calling one's well-prepared party opponent as a witness in civil cases is fraught with risk. If parties' own hearsay statements were also inadmissible against them, they could entirely avoid the jury's learning what they once said that was relevant to the case. This seems unfair, and the jury might be deprived of important information. If the statement is admitted, not only does the jury learn what the party once said, but it can also hear the party's explanation of why he made a statement he now disavows.

The fairness rationale is substantially weakened when it is an employee's hearsay statement that is offered against the employer. An employer *can* reasonably complain about his inability to question an employee, because employing someone does not mean trusting their judgment, observational capacity, or even honesty in all things, particularly if the statement was an opinion, or lacked personal knowledge, or was self-serving. Moreover, employment is often transient, and there is no guarantee that an employer will be able to produce the employee to explain a statement that harms the employer.

***The Fairness of Holding Employers Accountable for Employee Statements.*** Faced with the Advisory Committee's disavowal of a trustworthiness rationale, and the failure of the Committee's "adversary system" rationale when applied to employee statements, other commentators have made additional fairness arguments to justify holding employers accountable for the risks of their employees' hearsay statements. None of these efforts has been very satisfactory.

The McCormick treatise has only this to say: "[I]f the admissibility of admissions is viewed as arising from the adversary system, *responsibility for statements of one's employee is a consistent aspect.*"[27] Professor Lilly expands this thought:

> [The]  broader test adopted in the Rules is consistent with a party's adversarial responsibility: since he has engaged the agent to act on his behalf and he has some control over the agent's duties, it is fair that the statements of the agent related to his employment be admissible against the party-principal.[28]

This argument may have intuitive appeal, but it does not explain why an employer's *degree of control* over an employee has no bearing on the admissibility of the employee's statements, or why statements by employees may be admitted even if the employer had told the employee not to speak, or why an employee's statements are admissible after the employee has left his job and no longer must cooperate by testifying for

---

[27] McCormick, supra note 13, § 267 at p. 641 (emphasis added).

[28] Lilly, supra note 16, § 58 at p. 206.

the employer. In short, the idea that an employer's control is robust enough to justify his accountability for the content of employee hearsay statements does not apply in most employer-employee relations.

Another attempt at justification draws on the equitable concept of *quasi-estoppel*, which precludes "a party from asserting, to another's disadvantage, a right *inconsistent with a position previously taken by him*."[29] Here, a party may be estopped from asserting his right to object to his opponent's use of the party's own prior hearsay statement at trial. In espousing this approach, Edward Lev argued:

> It is a punishment for inconsistency, an estoppel to prevent exclusion of [statements made] on another occasion differing from his present cause. The relative trustworthiness is immaterial; the party has contradicted himself and the trier may treat either position as the truth ... one's standing in court is lessened when he has, at another time, made statements inconsistent with his present position ... one must sleep in the bed he has made.[30]

Sixty years before Lev, Gillet wrote that a societal duty underlies this position:

> Every individual is under an applied compact with society to speak the truth. He ought not to complain, therefore, if a court of justice should adjust his affairs, when required to do so, in accordance with his statements concerning them, even if he had no interest at the time which was disserved by what he said.[31]

Lempert, Gross and Liebman elaborate a moral theory:

> The exception [for party admissions] is best seen as rooted in ideas about the *responsibility* which individuals have for their actions. People are expected to tell the truth as a matter of course, not because the law requires veracity in everyday speech, but because accepted notions of morality require it. The law recognizes in the hearsay rule the fact that people do not always speak the truth, but recognizing this does not mean that parties before the court will be assumed to have failed in their moral duty to tell the truth or be relieved of the responsibility for their actions if they have failed. [32]

The problem with these equitable, societal and moral theories is that while they might justify admitting a party's own personal admissions, their extension to admitting an employee's statements against an em-

---

[29] BLACK'S LAW DICTIONARY (4th ed. 1951) (emphasis added).

[30] *The Law of Vicarious Admissions—An Estoppel*, 26 U.Cin.L.Rev. 17, 29–30 (1957).

[31] Gillett, INDIRECT AND COLLATERAL EVIDENCE § 2 (1897).

[32] Lempert, Gross, & Liebman, A MODERN APPROACH TO EVIDENCE 537 (3d ed. 2000) (emphasis in the original).

ployer is less satisfying. If the employee has adhered to his duty to speak the truth, holding the employer responsible for the employee's hearsay statements makes evidentiary sense, but no more sense than allowing the employer to use the same statements for his own benefit at trial, which the hearsay rule does not allow. If the employee had breached his duty to speak truthfully, it is the employee who should be punished. Would Lev's argument be persuasive had he written "The employee has made his bed; now the employer must lie in it?" In addition, none of these theories is responsive to the situation which concerned Judge Wangelin in *Mahlandt*, where an employee's unauthorized statements, due to lack of personal knowledge, may well be inaccurate.

***The Employer's Enterprise***. In his article cited above, Edward Lev developed the idea that the employer's voluntary act of selecting his employees and choosing to act in concert with them justified imposing an estoppel against the employer's right to object to the admissibility of their hearsay statements. He wrote: "The act of employment vindicates the imposition of responsibility for declarations of the employee relating to his work,"[33] and he later argued that a "voluntary alliance may draw with it [the employer's] responsibility."[34]

This is not, by itself, a satisfying justification for imposing the risks and burdens of employee statements on employers. We must look beyond the employer's act of employing others *vel non* to the benefits that employers, particularly corporate and institutional employers, receive from the structure of their enterprise.

Employers act in their self-interest in employing others, and benefit from the work their employees do. Individuals use employees to expand their operations and profits; corporate and other institutional employers can only conduct business through employees. Since employers *benefit* from having employees who interface with others, conducting and speaking about their employers' business, perhaps it would be unfair to permit employers wholly to *disclaim* what their employees have said and done. The limit to this principle under Rule 801(d)(2)(D) is that the employee's statement must at least *concern* a matter within the scope of his employment, though the employee need not be speaking as part of his job.

Employers, in other words, profit from their employees' behavior, including, over the long run, behavior which runs risks for others. The employer is held accountable for the conduct of employees who are part of his enterprise. There may be no principled distinction between employee behavior that takes the form of inculpatory statements and the

---

[33] Lev, supra note 30, at 45.

[34] Id. at 37, 49.

whole mass of other behaviors for which the employer is responsible. Absent such a distinction, it is arguably fair to impose on employers the risk of paying for an employee's irresponsible statement, just as the employer must pay, in a more literal sense, for the consequences of other risks the employee has created. As with other risks, employers can pass on and spread the costs of whatever additional liability they bear as a result of the admissibility of employee admissions. The class of customers, contractors and others which ultimately pays these costs is also treated fairly as a group because each individual may have a slightly better chance of recovering by using employee admissions, should he or she have a cause of action against an employer.

This sounds like a *respondeat superior* theory of employer accountability and cost-spreading, and it is. As a justification for employee admissions, it was perhaps adverted to in the Advisory Committee Note to Rule 801(d)(2) as a "necessity," but it is here elaborated as a fairness theory as well. If it is not wholly satisfying, it may be because extending the admissibility of employee admissions as far as subsection (D) of Rule 801(d)(2) does is not conclusively justifiable with rational arguments about accuracy and fairness. There remains an element of expedience in its reach, which is unsettling, but perhaps no more than other forms of the law's loss-spreading.

### Conclusion

All three encounters that make up the story of the *Mahlandt* case may leave the reader unsatisfied. We really do not know what happened between Danny and Sophie. If Sophie was responsible, then Danny was badly under-compensated for his injuries. If she was not responsible, then she lost her home and her eventual role within the Wild Canid Survival and Research Center for no good reason. The encounter between Judge Wangelin and Rule 801(d)(2) is also unsatisfying. The legal issue was sketchily briefed and argued, and the Judge did not appear to be interested in the technicalities of the Rule. He thought he was serving the interests of justice, but he was not interested in reconciling his vision of justice with the vision of wholesale admissibility found in the Federal Rules. Perhaps most unsatisfying is the encounter between Rule 801(d)(2)(D) and our desire for a comprehensive justification that fully allays concerns about accuracy, fairness and justice. The arguments marshaled above are well-reasoned as far as they go, and they do justify the admission of many employee statements. But each may fall short of a theory for the whole.

The missing factor in this search for a comprehensive justification is arguably an acknowledgement of the limits of the judicial role. It may be too much to expect that a trial judge, in the middle of a case like *Mahlandt*, could draw fine distinctions that would establish the reach of subsection (D) at just the right length, even if such distinctions could be reduced to doctrinal terms. Too may complexities must be balanced: lines between firsthand knowledge of an event and knowledge sufficient for an inference; lines between statements of fact and statements of opinion; and lines between speech that benefits an employer's enterprise or reflects the employee's authority and that which does not. Perhaps evidence law, applied on the spot in trials, cannot operate as intended, or consistently, if judges are faced with such fine doctrinal distinctions. The alternative, to treat the reach of Rule 801(d)(2)(D) as a discretionary judgment about trustworthiness, imposes its own risks of bias and error, of inconsistency and unfairness. The drafters of the Rule drew broader doctrinal lines that they thought judges could readily apply (*during* the relationship, *concerning* a matter within the scope of employment) and rejected judges' use of their own discretion.

The *Mahlandt* story thus exemplifies a fourth encounter, this one between law students and the law of evidence. It illustrates what values are at stake in the ever-present tension between the doctrinal mandates set by the Federal Rules and the dynamic role of trial court discretion in the administration of those Rules.

\*

# 11

## *Mutual Life Insurance Company v. Hillmon**

### Mr. Justice Gray

In each case the declaration alleged that Hillmon died on March 17, 1879, during the continuance of the policy, but that the defendant, though duly notified of the fact, had refused to pay the amount of the policy, or any part thereof; and the answer denied the death of Hillmon, and alleged that he, together with John H. Brown and divers other persons, on or before November 30, 1878, conspiring to defraud the defendant, procured the issue of all the policies, and afterwards, in March and April, 1879, falsely pretended and represented that Hillmon was dead, and that a dead body which they had procured was his, whereas in reality he was alive and in hiding.

On February 29, 1888, after two trials at which the jury had disagreed, the three cases came on for trial, under [an] order of consolidation.... At the impaneling of the jury each defendant claimed the right to challenge peremptorily three jurors. But the court ruled that, the cases having been consolidated, the defendants were entitled to three peremptory challenges only, and, after each defendant had peremptorily challenged one juror, ruled that none of the defendants could so challenge any other jurors; and to these rulings each defendant excepted.

At the trial plaintiff introduced evidence tending to show that on or about March 5, 1879, Hillmon and Brown left Wichita, in the state of Kansas, and traveled together through southern Kansas in search of a site for a cattle ranch; that on the night of March 18th, while they were in camp at a place called "Crooked Creek," Hillmon was killed by the accidental discharge of a gun; that Brown at once notified persons living in the neighborhood, and that the body was thereupon taken to a neighboring town, where, after an inquest, it was buried. The defendants

---

* The case of *Mutual Life Insurance Company v. Hillmon,* 145 U.S. 285 (1892), considered an appeal from a trial court's judgment in favor of the plaintiff, a young woman who had sued three life insurance companies for payment of the proceeds of policies they had issued against the life of her husband, John Hillmon. The Supreme Court's decision is one of the most famous texts in the law of evidence. The portion of the case in which Mr. Gray presents the Supreme Court's version of the *Hillmon* story is reproduced here.

introduced evidence tending to show that the body found in the camp at Crooked creek on the night of March 18th was not the body of Hillmon, but was the body of one Frederick Adolph Walters. Upon the question whose body this was there was much conflicting evidence, including photographs and descriptions of the corpse, and of the marks and scars upon it, and testimony to its likeness to Hillmon and to Walters.

The defendants introduced testimony that Walters left his home at Ft. Madison, in the state of Iowa, in March, 1878, and was afterwards in Kansas in 1878, and in January and February, 1879; that during that time his family frequently received letters from him, the last of which was written from Wichita; and that he had not been heard from since March, 1879. The defendants also offered the following evidence:

Elizabeth Rieffenach testified that she was a sister of Frederick Adolph Walters, and lived at Ft. Madison; and thereupon, as shown by the bill of exceptions, the following proceedings took place:

"Witness further testified that she had received a letter written from Wichita, Kansas, about the 4th or 5th day of March, 1879, by her brother Frederick Adolph; that the letter was dated at Wichita, and was in the handwriting of her brother; that she had searched for the letter, but could not find the same, it being lost; that she remembered and could state the contents of the letter.

"Thereupon the defendants' counsel asked the question, 'State the contents of that letter;' to which the plaintiff objected, on the ground that the same is incompetent, irrelevant, and hearsay. The objection was sustained, and the defendants duly excepted. The following is the letter as stated by witness:

> Wichita, Kansas, March 4th or 5th or 3d or 4th,—I don't know,—1879. Dear Sister and All: I now in my usual style drop you a few lines to let you know that I expect to leave Wichita on or about March the 5th with a certain Mr. Hillmon, a sheep trader, for Colorado, or parts unknown to me. I expect to see the country now. News are of no interest to you, as you are not acquainted here. I will close with compliments to all inquiring friends. Love to all. I am truly your brother, FRED. ADOLPH WALTERS."

Alvina D. Kasten testified that she was 21 years of age, and resided in Ft. Madison; that she was engaged to be married to Frederick Adolph Walters; that she last saw him on March 24, 1878, at Ft. Madison; that he left there at that time, and had not returned; that she corresponded regularly with him, and received a letter about every two weeks until March 3, 1879, which was the last time she received a letter from him; that this letter was dated at Wichita, March 1, 1879, and was addressed to her at Ft. Madison, and the envelope was postmarked 'Wichita,

Kansas, March 2, 1879;' and that she had never heard from or seen him since that time.

The defendants put in evidence the envelope with the postmark and address, and thereupon offered to read the letter in evidence. The plaintiff objected to the reading of the letter. The court sustained the objection, and the defendants excepted.

This letter was dated "Wichita, March 1, 1879," was signed by Walters, and began as follows:

> "Dearest Alvina: Your kind and ever welcome letter was received yesterday afternoon about an hour before I left Emporia. I will stay here until the fore part of next week, and then will leavo here to see a part of the country that I never expected to see when I left home, as I am going with a man by the name of Hillmon, who intends, to start a sheep ranch, and, as he promised me more wages than I could make at anything else, I concluded to take it, for a while at least, until I strike something better. There is so many folks in this country that have got the Leadville fever, and if I could not of got the situation that I have now I would have went there myself; but as it is at present I get to see the best portion of Kansas, Indian Territory, Colorado, and Mexico. The route that we intend to take would cost a man to travel from $150 to $200, but it will not cost me a cent; besides, I get good wages. I will drop you a letter occasionally until I get settled down. Then I want you to answer it."

. . . .

The court, after recapitulating some of the testimony introduced, instructed the jury as follows: "You have perceived from the very beginning of the trial that the conclusion to be reached must practically turn upon one question of fact, and all the large volume of evidence, with its graphic and varied details, has no actual significance, save as the facts established thereby may throw light upon and aid you in answering the question, whose body was it that on the evening of March 18, 1879, lay dead by the camp fire on Crooked Creek? The decision of that question decides the verdict you should render."

The jury, being instructed by the court to return a separate verdict in each case, returned verdicts for the plaintiff against the three defendants respectively for the amounts of their policies and interest.

**[The Court, after some consideration, decided that the trial court had erred in failing to allow the defendant companies three peremptory challenges apiece (rather than three altogether). But it did not stop there; it went on to hold that it was also error for the trial judge to exclude from the jury's knowledge evidence of the letters from Frederick Adolph Walters to his**

sister Elizabeth Rieffenach and fiancée Alvina Kasten. Although the letters were undeniably hearsay, the Court found they should have been admitted because they described the intentions of the writer, and thus were proper proof as tending to make more likely not only that he had those intentions, but also that they were carried out.]

# 12

# The Hillmon Case, The Supreme Court, and The McGuffin

**Marianne Wesson**

*McGUFFIN*: In film theory, especially in the films of Alfred Hitchcock, an essential object of no significance or function other than to explain the characters' behavior to suit the author's narrative purposes. Often introduced with a flourish, the McGuffin is sometimes later revealed to have been misunderstood or even nonexistent.

It says a great deal about the unnatural reverence with which the American law of evidence has regarded the Hillmon case that the canonical work of scholarship about that 1892 decision was written in 1925. In that year, Professor John MacArthur Maguire published an admirable analysis[1] in which he correctly observed that *Hillmon*'s reach remained unsettled at the time he wrote; he was also prescient in predicting that this uncertainty would generate later controversies. Professor Maguire's thoughtful exegesis did not, however, take issue with a conviction that then prevailed (and still prevails) among students of the Hillmon case: that the man who died in the incident at Crooked Creek was not John Hillmon. This implicit belief, indeed, animates nearly all of the commentary on the famous controversy and the precedent that it became.

The debate thus continues about whether an out-of-court declarant's description of his intention to meet or conclude a transaction with someone else may be employed to prove that the other party shared these intentions (or that the two had discussed their shared plan at some moment in the past).[2] So too does speculation about how a court might

---

[1] John MacArthur Maguire, *The Hillmon Case—Thirty Three Years After*, 38 Harv. L. Rev. 709 (1925).

[2] *See, e,g.,* United States v. Pheaster, 544 F.2d 353 (9th Cir. 1976), *cert. denied*, 429 U.S. 1099 (1977). After the disappearance of sixteen-year-old Larry Adell, both Hugh

enforce a negative answer to the latter questions while admitting the statement to prove the speaker's own intentions. How exactly is a jury to make use of an instruction that it may consider the statement "I intend to go traveling with John pursuant to our agreement" as evidence of the speaker's intentions, but not as evidence of either John's intentions, or that the speaker and John had discussed the plan?

This uncertainty was not resolved, but only made more consequential, when the Federal Rules of Evidence were adopted in 1975. The rule of *Hillmon* was incorporated, eighty-three years after its creation, into Federal Rule 803(3): "*The following are not excluded by the hearsay rule, even though the declarant is available as a witness:.... A statement of the declarant's then existing state of mind, emotion, sensation, or physical condition (such as intent, plan, motive, design, mental feeling, pain, and bodily health), but not including a statement of memory or belief to prove the fact remembered or believed....*" By itself (especially in light of the qualification of the last phrase) this rule might be read to exclude such materials as the letter that Frederick Adolph Walters wrote to his sweetheart, saying that he had met a man named Hillmon and formed a plan with him to travel together to "Colorado or parts unknown"—or at least to require strict confinement of its use to proving the intentions of the declarant, and prohibit its employment to prove any past acts, or anyone else's intentions. But it has often not been been read that way, in part because the influential Advisory Committee's Note to that rule states: "The rule of *Mutual Life Insurance Co. v. Hillmon*, ..., allowing evidence of intention as tending to prove the doing of the act intended is, *of course*, left undisturbed."

Since the Hillmon decision itself seemed to permit all uses of the Walters letters, it is not surprising that most judges have interpreted the case to mean that a declaration of the speaker's intentions is admissible over a hearsay objection, even if it includes assertions about past conduct of the speaker or another, and even if it contains a claim about the intentions of someone else. This doctrinal result grows largely out of reverence for the rule of *Hillmon*—and the fact that the disputed

---

MacLeod Pheaster and Angelo Inciso were convicted of kidnapping, conspiracy to kidnap, and the mailing of ransom demands and extortionate threats. Of Pheaster's involvement in Adell's disappearance there seems to be little doubt, although there was some evidence that Adell, a young man with a drug problem and a wealthy father, may either have participated in his own disappearance or decided to stay away from home even after he was free to return. There was much less evidence, however, against Angelo Inciso; the main item was a statement made by Adell to a group of his friends in a restaurant moments before he vanished, to the effect that he was going to out into the parking lot to obtain some drugs from "Angelo"—a statement admitted under the "state of mind" exception. The court affirms Inciso's conviction, noting that the Walters letters crucial to the *Hillmon* holding had the same tendency to prove not only the speaker's intentions, but those of someone else and the nature of a past conversation between the two.

evidence in *Hillmon* itself described not only the intentions of the declarant Walters, but also Walters' past dealings with Hillmon. Note the emphatic *of course* deployed in the midst of the comment. Although other Advisory Committee Notes are thoughtful, analytical, occasionally critical—even of Supreme Court precedents[3]—in this note the invocation of *Hillmon* begins and ends the discussion. Most decisions of that era enjoy little continuing vitality, but *Mutual Life Ins. Co. et al. v. Sallie Hillmon* is different. The state of mind exception to the hearsay rule, at least as it pertains to expressions of intention, rests on very little ground other than the authority of *Hillmon*. More than nearly any other rule of evidence, it owes its existence to a single decision.

\* \* \*

The first two Hillmon trials, in 1882 and 1885, produced hung juries, but the third resulted in the victory for Sallie Hillmon that led to the famous Supreme Court decision of 1892, reversing the judgment in her favor. Three more trials ensued, two ending with hung juries and the last in another verdict for Sallie Hillmon, destined to be once again overturned by the Supreme Court. The ultimate contested factual issue in all the trials was the identity of the man who died of a gunshot wound in March of 1879 at a campsite near Medicine Lodge, Kansas, leaving behind a body whose death far predated the availability of twentieth-century methods of identification. Sallie Hillmon and her attorneys insisted that the corpse was her husband's, and there was evidence that this was the case, including identifications of the body shortly after its demise by Sallie Hillmon and many of those who knew Hillmon when he was alive, and statements made on some occasions by Hillmon's traveling companion at the time, one John H. Brown. In Brown's original account, given within hours of the death, he said he had shot Hillmon accidentally when unloading a rifle from a wagon, while the two men were making camp at a place called Crooked Creek.

But there were doubts. Life insurance fraud was common, if not rife, in late nineteenth century America, and the insurance companies seem to have been suspicious about the reported death of Hillmon from the beginning. They took the position that the deceased was not Hillmon but an innocent victim, a man whom they claimed Hillmon and John H. Brown had lured to Crooked Creek for the precise purpose of killing him and leaving his body behind to be passed off as Hillmon's. There was some evidence that *this* was the case, including witnesses who knew

---

[3] In the advisory committee's note after Fed. R. Evid. 804(4), the Committee rejected the rule of *Donnelly v. United States*, 228 U.S. 243 (1913) (statement against penal interest is not an exception to the hearsay rule, even if declarant is unavailable). See also the nuanced consideration of *Palmer v. Hoffman*, 318 U.S. 109 (1943) in the advisory committee's note to Fed. R. Evid. 803(6), and of *United States v. Dumas*, 149 U.S. 278 (1893) in the note to Fed. R. Evid. 803(8).

Hillmon in life and swore that the body (or a photograph of it) could not have been he, and a written statement sworn to by John H. Brown a few months later, after a coroner's inquest had concluded that the dead man was not Hillmon. In this statement, Brown supported the companies' theory and admitted that the victim was an individual named "Joe" whom he and Hillmon had encountered in Wichita and persuaded to accompany them west. But before the first trial, John Brown repudiated this story and returned to his original one, saying that the insurance companies' lawyers had coerced him into signing a false affidavit.[4]

In all six trials the companies maintained that the corpse was that of Frederick Adolph Walters, once a citizen of Ft. Madison, Iowa, and the betrothed of a Miss Alvina Kasten, also of Ft. Madison. They produced witnesses, including Miss Kasten and various Walters family members, who identified the corpse from photographs as Frederick Adolph. It was undisputed that young Mr. Walters, a cigarmaker by profession, had left Ft. Madison in March of 1878 for the purpose of bettering his condition and traveled widely in the Midwest for a year or so. The defendant insurance companies claimed that Walters found himself in Wichita in March of 1879, and it is here that the famous letter to Alvina Kasten, a document that a film theorist might call the McGuffin of the story, first makes an appearance.

Miss Kasten testified in a pretrial deposition that she had received a letter from her fiancé dated March 1st from Wichita; in it he wrote that he planned to leave that city soon with a "man by the name of Hillmon," a sheep trader. The letter, which was attached to the Kasten deposition transcript as an exhibit, explained the writer's decision to accompany this stranger by confiding that Hillmon had "promised me more wages than I could make at anything else." Miss Kasten described this letter as the last communication she ever enjoyed from Mr. Walters. (The later testimony of Walters' sister Elizabeth that she and the family had received a similar letter from him was merely cumulative, and not nearly so persuasive because the letter itself was never produced, having allegedly been lost.)

The Kasten letter was exceedingly helpful to the defense, both in suggesting an alternate identity for the corpse and in corroborating

---

[4] For portions of Brown's pretrial deposition, which was taken over a period of weeks in December of 1881 and January and February of 1882, see Transcript of Record, Supreme Court of the United States, The Mutual Life Insurance Co. of New York, The New York Life Insurance Company, and the Connecticut Mutual Life Insurance Company of Hartford, Connecticut (Consolidated), Plaintiffs in Error, vs. Sallie E. Hillmon, at 190, filed Oct. 8, 1888 [hereinafter 1888 Transcript]. A transcript of the entire deposition may be found in the record of the second appeal. Transcript of Record, Supreme Court of the United States, Conn. Mutual Life Insurance Co. v. S.H. Hillmon, No. 94 (1903), at 342 [hereinafter 1899 Transcript].

Brown's statement that he and Hillmon had lured a victim to accompany them on their journey. It's difficult for any reader of the Supreme Court's 1892 decision to resist the conviction aroused by Mr. Justice Gray's description of the letter: the Crooked Creek corpse must have belonged to Frederick Adolph Walters. John Brown's conflicting accounts might cancel one another out and leave one in doubt, as might various witnesses' identifications of the corpse as Hillmon or Walters, but the letters are a decisive tiebreaker. It is insupportable as coincidence that Frederick Adolph Walters encountered a man named Hillmon in Wichita shortly before the death at the campground, left that town with him, and was never heard from again; murder is the obvious explanation.

Still, the first two juries were unconvinced, or at least enough of the jurors were to produce two mistrials. But in the third trial, Judge Shiras excluded the Kasten letter and the sister's testimony from evidence, accepting the arguments of Mrs. Hillmon's lawyers that they were inadmissible hearsay.[5] The jury, innocent of any knowledge of the letters, returned a verdict for Mrs. Hillmon, and the insurance companies appealed. The Supreme Court's decision overturning that verdict contains its famous language about what has become known as the "state of mind" exception to the hearsay rule:

> A man's state of mind or feeling can only be manifested to others by countenance, attitude, or gesture, or by sounds or words, spoken or written. The nature of the fact to be proved is the same, and evidence of its proper tokens is equally competent to prove it, whether expressed by aspect or conduct, by voice or pen. When the intention to be proved is important only as qualifying an act, its connection with that act must be shown, in order to warrant the admission of declarations of the intention. But whenever the intention is of itself a distinct and material fact in a chain of circumstances, it may be proved by contemporaneous oral or written declarations of the party. . . .
>
> The rule applicable to this case has been thus stated by this court: "Wherever the bodily or mental feelings of an individual are material to be proved, the usual expressions of such feelings are original and competent evidence. Those expressions are the natural reflexes of what it might be impossible to show by other testimony. If there be such other testimony, this may be necessary to set the facts thus developed in their true light, and to give them their proper effect. As independent, explanatory, or corroborative evidence it is often indispensable to the due administration of justice. Such declarations are

---

[5] 1888 Transcript, *supra* note 4, at 190 (Alvina Kasten letter), 189–90 (Elizabeth Rieffenach testimony).

regarded as verbal acts, and are as competent as any other testimony, when relevant to the issue. Their truth or falsity is an inquiry
for the jury."[6]

With this reasoning, the Court reversed the trial judge and sent the case
back to be tried anew, directing that the evidence about the letters be
allowed.

\* \* \*

Professor Maguire makes clear that he joins most students and
scholars of the case in believing that the dead man was Frederick Adolph
Walters. " 'Parts unknown,' " he writes (quoting the Walters letter),
"evidently included eternity." Not only American commentators, but
those overseas (by whom *Hillmon* was much remarked) have found
irresistible the conclusion that the corpse belonged to the young cigarmaker of Iowa.[7] But is it possible that the case itself, as well as the
penetrating commentaries of Professor Maguire and others, rest on a
misunderstanding of what really happened at that Kansas campsite near
a place called Crooked Creek?

Having taught the case many times to students in my Evidence
class, I recently found my curiosity aroused by the unconvincing nature
of the reasons the Court gave for its decision, as well as discrepancies in
the accounts I had read of the case; I decided to investigate further. I
also thought that closer scrutiny might illuminate the Court's real
reasons for inventing a rule that seemed to be so little grounded in logic,
policy, or psychology. For the Court's explanation of why the letter
should have been admitted is not persuasive, especially to the eye of a
reader a century later. It borrows from an earlier case the proposition
that the "truth or falsity" of statements like those in the letters is "an
inquiry for the jury." But the rule excluding hearsay, which the Court
does not purport to repeal in this case or any other, rests precisely on
the notion that determining the truth or falsity of some extrajudicial
utterances is too challenging a task for a jury that has been deprived of a
chance to observe the declarant and hear him cross-examined under
oath. The Court has, in fact, invented an exception to the hearsay rule.

But even a modest version of a hearsay exception for the expressed
intentions of a hearsay declarant—that is a version allowing expressions
of intention to prove only the genuineness of the intention—does not
rest on any plausible theory of reliability, as Professor Maguire implicitly

---

[6] Mutual Life Ins. Co. v. Hillmon, 145 U.S. 285, 295–96 (1892), *quoting* Travelers'
Insurance Co. v. Mosley, 8 Wall. 397, 404–05 (1869).

[7] A British scholar who investigated the case opines that "no impartial reader can fail
to be persuaded by the account of the facts retailed by Wigmore that the body presented
was not that of Hillmon, but that of one Walters." Colin Tapper, *Hillmon Rediscovered and
Lord St. Leonards Resurrected*, 106 L.Q.Rev. 441, 459–60 (1990).

acknowledges by observing that the danger of "misstatement" persists as to such expressions. It lacks any justification in the sort of armchair psychology that prompted the invention of, say, the exceptions for dying declarations or statements against interest. The former were thought reliable because "no man would meet his Maker with a lie upon his lips," and the latter because persons who say things that disadvantage them must be motivated by a powerful need to tell the truth. But it would seem to be easier to lie about one's intentions than about nearly anything else, since the likelihood of being caught out in a lie is small, and later acts incompatible with the expressed intention can always be explained by the simple phrase "I changed my mind." The more robust version of the exception endorsed by the *Hillmon* Court—that is, one allowing an expression of intention as evidence that the intention was accomplished—is even less grounded in reliability, disregarding as it does the folk wisdom that there is "many a slip 'twixt cup and lip.'"

One could ascribe the Court's curious misstep in the Hillmon case to generalized hostility toward Sallie Hillmon and her victory, but the Court did not need to reach out to invent the state of mind exception to send her case back for retrial. It had already decided, before addressing the matter of the Walters letter, that Judge Shiras erred reversibly by granting the insurance company defendants too few peremptory challenges. Indeed, the dispute about the letter seems to have been a secondary consideration in the minds of the defendants' lawyers. The companies' principal argument before the Court concerned the peremptory challenge question, and they placed the matter of the letters far down their list of assigned errors. Moreover, their only argument for the admissibility of the letter consisted of the claim that it was a business record, an obviously meritless proposition. Nevertheless, after disposing rather briskly of the challenge issue, the Court observed that "[t]here is ... one question of evidence so important, so fully argued at the bar, and so likely to arise upon another trial, that it is proper to express an opinion on it,"[8] and then proceeded to consider the trial court's decision to exclude evidence of the Walters letter.

Professor Maguire's account does give us some information about the circumstances in which the Hillmon case was heard by the Supreme Court. He relates that Justice Horace Gray, who was assigned to write the opinion of the Court, had at the time a remarkably competent secretary (today we would say law clerk): Ezra Ripley Thayer, later to become Dean of the Harvard Law School and a noted evidence teacher and scholar. Maguire relates that Thayer's "rough working notes on evidence" (to which Maguire apparently had access) reveal that the Court in conference voted to overturn the trial court's evidentiary ruling

---

[8] 145 U.S. at 294.

on "general principles" without specifying what those might be. Thayer's notes also claim that Justice Gray was in "dense darkness" about how to undo the ruling excluding the letter until Thayer "fed him with matter obtained with J.B.T."—that is, from James Bradley Thayer, the young secretary's father, himself a Harvard law professor and Wigmore's predecessor as the nation's preeminent treatise writer on the law of evidence.

What an imbroglio! At the time the Hillmon case was argued, it seems the Supreme Court building housed a Court that would object to the exclusion of the Walters–Kasten letter on principles too general to be articulated but too powerful to be omitted from its holding, a Justice assigned to author an opinion but more than willing to leave the fine points to his clerk, and a young scholar so eager to leave his mark on the law of evidence that he would seek guidance in *ex parte* correspondence with his famous father, incorporate their invention into the Court's opinion, and later boast that it was he, and not the clueless Justice Gray, who had invented this important new exception to the hearsay rule.

And yet these converging antagonists to Sallie Hillmon's lawsuit, whose apparent motives were no more nefarious than professional exhaustion or ordinary ambition, cannot altogether account for the invention of the state of mind exception. There is something more powerful at work: the urge to complete a just and intelligible narrative. It is impossible to come away from an encounter with the Supreme Court's opinion without the impression that the trial judge's exclusion of the evidence concerning Walters' letter—the story's McGuffin—disserved the cause of truth. Once a reader of the Court's opinion knows of the letter, it seems offensive to the idea of justice that the law would countenance a retrial in which the verdict could once again rest on the jurors' ignorance of evidence that seemed to prove, with near certainty, that the corpse belonged to Frederick Adolph Walters. The story, the true story, has to be the one that Brown told in his affidavit: Hillmon persuaded the credulous "Joe" (obviously, from the evidence of the letters, Frederick Adolph Walters) to accompany them on their journey and later killed him at Crooked Creek, leaving Walters' body to be taken for his.

If the opinion's reader is left with this narrative anxiety about the availability of the indispensable McGuffin, could the Court have been unmoved by the corresponding need to participate in the creation of an acceptable story—a story in which truth and justice are served in the end, rather than mocked? Inattentive though they may have been to the details of their decision, the Justices must have believed they were doing justice by inventing a hearsay exception for statements describing the intentions of the speaker. For truth to prevail (and for Hillmon's swindle to be thwarted), the letters had to be part of the story; for the letters to be part of the story, they had to be admissible; for the letters (unquestionably hearsay) to be admissible, some suitable exception to the hearsay rule had to be found; if one could not be found, it must be invented.

* * *

The power that this single letter seemed to hold over the development of the law of evidence eventually led my inquiry in this direction: suppose a case were to be made for the truth of quite a different narrative, one in which the corpse belongs to John Hillmon after all? In particular, suppose that the story's McGuffin, the famous letter, were full of lies? What would this circumstance, if proven, bode for the state of mind exception? The possibility of any such plausible narrative may seem small given the foregoing discussion, but that is in part because the provenance of the Walters letter is taken for granted; the lawyers' quarrel over its admissibility as hearsay seems to have exhausted any skepticism about the circumstances of its creation. And it is also in part because partisans of the defendants played a suspiciously large role in constructing the Hillmon story in historical memory.

Most persons familiar with the Hillmon case take their understanding of it from a few sources: the Supreme Court's opinion; a lengthy account of the case (cited approvingly by Maguire) found in the 1913 edition of Dean Wigmore's famous treatise on the law of evidence, THE PRINCIPLES OF JUDICIAL PROOF; and an engaging account published in AMERICAN HERITAGE magazine in 1968 by historian Brooks Maccracken. But the last two accounts rest on essentially the same source, and that source is one of the attorneys for the defendant insurance companies. Maccracken confesses that his "principal authority" was a report prepared by the Kansas State Superintendent of Insurance[9]; that report, reproduced verbatim, is also the only account of the case given in the Wigmore treatise. In fact the Superintendent of Insurance, a lawyer and businessman named Charles Gleed, was at the time of its preparation and release an attorney of record for the defendant insurance companies. He and his law firm represented one of the insurance companies from the second trial to the sixth and last one, as well as in both Supreme Court appeals.[10]

Apparently the Kansas Superintendent of Insurance was free, during his term of office, to represent at a month-long trial three of the insurance companies that he was charged with regulating, a rather

---

[9] Brooks W. Maccracken, *The Case of the Anonymous Corpse*, XIX AMERICAN HERITAGE 75 (June 1968).

[10] Annual Report of the Kansas State Superintendent of Insurance, *reproduced in* JOHN H. WIGMORE, THE PRINCIPLES OF JUDICIAL PROOF 856 (1913) [hereinafter Annual Report] (Gleed lists himself as attorney for defendants on both second and third trials); *see also* 884–87 (Gleed quotes at length from his own closing argument).

stunning instance of what we would today call "regulatory capture." Considering the bias that colored this canonical source, I concluded that the most instructive information about the Hillmon case was to be found in contemporaneous newspaper accounts, which were fortunately available because of Kansas' lengthy and proud journalistic tradition and its excellent newspaper archives.

When I visited those archives, there was plenty to read. The Hillmon trials were press sensations, and the Kansas newspapers of that time were neither restrained nor what we would today call "objective" in their coverage. But this is not to say they were indifferent to facts. Indeed, the daily stories in many papers resembled transcripts, with minute, almost question-and-answer, reportage of the testimony. Almost all of the newspaper stories employed this near-transcription method, and these close accounts of testimony comprised the bulk of any paper's coverage of a trial. These accounts are especially important because official transcripts of much of the testimony are nonexistent or unavailable.

Putting aside the partisan arguments of the various newspapers, their more particular reports of the testimony and evidence tell a rather clear story.

* * *

After John Brown reported the shooting death at Crooked Creek to some nearby rural residents, two inquests were conducted under the auspices of the coroner at Medicine Lodge. The first coroner's jury failed to agree whether the death was accident or otherwise; the second concluded that the shooting was accidental.[11] The body was then buried at Medicine Lodge, and Brown wrote a letter to Sallie Hillmon explaining what had happened and conveying his regret and condolences.[12]

When the insurance companies that had issued policies on Hillmon's life learned of the reported death of their policyholder, they lost no time moving into action. Agents of two of the companies, Major Theodore Wiseman and a Mr. C. Tillinghast, traveled to Medicine Lodge and demanded that the body be exhumed for their examination. These gentlemen told the Medicine Lodge coroner that they knew Hillmon and wanted to assure themselves that the deceased was he. According to a contemporaneous report in The Medicine Lodge paper, the *Cresset*, "the identification was satisfactory" and the body, presumptively Hillmon's, was dispatched "to be returned to his relatives near Lawrence."[13] But

---

[11] LAWRENCE STANDARD, Apr. 10, 1879, at 2.

[12] LEAVENWORTH TIMES, June 17, 1882, at 1.

[13] MEDICINE LODGE CRESSET, Apr. 3, 1879, at 2. At later proceedings, Major Wiseman and Mr. Tillingast would testify that they knew and said, immediately on seeing the body, that

when the body reached Lawrence it was not returned to Sallie Hillmon or any other relative; instead it was delivered to two physicians representing the insurance companies. These physicians were reported to be in doubt about whether the body, by then nearly a month dead and partially decomposed, was that of Hillmon. Three other persons who knew Hillmon were asked to look at the exhumed body, and all said they could not be certain whether or not it was he. Mrs. Hillmon declined at first to examine the body, saying she preferred to remember her husband as he was in life, but later she did look at it, and affirmed that it was her John.[14] The body was then sent to a funeral home to be embalmed, although it was apparently shown to various persons over the ensuing days. The next day the coroner of Leavenworth County summoned a coroner's jury and commenced a third inquest. Douglas County Attorney J.W. Green and his assistant George Barker performed the office of examining the witnesses. The inquest proceedings were reported for the *Lawrence Standard* in great particularity.

There must have been some buzz of citizen dissatisfaction about the role of the insurance companies in orchestrating the Lawrence inquest after the Medicine Lodge coroner had found the death to have been accidental, for the *Standard*'s reporter took time out from reporting the testimony to castigate in print some of the critics of the proceedings: "The mistake is made by some, of supposing that the inquest now being held is managed by the representatives of the insurance companies. The inquest is, of course, by the State to determine whether the body brought here is that of Hillmon, and the manner of that death. County Attorney Green and Geo. J. Barker represent the State and not the insurance companies in the examination now being held."[15]

This rather impatient admonition takes on some significance in light of later events. Not only did Mr. Charles Gleed, the Insurance Commissioner, represent the insurance companies at the later trials of Mrs. Hillmon's suit; his co-counsel in those trials were J.W. Green and George J. Barker. Barker and Green also represented the companies at the first trial, as well as in both appeals, serving these clients altogether for nearly a quarter of a century. Green, the County Attorney, later became Dean of the University of Kansas Law School, but even after taking that post he continued to represent the companies in the Hillmon litigation.

---

it was not Hillmon's. *See* TOPEKA DAILY CAPITAL, Mar. 18, 1895, at 1 (testimony of Major Wiseman), but this was not the *Cresset* reporter's impression.

[14] She later said that the insurance company's men discouraged her from viewing the corpse; they denied that they had, but another witness who had been with her on the occasion confirmed her account. *See* LEAVENWORTH TIMES, June 30, 1882, at 4 (testimony of Mrs. Judson).

[15] LAWRENCE STANDARD, Apr. 10, 1879, at 1.

And despite the reporter's claim, Green and Barker seem to have been employed by the insurance companies even at the time of the inquest, as were almost all of the other participants. At the fourth trial of the case, in 1895, the coroner testified that he had received his pay for conducting the inquest from the insurance companies, that he believed the witnesses and jurors had been compensated from the same source, and that "as far as he knew the coroner's inquest had not cost the county of Douglas a single dollar." He also recalled "the fact of the examination of witnesses being conducted by George J. Barker in behalf of the insurance companies and that to this, [I] offered no objections."[16] Testifying in the same trial, Major Wiseman corroborated this account: he said that he had "employed Mr. Barker at the time of the inquest to assist him in establishing the fact that the body was not Hillmon's."[17]

In any event, despite citizen grumbling about its justification the Lawrence inquest proceeded, an arduous affair of several days. Many witnesses testified, including John Brown, who gave the same account of an accidental shooting that he had given at Medicine Lodge. Mrs. Hillmon testified that she had looked at the corpse after it was brought to Lawrence and knew it for her husband's. Similar testimony about the corpse's resemblance to Hillmon was given by Levi Baldwin, a cousin of Sallie and erstwhile employer of John Hillmon who had gone to Medicine Lodge and accompanied the body back to Lawrence. The proprietor of the rooming house where Sallie and John maintained their household also said he had seen the corpse and it was Hillmon. The chief controversies seemed to concern the questions of Hillmon's height, the condition of his teeth, and the age of a smallpox vaccination scar. (Controversies over these matters—teeth, height, scars—would mark each of the later trials as well.) The corpse was five-eleven, and Hillmon had reported exactly that height when he first applied for one of the insurance policies. But the doctor who had examined him for the company at the time testified that Hillmon had come back a few days later to say that he was really only five-nine, and that the doctor had only then proceeded to measure him, and had found that the shorter height was correct. He explained the obvious alteration of the application to reflect the shorter figure by saying he had made the correction after Hillmon's second visit. Hillmon had been vaccinated for smallpox on the eve of his journey, about three and a half weeks before the shooting, and the corpse had a scar from a recent vaccination. But various doctors called by Green and Barker testified that the scar was too fresh for the body to be Hillmon's; one said Hillmon's scar would have hardened and dropped off by the

---

[16] TOPEKA DAILY CAPITAL, Feb. 16, 1895, at 6.

[17] TOPEKA DAILY CAPITAL, Jan. 31, 1895, at 4. The information in the following paragraph is all taken from this same source.

time of the Crooked Creek shooting. The physicians who had performed the post-mortem of the corpse noted its excellent teeth and one of them, who had examined John Hillmon in connection with his policy application, said that by contrast "one or two" of Hillmon's front teeth were "broken or out." Levi Baldwin and the Hillmons' landlord Arthur Judson, however, said that John Hillmon's teeth were not defective, and one of the other physicians said he had noticed nothing unusual about Hillmon's teeth when he had examined him.

Toward its conclusion the inquest became an occasion for the newspapers to suggest a number of different individuals who might have been the victim of Brown and Hillmon's criminal conspiracy. First a Mrs. Lowell thought from the body's description it might have been her missing brother, but when the corpse was dug up for her inspection she said it was not[18]; then there was a "young man of Indiana" said to be missing[19]; and later Colonel Wiseman was said to have located some friends of a man named Frank Nichols, also known as "Arkansaw." The friends said that Arkansaw had told them he had agreed to go herd cattle with men named Brown and "Hillman," and had never been heard from again.[20] Major Wiseman, Colonel Walker, and the insurance companies' other agents were seemingly tireless in their efforts to locate a convincing actor to cast in the role of the corpse, and the details of their story (the victim meeting up with Hillmon and agreeing to travel west with him) were already becoming clear, even though the agents had not at this point ever heard of the cigarmaker from Iowa, Frederick Adolph Walters.

It was mid-May when the coroner's jury returned its verdict, finding that the death was "of an unknown man," and moreover caused "feloniously" by J.H. Brown.[21] (Curiously, it did not mention Hillmon as murderer or accomplice.) Brown must have been feeling alarmed, but he was not immediately arrested, or charged. Instead, he was approached not long afterward by a lawyer named W.J. Buchan. Buchan sought Brown out at several locations in Missouri, to where John Brown had repaired after testifying in the proceedings at Lawrence. Buchan claimed to have come into the case at the request of John Brown's father, and held several conversations with Brown over the summer. In September, Brown signed and swore to a lengthy statement that repudiated the story he had told originally about Hillmon's death and gave quite a different account.

---

[18] LAWRENCE STANDARD, Apr. 17, 1879, at 4.

[19] Id.

[20] LAWRENCE STANDARD, June 26, 1879, at 4.

[21] LAWRENCE DAILY TRIBUNE, April 14, 1879, at 4.

The affidavit averred that John Hillmon and Sallie Hillmon's cousin Levi Baldwin had entered into a conspiracy to commit insurance fraud, Baldwin's part being to pay the premiums and Hillmon's (and Brown's) being to journey to the southwest with the object to "find a subject to pass off as the body of John W. Hillmon, for the purpose of obtaining the insurance money." The affidavit said that after leaving Wichita, the two men had encountered a stranger "the first day out of Wichita, about two or two and one half miles from town." The stranger "said his name was either Berkley or Burgess, or something that sounded like that," but Brown and Hillmon "always called him Joe." Hillmon told Brown that Joe "would do for a subject to pass off for him," but Brown objected that murder was "something that I had never before thought of, and was beyond my grit entirely." Nevertheless, by the statement's account, Hillmon proceeded with his plan, most foresightedly by persuading "Joe" to allow Hillmon to vaccinate him for smallpox. Hillmon accomplished this rather remarkable feat by taking the virus from his own arm and using a pocket knife to insert it into the other man's. Hillmon also persuaded the other man to trade clothing with him, and measures were taken to avoid any passersby seeing three men, rather than two, in the wagon: "sometimes one and then the other would be kept out of sight." Apparently as a hedge against any impression of implausibility a reader might form of these events, the statement explained that the stranger was "a sort of an easy-go-long fellow, not suspicious or very attentive to anything."

The affidavit then related that Hillmon shot and killed the stranger at the Crooked Creek campground, dressed the dead man in his clothes and put his own day book into the jacket pocket, told Brown to ride for assistance, and then vanished north with "Joe's" valise. Later back in Lawrence, according to the statement, Brown had a conversation with Sallie Hillmon in which she assured him that "she knew where Hillmon was, and that he was all right."[22]

From the insurance companies' point of view, a more useful document than this affidavit could scarcely be imagined. It accounted for all the facts then known, including the inconvenient vaccination scar, discredited not only Brown's earlier testimony but two of the most important witnesses (Levi Baldwin and Sallie Hillmon) who identified the corpse as Hillmon, and made excellent use of what had before been the most suggestive circumstance in favor of the company's position: the suspiciously large amount of life insurance carried by a poor man like Hillmon. And at about the same time Brown also wrote another document highly useful to the insurers: a letter to Sallie Hillmon. In it he said, "I would like to know where John is, and how that business is, and

---

[22] *See* Aff., John H. Brown, 1888 transcript, *supra* note 4, at 165.

what I should do, if anything. Let me know through my father. Yours truly, John H. Brown."[23]

But one's estimate of the probative value of these two documents—the affidavit and letter—must take account of John Brown's inconstancy. Brown later would say that the letter was dictated to him by Buchan. And by the time of the first trial of the Hillmon case in 1882, Brown had returned to his original account of the death at Crooked Creek, testifying for Sallie Hillmon and claiming that Buchan and the insurance companies had pressured him into swearing to the affidavit, which Buchan had composed.[24]

Brown's inconsistent narratives are described in the Court's 1892 opinion. I imagine most readers will likely have the same reaction that this writer did on first reading: Brown was a weasel and a turncoat, but his affidavit was probably true. For (I reasoned) there could have been many motivations for Brown to lie when he said he had killed Hillmon accidentally, chiefly an expectation that he would share in the insurance proceeds when they were paid. But it seemed unlikely that he had lied in confessing to the plot as he did in the affidavit. Pressure from the insurance companies seemed inadequate to account for that narrative or his willingness to give it, as it would have exposed him to prosecution as an accomplice to murder. Buchan's actions seemed questionable; nevertheless I was at first willing to ascribe my reaction to a perhaps excessively nuanced sense of the boundaries of acceptable professional conduct, instilled in me a century later in a far different legal environment. But further reading led me back to Buchan's behavior, and caused me to re-examine my initial conclusion.

Buchan, it seems, had more than one client in the Hillmon matter. An agreement executed by Brown on the same day he signed the affidavit authorized Buchan to "make arrangements, if he can, with the insurance companies for a settlement of the Hillmon case, by them stopping all pursuit and prosecution of myself and John H. Hillmon, if suit for money is stopped and policies surrendered to the companies."[25] A second agreement, dated the next day, was executed by an agent of the insurance companies; it "authorized and employed" Buchan to procure and surrender the policies of insurance on the life of John Hillmon. Buchan himself would testify later that the only pay he received in the

---

[23] This is the form in which the letter is reported in some newspaper accounts. *See, e.g.,* LEAVENWORTH TIMES, June 18, 1882, at 5. But Gleed's quotation of the letter in the "Report," which purports to be verbatim, contains a number of comical misspellings and other errors: "Mirs" for "Mrs.", and "Let me now threw my Father."

[24] LEAVENWORTH TIMES, June 17, 1882, at 1.

[25] *Id.*

matter came from the insurance companies.[26] (He bridled at the suggestion that there was anything improper about this, saying that he "was in the habit of taking fees for his work."[27])

John Brown testified in his deposition that over the summer Buchan had shown up, unbidden, at a farm in Missouri where Brown was working; he came back at least twice more, approaching Brown at various places where he was employed and finally at his brother Reuben's house. On the last occasion, Buchan brought with him a man named Ward, whom he said was a deputy sheriff.[28] On each occasion Buchan pressed Brown to sign a statement saying that the dead man was not Hillmon but another, informing Brown that there was a warrant for his arrest, but promising that he could protect Brown from any consequences for his role in the Crooked Creek death if he would but sign.[29] Reuben, in his testimony at the first trial, seconded his brother's account. He said that after listening to Buchan, he undertook to convince his brother that it would be better for him to do as the lawyer urged him in order to avoid further difficulties, and that John Brown then gave in to these arguments and agreed to sign a paper that Buchan would prepare. John Brown later claimed to have been told that the paper would only be used to persuade Sallie Hillmon to drop her suits.[30]

After this capitulation there followed John Brown's preparation and signing of the letter to Sallie Hillmon saying that he would "like to know where John is." Mrs. Hillmon testified that she did not receive this letter, and Buchan (although he denied having dictated it to Brown) admitted that he did not send it on to her; instead he gave it to the insurance companies' representatives.[31] Apparently it was never intended as an actual communication; it was a piece of evidence whose manufacture was solicited by Buchan, at a time he purported to be representing Brown, in favor of the insurance companies' theory that Brown and Sallie Hillmon were united in a continuing conspiracy.

A couple of days later, in the presence of a notary, Brown signed the lengthy affidavit prepared by Buchan. A few days after that the docu-

---

[26] LEAVENWORTH TIMES, June 14, 1885, at 4 (second trial)

[27] Id.

[28] LEAVENWORTH TIMES, June 17, 1882, at 1. Buchan acknowledged that the deputy accompanied him on the drive over to Reuben Brown's place, but testified that his companion's law enforcement credentials were mere coincidence; the sheriff's office just happened to have the best team of horses around, and "little use for it." LEAVENWORTH TIMES, June 22, 1882, at 1.

[29] LEAVENWORTH TIMES, June 17, 1882, at 1

[30] Id.

[31] LEAVENWORTH TIMES, June 22, 1882, at 1 (first trial).

ment's history became even more bizarre: after it was shown to Mrs. Hillmon, it was torn to pieces and thrust into a stove in Buchan's office. Brown (backed up by Sallie Hillmon) claimed that it was he who treated the paper thus, saying the reason for this destructive act was the agreement between him and Buchan that the document was to be used only to encourage Sallie to relinquish her claim.[32] Buchan maintained on the other hand that the statement was prepared "as a guarantee that Brown would testify in case suit was brought that the statement was true,"[33] a description that implies the possibility of use in court to impeach a discrepant statement (and of course that is the very use to which the affidavit eventually was put). In any event, after the stove incident Brown must have believed that the statement had been destroyed.

Buchan, however, later acknowledged that between the time Brown signed it and the stove incident, he had given a copy of the affidavit to the insurance companies' attorneys.[34] (Copies were made by hand at the time, so the preparation of a copy was not a casual act.) Buchan could then destroy the original affidavit or permit its apparent destruction to reassure Brown of his good faith, secure in the knowledge that his colleagues representing the companies had access to a copy. But he seems even to have anticipated the possibility that a handmade and unsigned copy might not be admissible to the same extent as an original: after Brown and Hillmon left his office, he rescued the torn original statement from the stove and placed the pieces into an envelope. These efforts were later rewarded: in the third trial the judge ruled that the copy made at Buchan's direction could not be admitted or described, and that the matters therein could not be proved unless the original document were produced. Thanks to Buchan's rescue it was produced (somewhat scorched and tattered, but apparently restored or at least pieced back together), and admitted into evidence for the impeachment of the man Buchan had claimed was his own client.[35]

---

[32] LEAVENWORTH TIMES, June 17, 1882, at 1 (John Brown); LEAVENWORTH TIMES, June 20, 1879, at 1 (Sallie Hillmon).

[33] LEAVENWORTH TIMES, June 22, 1882, at 1.

[34] *Id.*

[35] 1899 Transcript, *supra* note 4, at 166–67. *See also* TOPEKA DAILY CAPITAL, Mar. 2, 1888, at 4. This enforcement of what we would today call the Best Evidence Rule prompts the question: why was not the testimony of Elizabeth Rieffenach—who said she could not produce the letter from her brother but proceeded to describe its contents in detail—subject to the same objection? Possibly the objection was not made, or possibly Judge Shiras thought the testimony fell within an accepted exemption from the Best Evidence Rule for documents that have been lost or destroyed.

Although Buchan denied or contradicted many aspects of the Brown brothers' testimony, his own account was scarcely less damning. By his own admission he prepared a document that, in exchange for Brown's affidavit, promised immunity from prosecution for both Brown and Hillmon.[36] But these negotiations were held only between Brown and representatives of the insurance companies; no public officials signed any of the documents, nor is there any visible evidence of their involvement. Either Buchan arranged for his "client" to confess to a crime (or more than one) in exchange for a promise that he knew was worthless, or the insurance companies really did dictate the administration of criminal justice in Lawrence and elsewhere (for if there was a murder it took place in Barbour County), and Buchan knew it and was willing to participate in their appropriation of the criminal justice system for their private purposes.

Even allowing for the possibility of a less rigorous set of professional expectations in 1880 Kansas than we might entertain today, the behavior of the lawyer Buchan was far beyond unprofessional. If the testimony of the Brown brothers is to be believed, his perfidy was shocking; but even if his own account is credited, his persistent persuasions might easily have caused a poor young man to sign a statement that he knew was not true in exchange for assurances that he would face no further trouble if he did so.

The central claim of the affidavit drafted by Buchan for Brown's signature was that a man who called himself "Joe Berkley" or "Joe Burgess" camped and traveled briefly with Brown and Hillmon and was later killed at Crooked Creek. In the first five of the Hillmon trials, the insurance companies' lawyers argued that the "Joe" of Brown's affidavit was really Frederick Adolph Walters, presumably using an assumed name. But testifying at the last trial, in 1899, Major Wiseman admitted that he had found "Joe Burgess," the same one mentioned in Brown's affidavit, quite alive before the first trial.[37] Apparently, at the time the affidavit was written, the companies knew of an actual young man named Joe Burgess who had dropped from sight, and hoped this identity could be attached to the dead man; only after the real Joe Burgess turned up and the Walters family reported their son missing did they begin to claim that "Joe" was an alias of F.A. Walters. What better proof

---

[36] TOPEKA DAILY CAPITAL, Mar. 10, 1888, at 4 (second trial). Buchan testified that Brown's insistence on immunity not only for himself but for his partner as well complicated the negotiations, and of course if true this would suggest that Brown knew Hillmon was still alive; but Brown's testimony was different.

[37] LEAVENWORTH TIMES, Nov. 11, 1899, at 6. Apparently by the last trial the defendants had more or less given up the claim that Frederick Adolph Walters was the "Joe Burgess" of Browns' affidavit. One of their own attorneys elicited from Major Wiseman that he had "found" both Francis Nichols (or "Arkansaw") and Joe Burgess in 1879. Id.

could there be that the affidavit was the product of Buchan's invention, and not a truthful account related to him by Brown?

These reflections are important not only to the judgment of history as it pertains to Mr. Buchan, but also to the credibility of Brown and, ultimately, to the significance of the letter from Frederick Adolph Walters to his sweetheart. Without Brown's affidavit, the defendants had little to rest their case on but claimed variations between Hillmon's and the dead man's bodies, the oddness of a man like Hillmon having purchased so much life insurance, and the Walters letter. The letter and the affidavit seem to reinforce one another: each tends to quell doubts about the reliability of the other. But if the Brown affidavit is judged to be the unreliable product of an unscrupulous lawyer's interactions with a frightened and unlettered young man, the Walters evidence justly falls under new scrutiny, together with the famous decision that legitimized it.

The career of the letter through the various trials rewards further attention. After the Lawrence inquest the insurance companies learned about the Walters family, their missing Frederick Adolph, and his fiancée. Soon afterward the companies' lawyers took the deposition of Miss Alvina Kasten, who (she said) furnished them with the famous "Dearest Alvina" letter. Judge Foster, presiding in the first trial, admitted the letter, together with the deposition in which she identified it; Kasten herself did not testify live at this trial (or any of the others).[38] After seven ballots the jury remained divided seven to five in favor of Mrs. Hillmon, and a mistrial was declared.[39]

In the second trial, the Kasten deposition was again received in evidence, together with the letter. Again the jury hung, this time six to six,[40] but this time the letter seems to have been more important in their deliberations. One juror (who had voted for the plaintiff) suggested afterward to a newspaper reporter that if Walters had been in Wichita, as the letter suggested,

> he would certainly have been seen and remembered by somebody. He would have had a boarding house; he became a cigarmaker, he would certainly have been remembered by someone of that craft. The fact that there was no attempt to bring anyone forward, who could say they had seen him in Wichita at that time, caused us to believe THAT THERE WAS SOMETHING CROOKED about that letter.[41]

---

[38] LEAVENWORTH TIMES, June 29, 1882, at 4.

[39] LEAVENWORTH TIMES, July 4, 1882, at 4.

[40] LEAVENWORTH TIMES, June 25, 1885, at 4.

[41] *Id.* (capitalization in original).

Concerning Brown's two accounts, this juror said that they "had considerable influence, although it was hard to tell which of his stories was true," and also that "it will be hard to make me believe but what Buchan worked him pretty hard, to get his evidence for the companies."[42]

Apparently heeding this juror's skepticism, at the third trial in 1888 the defendants called several witnesses to testify that they had seen Walters, or someone who resembled him, in Wichita in early March, 1879.[43] And again they offered the Kasten deposition, together with its attached copy of the letter she said Walters had sent her. But this new and revived evidence availed the defendants little because Judge Shiras forbade any mention of the contents of the letter, reasoning that its assertions were hearsay (as they undeniably were).[44] The jury found unanimously for Mrs. Hillmon—the verdict destined to be overrruled by the Court's famous decision.

The three trials that ensued after the Supreme Court's 1892 decision all included, of course, proof of the Kasten letter, and they produced outcomes that eerily replicated the first three trials': two more hung juries, followed by a verdict for Mrs. Hillmon, to be overturned by the United States Supreme Court when the litigation reached it for the second time. But the letters, having by then enjoyed the Supreme Court's attention, sustained a more focused and searching scrutiny in the last three trials than in the first two.

The fourth trial, which took place in Topeka in 1895, was the longest of any, occupying nearly three months of the court's time. (The Topeka newspaper, recounting the case's previous history with some awe, prematurely called the proceeding "this final Titanic contest."[45]) On this occasion the insurance companies called three citizens of Lawrence who had served as jurors at the inquest there, who swore with remarkable unanimity that during the inquest Mrs. Hillmon had testified that she could not remember or did not know the color of her husband's hair and eyes, nor his height.[46] As no official transcript was preserved of the inquest, Mrs. Hillmon's lawyers were not in position to impeach this testimony, but this author (having read the newspaper accounts) is: she described the color of his hair and eyes (eyes dark brown, hair brown, whiskers lighter than hair) in addition to many other features of his appearance (dark complexion, sometimes wore chin whiskers and some-

---

[42] Id.

[43] Id.

[44] See 1888 Transcript, supra note 4, at 189–90.

[45] TOPEKA DAILY CAPITAL, Feb. 5, 1895, at 4.

[46] TOPEKA DAILY CAPITAL, Feb. 2, 1895, at 5; TOPEKA DAILY CAPITAL, Feb. 6, 1895, at 4.

times only a moustache, hair quite straight and tolerably long, cheek bones quite prominent at times, depending on his weight).[47] It is true that she said she could not certainly state his height, never having measured him.[48]

More new evidence arrived in the testimony of a Walters brother, C.R. Walters, who lived at the time of Frederick Adolph's disappearance in Missouri, and who remembered (as he had in the first trial) a letter he said he had received during February of 1879, postmarked Wichita. He could never produce this letter, but his memory of it had grown a bit more particular with time: in the fourth trial he said it related that his brother "had made arrangements to drive cattle for a man by the name of Hillmon" in Colorado, and wished to postpone plans the two brothers had made to meet and go to Leadville for the gold mining until after his engagement with Hillmon.[49] Another letter was produced, by Mrs. Hillmon's lawyers: a letter that C.R. Walters had written to the sheriff of Leavenworth in 1880, after the inquest but before any of the trials, stating that his brother Frederick Adolph had a gold filling in his teeth.[50] This letter was inconvenient to the defendants, as their proof had been as adamant on the untouched perfection of the corpse's teeth as on any point in the litigation. The jury in this trial hung eleven to one in favor of Mrs. Hillmon.[51]

The fifth trial followed the fourth by a year; it began and ended in March of 1896. The jury hung again, a majority of the jurors apparently in favor of the defendants.[52]

The sixth trial began in a manner that resembled the others, but offered several significant new revelations. Major Wiseman finally confessed that he had found Joe Burgess—the same Joe "of whom there was some talk of [his] having been the body which was shipped back for that

---

[47] LEAVENWORTH STANDARD, Apr. 10, 1879 at 1.

[48] Id.

[49] TOPEKA DAILY CAPITAL, Feb. 23, 1895, at 5.

[50] Id.

[51] TOPEKA DAILY CAPITAL, Mar. 21, 1895, at 1.

[52] TOPEKA DAILY CAPITAL, Apr. 4, 1896, at 1. The Capital reported that the last poll taken of the jurors was seven to five, although one juror later claimed they had been evenly divided. It also reported that the jurors had thereafter agreed to some sort of numerical system to calculate the weight of evidence on each side by assigning a value from zero to five for each witness. On this system, the Capital's source said, the insurance companies were far ahead until one holdout juror refused to vote according to this system, and this defection caused the foreman to inform the judge that they were at an impasse. The paper also reported that the insurance companies had proposed to the Hillmon side, after this outcome, to "try the case before the five federal judges who have tried the case and abide by the decision of the majority." Id. Nothing seems to have come of this proposal.

of Hillmon"—alive more than twenty years before.[53] There was a blatant effort at corruption reported by a juror about midway through this last trial, but it is impossible to tell which side might have been responsible, as Judge Hook handled the event with extraordinary discretion, issuing a stern admonition against further such attempts but declining to interrupt the trial or dismiss the jury.[54] Then there was a surprise rebuttal witness for the plaintiff, a man named Arthur Simmons, who owned a cigar factory in Leavenworth.

Simmons testified that for three weeks in May of 1879—that is, two months *after* the death at Crooked Creek—he employed Frederick Adolph Walters in his factory as a cigarmaker. Nor was his testimony the only proof of these events; Simmons produced records of employment corroborating this claim. He knew his employee as F. Walters, and he identified a photograph of Frederick Adolph as a likeness of the man who had made cigars for him. He testified that even after the intervening years he had a good recollection of the young cigarmaker because

> [h]e was a man who was all the time talking to the men about him and telling of his many travels. He had been in a large number of towns in different places and he also talked a great deal of his love scrapes and how he had gotten out of them.[55]

This testimony apparently made an impression on the sixth jury; they returned a unanimous verdict for Sallie Hillmon.[56] And although the companies continued their appeals to higher courts, and eventually succeeded in overturning this victory as well in the Supreme Court, in the end they all settled with her.[57] It was then nearly twenty-five years after the death at Crooked Creek.

---

[53] *See supra* note 43.

[54] LEAVENWORTH TIMES, Oct. 27, 1899, at 4.

[55] LEAVENWORTH TIMES, Nov. 14, 1899, at 4.

[56] LEAVENWORTH TIMES, Nov. 19, 1899, at 4.

[57] The New York Life Insurance Company had paid Sallie Hillmon Smith's claim before the sixth trial commenced. *See* LEAVENWORTH TIMES, Oct. 15, 1899, at 4. Mutual of New York paid the judgment against it from the sixth trial. *See* Satisfaction in Full of Judgment, August 8, 1900 (NARA Archive). But the Connecticut Mutual Life Insurance Company again appealed. A Circuit Court of Appeals having been created since the previous appeal, the appeal was first argued and decided there, in favor of affirmance. Conn. Mut. Life Ins. Co. v. Hillmon, 107 F. 834 (1901). Certiorari review was granted by the United States Supreme Court, with the same result as a decade earlier: the Court overturned Mrs. Hillmon's victory and remanded the matter for a new trial. On this occasion the bases for reversal were again issues pertaining to the law of evidence. The Court held that John Brown's affidavit, introduced by Mrs. Hillmon for the limited purpose of showing why she had at one time said she would release the defendants from her claims, should have been received as the truth of the matters it recited and the jury so instructed. It also held that certain statements that witnesses claimed Levi Baldwin had made about a scheme he and

But I have not forgotten that I undertook to persuade you that the Dearest Alvina letter was full of lies. Consider the testimony of Arthur Simmons. If this testimony was true (and no reason appears that a cigar factory owner should have perjured himself for Sallie Hillmon's sake, much less manufactured business records), then of course Walters did not die at Crooked Creek. And if he did not, the same argument against coincidence that made the "Dearest Alvina" letter such convincing proof of his death at the hands of Hillmon must be reconsidered—as an argument that the letter was not truthful. Curiously, Mrs. Hillmon's lawyers do not seem to have pursued the possibility that the "Dearest Alvina" letter was mendacious, perhaps because they had had an opportunity to compare the letter's handwriting with exemplars and concluded that the letter was written by Walters' hand. But that circumstance does not necessarily imply that the letter was written when it is dated, nor that the assertions in it are true.

Walters' long absence from home and failure to write to his loved ones, which the insurance companies learned of at about the same time their agent Major Wiseman reported the disappointing news that Joe Burgess was alive and well, must have been circumstances too suggestive for the defendants not to make use of them. As they had to the earlier rumored disappearances of various young men, they responded with a determination to turn these events to their advantage. All that was needed to transform the cigarmaker's disappearance into strong proof that Hillmon had not died at Crooked Creek was a document to tie Walters to the Crooked Creek corpse, and a witness to authenticate it. The Kasten letter and Miss Alvina Kasten satisfied this need almost perfectly—if the letter could be manufactured, and if she could be persuaded to testify in a deposition that she had received the letter by post shortly after the date that appeared on it.

The mind resists this last possibility, because it requires us to conclude that Alvina Kasten lied when she testified in her deposition that she had received the letter on March 3, 1879. We must also credit the insurance companies' agents and lawyers with sufficient dishonesty to create a brazenly inauthentic document and suborn the perjury of these witnesses. Can this rather extravagant hypothesis be supported?

---

John Hillmon had conceived, a scheme that Baldwin said would make him rich, were admissible against Mrs. Hillmon as co-conspirator's statements. Conn. Mut. Life Ins. Co. v. Hillmon, 188 U.S. 208 (1903). To the twenty-first century litigator these seem very dubious propositions, and they never achieved the prominence of the rule created in the first decision. (Two Justices dissented without opinion; one of them was Justice David Brewer, who eighteen years earlier had presided over the second Hillmon trial.) Before the case could be tried for a seventh time, the Connecticut Mutual Life Insurance Company settled Mrs. Hillmon's claim.

We know that the lawyer Buchan, an attorney who conceded that he worked for and was paid by the insurance companies, employed coercion to persuade John Brown to sign the "Joe Burgess" affidavit, a document shown to be false by the later testimony of Major Wiseman. We also know that not long before Alvina Kasten gave her deposition, Buchan dictated to John Brown (or at the very least, directed him to write) an incriminating letter addressed to Sallie Hillmon. The circumstance that there was never even any pretense of actually mailing this letter to Mrs. Hillmon—that Buchan sent it directly to the insurance company lawyers—suggests both the nakedness of Buchan's motive for having Brown write it, and the clumsiness of his methods. Mr. Buchan was no stranger to the fabrication of evidence—epistolary evidence—nor was he too scrupulous to pressure an individual into swearing to propositions that were not true.

Neither was Buchan the only attorney in the employ of the companies who participated on the presentation of false evidence. At least three witnesses who testified at the second and fourth trials—the three jurors from the Lawrence inquest—testified falsely about what Mrs. Hillmon had (or had not) said at the inquest. The witnesses were examined in these trials by attorneys Green and Barker, both of whom were present at the inquest—indeed conducted it—and surely knew that these witnesses' testimony was untrue. Other testimony presented by the defendants—such as that of the doctor who said that John Hillmon reported his height to be 5'11" (the length of the dead body) when examined for his insurance policy, but came back a few days later to say he was in fact only 5'9"—is far enough beyond implausible to arouse a serious suspicion of subornation. And it surely reflects on the ethics of the companies' lawyers that they continued to maintain for years after their agent had located "Joe Burgess" alive that he and Frederick Adolph Walters were the same (dead) man.

But even if the defendants' lawyers were capable of such chicanery as document fakery and subornation, what would have induced such a respectable woman as Alvina Kasten and various Walters family members to perjure themselves? Of Kasten more later, but as to the Walters family, a possible explanation appears in a newspaper account of the second trial. The reporter concludes an account of the day's testimony with the following:

> It is not generally known that there was an insurance on the life of young Walters, who is said to have been the dead body taken to Lawrence and passed for the body of Hillman. A reporter for THE TIMES was informed yesterday afternoon that Walters' life was insured and that the insurance money was paid, on the evidence elicited in the Hillman trial, of his death.[58]

---

[58] LEAVENWORTH TIMES, June 14, 1885, at 4.

If the defendants wished to induce members of the Walters family to testify (as they did) about correspondence from Frederick Adolph that mentioned the name Hillmon, what better method of compensating them for their trouble than retrospectively issuing a policy of insurance on his life, then paying the proceeds to his bereaved family—a gesture splendidly in sync with their insistence that he had died at Crooked Creek? But beyond pecuniary motives, I credit that the Walters family did truly come to believe that the photographs of the dead man were those of their lost son and brother Frederick Walter. A little suggestion and an adroit presentation of the photos of the corpse would go a long way toward persuading a baffled and worried family, whose loved one had suddenly ceased writing, that his death at the hands of the murderer John Hillmon was the explanation. If they believed this much, they would also have believed that John Hillmon was in hiding, waiting to enjoy the proceeds of his crime. Their conviction that Frederick Adolph had died at Crooked Creek may have nudged the family toward participation in perjury, if they thought it would produce justice for their missing loved one.

Consider Alvina Kasten: her deposition was taken in June of 1881, a year before the first trial, in her home town of Ft. Madison, Iowa, and it is this deposition that served thereafter as the defendant's evidence concerning the famous letter. She identified the letter containing the familiar description of an encounter with "a man by the name of Hillmon" as one received by her on the 3rd of March, 1879; she swore she recognized the handwriting as that of her fiancé F.A. Walters. Kasten testified that she had given this letter to Mr. Tillinghast, representing the New York Life Insurance Company, in January of 1880. (Of the other twenty-five or so letters she had received from her swain, she claimed in the deposition that she had destroyed them because she was "was sick at the time and did not expect to get over my sickness and destroyed all my letters.")[59]

What might have been Miss Alvina Kasten's motives for lying under oath? If threats or inducements prompted her deposition testimony identifying the letter, they are not evident from the record. But her account of her relationship with Adolph, as she said she called him,

---

[59] 1899 Transcript, *supra* note 4, at 1694. At first she said she had destroyed the letters shortly after giving the Wichita letter to Tillinghast; on further questioning she said it had been a year later than that, which would have been only shortly before giving the deposition. She appears, from the transcript, to have been flustered by the questioning, explaining her lapses by saying she was "bothered" (worried, presumably) about her sister, who was ill.

suggests some modest pride in her betrothed status. Perhaps it would have been hard for her to acknowledge that her fiancé had simply chosen not to come home to her, and to stop writing; his death at the hands of Hillmon may have been a less painful explanation for his disappearance, not to mention one that would spare her public humiliation. And once recruited to this theory, perhaps she (like the Walters family) was not difficult to enlist in the enterprise of denying the wicked Hillmons the proceeds of their crime, in her case by agreeing to say that a letter she was actually given by the lawyers had instead been received by her in the post shortly after the date shown on it. She may have been persuaded that the letter was intended for her and had somehow gone astray, and told that it would benefit the wicked, lying Hillmons were she to say truthfully how it had come to her. She may also have been promised that she needed only to testify at a deposition and would never have to appear before a judge (for as a resident of Iowa she was not susceptible to a subpoena to appear in federal court in Kansas). She may even have been offered assurances similar to those John Brown said he was offered— that his affidavit would never be used in court, but only employed to persuade Sallie Hillmon to abandon her claim. We know that Kasten never *did* appear in court, which prompts the question, why not? Would it not have behooved the defendants (who brought in many witnesses from much further away than Iowa) to persuade the bereaved fiancée to travel to the trial? Yet they did not do so. The suggestion that wounded romantic pride might account for a respectable young woman's small bout of perjury may seem fanciful, but Mr. Arthur Simmons' description of F.A. Walters as a seducer suggests that being his fiancée must have been a rather dodgy business, requiring a certain capacity for self-deception.

But how would the companies have persuaded young Walters to write the famous letter? We know that the companies' agents started looking for him after they learned from his family that he had stopped writing home at about the time of the death at Crooked Creek. If they had found him shortly after that time working for Simmons' cigar factory in Leavenworth and explained their interest to him, why would not Walters then have written home, and by this act relieved the sorrow of those who loved him and mourned his supposed demise? If he was the young man described by Arthur Simmons, an adventurer and traveler and a bit of a rake with a tiresome fiancée back home, perhaps he would have preferred to remain lost, especially if the insurance companies who had placed so much stock in his death were eager to subsidize his adventures away from home. And if this deal were struck, what would have been more sensible than for one of the companies' agents (my money would be on Mr. Buchan) to require Walters for his part to write out a letter, its contents partly dictated, to someone back home? (The dictation technique was precisely the method employed by Buchan to obtain a letter from John Brown addressed to Sallie Hillmon, a document that was then employed to suggest the existence of a Hillmon/Brown conspiracy.) The letter penned by Walters could then serve as evidence for the companies' propositions about the corpse at Crooked Creek. In such a case, the handwriting similarity between the Dearest Alvina letter and the letters later produced by Elizabeth Rieffenach need not be explained by coincidence or forgery; they would indeed have been written by the same hand. And the mystery of why F.A. Walters, if he were still alive, had not in so many years turned up would be solved.

Of course the letter to Alvina Kasten, having been created some time after the inquest, would have to be supplied with a Wichita postmark of a date some months earlier. Unfortunately the original cannot be examined; both the letter and the envelope made an exhibit to the Kasten deposition spent many of the years between the 1880 deposition and the later trials in the safekeeping of defense counsel J.W. Green, after he supplied the record with a substitute copy. This copy, having been made before the advent of copying machines, was written by hand; the original is missing from the court's archive. The copy that remains available for inspection represents that the original was postmarked "Wichita—Mar 2, 1879." But nineteenth century American postmarks, or cancellations, were neither distinctive nor uniform.[60] Forging one would not have been much of a challenge, and there is no suggestion that any of Mrs. Hillmon's lawyers scrutinized the cancellation or the letter with any suspicion.

As for Sallie Hillmon, by the time the case was over she retained none of the settlement proceeds; before the last trial she had assigned her interest in them to other parties.[61] Perhaps the decision whether to

---

[60] See the examples in THE NEW HERST-SAMPSON CATALOG: A GUIDE TO 19TH CENTURY UNITED STATES POSTMARKS AND CANCELLATIONS (Kenneth L. Gilman ed., 1989) (copy available from author).

[61] On the question of who owned what interest in the eventual proceeds, there is a great deal of conflicting evidence. In 1882 Sallie Hillmon swore that she had not parted with her interest in any of the cases. See Affidavit of Sallie Hillmon, June 1882, Hillmon Case file at National Archives and Records Administration, Kansas City, Missouri (hereinafter NARA Archive). In 1888 William Sinclair, the individual who had provided the bond securing any costs Mrs. Hillmon might be required to pay in connection with the litigation, had prayed to be released from his obligation, averring in part that "Sallie E. Hillman has assigned and parted with all of her interest in said several suits," naming her attorneys and H.S. Clark as the purchasers. Affidavit of Wm. T. Sinclair, January 6, 1888 (NARA Archive). (An H.S. Clark was in 1879 the Sheriff of Douglas County, where Lawrence is located., see TOPEKA DAILY CAPITAL, Mar. 12, 1895, at 6). See TOPEKA DAILY CAPITAL, Feb. 19, 1895, at 4, where reference is made to a document (excluded from evidence) conferring a certain interest in the litigation on the plaintiff's attorneys. But see Appearance of Attorneys Representing James T. Lord, January 22, 1898, (NARA Archive), in which it is

continue an exhausting quest for affirmation that her husband was no murderer was by then not hers to make. But of her we do know this one thing: years earlier, before the Supreme Court first heard the Hillmon case and while there was still some prospect that she would collect the insurance, Sallie Hillmon remarried.[62] It is possible that an unschooled waitress in her twenties pulled off a devastating double-cross of her first husband, knowing that he would be compelled to remain hidden while she and her second husband enjoyed their bigamy and Hillmon's life insurance proceeds. But isn't it far more likely that she always knew the truth of what she had claimed from the first moment she viewed the body that had been brought to Lawrence from Crooked Creek—that John Hillmon was dead?

* * *

One proponent of narrative legal theory quotes the maxim *Da mihi facta, abo tibi jus* ("give me the facts, then I will give you the law"), and several scholars have remarked the inseparable character of the activities of law-making and fact-finding (or storytelling). I have suggested that the legal rule propounded by the Court in the Hillmon case was created because the only story the Court could bring itself to endorse demanded it. And I have undertaken to persuade my readers that this story was untrue.

Of course, I cannot claim to be immune myself from the seductions of narrative. I have here only told another story, albeit one that I believe to be better justified by the evidence than the understood version. I have tried in telling my version to lash myself to the mast of truth, but I confess I've enjoyed telling what I believe to be an excellent tale, and possibly its siren call has deceived me as well.

But what if I am right? What if the letter from Frederick Adolph Walters to Alvina Kasten was written not when it was dated and postmarked but later, and not because the writer really wished to inform Miss Kasten of his whereabouts and plans, but because some agent of the three insurance companies manufactured this evidence with the assistance of Mr. Walters, who was paid for his contribution? At the very least, if we are persuaded of this proposition, we might be able to look at the exception to the hearsay rule for statements of intention with an eye

---

averred that Sallie has sold her interest in the litigation against the New York Life Insurance Company to Mr. Lord.

[62] Newspaper accounts of the third trial, in 1888, report that "Mrs Hillman was married some time ago and her name is now Smith," and that her husband attended the trial with her. LAWRENCE TRIBUNE, Mar. 16, 1888, at 4. The same story says that the jury is unaware of her remarriage because "the attorneys on each side fear to introduce" evidence of it. *Id.*

less deceived by the McGuffin that has always bound this fragment of legal doctrine to a charming but mendacious story.

Recent Supreme Court discussions about other hearsay exceptions have cast a severely critical eye on proponents' easy claims about the inherent credibility of certain categories of extrajudicial statement.[63] Suppose this renewed skepticism were applied to statements of a declarant's intentions, as exemplified by the Walters letter. Those I have persuaded of my theory about the letter's origins must look soberly at the statements of Frederick Adolph Walters in the letter to his Dearest Alvina, for if I am correct it is full of falsehoods from the implicit assertion contained in the date at the top ("Today is March 1, 1879"), to its assurance to Miss Kasten that "I am about as Anxious to see you as you are to see me," to its recitation of the writer's intentions to look for a place to start a sheep ranch with John Hillmon, who had promised him "more wages than I could make at anything else." One might respond that a single counterexample does not unmake the wisdom of a general rule, but at least the wisdom of the rule must be defended without reference to that particular example. This enterprise is one that the law of evidence, in the one hundred fourteen years post-*Hillmon*, has not seriously undertaken.

## SUGGESTED READINGS

Eustace Seligman, *An Exception to the Hearsay Rule*, 26 HARV L. REV. 146 (1913).

Annual Report of the Kansas State Superintendent of Insurance, *reproduced in* JOHN H. WIGMORE, THE PRINCIPLES OF JUDICIAL PROOF 856–896 (1913).

John MacArthur Maguire, *The Hillmon Case—Thirty Three Years After*, 38 HARV. L. REV. 709 (1925).

Brooks W. Maccracken, *The Case of the Anonymous Corpse*, XIX AMERICAN HERITAGE 50 (June 1968).

---

[63] *See* Crawford v. Washington, 541 U.S. 36 (2004); Williamson v. United States, 512 U.S. 594 (1994); Idaho v. Wright, 497 U.S. 805 (1990).

*

# 13

## The Wisdom of *Dallas County*

### Dale A. Nance*

The hearsay rule is a strange beast. Its prohibition sweeps quite broadly, only to be offset by a bewildering array of exceptions. Further, the Federal Rules of Evidence include an important and controversial provision, Rule 807, granting authority to trial judges to admit some hearsay that is not admissible under one of the other, more specific exceptions. Generally known as the "residual" exception to the hearsay rule, and replicated in most, but not all, state evidence codes, Rule 807 sets forth a multi-factored standard to guide decision-making. The drafters of the original rule cited only one authority for the idea that courts should have such residual discretion—a 1961 decision by a panel of the Fifth Circuit in the case of *Dallas County v. Commercial Union Assurance Co.*[1]

The opinion in that case, authored by Judge John Minor Wisdom, reflects two fundamental and recurring issues in the law of evidence. The first is the question to what extent rulings on admissibility should be governed by abstractly stated rules, applicable to a range of cases and stated in relatively specific and determinate language. Predictability by advocates and control by appellate courts argue against a residual authority in trial judges to admit evidence in particular cases when such categorical rules, like the prohibition of hearsay together with its various specific exceptions, would otherwise exclude that evidence. On the other hand, the need for trial judges, as decision-makers "in the trenches," to tailor admission practices to the equities of the particular case argues in favor of residual discretion.

The second issue is more substantive. On what grounds should relevant hearsay be admitted or excluded? Unlike the first issue, which speaks to the allocation of authority between rule-maker and trial judge,

* I am grateful to Robert Myers and Rebecca Glick for assistance with research in preparing this chapter. For commentary on earlier drafts, thanks are due to my colleagues, Paul Giannelli and Max Mehlman, and to our diligent general editor for this volume, Richard Lempert.

[1] 286 F.2d 388 (5th Cir. 1961), cited in the advisory committee note to Fed. R. Evid. 803(24), precursor of Rule 807.

this issue speaks to the reasons that would motivate any rational decision-maker confronting a hearsay issue, whether a rule-maker crafting an exclusionary rule, an appellate court deciding a hard case, or a trial judge exercising discretion to admit or exclude particular hearsay evidence. Although considerations relating to one issue may affect how the other is addressed, still the two issues are distinguishable.

It is widely accepted that the hearsay rule's exclusion of out-of-court assertions rests primarily on the absence of one or more of three safeguards that characterize live in-court testimony: (1) the taking of an oath subject to the penalty of perjury; (2) the possibility, and often the actuality, of cross-examination, and (3) the fact finder's opportunity to observe the witness's demeanor as the witness testifies and is cross-examined. Yet all evidence is subject to sources of unreliability and is likely to be less probative than some imaginable alternative piece of evidence. For example, an eyewitness's identification of a criminal defendant based on a brief glimpse in poor light is less reliable than a hypothetically similar identification after having clearly seen the perpetrator in bright light. Why then do the deficiencies of hearsay call for exclusion, when other kinds of less-than-perfect evidence are routinely admitted? And why are so many hearsay statements admissible nonetheless, even when the three safeguards of live testimony are all absent? Plainly, there is an important missing premise in the argument for excluding or admitting hearsay. Bringing it into the open facilitates informed judgments about the admission or exclusion of hearsay.

There is, perhaps, no better vehicle for exploring these issues than the *Dallas County* case. In this essay, I shall tell the story of the case and its much-cited opinion, highlight its contributions to thinking about the reasons and criteria for excluding hearsay, and comment on the case's legacy for the law of evidence.

## The Case

*The Trial of an Insurance Claim*

Great cases often have humble beginnings. The *Dallas County* case arose from a fairly mundane, if somewhat unusual insurance claim.[2] On the bright, sunny morning of July 7, 1957, the clock tower of the Dallas County Courthouse, at Selma, Alabama, collapsed. The County undertook an investigation of the incident, which led to the filing of insurance claims for the property damage. The insurance in question provided coverage for damage resulting from lightning, and the County had evidence of a lightning strike during a thunderstorm five days before the collapse. The evidence included an eyewitness who said she saw lightning hit the courthouse, government employees who described a ball of light jumping from one place to another within the building during the storm, and charred timbers found amidst the debris several days later. The insurance companies (hereafter, "defendants") undertook their own investigation and found evidence that a lightning strike did not occur

---

[2] The description of the case that follows is taken from the trial transcript, the briefs on appeal, and Judge Wisdom's opinion.

and that, even if it did, the cause of the collapse was faulty design, construction, and maintenance of the building, a cause not covered by the insurance. The trial of the resulting federal claim,[3] before District Judge Daniel H. Thomas, involved "ample evidence to support a jury verdict either way" (p. 390). (Page references in the text refer to Judge Wisdom's opinion on appeal.)

Some of the evidence presented at trial by defendants was intended to explain away, without necessarily controverting, the evidence offered by the plaintiff county. For example, the plaintiff's testimony that balls of electrical charge jumped from place to place in the building during the storm was explained by expert testimony to the effect that this was a common discharge of static that would develop during a storm without regard to lightning striking the courthouse tower. In a similar vein, without denying that charred timbers were found within the debris, defendants introduced evidence that termite damage to the charred timbers must have occurred after the charring, which implied that the charring had occurred long before any July storm in 1957. They also provided expert testimony to the effect that lightning could not cause such charring without having produced flames, yet no fire was reported in the aftermath of the storm.

Still, the defendants thought they needed to explain how charred timbers might have been found among the debris if there had been no lightning strike. To do this, they presented a short newspaper article from *The Morning Times* of Selma, dated June 9, 1901—fifty-six years before the collapse of the tower—and authenticated by the editor of the successor newspaper as retrieved from the paper's archives. The article, written by an unnamed reporter, read simply:

---

New Courthouse
Badly Damaged by Fire This Morning—Dome Burned Off
Incendiary Origin

At a few minutes past two o'clock this morning the alarm was sent in from box 21, calling the firemen to the corner of Lauderdale and Alabama streets. The unfinished dome of Dallas county's new courthouse was in flames near the top, and before a stream could be brought to bear upon it the structure was a mass of flames and soon fell in. The fire was soon under control and the main building was saved. The fire was evidently the work of an incendiary. When first seen the fire was in the top of the dome. We could not learn whether there was any insurance on the building, but presume that the county is protected against loss.

---

[3] There were actually fifteen different suits against fifteen insurance companies, only seven of which could be removed to federal court under the then existing $3,000 minimum amount in controversy for diversity jurisdiction. These seven were tried together, as all presented the same factual issue, the cause of the collapse.

In offering this evidence, defendants likely were responding to the possibility that the jurors would find the county's claim more credible if they were given no evidence of an explanation for the charred timbers other than lightning.

Judge Thomas overruled the county's objection that this article was inadmissible hearsay, and when the jury decided for the defendants after a seven day trial, the county appealed on this single evidentiary issue.

*An Innovative Ruling on Appeal*

Appeal went to the Fifth Circuit, which at the time embraced the State of Alabama. There the case landed in a veritable nest of progressive judges. On the panel were Judges John Minor Wisdom, Richard Taylor Rives, and John R. Brown. These men were three of the federal

Top Row: Judges JONES, CAMERON, BROWN and WISDOM.    Bottom Row: Judges RIVES, HUTCHESON and TUTTLE.
FIFTH CIRCUIT—MAY 9, 1959.

Photo courtesy of the U.S. Fifth Circuit Court of Appeals Archives

judges most responsible for desegregation decisions in the South. They and Judge Elbert P. Tuttle were disparagingly labeled "The Four" by fellow judge Ben Cameron, who saw them as attempting to destroy the Old South. Three of the four, including Wisdom, were Republicans who had worked hard to create a real two-party system in the South and, specifically, to elect Dwight Eisenhower to the presidency. Their reward was to find themselves appointed to the federal bench at a time when the Fifth Circuit had the difficult task of implementing the equal protection guarantee in the wake of *Brown v. Board of Education*. This they did with determination.

The *Dallas County* case hardly posed the kind of urgent issues of social justice involved in the desegregation cases. And at one level, the panel's decision to affirm the admission of the newspaper account proceeds through a fairly uncontroversial analytical path. It can be summarized in the following propositions:

1.  Questions about the admissibility of hearsay in trials of diversity actions are governed by federal, not state, evidence law; specifically, the *Erie* doctrine does not compel recourse to Alabama hearsay law (pp. 392–94).

2.  The (then) controlling federal rule of procedure favors liberal admissibility and provides wide discretion to courts to decide admissibility (pp. 394–95).

3.  Newspaper accounts of events are hearsay, when offered to prove the events recounted, and are ordinarily inadmissible (pp. 391–92).

4.  The prohibition of hearsay evidence is not absolute; "[a]ll too often primary evidence is not available and courts and lawyers must rely on secondary evidence" (p. 392).

5.  The present newspaper account is admissible on the ground that it is both necessary and trustworthy evidence (pp. 395–98).

But behind this straightforward reasoning lay reformist zeal. To begin with, the Fifth Circuit panel chose not to take the easy way out by ducking the admissibility issue. As the defendants had urged in their briefs, there was substantial non-hearsay evidence that lightning was not the cause of the charred timbers, so it would have been reasonable to hold that, if an error had been made in admitting the newspaper article, it was harmless. But the court was having none of that; it squarely addressed the merits of the hearsay issue.

More important, however, is exactly how the court responded on the merits. To the County's argument that "you cannot cross-examine a newspaper," Judge Wisdom replied, "This argument, a familiar one, rests on a misunderstanding of the origin and the nature of the hearsay rule. The rule is not an ancient principle of English law recognized at Runnymede. And gone is its odor of sanctity" (p. 391 n.1). Quoting extensively from the reformist opinions of two great evidence scholars, John Henry Wigmore and Edmund Morgan, Judge Wisdom's opinion emphasizes the court's need to utilize the best available evidence (pp. 391–92). Further, in addressing the then applicable federal rule of civil procedure—Rule 43(a)—Wisdom goes out of his way to observe that its specification of the rules of evidence for federal courts was "so uncertain in its meaning as to give broad latitude to a trial judge," "unencumbered by common-law archaisms" (pp. 394–95). Consequently, when one reaches the end of Wisdom's opinion, one is hardly surprised by its willingness to break free of the chains of tradition:

> We do not characterize this newspaper as a "business record", nor as an "ancient document", nor as any other readily identifiable and happily tagged species of hearsay exception. It is admissible because it is necessary and trustworthy, relevant and material, and its admission is within the trial judge's exercise of discretion in holding the hearing within reasonable bounds. (Pp. 397–98.)

There is some dispute about whether Judge Wisdom's recourse to general principles of admissibility was necessary to the decision. Some have suggested that the case presented nothing that could not have been resolved, with the same result, by application of the common-law hearsay exception for ancient documents. Others reject this view, arguing that the newspaper account, because it asserted facts the reporter did not personally observe, must have presented at least two levels of hearsay. If the ancient document exception was understood as only satisfying one level of hearsay—that presented by the fact that the article was introduced rather than the testimony of the reporter who wrote it—then it would not suffice to render the article admissible.

This is an interesting difference of opinion, but it is somewhat anachronistic. In 1960 there was considerable controversy about whether there was an ancient document exception to the hearsay rule at all and, if so, what the contours of such an exception might be. Under fairly well-developed case law, certain ancient documents were considered immune from the requirement of an authenticating witness, but the matter of the hearsay objection was still clouded, a fact of which both the parties and Judge Wisdom were well aware. The county denied that such a hearsay exception existed, and even the defendants did not dispute the matter. Rather, in two extensive and well written briefs, defendants argued for an exception only for those ancient documents that meet the twin tests of necessity and trustworthiness. For his part, Judge Wisdom had not only these briefs, but also the work of academicians who had considered the point in recent decades (p. 396 n.16).

In any event, Judge Wisdom chose not to rely on any application of canonical language of a former opinion or secondary authority laying out the precise boundaries of a supposedly extant exception, and he did not purport to modify such boundaries or to establish a new categorical exception. His opinion instead endorses judicial discretion to admit hearsay—any hearsay—when the underlying principles warrant doing so. Though not completely unprecedented, Wisdom's was a courageous move, more radical than anything even the defendants had endorsed.

## The Principles

As noted in the introduction, Judge Wisdom's willingness to engage in what today might be labeled—pejoratively—"activist" judging raises two fundamental issues.

### Tailored Justice Versus Rule–Based Predictability

Judge Wisdom came down squarely on the side of judicial discretion to admit hearsay evidence that will help to do justice in a particular case. He did not attempt to explain or justify this choice in favor of ad hoc justice, nor did he explicitly acknowledge the competing interest in predictability. To be sure, he did explain his reasons for admitting the newspaper account, and these explanations were surely intended to provide a significant element of generality and predictability. Just how predictable and consistent decisions under Wisdom's rather antinomian philosophy can be depends, however, on the intelligibility and coherence of the reasons given. As we will see, there is considerable confusion on that score.

Before turning to these matters, however, it is worth noting that the drafters of Federal Rule 807, not content with the predictability that comes from reasoning articulated in judicial opinions or their own general standards crafted to capture the desirable essence of *Dallas County*, eventually settled on a provision designed to ensure that opponents would be given adequate notice of a proponent's intent to use hearsay that does not fall within one of the standard exceptions. Rule 807 provides, in part:

> However, a statement may not be admitted under this exception unless the proponent of it makes known to the adverse party sufficiently in advance of trial or hearing to provide the adverse party with a fair opportunity to prepare to meet it, the proponent's intention to offer the statement and the particulars of it, including the name and address of the declarant.

Although there are inevitable disputes about how early this notice must be given and what constitutes the giving of notice, this provision makes the potential admissibility of hearsay under the residual exception in one important respect *more* predictable than admissibility under the categorical exceptions. The use of a categorical exception does not require pretrial notice, even when the applicability of the exception is contestable, but when hearsay is offered under the residual exception, an attorney knows before trial that his opponent intends to offer it and, through a motion *in limine*, may even be able to learn how the judge will rule on it. As a practical matter, the availability of the residual exception should not hamper trial preparation more than the availability of any other hearsay exception.

The concern for rule-generality reflects not only trial preparation concerns, but also a concern that judges maintain legitimacy, applying—and being seen by the public to apply—existing rules, rather than making things up on the fly. This concern is, however, ameliorated by the fact that norms governing the admissibility of hearsay fall very close to the administrative sphere of courts, where the judicial need for flexibility is acknowledged by the bar and lay scrutiny is at a minimum. Most evidence law, including that which defines the contours of hearsay exceptions, is unlike the substantive law that courts apply. The latter provides norms for the conduct of life outside the courtroom, where the virtues of generality, definiteness, and transparency to the public are most important.[4] By comparison, it is difficult to imagine these "rule of law" virtues being significantly undermined by the exercise of judicial discretion in admitting hearsay at trial.

More difficult to assess is the question whether appellate courts are willing and able to exercise appropriate control over discretionary admissibility decisions. This seems not to have concerned Judge Wisdom or the other members of his panel. Today, with thirty years of experience under the Federal Rules, this concern is muted by the reasonably successful appellate supervision of the substantial provisions for discretion under those rules. There is no serious movement to reduce the scope of trial judge discretion, even though it is fair to say that appellate courts, in reviewing the rulings of trial judges, could do more to articulate the value choices embedded in admissibility decisions. This concern seems most pressing in the context of a broad discretionary provision, such as Rule 403, which applies to nearly all types of evidence and potentially subsumes an enormous breadth of competing values. Just how serious the problem is in the context of Rule 807 depends on the clarity of the

---

[4] Ironically, that portion of the evidence law where the norms most likely affect the non-litigative behavior of parties—namely, the law of privileges—is the one context in which Congress left the law of evidence entirely to the vagaries of common-law development.

substantive grounds for admitting hearsay and the specificity with which such grounds are reflected in the standards that guide trial court decision making. I now turn to that topic.

## The Grounds For Admitting Hearsay

Judge Wisdom accepted the premise that there must be a special reason to admit hearsay, noting simply that "[i]n the Anglo–American adversary system of law, courts usually will not admit evidence unless its accuracy and trustworthiness may be tested by cross-examination" (p. 391). Wisdom's opinion then adopted Wigmore's influential analysis of the reasons motivating those hearsay exceptions that had evolved through the common-law process, reasons relating to the necessity and trustworthiness of various classes of hearsay. Wisdom, however, applied these principles to the analysis of an individual item of hearsay, rather than to the analysis of class-based exceptions. I shall first discuss each principle separately, identifying what each says about the basic reason to admit or exclude hearsay, and then address the important relationship between them.

*The Necessity Principle.* What exactly is meant in the hearsay context by "necessity"? It does *not* mean that the proponent needs the hearsay in order to win at trial, although proponents tend to argue as if it did. If, for example, an advocate believes that she would have a much stronger case if her opponent could not cross-examine a declarant, no court would recognize her "need" to avoid cross-examination as justification for admitting the declarant's out-of-court statement no matter how central it was to the advocate's case. Rather, necessity signals that the *tribunal* needs the hearsay in order to make a well-informed decision.

Necessity might then simply mean, as it does in Federal Rule 804(a), that a declarant is not reasonably available to testify because of death, illness, or other consideration. After all, rational decision-makers, whether judge or jury, presumably want the best information they can get. Testimony by the declarant, under oath and subject to cross-examination, would be nice if available, but if not, why ignore the best that is available, even if it is hearsay? On this point Judge Wisdom quoted Wigmore's influential analysis:

> [T]he [hearsay] rule aims to insist on testing all statements by cross-examination, *if they can be.* * * * No one could defend a rule which pronounced that all statements thus untested are worthless; for all historical truth is based on uncross-examined assertions; and every day's experience of life gives denial to such an exaggeration. What the Hearsay Rule implies—and with profound verity—is that all testimonial assertions *ought to be* tested by cross-examination, as the best attainable measure; and it should not be burdened with the

pedantic implication that they must be rejected as worthless if the test is unavailable. (P. 391 n.1.)

This root idea of necessity (unavailability of the declarant) can be modified in two important ways. First, it can be constricted, so as to further limit admissibility, by recognizing that even if the declarant is unavailable to testify, there might be alternative admissible means of proving the facts asserted in the hearsay or inferable therefrom. So long as alternative means of proof are available, it may be unnecessary to require the trier of fact to grapple with the assessment of the credibility of the out-of-court speaker. Excluding the hearsay encourages the presentation of the alternative proof in order to take advantage of that possibility. In what follows, I will refer to this as a notion of "comprehensive necessity," for it looks not only to the availability of the declarant but, comprehensively, to the availability of other sources of proof. It is more demanding than the standard of Rule 804, which conditions the admissibility of certain categories of hearsay only on the unavailability of the declarant.

Judge Wisdom, without explicitly endorsing a test of comprehensive necessity, cited Wigmore on the importance of considering the availability of "evidence of the same value from the [declarant] *or from other sources*" (p. 396; emphasis added). And in applying the necessity principle to the case, he rejected as impractical and improbable the idea that an eyewitness with memory of the fire might be found, even if that eyewitness was not involved in the chain of declarations that led to the newspaper article (p. 396). That Wisdom thought it necessary to reject such possibilities confirms that he had a comprehensive notion of necessity.

In contrast, one can justify broadening the admissibility of hearsay beyond the test of declarant unavailability. After all, in some circumstances the testimony of an available witness might be *less* reliable than what he said out of court. A spontaneous and contemporaneous statement by a possibly interested witness to a confidant can be more reliable than later sworn testimony, when memories have faded and the witness realizes the implications of his statements for a law suit. Beyond that, if hearsay is excluded by way of expressing a preference for the declarant's live testimony, such testimony might not be forthcoming if the court is wrong in thinking that the declarant is available, a result that would entail the loss of both sources of information, the hearsay and the live testimony. By this analysis, recourse to the hearsay becomes permissible—as far as the necessity requirement is concerned—because it is better, or at least not discernibly worse, than the anticipated alternative. I shall call this relaxed necessity principle "relative necessity."[5] As we

---

[5] Because it involves a comparative assessment of reliability, it could also be considered a version of the requirement of trustworthiness, but Wigmore instead discussed it (perhaps

will see, the Rule 803 exceptions, which are not conditioned on a judicial determination of declarant unavailability, were justified in such terms.

Judge Wisdom explicitly drew on this perspective. He noted that, even if the newspaper reporter, the reporter's sources, or others who claimed to have seen the fire were living and could be identified after fifty-eight years, their testimony was very unlikely to be as reliable as the contemporaneous newspaper account (p. 396).

Judge Wisdom thus blended two distinct ways of thinking about the necessity principle. He considered the availability of evidence other than the hearsay declarant, and in this sense took a relatively strict view of necessity. But he also considered whether any epistemic advantage was likely to be gleaned from these alternative sources, and in this sense he used a relatively permissive form of necessity. I shall call this combination of restrictive and expansive ideas "functional necessity." The relationships among these versions of the necessity principle are summarized in the following table:

| Alternative Forms of the Necessity Inquiry | Only declarant considered as alternative source of information. | All alternative sources of information considered, including declarant. |
|---|---|---|
| Condition satisfied if alternative source not reasonably available. | Declarant Unavailability | Comprehensive Necessity |
| Condition satisfied if alternative source either (1) not reasonably available, or (2) not more reliable than the hearsay. | Relative Necessity | Functional Necessity |

Of the four variants, comprehensive necessity most strictly constrains the admissibility of hearsay, while relative necessity is the most permissive standard. Declarant unavailability and functional necessity are intermediate standards, neither of which can be said to be uniformly stricter than the other. Functional necessity, as we shall see, is embodied in Rule 807(B), which conditions employment of the residual exception on a finding by the trial judge that the proffered hearsay is "more probative on the point for which it is offered than any other evidence which the proponent can procure through reasonable efforts."

The necessity principle provides one way to fill in the missing premise in the argument for or against excluding hearsay. If hearsay is

---

unfortunately) as a form of necessity. See 5 John H. Wigmore, A TREATISE ON THE ANGLO-AMERICAN SYSTEM OF EVIDENCE IN TRIALS AT COMMON LAW § 1421 (3d ed. 1940).

excluded when it is not the most probative evidence a party can produce on the point, the party will have an incentive to present the factfinder with the more probative evidence, whether that be testimony by an available declarant or some other evidence. The alternative of relying on the opposing party to produce the better evidence may be inferior, either because the opponent is unable to acquire the better evidence, or because the time lag between the presentation of the hearsay and its rebuttal by better evidence may be so great that the hearsay will have become embedded in a coherent story that later evidence cannot shake, at least not without unnecessary inconvenience for the trier of fact. Conversely, when the hearsay is the best the proponent can offer on the point, the very rationale of exclusion is muted.

In an adversary system, where parties have primary control of the evidence that is presented to the tribunal, this way of understanding the exclusion of hearsay has much to commend it. At least this is so if the goal of a trial is to arrive at the best possible approximation of the truth. And as Judge Wisdom put it, "If they are worth their salt, evidentiary rules are to aid the search for truth" (p. 395). This theme is, of course, reiterated in the Federal Rules. Rule 102, for example, directs that the rules be interpreted to serve "the end that the truth may be ascertained and proceedings justly determined."

*The Trustworthiness Principle.* The second idea employed by Judge Wisdom is trustworthiness. The core idea is that hearsay is presumptively unreliable and so should be admitted only in those special contexts where reliability is likely. Although the idea sounds plausible and is frequently encountered in discussions of hearsay, its precise meaning is hard to pin down. The problem can be easily grasped. In our discussion of relative necessity, one point was conspicuous: the application of that principle requires comparing the degree of reliability of alternative forms or sources of evidence. For example, testimony by a person under oath subject to cross-examination is generally considered more reliable than a hearsay report of what that person said out of court. This conceptual framework views reliability as a likelihood that evidence can be trusted, which ranges from very low to very high. Evidence, then, cannot be said to be "reliable" or "unreliable," because reliability is not a dichotomous characteristic of evidence but rather a matter of degree. Whether an evidentiary item is *reliable enough* for a court to consider depends on the purpose to be served by admission and the degree of reliability that purpose requires.

Once again, the general goal is to admit hearsay when doing so facilitates reaching an accurate verdict, subject to any ancillary restraints that justice may require. So the challenge is to formulate a reliability criterion, distinct from necessity, that will guide courts in achieving this goal. Many alternative formulations have been advanced, but when examined closely most turn out to be inadequate to the task. We will consider only the most plausible of these alternatives, some of which are reflected in Wisdom's opinion.

(1) *Hearsay is reliable enough to be admitted only when "even a skeptical caution would look upon it as trustworthy (in the ordinary instance) in a high degree of probability."* The quoted language is Wigmore's.[6] The phrase "high degree of probability" is imprecise and unsatisfactory, for it merely translates the question of how reliable is reliable enough into the question of how probable is probable enough. Wigmore must have meant, at least, more probable than not, a standard compatible with an opinion by Judge Learned Hand upon which Judge Wisdom relied.[7] Hand had referred to circumstances rendering the hearsay declaration "presumptively true," which means at least probably true in the absence of rebuttal evidence. Thus reformulated, the test sounds plausible. But it is too stringent. We need to allow for the possibility that weak hearsay, when taken together with other independent evidence favoring its proponent, might make the proposition asserted by the hearsay, or some other fact to be inferred therefrom, highly probable or presumptively true. Many statements admitted pursuant to standard hearsay exceptions work like that, and none of the well-recognized exceptions requires that the hearsay it admits, considered alone, be more likely than not true. Indeed, if all admitted hearsay were treated as presumptively true, then we would see many more directed verdicts or preemptive jury instructions than in fact we do. Nor will it do to construe this theory as merely requiring that the hearsay (by itself, in context) be reliable enough to raise a "permissible inference" of the fact asserted, one that the trier of fact must be permitted but not required to make. The case law is replete with references to the dubious reliability of admitted reports of unsworn out-of-court statements, and it was established well before the *Dallas County* decision that introducing admissible hearsay does not necessarily preclude a directed verdict against its offeror, even under the lenient standard for such decisions in civil cases. In the end, this theory of the trustworthiness requirement confuses the question of the admissibility of evidence with that of its sufficiency, exaggerating the stringency of the test for the former.

(2) *Hearsay is reliable enough to be admitted only when it has "more than the ordinary" degree of reliability associated with hearsay.* Once again, the quoted language is Wigmore's.[8] Judge Wisdom did not cite this language in *Dallas County*, but he quoted Professor Morgan to the same

---

[6] 105 Wigmore, supra note 9, § 1420 at 203.

[7] 286 F.2d at 395–96 (relying on G. & C. Merriam Co. v. Syndicate Pub. Co., 207 F. 515 (2d Cir. 1913)).

[8] 5 Wigmore, supra note 9, § 1420 at 202.

effect. Morgan's idea that hearsay should be admissible when it is "less unreliable than hearsay in general" (p. 391, n.1) might seem appealing, but it is a standard that is impossible to apply, except perhaps in the most extreme cases. The enormous range of reliability of hearsay statements precludes the specification of an "ordinary" instance of hearsay to use as a standard, and it is not realistically possible to determine an average level of reliability with the precision necessary to handle hard cases. Nor would it suffice if we could; it is simply too fortuitous to think that typical or average hearsay, however determined, is just at the tipping point between the properly admitted and the properly excluded.

(3) *Hearsay is reliable enough to be admitted only when the jury will not be misled into crediting the hearsay more than is rationally warranted.* The idea that we exclude evidence out of a fear that the jury will over-value it is a familiar theme in evidence law, and particularly the law of hearsay. Few, if any, informed observers would claim that jurors never make mistakes by overvaluing hearsay. But then the same can also be said about most categories of admissible evidence, hearsay or otherwise, so the mere potential for jury overvaluation is clearly not enough to warrant exclusion of evidence. Thus, there are several problematic assumptions underlying this theory, including (a) that jurors are generally more likely to err if they are allowed to consider hearsay (with the risk of its overvaluation) than if they are not (in which case they lose whatever legitimate probative value the hearsay possesses), and (b) that judges (or rule-makers) are able to identify those special situations in which this generalization is false so that exceptions to the rule, either categorical or case-specific, are warranted. Empirical studies of how mock jurors treat hearsay, conducted long after Judge Wisdom wrote, have so far failed to support the first assumption, and none have even tried to test the second. To be sure, at the time of *Dallas County*, jury distrust theory was in its heyday, and it is not dead even now. Wisdom was, however, alive to emerging criticisms of this line of hearsay justification, particularly the work of Professor Morgan. In citing Morgan's commentary on the American Law Institute's Model Code of Evidence, Judge Wisdom quotes passages that reject the jury distrust theory of the hearsay rule (pp. 391–92 nn. 1 & 3).

(4) *Particular hearsay is reliable enough to be admitted only when it is at least as reliable as other hearsay already known to be admissible.* Obviously, this standard is not viable as a general approach to the admissibility of exceptional hearsay, because (unlike the other candidates discussed here) it presupposes the existence of admissible hearsay with which the challenged hearsay can be compared. But in the context of established exceptions, it is a seemingly plausible strategy. Although Judge Wisdom did not write in these terms, it is perhaps the most obvious interpretation of Rule 807, which refers to the 803 and 804

hearsay exceptions and conditions admission under Rule 807 upon a
determination that the proffered hearsay has "equivalent circumstantial
guarantees of trustworthiness." As with alternative (2), however, this
seeming plausibility evaporates when one reflects upon the enormous
range of reliability reflected in the categorical exceptions, such as those
articulated in Rules 803 and 804. A plaintiff's self-interested statements
about his emotional condition, made to a testifying physician retained
solely to give an opinion at trial, has about as little reliability as one can
imagine, but it is nonetheless admissible under the Federal Rules (Rule
803(4)). At the other extreme, a regularly kept public record prepared by
a person with no interest other than to do his job by keeping accurate
records seems highly reliable (Rules 803(6)–(12)). If we use for comparison purposes the former, then the reliability test will exclude virtually
nothing; if we use the latter, the reliability test will exclude nearly all
hearsay not within a particular exception. Nor is there any practicable
way to construct an "average" degree of trustworthiness from all the
evidence that is now admitted under the established exceptions. Interpreted in this manner, Rule 807's trustworthiness directive is little more
than a license for judges to select positive or negative features of the
situation that support a choice about admission made on other (perhaps
justifiable) grounds.

(5) *Hearsay is reliable enough to be admitted only when it is sufficiently probative that considering it will not waste the time or other
resources of the tribunal.* This criterion treats the hearsay rule simply as
a concession to the inevitable limits on time and energy that can be
devoted to litigating a dispute (an efficiency concern) and to the conse-
quent need to focus these resources on the most valuable evidence (an
accuracy concern). It accepts the premise that abolition of the hearsay
rule might create perverse incentives to flood the courts with (possibly
fabricated) hearsay, and demands on that account a showing by the
proponent that offered hearsay is practically useful to a rational decision-maker. For this, the judge may use himself or herself as the
standard of rationality, without any need to second guess jurors' inferences. One can think of it as a (limited) "reverse–403" test. Whereas
Rule 403 overrides the presumptive admissibility of relevant evidence
when various negative factors substantially outweigh its probative value,
this "reverse" test would override the presumptive inadmissibility of
hearsay when its probative value clearly (or "substantially") outweighs
the potential of the hearsay to divert the tribunal's limited time and
cognitive resources from the assessment of other evidence. This is not a
particularly stringent trustworthiness constraint, nor is it the most
obvious interpretation of Rule 807's trustworthiness requirement. Still,
there is respectable authority favoring something like this approach to

admitting hearsay, and it is has the twin advantages of being reasonably intelligible and comparatively workable.

*The Relationship Between the Two Principles.* Judge Wisdom's trustworthiness analysis in *Dallas County* reflects these persistent difficulties. Drawing on a characterization by Wigmore, he began by stating that the question was whether the circumstances indicated that the hearsay was "trustworthy enough" to serve as a "practical substitute for the ordinary test of cross-examination" (p. 397). He then identified factors—also taken from Wigmore's more general analysis—tending to minimize concern about the reliability of the newspaper account, such as the low probability of a motive to falsify and the high probability that a false report would have been identified (p. 397).[9] But when it came time for a final assessment of the trustworthiness factor, Wisdom apparently realized that it was not enough to point to positive indicators of reliability, nor to say simply that the hearsay was "unusually" reliable or "very" reliable. He needed to answer the question, "How reliable is reliable enough?"

Wisdom's response to this conundrum speaks volumes. He wrote: "To our minds, the article published in the *Selma Morning–Times* on the day of the fire is more reliable, more trustworthy, more competent evidence *than the testimony of a witness called to the stand fifty-eight years later*" (p. 397; emphasis added). Here we have a meaningful comparison between the reliability of two specific pieces of evidence, even if one exists only hypothetically. What we also have is a straightforward application of the necessity principle, specifically what I have called functional necessity. The newspaper account, Judge Wisdom tells us, is reliable enough because it can be expected to be more reliable than any alternative sources not presented to the court. This subtle shift from trustworthiness to necessity illustrates an important point: trustworthiness, if strictly distinguished from considerations of necessity, is of little help in determining admissibility, apart from setting a lower bound that mandates the exclusion of evidence so weakly probative that it is unlikely to be helpful to the tribunal.[10]

---

[9] Unnoticed by the parties and the court were two brief notes in *The Morning Times* two days after the alleged fire. The first stated that the Knoxville architect (named Chamberlain) was in town to inspect the damage from the fire of the previous Sunday; the second reported that the *Times* had "received a great many compliments on its exclusive publication of the damage to Dallas County's new court house building by Sunday morning's fire." *The Morning Times*, Selma, Ala., June 11, 1901. Neither of these notices had an identified author.

[10] This is the sort of thing that caused Wigmore to observe that the courts routinely blend the requirements of reliability and necessity and that it is meaningless to try to analyze one without considering the other. See 5 Wigmore, supra note 9, § 1420 at 203.

Writing not long after *Dallas County*, Professor Morgan endorsed what he considered to be a crisp summary of Judge Wisdom's test. Morgan argued that the hearsay rule should not bar evidence if: (a) "the hearsay is such that the trier can put a reasonably accurate value upon it as evidence of the matter it is offered to prove," and (b) "direct testimony of the declarant is unavailable or, if available, is likely to be less reliable."[11] While Morgan's version of the trustworthiness idea— component (a)—has no explicit counterpart in the language of Wisdom's opinion, it is consistent with Wisdom's assessment of the newspaper article, and it is functionally identical to the reverse 403 test that I have argued is the most plausible form of the trustworthiness principle. If the information available does not allow the trier to assess the probative value of proffered hearsay with reasonable accuracy, then its probative value is too indeterminate to be practically useful. Conversely, if the trier can be reasonably accurate in assessing the probative value of hearsay, then the hearsay is practically useful, even if its probative value is relatively low, so long as it is not so weakly probative as to make its consideration a waste of time. (Morgan did not explicitly allow for this last qualification, perhaps because he knew that this reason for exclusion existed independently of the hearsay rule, as in the modern Rule 403.)

With regard to necessity, Morgan characterized Judge Wisdom's opinion as employing what I have called relative necessity. In this, Morgan failed to follow Wisdom in considering the implications of sources of evidence beyond the hearsay declarant. Perhaps Morgan believed that such attention was not necessary to the result in the case and that Wisdom would have admitted the article even if there had been an available eyewitness other than the reporter or his informant. In any event, Morgan may have been right to prefer relative necessity to functional necessity. After all, looking to other sources of information makes the decision making on admissibility more complicated and presents problems of determining when such alternative sources address the same point as the hearsay. However that may be, Wisdom's opinion clearly speaks in terms of functional necessity. And it is easy to imagine cases in which that approach has a strong appeal. For example, absent unusual circumstances, why admit the hearsay of a deceased expert when a live expert can be called and made subject to cross-examination?

Details aside, both Judge Wisdom and Professor Morgan articulated a two-prong test designed to achieve seemingly conflicting but entirely complementary objectives. The necessity principle seeks to *expand* the information available to the trier of fact by demanding, as a condition of admitting proffered hearsay, the exhaustion of alternative sources anticipated to be superior. At the same time, the trustworthiness principle

---

[11] Edmund M. Morgan, Basic Problems in Evidence 254 (1963).

seeks to *contract* the information available to the trier of fact. In its most plausible form, this is done so as to keep fact-finding in trials focused on practically useful information. Together, these principles push and pull in an attempt to optimize the information available to the trier of fact.[12] How well they do this and how they might be modified to better regulate the information flow and to serve other values, such as fairly allocating among the parties the costs of producing alternative evidence, are complicated matters that I shall not pursue here.

## The Legacy

We are poised now to consider the legacy of the *Dallas County* decision. First, we will consider how and to what extent its philosophy was adopted in the drafting of the Federal Rules. Then we will consider more briefly the impact of the residual exception on the continued potency of the hearsay objection.

### The Curious Legislative History of the Federal Rule

The adoption of the Federal Rules of Evidence in 1975 was a watershed event in the history of the law of evidence. The new rules were intended to liberalize the admissibility of evidence generally, and hearsay was no exception. In particular, the decision in *Dallas County* was well known to the drafters of the new rules, if only because it was featured in a number of evidence casebooks of that era. They understood that "[i]t would be presumptuous to assume that all possible desirable exceptions to the hearsay rule have been catalogued and to pass the hearsay rule to oncoming generations as a closed system," and that they needed to "provide for treating new and presently unanticipated situations which demonstrate a trustworthiness within the spirit of the specifically stated exceptions."[13]

In the original 1969 draft, Rule 8–03(a) provided:

(a) General Provisions. A statement is not excluded by the hearsay rule if its nature and the special circumstances under which it was made offer assurances of accuracy not likely to be enhanced by calling the declarant as a witness, even though he is available.

(b) Illustrations. By way of illustration only, and not by way of limitation, the following are examples of statements conforming with the requirements of the rule:. . . .

---

[12] Going beyond just the domain of hearsay law, I have elsewhere referred to these twin objectives as the "expansionary" and "contractionary" aspects of the best evidence principle, the principle that parties have a duty to present to the tribunal the best evidence reasonably available to them, qualified by a limited adversarial privilege. See Dale A. Nance, *The Best Evidence Principle*, 73 Iowa L. Rev. 227 (1988).

[13] FED. R. EVID. 803(24), advisory committee note.

Then followed various familiar hearsay exceptions, such as the excited utterance and business records exceptions, often revised somewhat to be more liberal than the common law.

Proposed Rule 8–04, had the same form as 8–03, except it conditioned admissibility on the declarant's unavailability:

(a) General Provision: A statement is not excluded by the hearsay rule if its nature and the circumstances under which it was made offer strong assurances of accuracy and the declarant is unavailable as a witness.

(b) Illustrations. By way of illustration only, and not by way of limitation, the following are examples of statements conforming with the requirements of this rule: . . .

The "illustrations" that followed here included those exceptions, like the dying declaration and statement against interest exceptions, that the common law had conditioned on unavailability.

Proposed Rules 8–03 and 8–04 would thus have relegated to judicial discretion decisions regarding the admission of hearsay, with the specifically enumerated exceptions serving simply as "safe harbors" for the proponent. If a hearsay statement came within one of these safe harbors, the hearsay objection would fail, but if it did not, the hearsay might still be found to have satisfied the one or the other "General Provision."[14]

While the two proposed rules had a common structure, they encapsulated quite different forms of necessity and trustworthiness. Proposed Rule 8–03 invoked what I have called relative necessity, but proposed Rule 8–04 relied on a combination of declarant unavailability and some form of the trustworthiness requirement.[15] The latter was apparently intended to be something like alternative (1), discussed above, in which the hearsay is required to be reliable enough so as to raise (by itself, in context) an inference or presumption of its truth.

---

[14] Note that the proposed hearsay structure was directly parallel to the structure of the authentication rule. Rule 901(a), both as proposed and as adopted, states a general rule for satisfying the requirement of authentication, while Rule 901(b) provides a non-exclusive list of ways the general standard may be satisfied.

[15] This difference was acknowledged by the drafting committee:

Rule 8–03, supra, provides for the admission of hearsay when its quality is considered to be at least as good as would be forthcoming if the declarant took the stand and testified. . . . The instant rule proceeds upon a different theory: hearsay which admittedly is not equal in quality to testimony of the declarant on the stand may nevertheless be admitted if the declarant is unavailable and if his statement meets a specified standard. The rule expresses preferences: testimony given on the stand in person is preferred over hearsay, and hearsay, if of the specified quality, is preferred over complete loss of the evidence of the declarant.

46 F.R.D. at 378–79 (advisory committee note).

In response to criticism, the advisory committee's 1971 draft changed the structure of Rules 803 and 804, so that they no longer were general principles followed by non-exhaustive lists of examples. Instead, the safe harbors became formal exceptions, and residual exceptions were added to both Rule 803 and Rule 804, each available to admit any "statement not specifically covered by any of the foregoing exceptions but having comparable circumstantial guarantees of trustworthiness." This standard is amenable to two, very different interpretations. It could mean that a statement admitted under the residual should have a *degree* of trustworthiness roughly equivalent to that of hearsay admitted under the other exceptions. We have already seen the formidable difficulties presented by such an interpretation. Alternatively, a more workable interpretation is that the drafters were attempting to maintain the reliability standards of the 1969 draft and intended that a "comparable" guarantee would be found under the Rule 803 residual whenever, in the language of the 1969 draft, "the special circumstances under which [the statement] was made offer assurances of accuracy not likely to be enhanced by calling the declarant as a witness." Under this interpretation, the 803 residual test would have been one of relative necessity: the court would have been directed to compare the reliability of the offered hearsay to the reliability of hypothetical live testimony by the declarant, *not* to the reliability of the diverse hearsay admitted under other exceptions. Similarly, though less intelligibly, a "comparable" guarantee would be presented under the Rule 804 residual whenever the circumstances "offer strong assurances of accuracy" (whatever that might mean), whether or not the degree of reliability was comparable to that of statements coming within the specific exceptions in 804.

But we did not have a chance to see the judicial interpretation of this language. Citing concerns about predictability, the House Judiciary Committee eliminated the residual exceptions entirely. In contrast, the Senate Judiciary Committee, concerned that without residual exceptions the enumerated exceptions would be "tortured" to admit necessary and reliable hearsay, retained them but added, as a compromise, certain restrictions noted below. The Conference Committee accepted the Senate's version with the further addition of a notice requirement, thus producing exceptions in substantially the same form we see today, albeit now consolidated in Rule 807.[16] As enacted, the residual exceptions, like the present version in Rule 807, imposed five distinct requirements, designated here so as to facilitate reference to the rule:

---

[16] The 1997 consolidation recognized what had become clear in the case law: any hearsay admissible under the 804 residual (then Rule 804(b)(5)) was also admissible under Rule 803(24), so having two residuals was unnecessary.

(I) the hearsay must have "circumstantial guarantees of trustworthiness" that are "equivalent" to those provided by the enumerated exceptions;

(A) the hearsay must be "offered as evidence of a material fact;"

(B) the hearsay must be "more probative on the point for which it is offered than any other evidence which the proponent can procure through reasonable efforts;"

(C) "the general purposes of these rules and the interests of justice" must be served by admission; and

(V) adequate pretrial notice of an intent to use the hearsay must be given to the adverse party.

Do these requirements give courts appropriate guidance? To begin with, as has often been observed, requirements (A) and (C) have no obvious function. Evidence not probative of a material fact is inadmissible under Rule 402, so the addition of (A) to Rule 807 seems pointless. Requirement (C) simply echoes Rule 102 and is basically empty of specific content. Hence, these provisions are deservedly ignored in the case law of Rule 807 and its precursors. If they have a purpose, it is simply to emphasize that the hearsay proponent must bear the burden of satisfying the other, more meaningful requirements and that courts should be cautious in their admission of evidence under the residual exception. Consequently, the three substantial restrictions in the federal rule are requirement (B) and the requirements I have labeled (I) and (V).

The notice provision in (V) has already been mentioned. It is the most important concession to the House's concern about predictability. The difficulties with the trustworthiness requirement in (I) have been discussed in some detail in the previous section. Much of the controversy surrounding the residual exception relates to the imprecision of this trustworthiness requirement and the tendency of those who wish to limit the use of hearsay to interpret that requirement much like the "strong assurances of accuracy" language appearing only in the original 1969 draft of Rule 8–04.[17] Suffice it here to reiterate that the only workable version of the trustworthiness requirement that is neither too

---

[17] Some support for this can be found in the legislative history. In its comment on the "more probative" requirement (B) that appeared in both 803(24) and 803(b)(5), the Senate Judiciary Committee stated: "This requirement is intended to insure that only statements which have high probative value and necessity may qualify for admission under the residual exceptions." S. Rep. No. 1277, 93d Cong., 2d Sess. (1974), 1974 U.S. Code Cong. & Ad. News 7051, at 7066. This unfortunate blending of the trustworthiness idea and the necessity idea conflicts with the language of the rule, however, for requirement (B) can be satisfied by hearsay that is more probative than alternatives even if the hearsay does not possess "high probative value." For example, if relevant hearsay is the only evidence on the point, then it is more probative than the alternatives no matter how weakly probative it is.

demanding nor parasitic on the notion of necessity seems to be some kind of "reverse 403" burden on the proponent to convince the trial judge that the hearsay is probative enough to be worth the time and energy of considering it.

Admittedly, this is not the most natural interpretation of requirement (I), which seems to call for direct comparisons between the reliability of the offered hearsay and the reliability of hearsay admitted under other exceptions. But it is not an implausible one. As I have noted, "equivalency" need not refer to equivalent reliability. Instead, if it is to be a workable standard, it must refer more broadly to an identification of equivalent positive indicators of reliability. And what makes indicators of reliability "equivalent" is a criterion of sufficient reliability shared with the other exceptions, if one can be identified. Given the superiority of the reverse 403 formulation of the criterion, it is not surprising that courts have gravitated toward it in their behavior, if not in their statements. On this account, positive indicators of reliability are equivalent when they render the hearsay practically useful in resolving a dispute.

But what about the "more probative" requirement in (B)? In this codification of the necessity idea, we have a legislative choice among meaningful and plausible alternatives: declarant unavailability; comprehensive necessity; relative necessity; functional necessity; and perhaps other hybrid conceptions. In the 1969 and 1971 drafts, the sense of necessity was fairly clear. Rule 803 contemplated relative necessity, while Rule 804 spoke in terms of declarant unavailability. In later versions, however, the "more probative" language (requirement (B)) appears—clearly tightening the necessity requirement by adding the comprehensiveness element. This change brought the rule more in line with Judge Wisdom's functional necessity test: it requires attention to sources of information including, but not limited to, the declarant, but it does not condition admission of the hearsay on a finding that such alternative evidence is unavailable when the alternative can be expected to be less probative than the hearsay. This functional necessity test is fairly demanding and helps to honor the Congressional will that the use of the residuals be constrained. Thus interpreted, the provision helps to allay the fears of those who would like to see a more demanding interpretation of the trustworthiness requirement than the one that seems most intelligible. Still, it is important to recognize that it is not the most demanding possible form of the necessity requirement. Comprehensive necessity would have been more demanding.

Indeed, another more demanding interpretation has been suggested. It has been argued that the "any other evidence" language in the "more probative" clause of the federal rule means just what it says, that the hearsay must be more probative than any other evidence on the point, even that which has been introduced in court, so that hearsay may not be admitted under the residual exception when it corroborates (or perhaps contradicts) evidence of greater probative value, such as direct testimony. But this construction of the rule is neither necessary nor desirable, and the courts have been right to avoid it. In *Dallas County*, the acknowledged model for the residual exception, defendants presented considerable non-hearsay evidence that the charred timbers pre-existed any lightning strike in July of 1957, but this did not bar the hearsay. Judge Wisdom's concern focused on the possibility of obtaining more probative evidence that was not before the court. He gave no attention at all to the corroborating evidence introduced by defendants. Similarly, requirement 807(B) is rightly understood as an *evidence producing* constraint, a restriction that forbids recourse to the hearsay only when other, more probative evidence on the point is likely to be available but has not been presented. When no such evidence can be identified, or when all such identifiable evidence has been presented, the necessity requirement serves no further purpose and thus should be considered satisfied.

A different, more complicated question is presented by the relationship between corroboration and trustworthiness. Courts and commentators have disagreed about whether the determination of "equivalent circumstantial guarantees of trustworthiness" may include consideration of independent evidence that corroborates the truth of the hearsay statement, with most courts reasoning from the premise that corroborative evidence counts in favor of trustworthiness.[18] There is merit on both sides of the debate. If the courts rightly employ a 403 type analysis of trustworthiness, there should be no rule that corroboration is always irrelevant to the determination of trustworthiness. Without corroboration, hearsay may be too weakly probative to be worth considering, but corroboration may increase its probative value to the point where it tips the 403 type balance. But if the independent evidence is much more decisive on the material fact in question, even reliable hearsay is likely to be a waste of time, so that powerful corroborative evidence counts against admission. Many cases, perhaps most, will fall in between, in which context corroboration is not needed to warrant the admission of the hearsay but also should not count against it.

Concerns about jury overvaluation of hearsay probably account for the tendency in some quarters to think of corroborative evidence as counting in favor of admission in a wider spectrum of cases. The argument would be that, although independent corroboration does not

---

[18] The opposite view (just barely) prevailed, however, in regard to the "particularized guarantees of trustworthiness" test under pre-*Crawford* Confrontation Clause doctrine, applicable only to hearsay offered by the prosecution. See Idaho v. Wright, 497 U.S. 805 (1990).

increase the "intrinsic" trustworthiness of the hearsay itself, as judged from the circumstances of its utterance, it nonetheless tends to make it more likely that the hearsay is true and thus to reduce the potential harm of the jury erroneously treating the hearsay as a source of truthful information. Aside from the general problems, already noted, for a jury distrust theory of hearsay, the main difficulty with this argument is that admission of the hearsay only matters in those cases in which the hearsay makes the difference in the verdict. As to these cases, overvaluation of the hearsay is no less a risk just because there is corroborating evidence. In the end, thinking of corroborative evidence as favoring admissibility in this way involves falling into the trap of thinking of hearsay as admissible when and because it is true, a form of analysis that once again confuses the roles of judge and jury, conflating admissibility with sufficiency.

As a final note, the legislative history sheds some light upon another persistent controversy surrounding the residual exception, the "near miss" problem. The issue arises when offered hearsay is found to lie close to, but not within, some enumerated exception and is then offered under the residual exception. Some have argued that such hearsay should be rejected under the residual because, in the language of Rule 807, the hearsay is still "covered by" (in the sense of "addressed by") the enumerated exception, making Rule 807 inapplicable. For example, it is argued that grand jury testimony of a person unavailable to testify at trial should not be admitted under the residual exception because it is a kind of prior testimony, and therefore is "covered" by Rule 804(b)(1) and should be admitted only if it complies with the requirements of that rule (which it generally will not). The familiar claim is that to do otherwise would give courts license to expand the parameters of the enumerated exceptions, contrary to legislative intent. The rejection of the 1969 draft, in which the enumerated exceptions were merely safe-harbor provisions, would seem to support this "near miss" theory.

Nonetheless, the near miss theory is seriously flawed unless carefully and narrowly understood, and the majority of courts have been right in rejecting it as a general doctrine. Any hearsay statement not within an enumerated exception can be analogized to at least one exception whose conditions are not all met. Were there no ancient document exception in the Federal Rules, a newspaper article like that in *Dallas County* could be seen as close to but not within the past recollection recorded exception (Rule 803(5)) or the business records exception (Rule 803(6)). Apparently, some near misses must be less problematic than others. In the final analysis, extending the residual exception to evidence that can be characterized as a near miss is a mistake only when that overrides clear Congressional decisions on the lines between admissible and inadmissible hearsay—which are *not* necessarily the same as the lines that mark the borders of the categorical hearsay exceptions.

For example, Congress's clear intent to make the official records exception unavailable in most criminal cases in which records are offered against the accused should bar the use of the residual exception in these circumstances, and it has been held to do so. On the other hand, the federal ancient document exception (Rule 803(16)) applies only to hearsay in documents that are at least twenty years old. Yet Congress's decision to make such hearsay automatically admissible (against a hearsay objection) does not suggest that Congress thought it important to exclude otherwise comparable hearsay in documents that are, say, only nineteen years and 364 days old. A better example of a "near miss" would be hard to find, but there is no Congressional policy or other good reason not to admit a document that otherwise satisfies the conditions of the residual exception just because it falls slightly short of the twenty-year threshold.[19] This particular line (twenty years of age), and many others in the law of hearsay exceptions, are best seen as marking off safe-harbors after all, in accordance with the drafters' original conception.

### The Demise of the Hearsay Rule?

Several commentators have claimed, and some of these have lamented, that we are experiencing the demise of the hearsay rule. The residual exception is often cited as an important cause of this phenomenon. Indeed, the residual exception has been used extensively. Rightly or wrongly, courts have relied on it to admit postmarks on letters, grand jury testimony of unavailable declarants, the results of social science surveys, statements in documents from foreign sources, reports of crimes by police officers, summaries of voluminous documents, medical and scientific articles, and much more. One might justifiably claim that the residual exception has worked something of a revolution in the law of hearsay.

Arguably, this doctrinal development ignores the oft-quoted admonition of the Senate Report during the drafting of the residual exception: "It is intended that the residual exceptions will be used very rarely, and only in exceptional circumstances. The committee does not intend to

---

[19] Try to make the near miss theory work here by imagining a threshold for how old a document must be, short of twenty years, such that it should be excluded because it is a near miss that is nonetheless "covered" by the ancient document exception. Then ask yourself why, if increasing age counts in favor of admission, a document *younger* than that threshold age should be a legitimate candidate for the residual exception while one *older* than that threshold age should not! For example, if a ten-year-old document is not a near miss, while a nineteen-year-old document is a near miss, then the near miss theory forces upon us a curious result. Why should the ten-year-old document receive *more* generous admissibility treatment than the nineteen-year-old document?

establish a broad license for trial judges to admit hearsay statements
that do not fall within one of the other exceptions contained in rules 803
and 804(b)." This statement, however, is curious in several respects. As
a prediction, it is obviously qualified by the committee's limited fore-
sight. How could they pretend to know, for example, that the patterns of
federal litigation would not shift so that undeniably legitimate residual
categories, like postmarks and survey results, would become dominant
evidentiary vehicles, used more frequently than the traditional exceptions? More importantly, what else could the residual be, if not a broad
license of the type described? To the extent that it goes beyond suggesting thoughtfulness and caution in the use of the residual exception, this
committee statement should be given little interpretive weight.

In any event, case reports do not show the hearsay prohibition in a
state of incipient collapse. Rather, one finds hundreds of appellate
opinions reversing verdicts for improper admission of hearsay or affirming a trial court's exclusion of hearsay. Roger Park has described the
situation aptly:

> There have been some very permissive cases, and some significant
> countercases. Even if the permissive cases win out, what may
> emerge is not death of the hearsay rule, but a discretionary hearsay
> rule in which trial judges will be upheld when they admit evidence
> under the residual exception, but will also be upheld when they
> refuse to use a residual exception to admit evidence. * * *
>
> * * * [E]ven if the trial judges have (or come to have) great
> discretion in administering the residual exceptions, the specifically
> enumerated exceptions could conceivably still serve a useful purpose.
> Those exceptions define what is admissible as well as attempting to
> say what is not. If half a loaf of certainty is better than none,
> perhaps it is worth retaining class exceptions for their value in
> carving out a predictable core of admissible hearsay, even if (argu-
> ably) there is no longer a predictable core of inadmissible hearsay.[20]

Professor Park's comment portrays a potential future hearsay regime
that would closely match the advisory committee's original 1969 proposal, substantial safe harbors of admissibility surrounded by a sea of
hearsay that may be admitted if the requisite necessity and trustworthiness are shown, with an extra measure of fair notice thrown in for good
measure. One has to think that such a regime would have been wel-
comed by Judge Wisdom.

Before closing, it should be noted that much of the angst over the
supposed decline of the hearsay rule reflects concerns over the misuse of
hearsay by the prosecution in criminal cases, especially the use of the

---

[20] Roger C. Park, *Hearsay, Dead or Alive?*, 40 Ariz. L. Rev. 647, 653–54 (1998).

residual exception to circumvent limitations grounded in distrust of governmentally created out-of-court statements. That context raises special concerns that generated the constitutional protection of the Confrontation Clause. The admissibility of such statements has been dramatically affected by the Supreme Court's 2004 decision in *Crawford v. Washington*,[21] which reinterpreted the clause to place tighter restrictions on the prosecution's use of "testimonial" hearsay. Importantly, these restrictions cannot be ignored just because the judge determines, in some conclusory and inevitably opaque way, that the hearsay is "reliable." Although it will be some time before the full implications of *Crawford* can be mapped out, it is safe to say that, in a broad category of cases, it will render inconsequential the statutory availability of the residual exception to the prosecution. The exception is, of course, trumped by the Constitution. This category will include most of the cases that have been of greatest concern, including victim statements solicited by the police, custodial accomplice statements to the police implicating another, and grand jury testimony. With the special protection of criminal defendants provided by this revitalized constitutional jurisprudence, there should be less need to fear a more liberal and discretionary nonconstitutional hearsay regime, like the one envisioned by Judge Wisdom.

————

This has not been the usual evidence story, for although there is an interesting tale to the *Dallas County* case, there is not much human drama to it. The real story has been one of the development of a rule that has dramatically changed the law of evidence. This is a story that has roots in the 19th Century, at a time when evidence law was a common law of trial procedure that varied considerably across jurisdictions. The need to make sense of these various rules and the principles behind them gave rise to a series of great treatises; in the 19th Century, by Greenleaf and Thayer, and at the turn of the century, the greatest and most influential of them all, by John Henry Wigmore. Other academics were also major figures, one of the stars being Edmund Morgan, a pioneer in the movement for codification and, like Wigmore, a critic of the many strictures of the common-law rule barring hearsay. John Minor Wisdom grew up as a lawyer at a time when the authority of Wigmore and Morgan and a few others like them was at its zenith. It is not surprising that he read these men and cited them and looked to them for guidance when confronted with novel problems of evidence.

What is surprising, and what took considerable judicial courage, was Judge Wisdom's willingness to articulate as case law the principles these

---

[21] 541 U.S. 36 (2004).

reformers espoused, without seeking, as almost any other judge would have, to ground the decision in some existing stretchable hearsay exception, and without taking some escape route like harmless error to avoid hard questions. In this sense, *Dallas County* is almost an "in your face" decision. One cannot avoid confronting the clear break with existing doctrine. Perhaps because of this, the case was more celebrated than precedential. But the power of Judge Wisdom's approach remained, and with the drafting of the Federal Rules of Evidence, it emerged from the legislative debates with the qualified endorsement of Congress. So this evidence story is not so much the story of a building hit or not hit by lightning as it is the story of an intellectual tradition, and of a judge, and how ideas come to be enacted into law, interpreted and developed. The same kind of story can be told of a number of changes in the law of evidence, but few are as important as this one.

## SUGGESTED READINGS

Edmund M Morgan, *The Jury and the Exclusionary Rules of Evidence*, 4 U. Chi. L. Rev. 247 (1937).

George F. James, *The Role of Hearsay in a Rational Scheme of Evidence*, 34 Ill. L. Rev. 788 (1940).

Jack Weinstein, *Probative Force of Hearsay*, 46 Iowa L. Rev. 331 (1961).

Edward J. Imwinkelried, *The Scope of the Residual Hearsay Exceptions in the Federal Rules of Evidence*, 15 San Diego L. Rev. 239 (1978).

David A. Sonenshein, *The Residual Exceptions to the Hearsay Rule: Two Exceptions in Search of a Rule*, 57 N.Y.U. L. Rev. 867 (1982).

Randolph N. Jonakait, *The Subversion of the Hearsay Rule: The Residual Hearsay Exceptions, Circumstantial Guarantees of Trustworthiness, and Grand Jury Testimony*, 36 Case W. Res. L. Rev. 431 (1986).

Eleanor Swift, *Abolishing the Hearsay Rule*, 75 Cal. L. Rev. 495 (1987).

Mirjan Damaška, *Of Hearsay and Its Analogues*, 76 Minn. L. Rev. 425 (1992).

Dale A. Nance, *Understanding Responses to Hearsay: An Extension of the Comparative Analysis*, 76 Minn. L. Rev. 459 (1992).

Richard D. Friedman, *Toward a Partial Economic, Game—Theoretic Analysis of Hearsay*, 76 Minn. L. Rev. 723 (1992).

Roger C. Park, *Visions of Applying the Scientific Method to the Hearsay Rule*, 2003 Mich. St. L. Rev. 1149.

# 14

# The Story of *Crawford*

## Richard D. Friedman

I never open most of the unsolicited e-mail messages I get. But the subject line of one I received on the afternoon of March 10, 2003—"Confrontation Clause cert petition"—caught my eye. For some years I had been contending that the Supreme Court should dramatically change its conception of what the Sixth Amendment means when it guarantees an accused "the right to be confronted with the witnesses against him." And so I opened the message immediately, and read:

> Professor Friedman—
>
> I graduated from Michigan Law School in 1997. Although I never had you as a professor, I became familiar with your Confrontation Clause scholarship in 1999, when I was clerking for Justice Stevens during the Lilly v. Virginia[1] case.
>
> I now practice law in Seattle and teach as an adjunct professor at the Univ of Washington School of Law. As part of my practice, I occasionally handle cases presenting constitutional criminal procedure issues for the NACDL (National Association of Criminal Defense Lawyers). After I learned of the Washington Supreme Court's interpretation of the Confrontation Clause in this case, I contacted the defendant's attorney, and he gave the case to me.
>
> I thought you might be interested in the cert petition that I filed in the case last Friday, so I've attached a copy. As you can see, I am urging the Court to adopt the testimonial approach you presented in Lilly in order to put an end to lower court opinions like this one. If you have any thoughts on this case or the issue in general, I would, of course, love to hear them. Otherwise, I will be sure to let you know if the Court takes the case. We hope to get an answer before the end of this Term.
>
> Sincerely,
>
> Jeff Fisher

---

[1] 527 U.S. 116 (1999).

Now, of course, I was intrigued, and so I opened the attachment and read the petition. Michael Crawford had been charged with assault. At his trial, the prosecution offered a statement made in the police station on the night of the incident by Crawford's wife Sylvia, who did not testify at trial. He objected, in part on the ground that this violated his right under the Confrontation Clause. The trial court nevertheless admitted the statement, and Crawford was convicted. The Washington Supreme Court ultimately affirmed the judgment. In rejecting the Confrontation Clause challenge, that court purported to apply the then-governing doctrine of *Ohio v. Roberts*,[2] under which the Clause posed no obstacle to admissibility if the statement was deemed sufficiently reliable. And the court concluded that the statement met this standard, in part because it "interlocked" with a statement Michael himself had made to the police the same night. In his petition, Jeff—as I will refer to Fisher, because we have become friends and close working colleagues—argued first that the "interlock" theory was in conflict with decisions of other jurisdictions and was an inappropriate application of *Roberts*. This part of the petition struck me as very, very good—well argued, precise, and professional. But it was the second part of the petition to which Jeff had referred in his message. There, he urged that the Court take the case so that it could throw out the whole *Roberts* doctrine. The Court should replace that doctrine, he said, by an approach under which an out-of-court statement that is testimonial in nature cannot be introduced against an accused if he has not had a chance to cross-examine the maker of the statement. As Jeff had indicated in his e-mail, this was the approach I had advocated in my scholarship, and the petition featured generous quotations from my work. Now, as you can imagine, I thought this was a *great* petition.

Indeed, I began salivating, at least figuratively. In response to *amicus* briefs in two prior cases, one of which was the *Lilly* case mentioned by Jeff, three justices had indicated their willingness to rethink the foundations of Confrontation Clause jurisprudence. But *amici*, friends of the Court, stand on the sidelines. Until a party to a case before the Court urged the Court to discard *Roberts*, we were probably going to be stuck with it for the foreseeable future. And here was a defendant, represented by an able lawyer, who was asking for just the change I had hoped, adoption of the testimonial approach. But three questions were immediately apparent:

- Would the Court take the case? Most petitions for *certiorari* are rejected.

- If the Court took the case, would it reach the broad issue, or would it simply continue to apply the *Roberts* framework? The Court

---

[2] 448 U.S. 56 (1980).

usually tries to avoid broad questions if it can decide a case on narrow grounds, and there was no doubt the Court could reverse Michael Crawford's conviction without needing to consider whether it should abandon *Roberts*.

• If the Court did reach the broad issue, would it actually adopt the testimonial approach, or would it stick with *Roberts*? The Court is generally hesitant to make dramatic changes in doctrine, and there was no doubt that rejecting *Roberts* would be dramatic. And, as in Crawford's case, the Court always *could* reach a sensible result while staying within the *Roberts* framework (The Court could reach just about *any* result within that framework, and that was part of the problem.)

All three questions would be answered in the affirmative over the next year. And so the story of *Crawford* is much more than the story of Mike and Sylvia Crawford and the knife fight with another man that landed Mike in prison. It is also the story of how the accused's right to be confronted with witnesses developed over the centuries and then atrophied, and of how a young lawyer with talent, gumption, and guts was able to persuade the Supreme Court to restore the right to its proper place at the center of our system of criminal justice. From my point of view as a scholar, it is a story that is enjoyable to tell in part because it is so gratifying.

* * *

Let's do a little thought experiment. It is 1220, and the young King Henry III has given you a hard assignment. Until recently, the criminal justice system in England, like that of most Christian countries, has relied to a considerable extent on various means to determine the judgment of God. Principal among these were the *ordeals*. For example, an accused person might be asked to carry a red-hot iron rod a fixed distance in his hand. If in three days his wound was healing nicely, then this was taken as judgment that he was innocent; if it was festering, he was deemed guilty. Alternatively, the accused might be bound up and lowered into cold water. If he sank, he was deemed innocent and pulled out, wet but happy; if he floated, that was taken as a sign of guilt.

This wasn't a bad system, if your principal concern was reaching a judgment that was swift and easy to determine. The problem, of course, was that to accept these ordeals one would have to have a lot of faith that God was in fact revealing judgment in these strange ways. In 1215, at the great Fourth Lateran Council, the Catholic Church forbade its clergy to participate in administering the ordeals. This limitation has impaired the practice, which had already lost much support in England. So your job is to devise a new system that does not rely on the ordeals. What will you do?

You probably will realize pretty quickly that a rational system of adjudication must depend to a large extent on witnesses, who have information relevant to the case to transmit to the adjudicator. But how will they pass that information on—that is, how will they *testify*? Probably requiring them to take an oath is a good idea, so that they know the seriousness of the matter and they understand they are at risk of damnation[3] if they testify falsely. Beyond that, various means are possible. You could follow the method used by the later Athenians, and have all the witnesses submit written testimony in a pot, which would be sealed up until the day of trial and then presented to the adjudicator. Or you could go along with a model being developed by most of the courts in Continental Europe, in which testimony is received and recorded in writing by an official out of the presence of the parties—for fear that otherwise the witnesses will be intimidated—but with the parties afforded an opportunity to pose questions in writing.

But you may be drawn to another model, the system used by the ancient Hebrews, by the earlier Athenians, and by the Romans: Witnesses give their testimony orally, in the presence of the parties, at an open trial. This system avoids any possibility that the witness's testimony has been transmitted incorrectly to the court. It gives the accused some assurance that the witnesses against him are not testifying as a result of coercion. It also may give the accused a chance to question the witness. And it puts a significant moral onus on the witness, telling her in effect: "If you're going to say that, look him in the eye."

Now of course this thought experiment does not reflect reality, in that nobody sat down and designed the common law system of criminal adjudication; rather, it evolved over centuries. But it is clear that by the middle of the sixteenth century the English courts were following the last of these models, the one requiring open, confrontational testimony, in which a witness gave testimony face to face with the accused. Indeed, repeatedly over the next few centuries, English commentators on the law proclaimed this method of giving testimony as the central glory of their criminal justice system. Repeatedly, too, Parliament passed statutes providing that in treason cases witnesses had to testify "face to face" with the accused.

This procedure was not uniformly followed. In some ·politically charged cases in the sixteenth and early seventeenth century, particularly treason cases, the Crown presented evidence that had been taken out of the presence of the petitioner. The case of Sir Walter Raleigh was the most notorious of these, but not the only one. Statutes passed under Queen Mary in the middle of the sixteenth century required justices of

---

[3] Under the softer conception of later times, the risk would only be of a perjury prosecution.

the peace to take statements from witnesses to felonies, and soon it
became established that a statement so taken could be admitted at trial
if it had been taken under oath and the witness was unavailable to
testify then. Finally, a set of courts, such as the Court of the Star
Chamber, followed the Continental style of taking testimony rather than
the English style.

By the middle to end of the seventeenth century, however, the right
to be confronted with adverse witnesses was firmly established. Courts
in treason cases not only ensured that the prosecution witnesses testified
live at trial but solicitously gave the accused the opportunity to cross-
examine. The practice permitted under the Marian statutes was not
expanded beyond the scope of those statutes, felony cases; in misdemean-
or cases, the notable case of *R v. Payne* ruled in 1696 that, even if a
witness were unavailable at trial, his prior testimony could not be
introduced against the accused if the defendant had not had an opportunity for cross-examination. And most of the courts following the Continental model, including the Star Chamber, did not survive the political
upheavals of the era. Equity courts continued to take evidence in the
Continental style, but they did not have criminal jurisdiction. If a
witness was unavailable at trial in a common law court, depositions
taken in equity could be admitted, but only if the adverse party had had
an adequate opportunity to pose questions in writing.

The confrontation right crossed the Atlantic, and it took strong root
in America. In England, until the nineteenth century, most criminal
cases were privately prosecuted, and the accused usually was not represented by counsel. But in America, the right to counsel became established sooner, and this intensified the benefit of the confrontation right,
because it made the ability to cross-examine witnesses more valuable.
Moreover, cases prosecuted by the Crown under the Stamp Acts were
assigned to the admiralty courts, which followed the Continental model,
operating without a jury and taking testimony in writing out of the
presence of the parties.[4] This practice became one of the colonists'
grievances leading to the Revolution.[5] Most of the early state constitu-

---

[4] This history is summarized in *Crawford*, 541 U.S. at 47–56.

[5] The Stamp Act Congress complained that "by extending the jurisdiction of the courts
of Admiralty beyond its ancient limits," the Act had "a manifest tendency to subvert the
rights and liberties of the colonists," one of which was trial by jury. Resolutions of the
Stamp Act Congress § 8th (Oct. 19, 1765), reprinted in SOURCES OF OUR LIBERTIES 270, 271
(R. Perry & J. Cooper eds. 1959). The Declaration of Independence made a similar
complaint, asserting in its enumeration of grievances against King George III:

He has combined with others to subject us to a jurisdiction foreign to our Constitution
and unacknowledged by our laws, giving his assent to their acts of pretended legislation: * * *

For depriving us, in many cases, of the benefits of trial by jury. . . .

tions included a guarantee that prosecution witnesses would testify live in the presence of the accused. Some used the time-honored "face to face" formula. Others used language very similar to that which was incorporated into the federal Constitution after its ratification, when the absence of an enumeration of rights was corrected by the first ten amendments, the Bill of Rights. The sixth amendment, ratified in 1791, provides that "[i]n all criminal prosecutions, the accused shall enjoy the right . . . to be confronted with the witnesses against him."

Note that in this account, the term hearsay has not played a role—just as it is not mentioned in the Confrontation Clause itself. Indeed, the rule against hearsay as we know it today was still inchoate at the time the Clause was adopted. The Clause was not a constitutional statement of the rule against hearsay, but rather a procedural rule about how prosecution testimony should be given.

Soon, though, the distinction became less apparent. Around the time of the adoption of the sixth amendment, and for several decades thereafter, the hearsay rule developed rapidly. The increasing role of criminal defense counsel seems to have been largely responsible for the change. Defense lawyers recognized the potential value of cross-examination whenever the probative value of adverse evidence depended in part on the capacities of an observer to perceive, remember, and describe an event or condition and on her inclination to communicate accurately. By the early years of the nineteenth century, then, something like the modern definition of hearsay—an out-of-court statement offered to prove the truth of a matter that it asserted—had emerged. And indeed, in 1838, the rule against hearsay reached its high-water mark, when the House of Lords held in effect, in the famous case of *Wright v. Doe d. Tatham*,[6] that the rule applied not only to statements but to any out-of-court conduct offered to prove the truth of a proposition apparently

---

And what were "the benefits of trial by jury"? In its Address to the Inhabitants of the Province of Quebec, of October 26, 1774 (drafted, like the Stamp Act resolutions, by John Dickinson), the First Continental Congress explained that this right

> provides that neither life, liberty, nor property can be taken from the possessor until twelve of his unexceptionable countrymen and peers of his vicinage, who, from that neighborhood, may reasonably be supposed to be acquainted with his character and the characters of the witnesses, upon a fair trial and full inquiry, face to face, in open court, before as many of the people as choose to attend, shall pass their sentence upon oath against him. . . .

http://www.ushistory.org/declaration/related/decres.htm

Thus, though neither the Resolutions of the Stamp Act Congress nor the Declaration of Independence explicitly mentions the confrontation right, it appears that the right is included in their references to trial by jury—the English style of adjudication, in contrast with the Continental style used by the admiralty courts. The Sixth Amendment articulates the two rights separately, side by side.

[6] 5 Cl. & F. 670, 7 E.R. 559, 47 Rev. Rep. 136 (H.L. 1838).

believed by the actor. Even without this extension, the rule described a vast category of evidence, including but reaching far beyond the relatively narrow category of testimonial statements that was the focus of the confrontation right. But the rule against hearsay was never absolute, and for nearly two centuries courts and rule-makers have developed an ever-expanding list of exceptions to it. These are designed to exempt from the rule hearsay that will be particularly helpful to the truth-determination process, because it appears highly probable that the statement in question is accurate and because there is no good substitute evidence for the statement.

With so much intellectual energy focused on the rule against hearsay, the independent role of the confrontation right—as a categorical prohibition of testimonial evidence offered against the accused without offering him an opportunity to be face-to-face with the witness and cross-examine her—became obscured. I believe many decision-makers still had a rough intuitive sense of where the right applied, and this sense almost unconsciously helped shape the rule against hearsay and helped prevent results from being altogether intolerable.[7] And so we muddled through. Any result a court should have reached by speaking of the accused's right to confront witnesses it could still reach by speaking of the rule against hearsay—until 1965. In that year, the Supreme Court held that the confrontation right is a fundamental one that is applicable against the states via the fourteenth amendment to the Constitution.[8] Now a federal court, whether on direct or collateral review, could hold that a state court conviction was invalid because it had violated the accused's confrontation right—but not because it violated the state's rule against hearsay. Therefore, it became crucial to understand the scope of the confrontation right.

The problem was that, with the confrontation right having been mixed together with the rule against hearsay for so long, the Supreme Court did not have a well developed and articulated understanding of what the right meant and where it applied. And so before long the Court started referring for guidance to the rule against hearsay—which meant that the confrontation right had very little force of its own. In *Ohio v. Roberts*, the Court tried to articulate a general framework, under which

---

[7] For example, many (but not all) American jurisdictions in the late twentieth century would not allow a confession made to the authorities by one confederate to be introduced against another confederate. The reason usually given was that such a statement was unreliable, because it may have been made to curry favor with the authorities. Sometimes these statements are indeed highly unreliable—but sometimes not. The real reason to exclude such statements is that they amount to testimony against the second confederate; this, I believe, accounts for the simple, categorical rule against such statements that was adopted by the twelve judges in *Tong's Case*, Kel. J. 17, 84 Eng. Rep. 1061 (1662).

[8] Pointer v. Texas, 380 U.S. 400 (1965).

*any* hearsay statement—not just testimonial statements—made by an out-of-court declarant posed a potential Confrontation Clause problem. On the one hand, the Court seemed to set up a general requirement that such hearsay could not be admitted if the declarant was available to be a witness at trial. On the other hand, the confrontation problem could be overcome by showing that the statement was reliable, and reliability could be demonstrated by showing that the statement fell "within a firmly rooted hearsay exception." Alternatively, the Court suggested, the reliability test could be satisfied by "a showing of particularized guarantees of trustworthiness."[9]

This framework was shaky from the start. The Court quickly drew back from the supposed unavailability requirement—which if taken seriously would have meant, for example, that a routine business record could not be introduced without showing that its makers were unavailable to testify at trial.[10] The Court continued to profess adherence to the reliability requirement, but it was highly problematic. Why should the fact that an exception from the ordinary (that is, non-constitutional) rule against hearsay had become "firmly rooted" (whatever that meant) relieve a statement fitting within the exception (as construed by the Supreme Court[11]) from the constitutional guarantee of confrontation? And what if a state interpreted a given exception in a way that was particularly generous to the prosecution? Moreover, the "individualized guarantees of trustworthiness" prong of the doctrine was highly manipulable. Regardless of whether a statement was made calmly or in excitement, soon after the events it described or after a period for reflection, to private persons or to police officers, lower courts tended to conclude that the statement was made in circumstances giving it sufficient reliability to warrant admission.

I became particularly interested in the confrontation right around 1990. I was working on a large project on the law of hearsay, and I became convinced that the confrontation right was the key to unlocking

---

[9] 448 U.S. 56, 66 (1980).

[10] *See* United States v. Inadi, 475 U.S. 387 (1986) (holding that a conspirator's statement may be admitted against an accused even if the declarant is available to testify at trial but does not do so); White v. Illinois, 502 U.S. 346 (1992) (holding that spontaneous declarations are admissible against an accused notwithstanding availability of declarant).

[11] Monitoring by the Court was necessary, because otherwise a state court could interpret a particular exception with undue generosity towards the state. In both *Lee v. Illinois*, 476 U.S. 530 (1986), and *Lilly v. Virginia*, 527 U.S. 116 (1999), the state courts had admitted confessions made by co-defendants to police officers, and in each case the Court refused to accept for Confrontation Clause purposes the state's characterization of the statement as a declaration against penal interest. In *Lilly*, a plurality explicitly stated that "accomplice's statements that shift or spread the blame to a criminal defendant" fall outside a "firmly rooted" hearsay exception.

the hearsay puzzle. Because the confrontation right had become dependent on the law of hearsay, the rule against hearsay was more restrictive than it should be in general, and the confrontation right was less strong than it should be. It became apparent to me that, *Roberts* notwithstanding, it was not true that any hearsay statement posed a potential confrontation problem; rather, it was only those statements made with the anticipation that they would aid in the investigation or prosecution of crime. And *Roberts* erred by holding that even this type of statement did not violate the confrontation right if it was deemed sufficiently reliable; there should be a categorical rule of exclusion. But I lacked a theory under which this one type of statement should be considered the focus of the Confrontation Clause. During two extended periods in Oxford in the 1990s, though, I found myself drawn, against my original inclination, back into the remote history I have just summarized. I had the great fortune of being able to work with Mike Macnair, an extraordinarily knowledgeable English historian who understood the materials far better than I did. And the picture clicked into place: The Confrontation Clause does not simply describe a species of statement that is subject to a stringent rule of evidentiary exclusion. Rather, it is a fundamental procedural rule designed to ensure that *testimony* is given under proper conditions, in the presence of the accused. Statements that perform the function of testimony, by providing information for use in investigation or prosecution of crime, are necessarily within the ambit of the Clause, and as to these the Clause provides a categorical rule of exclusion—for otherwise, our system would countenance a method of giving testimony against an accused that did not require confrontation.

I was not the only scholar, nor the first (though I may have been the most persistent and obsessive), to argue that *Roberts* erred by diluting the confrontation right—on the one hand by giving it the breadth of hearsay law rather than grappling with the meaning of the phrase "witnesses against", and on the other by allowing the right to be defeated upon a finding that the statement was reliable. Michael Graham, Akhil Amar, and Margaret Burger all articulated theories that resembled mine to some extent, though in each case there were significant differences as well. Moreover, the United States Government played a significant role. In *United States v. Inadi*, in a brief co-authored by a young Assistant Solicitor General, Samuel A. Alito, Jr., the Government argued that the Confrontation Clause, having been intended to prohibit trial by affidavit and comparable practices, "closely regulated the admission of hearsay, such as former testimony, that is broadly analogous to an affidavit or deposition,"[12] but did not seriously limit the admission of other hearsay. The Court ruled in favor of the Government—holding that a statement fitting within the hearsay exemption for declarations of

---

[12] Brief for the United States 25, United States v. Inadi, No. 84–1580.

a conspirator could be admitted against an accused even absent a showing that the declarant was unavailable—without reaching the essence of the Government's argument. In 1992, in *White v. Illinois,* the Solicitor General's office tried again, submitting an *amicus* brief that argued that the Confrontation Clause should apply only to "those individuals who actually provide in-court testimony or the functional equivalent—i.e., affidavits, depositions, prior testimony, or other statements (such as confessions) that are made with a view to legal proceedings."[13] The Court, in an opinion by Chief Justice William Rehnquist, said this argument came "too late in the day"; "[s]uch a narrow reading of the Confrontation Clause," the Court said, "would virtually eliminate its role in restricting the admission of hearsay testimony," and it was barred by the Court's precedents.[14] But Justice Clarence Thomas, joined by Justice Antonin Scalia, wrote a concurring opinion, saying the Court had rejected the Solicitor General's approach too hastily. While not endorsing that approach in its entirety, Thomas suggested that "the Confrontation Clause is implicated by extrajudicial statements only insofar as they are contained in formalized testimonial materials, such as affidavits, depositions, prior testimony, or confessions."[15] (But why, one might ask, is a confession necessarily "formalized"?)

In May 1998, in part by virtue of another stroke of luck, I was seated next to Justice Stephen Breyer at a dinner in Oxford. He spoke favorably about the value of *amicus* briefs from academics. I thought of that conversation several months later when the Supreme Court granted *certiorari* in *Lilly v. Virginia,* a case in which the state courts had held the Confrontation Clause did not preclude admitting a statement made to the police accusing the declarant's brother of being the trigger man in a murder. Margaret Burger and I co-authored an *amicus* brief for the American Civil Liberties Union, urging the Court to discard *Roberts* and adopt a doctrine under which the Confrontation Clause applied categorically to out-of-court statements by those deemed to be witnesses against the accused (however that term might be understood). By a 5–4 vote, the Court held that the challenged statement should not have been admitted against Lilly. (The minority agreed that the conviction should be reversed, but would have left it to the Virginia courts to decide whether there were particularized guarantees of trustworthiness.) What I found most exciting was that Justice Breyer, a member of the majority, wrote a concurrence saying quite explicitly that he found the arguments in our

---

[13] Brief for the United States as Amicus Curiae Supporting Respondent, White v. Illinois, 502 U.S. 346 (1992) (No. 90–6113), microformed on U.S. Supreme Court Records and Briefs 1991/92 FO, Card 4 of 7 (CIS).

[14] 502 U.S. at 352–53.

[15] 502 U.S. at 365.

brief appealing. There was no need to re-examine the link between hearsay law and the Confrontation Clause in that case, he concluded, but the question was "open for another day."

And so that made three justices who had expressed willingness to consider a revamp of Confrontation Clause doctrine. But, especially given that *Roberts* was so manipulable that it almost always would allow the Court to reach whatever result it wanted, a change was unlikely to occur at the urging of *amici*. Transformation would not occur unless a defendant made a point of asking for it.

* * *

Michael and Sylvia Crawford, both 21, were married and had a small child. But life was hardly idyllic. They had recently re-united after a period of separation, and neither of them was employed. They spent the afternoon of Thursday, August 5, 1999 as they spent much of their time, drinking with friends in downtown Olympia, Washington. At some point, they decided that they needed to settle an old score with an acquaintance whom they knew as Kenny Lee. And so the two set off to find him. They may have searched first at several taverns that Kenny frequented, but in any event they soon wound up at Kenny's apartment; Sylvia, who had been there before, showed Mike the way.

When they saw Kenny, Mike immediately mentioned several hundred dollars—drug money, perhaps?[16]—that he said Kenny owed him. Whether this was just a rather clumsy conversation-opener, or whether, contrary to the accounts that Mike and Sylvia later gave police, this was the only grudge that Mike had against Kenny, is unclear. In any event, the encounter almost immediately became violent. Mike pulled a knife from a sheath on his belt and stabbed Kenny in the midsection, injuring him seriously. Mike and Sylvia quickly left the scene, but Kenny managed to make a 911 call and gave the operator enough identifying information about them that they were promptly picked up by police.

Sylvia first told a police officer informally that she, Mike, and Kenny had come to Kenny's apartment together, that Mike had gone to the store to buy liquor, and that while he was gone, Kenny had sexually assaulted her, pinning her to the ground and trying to remove her clothes; the knife fight began when Mike came back to see Kenny on top of Sylvia. She repeated this account at around 7 p.m. in a more formal interview at the police station. This interview was audiotaped, and Sylvia was given the *Miranda* warnings and asked a series of identifying questions before the interview began. Soon after, Mike—whom the police

---

[16] One of the interviews with Mike contains this passage:

Q . . . [H]e apparently owed you some money for perhaps some marijuana or drugs

A I (won't?) (inaudible) specify.

had separated from Sylvia—was subjected to a similar interview, and he gave an account that was similar in many respects but not in all: According to Mike, Sylvia had mentioned a prior sexual assault committed by Kenny while Sylvia was living apart from Mike, and so the incident on the evening of August 5 was the second of its type.

Suspicious because of the inconsistencies, and also perhaps dubious that Mike would leave his wife alone with a man who had allegedly assaulted her, the police pressed Sylvia and Mike further. They each agreed to give another statement, again audiotaped and under considerable formality. Now their stories were more congruent with each other, and put them in a far more aggressive light: The sexual assault had occurred several weeks earlier, during the period of estrangement, and Mike had been nowhere near the scene. But mention of it during the afternoon's bout of drinking had prompted Mike to say that Kenny "deserve[d] a ass-whoopin'." And so they set off to find Kenny. He came to the door of his apartment, and there the fight occurred. On one crucial issue, however, Mike and Sylvia's accounts were subtly different. Mike indicated that before the stabbing he thought Kenny had reached inside his pocket for something, though he admitted he could not be sure. Sylvia seemed not to believe that Kenny had reached for anything before Mike stabbed him. But Syliva acknowledged some difficulty in giving a detailed rendition of the incident: "I shut my eyes and I didn't really watch. I was like in shock ..."

* * *

In preparing for Mike's trial, before Judge Richard Strophy of Thurston County Superior Court, the prosecution subpoenaed Sylvia. But Sylvia did not want to testify at trial. She could have invoked her Fifth Amendment right not to do so, because the state was considering filing charges against her (and eventually did). She never did formally invoke that right. But after the jury was selected, on October 18, 1999, Mike's trial lawyer, Hugh McGavick, reported to the court that she was invoking the spousal privilege. Washington law provides that one spouse may not testify against another in a criminal case unless the defendant spouse consents, so a more accurate statement—putting aside the unexercised Fifth Amendment—would have been that Mike was declining to waive his right to prevent Sylvia from testifying. Nobody made an issue of the difference at the trial level, and the parties agreed that Sylvia was unavailable to be a witness at trial. McGavick contended that introducing Sylvia's statements against Mike would violate the spousal privilege and—relying heavily on *Lilly*, which had been decided four months earlier—the Confrontation Clause. After reading *Lilly* and the statements overnight, the judge ruled the statements admissible. He spent little time explaining his view that the privilege did not apply to out-of-court statements made to third parties. But then at greater length, he ruled that Sylvia's statements were sufficiently reliable to be admitted. In part, he relied on the similarities of her statements to Mike's own. Were he to make the assessment without taking Mike's statements into account, he indicated, the case would be a much closer call, and he suggested that to avoid creating an issue for appeal the prosecution should consider not using Sylvia's statements in its case-in-chief.

The prosecution did not heed this advice. It introduced Sylvia's statement at trial. The jury found Michael guilty, and he was sentenced to fourteen years in prison.

Through a new attorney, Thomas E. Doyle, Crawford took the case to the Washington Court of Appeals. Steve Sherman of the Thurston County Prosecutor's Office—who eventually would argue the case in the United States Supreme Court—argued for the state. He contended that Mike had waived his confrontation right by not allowing Sylvia to testify. The court rejected the contention—Mike had a statutory right to prevent Sylvia from testifying against him at trial, and he should not have to choose between that right and the right not to be convicted in violation of the Confrontation Clause. On the merits, the court held that the admissibility of Sylvia's first statement rested on whether the second statement was admissible, because the first was admitted not for its truth but to show evasive conduct by the couple. As for the second statement, two members of the three-judge panel held that parts were too unreliable to satisfy either the Confrontation Clause or Washington's hearsay exception for statements against penal interest. In reaching this conclusion, the court attempted to apply a nine-factor test for reliability that the Washington Supreme Court had developed. Concluding also that the error was not harmless, the court reversed Mike's conviction on July 30, 2001. One judge dissented, concluding that the majority had erred, according to another decision of the state supreme court, by assessing credibility without taking into account the fact that Sylvia's statement "interlocked" with Mike's own.

Not surprisingly, the State sought review of the decision in the state supreme court, and on March 5, 2002, that court decided to take the case. On September 26, the nine-justice court issued its decision, unanimously reversing the court of appeals and reinstating Crawford's conviction. The state supreme court agreed with Crawford, and with the court of appeals, that he had not waived the confrontation right. On the merits, though, the supreme court concluded that Sylvia's second statement was sufficiently reliable to overcome the confrontation right. In this case, the court did not believe it needed to work through all nine factors of its elaborate reliability test. Rather, it grounded its decision on the facts that Sylvia's statement was self-inculpatory and that it overlapped, or interlocked, substantially with Mike's own statement.

* * *

Enter Jeff Fisher. A young associate with a large Seattle firm, Jeff did *pro bono* work for the National Association of Criminal Defense Lawyers. He sat on a committee that looked for potentially important cases in which to write *amicus* briefs. Jeff spotted the *Crawford* case and called Doyle, Crawford's lawyer, to offer the committee's help if Doyle prepared a petition for *certiorari*. But he found that Doyle was uninterested in preparing a *cert* petition; it would be an enormous amount of work offering a flimsy chance of success, and (given that Doyle had already worked through the state's $2000 cap on fees for appointed appellate counsel) no chance of financial gain. With the support and resource of his firm behind him, Jeff offered to take the case over. Doyle readily agreed. Jeff then wrote the petition that he sent me by e-mail in March 2003.

When you write a *cert* petition, you always want to find a conflict among the lower courts, for if there is none the Supreme Court is likely to conclude that there is no need for it to intervene. And Jeff had a pretty good conflict. The Supreme Court had held that in applying the "particularized guarantees of trustworthiness" test under *Roberts* a court could not rely on evidence corroborating the challenged statement but instead had to limit itself to circumstances "that surround the making of the statement and that render the declarant particularly worthy of belief."[17] In holding that Sylvia's statement was reliable, the state supreme court, like the trial court, relied heavily on the interlock with Mike's own statement. That seemed to fly in the face of the no-corroboration rule, and several other courts had so held. It was reasonable to suppose, therefore, that the Supreme Court might want to take the case to clean up application of *Roberts*.

But Jeff did not rest there. As I mentioned at the beginning of this story, his petition included a second part that asked the Court to discard the entire *Roberts* doctrine and replace it with a "testimonial" approach. So we were not only rooting for the Court to grant *certiorari* but for it to do so without limiting the grant to the first question presented, the narrow and highly technical matter of how *Roberts* should be applied. The state did not bother to file a response to the *cert* petition, but the Court called for one. That was a good sign; it meant that at least someone was paying attention, and as Jeff explained to me the Court would not grant the petition without calling for a response. On June 9, we got our answer. The Court granted the petition—a simple grant, without limitation to one question or the other. We were in business: The testimonial approach would now be presented to the Supreme Court by a party.

---

[17] Idaho v. Wright, 497 U.S. 805, 819 (1990).

As Jeff prepared his brief on the merits, he told me he was thinking of flipping the issues, of arguing first the broad question of whether the testimonial approach should replace *Roberts* and just addressing the narrow, technical issue towards the end of the brief. I encouraged him to do so. I thought it made sense, and that it would not diminish Jeff's chance of achieving a reversal for his client. Of course, I was self-interested: I was eager for the testimonial approach to be considered by the Court, and I regarded the "interlock" issue as just one of many odd questions that were bound to arise under the utterly unsatisfactory *Roberts* framework. Jeff later told me that I was the *only* person who advised him to switch the issues. Some of the wiser heads whom he consulted thought that doing so—putting greatest weight on a request that the Court should completely discard a long-established doctrine, replacing it with a broad categorical rule, when there was a narrow and straightforward way of ensuring reversal under the prevailing frame-work—was foolhardy. And this seemed especially so given that on so many issues the swing vote was Justice Sandra Day O'Connor, who had an aversion to broad rules. In a brave move—especially for a young rookie preparing his first Supreme Court case—Jeff made the switch. The first and longest part of his brief, which contained a powerful showing of how lower courts had manipulated the *Roberts* standard, asked for adoption of the testimonial approach, and only towards the end of the brief did Jeff address the interlock issue.

Meanwhile, I prepared an *amicus* brief, arguing from the academic perspective why the testimonial approach should be adopted. After completing a draft, I asked law professors around the country if they were interested in signing on, and eight of them did; David Moran of the Wayne State faculty, a brilliant former student of mine, made particular-ly valuable contributions, and I designated him as "of counsel" on the brief. As the argument date approached, Jeff asked me to be "second chair"—that is, to sit next to him at counsel table during the argument. I accepted with delight; on November 10, 2003, I would get to sit up front and almost at the center as the merits of the testimonial approach were discussed in the highest court of the land.

* * *

The Supreme Court justices do not file into the courtroom in a single line. They emerge almost all at once from curtains behind their chairs, and they take their seats immediately. Jeff's nerves were eased a little by a reassuring smile from his old boss, Justice Stevens, but when he rose to argue *Crawford*, he was hit promptly with pointed questions. Notably, although Jeff mentioned the interlock question in passing at the outset, the justices seemed uninterested in it; instead, they, as well as Jeff, focused entirely on the testimonial approach. Justice Anthony Kennedy posed a clever hypothetical that we had not anticipated. There

is a serious auto accident, and insurance investigators take statements
from witnesses; if a criminal prosecution later emerges from the accident, are those statements testimonial? Jeff hesitated, saying that such a
statement was "likely not to be testimonial," but that if the statement
was made to a police officer that would "tip the balance." I wasn't happy
with the response. It seemed to me that even though the insurance
investigator is a private individual the statement should probably be
deemed testimonial because it was made in clear anticipation of use in
litigation.[18] Chief Justice Rehnquist jumped on Jeff's answer; if he was
balancing, how much certainty would be gained by adopting a testimonial approach? Justice O'Connor joined in. Wasn't the *Roberts* framework
working well enough? Why change? ("[W]hy buy a pig in a poke?" she
asked later in the argument.) Jeff argued effectively that actually *Roberts* was leading to very bad results in the lower courts.

Justice Breyer soon broke in to ask Jeff to clarify his standard of
"testimonial". Echoing the Government's brief in *White,* Jeff had spoken
of the "functional equivalent" of in-court testimony. But that, as Justice
Breyer pointed out, was a little vague. Did Jeff agree with the standard
articulated in the law professors' brief, whether "a reasonable person in
the position of declarant [would] anticipate that the statement would
likely be used for evidentiary purposes"? I held my breath. The "functional equivalent" was his starting point, said Jeff, but he thought the
"reasonable expectation" standard was "a good test." Trying to make
the testimonial approach appear unthreatening, though, he worked hard,
perhaps too hard, to emphasize its narrowness. In "99 cases out of
100 "a testimonial statement would be made to the authorities; there
might be "a rare, rare case" in which a statement made to a private
audience could be considered testimonial. Not so rare, I was thinking—
but that was a matter that could be cleared up in later cases.

Why should the decisive consideration be the anticipation of the
declarant, Justice Scalia wanted to know; what if the statement were
made to an undercover police officer? Jeff—not wanting to go further
than necessary in any direction for fear of impairing the formation of a
majority—suggested that this posed a difficult case. Uh-oh, I thought.
The Court is never going to accept the testimonial approach if doing so is
going to put in doubt the admissibility of conspirators' statements to
undercover officers or informants. Justice John Paul Stevens asked
whether it was the intent of the speaker or the intent of the person
taking the statement that mattered. Jeff noted correctly that this was a
question that the Court did not have to reach, but Justice Scalia
interjected: "I really object to saying, . . . 'We'll worry about it later.' I

---

[18] I further elaborate on this point in *Grappling with the Meaning of "Testimonial"*, 71
BROOK. L. REV. 241, 249 n.26 (2005).

mean, if there are real problems that come up later, I'm not going to buy your ... retreat from *Roberts*."

Well, that sounded ominous—though I thought Scalia was just playing law professor with Jeff. Jeff tried to suggest that a statement should be testimonial if the speaker anticipated use in a criminal case and that in some circumstances it would be testimonial if the recipient did. But that did not relieve the problem. Justice Breyer pointed out that under prevailing law an informant's testimony of a statement made by a conspirator would be admissible, and that he would be "a little nervous" about a test that seemed to throw that result into doubt. But there was no need to do that. The law professors, he said, seemed to be thinking that "this isn't difficult." Referring to the standard we suggested in our brief, which referred to the anticipation of a reasonable person in the position of the declarant, he said, "I think they wrote these words in this brief thinking about [the case of a conspirator's statements to an undercover police officer or informant]." As second chair, I was not permitted to say a word audible to the bench. But while Justice Breyer was speaking to Jeff I was well within his line of vision, and he may have noticed that I was nodding my head, subtly perhaps but as vigorously as I could within the bounds of decorum.

And to my relief Jeff soon agreed with Breyer that "the law professors have it right." I am not sure that Justice Scalia's question, as to why the proper perspective was that of the witness, had been satisfactorily answered, but at least it was clear that Jeff was contending that the witness's perspective was the proper one, and that conspirator statements to undercover officers or informants were not testimonial. And when Justice Breyer referred to "the new rule," it seemed to me that he was treating it almost as a foregone conclusion that the Court would adopt the testimonial approach.

The Court continued to pepper Jeff with questions as to the consequences of that approach. Jeff did a deft job of reassuring the Court that adopting the approach would leave untouched most of the results of the Court's own decisions. At one point, he seemed to say flatly that excited utterances are not testimonial—a statement having no relation to the case at hand that he would later regard as overly broad, a practicing lawyer's counterpart to judicial dictum.

There was just one other set of questions that worried us: Justice Ruth Bader Ginsburg pointed out that the reason that Sylvia was unavailable for cross-examination at trial was that Mike refused to waive his spousal privilege to prevent her from being a live witness. We had been concerned that the Court might decline to reach the merits, rejecting the view of the Washington courts that Mike could not be forced to elect between his confrontation right and his spousal privilege.

But this, it turned out, was not Justice Ruth Bader Ginsburg's point at all. If Mike had a privilege to prevent Sylvia from testifying at trial, she wondered, what sense did it make not to apply the privilege to the out-of-court statement that was a substitute for her in-court testimony? It was a good question, but it would have been better addressed to the Washington Supreme Court, for it concerned only a matter of state law and had nothing to do with the issue before the United States Supreme Court.

Michael R. Dreeben, a Deputy Solicitor General and an extremely skilled and experienced Supreme Court advocate, then spoke for fifteen minutes. *Amici* generally do not make oral arguments in the Supreme Court, but there is one big exception—the United States. When Michael had asked for seven and one half minutes from each side, the parties had little choice but to agree, because if they had resisted the Court surely would have granted the time anyway. Michael argued that the reach of the Confrontation Clause should be limited to testimonial statements, but that within that ambit the Clause should not be absolute; if the declarant was unavailable, the statement should be admitted if it was sufficiently reliable. I had characterized this position as taking the bitter without the sweet. To my relief, the Court seemed not to be buying it. When Michael pointed to other areas in which the Sixth Amendment had not been interpreted absolutely, Justice Scalia gave the right response—those decisions, he said, were matters of the scope of the particular right, not decisions in which the Court allowed other considerations to over-come exercise of the right within its proper scope. Michael mentioned in passing that adopting the testimonial approach would require develop-ment of a jurisprudence of what "testimonial" means. Justice Scalia asked: "Do you think that developing a jurisprudence to decide what constitutes testimonial statements is any more difficult than developing a jurisprudence to determine what are sufficient indicia of reliability to overcome the text of the Confrontation Clause?" I liked that. Justice Scalia seemed to be signaling that he would reject any theory that allowed a confrontation claim to be overcome by a determination of reliability. As Michael sat down, it seemed to me that he had made very little headway.

Steve Sherman, arguing for the state, had an even more difficult time. Justice Breyer joined Justice Scalia in expressing skepticism about the constitutional validity of a reliability test. And even if *Roberts* applied, the justices suggested, it did not appear Sylvia's statement should have been admitted. Justice Ginsburg expressed puzzlement as to how Sylvia's statement could be deemed reliable given that Sylvia said she had her eyes closed part of the time—and suggested that the fact that the Washington Supreme Court nevertheless deemed the statement reliable reflected the arbitrariness of the reliability test. And the justices also doubted that her statement and Mike's should qualify as interlocking, given that they differed on the crucial point for which Sylvia's was offered, or that *Lee v. Illinois*, a case involving confessions by two suspects, left any space for the admission of Sylvia's statement on an interlock theory. Steve conceded the difficulty, and said weakly that the Washington Supreme Court had interpreted *Lee* to permit admission. "Well, maybe they better re-read it," said Justice O'Connor, to laughter in the courtroom. And at that moment I suspect that Steve Sherman realized there was not much chance that Michael Crawford's conviction would be upheld. Jeff treated his rebuttal time the way a quarterback with a ten-point lead treats the last thirty seconds of play; he took no chances, offering an historical overview of why a reliability test was inappropriate.

As we reflected on the argument over lunch, we had reason for confidence. Not a single justice seemed inclined to uphold the conviction, but of course our interest went far beyond that. More significantly, none of the justices seemed drawn to the Solicitor General's approach. The questioning of Jeff, which had focused entirely on the testimonial approach, gave us reason to think that as many as seven justices might join an opinion adopting that approach: Only two justices, Rehnquist and O'Connor, had expressed doubts about the need for making a wholesale change in doctrine; the others seemed primarily interested in exploring the contours of the doctrine. And if some of Jeff's answers exploring those contours were not the ones I would have given (easy to say from the second chair!), that was a relatively small matter; it was clear enough, Justice Scalia's jab notwithstanding, that if the Court were going to adopt the testimonial approach in this case it could not resolve all the difficult issues at once. Maybe, I said to Dave Moran over lunch, even Rehnquist and O'Connor would go along with an opinion adopting the testimonial approach. Dave's optimism didn't carry that far.

* * *

Now we just had to wait. On December 15, Jeff sent me a message saying that the justices had heard nine cases in the November sitting, so he expected each justice to write for the Court in one case—and the first decision had just been handed down, with the Court's opinion by Rehnquist! As the cases came down, eliminating the justices one by one as potential authors of the *Crawford* opinion, we played a little game, adjusting up or down our assessment of the odds that the Court would adopt the testimonial approach. With a flurry of decisions issued on February 24, there was only one case left from the sitting, *Crawford*, and only one justice who had not written a majority opinion, Scalia. Maybe, Jeff speculated, the decision was taking so long because O'Connor was writing a long historical dissent.

* * *

At last, on March 8, 2004, the decision came down. Sure enough, the Court unanimously reversed Crawford's conviction, Justice Scalia wrote the Court's opinion, six other justices joined in, and the Chief Justice, joined only by Justice O'Connor (not the other way around), concurred separately. Most importantly, the majority opinion, over the objection of those two justices, explicitly adopted the testimonial approach.

After reviewing the historical background of the Confrontation Clause, Justice Scalia concluded that "testimonial hearsay" was the principal, if not the only, object of concern of the Clause. And, he wrote, "the Framers would not have allowed admission of testimonial statements of a witness who did not appear at trial unless he was unavailable to testify, and the defendant had had a prior opportunity for cross-examination." And in these two propositions was the essence of the testimonial approach to the Clause. Although the actual results of Supreme Court decisions were largely in accordance with these principles, Justice Scalia wrote, the rationale stated by the Court under *Roberts*, based on an assessment of reliability, was unsound. A judicial determination of reliability could not replace the constitutionally prescribed procedure, cross-examination—and as this case and many others in the lower courts demonstrated, judicial assessments of reliability were unpredictable and sometimes resulted in admitting statements that should have been deemed to be at the center of the Confrontation Clause's concerns. Without deciding what the fate of the *Roberts* standard should be with respect to statements not deemed to be testimonial, the Court was utterly clear with respect to statements that are testimonial: They could not be admitted against an accused unless he has had a chance to cross-examine the witness and the witness is unavailable to testify at trial.

But what are testimonial statements? Here was an irony, and one that Jeff particularly relished, given Justice Scalia's jab at him during the oral argument: "We leave for another day any effort to spell out a comprehensive definition of 'testimonial.' Whatever else the term covers, it applies at a minimum to prior testimony at a preliminary hearing, before a grand jury, or at a former trial; and to police interrogations." And the statement here, "knowingly given in response to structured police questioning, qualifies under any conceivable definition" of interrogation. I thought the Court acted sensibly in taking this general approach—avoiding the articulation of a general standard in the first case transforming the law of the confrontation right, but reciting some clear instances of statements that are testimonial, and holding that the statement at issue clearly fell into one of those categories. To what extent the approach was a necessary compromise to achieve a majority opinion and to what extent it was a product of simple caution I do not know.

There were other relatively narrow points that I was glad to see in the opinion (even apart from the citation of one of my articles!). The Court said that it was "questionable whether testimonial statements would ever have been admissible on [the] ground [that they were spontaneous] in 1791 [when the Sixth Amendment was adopted]; to the extent the hearsay exception for spontaneous declarations existed at all, it required that the statements be made " 'immediat[ely] upon the hurt received, and before [the declarant] had time to devise or contrive any thing for her own advantage.' *Thompson* v. *Trevanion*, Skin. 402, 90 Eng. Rep. 179 (K.B.1694)." That struck me as exactly right—and language that should be heeded by courts that have allowed prosecutors to prove their cases on the basis of accusations assertedly made under excitement by complainants who for one reason or another do not testify at trial.[19] The Court noted that, though there have always been exceptions to the rule against hearsay, the only exception that was established in 1791 that would admit testimonial hearsay against a criminal defendant was the one for dying declarations. Exactly right again. "If this exception must be accepted on historical grounds," the Court said, "it is *sui generis*." I was glad to see the contingent nature of this statement; the Court reserved the question whether the Confrontation Clause "incorporates an exception for testimonial dying declarations,"and I think the answer should be negative. Rather, I believe many dying declarations should be admissible on the grounds that if the reason the witness cannot testify at trial is that the accused murdered her, then the accused has forfeited the right to demand that the statement be excluded for want of confrontation. And the Court expressly preserved the concept of forfeiture, not on a reliability rationale but "on essentially equitable grounds."

There were also aspects of the opinion that I wish I could change. Some stray language might be taken to suggest that a statement could not be testimonial unless it was made to a governmental agent—a bad result, and one that would open the door to the evasion of the confrontation right by the intercession of private organizations that would take statements from witnesses and relieve them of the burden of testifying subject to confrontation. And the Court's apparent emphasis on prosecutorial abuse raised the danger that statements would not be deemed testimonial absent such abuse, which would be a most unfortunate construction (and therefore ultimately one that I do not believe the Court will adopt).

---

[19] In fact, it now appears clear that the hearsay exception for spontaneous declarations did *not* exist in 1791; this is a point that Jeff and I are making in the pending cases of *Davis v. Washington* and *Hammon v. Indiana*, respectively. Also, though not of great importance, with the help of my superb research assistant, Josh Diehl, I have determined that *Thompson* was decided in 1693 not 1694.

Important as these matters were, they were relatively trivial in context, especially because they could be straightened out later. Overwhelming all other considerations was the fact that the Court had transformed the Confrontation Clause by adopting the testimonial approach.[20]

* * *

In October, Justice Scalia spent two days at our law school. He attended a lunchtime presentation I made to our faculty of a paper I had written before *Crawford* but that was published after. My main argument was that evidentiary discourse relies too much on the notion that the jury is unable to deal satisfactorily with some types of evidence. One of my illustrations was the Confrontation Clause as it was applied before *Crawford*. I noted that the change I advocated in the paper had "just happened." Justice Scalia appeared amused, and I noted further that with the author of the opinion that had achieved this great change in attendance, the gracious thing to do would be to acknowledge his contribution and move on. But being an academic, I could not resist the opportunity to carp about one aspect of the opinion that I did not like, the apparent emphasis on prosecutorial abuse. During the question period, Justice Scalia pressed me on the point. Why should the question of whether a statement is testimonial be determined from the perspective of the speaker rather than that of, say, a police officer who took the statement? I was able to say that this was the second time I had heard him ask that question, and the first time—when I was sitting in front of his Court at the *Crawford* argument—I was not allowed to say a word. Now I had my chance. I told Justice Scalia that making the role of government agents decisive is wrong on several grounds. It is wrong historically, for the confrontation right predated the existence of police officers and prosecutors. It is wrong analytically, for a police officer or prosecutor does nothing wrong in taking statements from witnesses in the defendant's absence. Indeed, this is how much police work is accomplished. It is the *court* that violates an accused's right by admitting an incriminating testimonial statement if the accused does not have an opportunity to cross-examine the person who made it. And it leads to very bad results: If a witness shoves an affidavit under the courthouse door, with no involvement by the police or prosecutor, and says, "Here is

---

[20] I will indulge here in a purely personal note. Shortly before the decision came down, I spoke about the case with my father, who had just turned 95. His powers of understanding were limited but he was eager to know about it; he couldn't much focus on the potential implications of the case for the administration of criminal justice, but his concern for his son's career remained as strong as ever. When I talked to him about the decision shortly after it was issued, the pride and delight in his voice were just what they would have been in his prime. Seven weeks later, he died swiftly and peacefully. The time was not too soon—but I was glad that it had not come two months sooner.

my accusation, but I don't want to come to court to talk about it," the affidavit is plainly testimonial, and it is just as plain that the statement should be inadmissible.

* * *

As a result of the Supreme Court's reversal of his conviction, Michael Crawford was able to negotiate a plea yielding a reduced sentence of ten years. But of course that did not end the story of *Crawford*; that story is just beginning. By transforming the jurisprudence of the Confrontation Clause, the case opened up an array of issues. Although some of the most egregious violations of the confrontation right that recurred before the decision—such as the use against defendants of statements made, without cross-examination, in grand jury testimony or in plea hearings—have pretty much ended, many courts have given the decision a grudging interpretation. Some courts have treated *Crawford*'s enumeration of core examples of testimonial statements as if it stated the outer bounds of that category. Some have insisted that only formal statements could be considered testimonial— thus admitting without cross-examination statements that were clearly made with the anticipation that they would be used in prosecution, so long as they were made informally. Some have said that only statements made in response to official interrogation can be considered testimonial, and have declined to characterize as interrogation any questioning that was not "structured."[21]

One recurrent issue involves accusatory statements made in 911 calls. Another, related, issue involves accusatory statements made at the scene of the alleged crime to responding police officers. On October 31, 2005, the Supreme Court granted certiorari in a 911 case, *Davis v. Washington*, and a responding officer case, *Hammon v. Indiana*, with Jeff Fisher and me, respectively, as counsel for the petitioners. We argued the cases in tandem on March 20, 2006, contending that any accusation of criminal conduct knowingly made to a police officer or other government agent with significant law enforcement responsibilities is necessarily testimonial within the meaning of *Crawford*. That proposition has strong intuitive appeal, and I am hopeful that the Court will accept it. Whether or not the Court does so will, to a very considerable extent, shape the future of the story of *Crawford*.

---

[21] I have begun the Confrontation Blog, www.confrontationright.blogspot.com, to allow me to comment rapidly on significant developments, good and bad.

*

# 15

## Chambers v. Mississippi: A New Justice Meets An Old Style Southern Verdict

### Stephan Landsman

#### A Hot Night in Strife–Torn Mississippi

The weather was hot on Saturday evening, June 14, 1969, in Woodville, Mississippi, a small town about 35 miles south of Natchez, not far from the Louisiana border. Although the vast majority of the people of Woodville and surrounding Wilkinson County were black, its law enforcement officials and elected leaders were overwhelmingly white. The county's claim to fame was that it had been the childhood home of Jefferson Davis, the one-time President of the Confederate States of America. It was a thoroughly segregated community whose public schools educated not a single white child and whose last movie theater closed in the late 1960s to avoid integration.

That evening two police officers, James Foreman and Aaron Liberty (who was African–American), sought to execute a warrant for the arrest of a young black man named C.C. Johnson.[1] As they attempted to take Johnson into custody a crowd of about 60 black residents formed in front of Hay's Café and Pool Hall, menaced the officers and refused to let them have their prisoner. The officers called for assistance. When three more policemen arrived another attempt was made to seize Johnson. Again, the crowd resisted, but this time a series of gunshots was fired. Officer Liberty was struck several times in the back and side. He turned to a fellow officer, Waldo Welch, and said he had been shot. Welch shouted that Liberty should "kill" his assailant. In response, Liberty turned and fired his double barreled sawed-off shotgun into an alley

---

[1] The facts of the case, unless otherwise noted, are drawn from the Index filed by the parties in United States Supreme Court Docket Index, Chambers v. Mississippi, 410 U.S. 284 (1973) (No. 71–5908) Documents in the index from which quotations are drawn include, in addition to portions of the trial transcript, defendants' motion for change of venue and defendants' motion for subpoena duces tecum. A version of this article with more specific citations to the portions of the index from which quotations are drawn is available from the author.

beside the pool hall. That shot was high but had the effect of scattering the crowd. Liberty then took what some observers claimed was more careful aim and fired again. The second blast struck a fleeing black man, Leon Chambers, in the back of the head and knocked him to the ground, apparently lifeless.

Officer Liberty staggered toward a nearby police car and collapsed. Fellow officers rushed him to a hospital in Centreville, Mississippi. There he was pronounced dead on arrival. The man he had shot, however, was still alive. A bystander, James Williams, with the help of two other men, Gable McDonald and Berkley Turner, placed the severely wounded Chambers in Williams's car and drove him to the Centreville hospital where he was treated and, later that night, placed under armed guard on the order of the county sheriff.

These shootings were another episode in the turbulent history of Mississippi during the 1960s. The passions of the state's citizens, both white and black, had been aroused by the efforts of local African–Americans and sympathizers from the North to secure minority residents the rights to vote, to be served in public establishments and, more generally, to be treated as equals. The shootings came less than two years after seven conspirators, including a police officer, were convicted in the so-called "Mississippi burning" case, of violating the civil rights of Michael Schwerner, James Chaney and Andrew Goodman, young men killed because of their efforts to advance the cause of integration.

While the main thrust of the integration effort undertaken by African–Americans was non-violent political protest, the murderous attitudes of the Ku Klux Klan and other white hate groups led some blacks in the region to organize armed self-defense organizations. Perhaps the most prominent such organization was the Deacons for Defense which was founded, not far from Wilkinson County, in Jonesboro, Louisiana, in 1964.[2] Another chapter was established in Bogalusa, Louisiana, where a Deacon opened fire on a menacing white mob. At its height, the Deacons may have had as many as 50 chapters throughout the South.

### Chambers Faces Prosecution

Leon Chambers and James Williams, the man who had driven him to the hospital, were charged with the murder of Officer Aaron Liberty in an indictment filed on October 7, 1969. The defendants were arraigned on March 16, 1970. They were represented by several white attorneys from the Natchez law firm of Mullins and Smith. Immediately after the arraignment defense counsel moved for a change of venue, claiming that the defendants could not get a fair trial in Wilkinson County "because of

---

[2] *See* LANCE HILL, THE DEACONS FOR DEFENSE: ARMED RESISTANCE AND THE CIVIL RIGHTS MOVEMENT 63 (2004).

the prejudgment of the case [and the] ill will, there existing against them." Counsel went on to assert that Clay Tucker, a particularly powerful local lawyer whose "influence in this matter is boundless" had been retained as a special prosecutor, that the two local newspapers (the NATCHEZ DEMOCRAT and the WOODVILLE REPUBLICAN) had "extolled the virtues of the deceased and condemned the defendants" and that local law enforcement officials were exerting "all influence possible" to secure a conviction. Circuit Judge James Torrey granted the defendants' motion, fixed bail at $15,000 for each defendant and moved the trial to Amite County, the jurisdiction directly to the east of Wilkinson.

Even before this legal maneuvering, defense counsel had been busy trying to strengthen their case. They discovered that one of the men who had taken Chambers to the hospital, Gable McDonald, had told several people that he, not Chambers, had shot Liberty. In early November, 1969, a black community leader and Natchez gas station owner named James Stokes, associated with the Deacons for Defense, contacted McDonald, who had left the area shortly after the shooting, and persuaded him to return to tell the lawyers his story. On November 10, 1969, McDonald appeared at defense counsels' office and under Stokes's watchful eye, provided a sworn statement about the events of June 14. He stated that he had hitched a ride into Woodville on the afternoon of Liberty's death. Once there he had witnessed the police attempts to take C.C. Johnson into custody. The officers "were handling [Johnson] pretty rough." Things got even rougher when police reinforcements arrived. Officer Liberty allegedly then fired his shotgun. McDonald claimed that in response he took out the .22 caliber pistol he was carrying and returned Liberty's fire. McDonald then slipped away but later returned to help get Chambers to the hospital. That night he gave "one of the spokesmen" (apparently a reference to one of the leaders of the Deacons for Defense) the murder weapon to dispose of.

Once McDonald had made his statement he was escorted to the Woodville jail where he was incarcerated until December 9, 1969. At that time a preliminary hearing regarding his legal status was held. At the hearing McDonald was represented by an attorney hired by his father. That lawyer led McDonald through a recital in which he recanted his confession and claimed that Stokes had persuaded him to make a false statement by promising that he would not go to prison and would share in the proceeds of a lawsuit to be filed by Chambers against various governmental bodies and officials. McDonald now denied being present at the scene of the shooting. When McDonald's lawyer had finished, the prosecutor, Mr. Foreman, cross-examined McDonald. He began by asking the witness how long he had known James Stokes. McDonald said that for a period of about two years (1967 to 1969) he had been "attending [Deacons] meetings" and that Stokes was a "spokesman" or leader of the group. The prosecutor asked McDonald if he and Stokes were "member[s] of the N double A CP," which both men apparently were. Having established that background the prosecutor went on to explore McDonald's recantation and Stokes's role in rehearsing the illiterate witness to make his original statement. The implication of all this in 1969 Mississippi was not hard to fathom—Stokes as leader of a militant and armed civil rights organization had ordered the unlettered Mc-Donald to swear falsely that he had shot Officer Liberty. This, in turn, was part of an elaborate plot to free the real culprit and lay the groundwork for a lucrative lawsuit. Shortly after the preliminary hearing the court ruled that McDonald should be set free.

On October 27, 1970, Chambers and Williams went on trial in the Circuit Court of Amite County for the murder of Officer Liberty. The State's case rested on the testimony of three police officers. The first, Herman Anthony, testified over objection, that he saw Officer Liberty "make a deliberate aim" before he fired and wounded Chambers.[3] The second, Gordon Geter, said he saw Chambers fire "a volley of shots, I would say five or six" at Liberty.[4] Finally, Waldo Welch testified that although he did not see a gun in Chambers's hand he did see what he thought was the recoil of shots break Chambers's "right hand down ... when the shots began." Welch also testified that he urged Liberty to "kill" his assailant which led the wounded officer to fire the shot that felled Chambers. Although the State's case appeared formidable with respect to Chambers, there was scarcely any proof against James Williams, and the Court eventually granted his motion for directed verdict.

Chambers's proof starkly contrasted with that offered by the State. The defendant presented the testimony of more than half a dozen witnesses. Several described their direct observation of the crime and their conclusion that the accused had not shot the officer. Several others either said that they had seen McDonald shoot the policeman or that they were aware of information that undercut his denial of responsibility. Four offered to testify that they had heard McDonald confess to the crime. The defendant also called Gable McDonald himself.

---

[3] Record from the Circuit Court of Amite County, State of Mississippi, State of Mississippi v. Chambers and Williams, Index at 62, *Chambers* (No. 71–5908). This material raises difficult opinion evidence problems. These are heightened by the fact that Liberty was shot in the back and side and may not have seen his assailant.

[4] The defendants would introduce evidence casting doubt on Geter's claim and indicating that he "spent the very next day after the murder nervously questioning members of the black community to discover who shot Liberty (R. 304–06)"; Brief for Petitioner in the United States Supreme Court at 7, n. 6, Chambers v. Mississippi, 410 U.S. 284 (1973) (No. 71–5908).

The first witness for the defense was Samuel Hardin who testified that he had been watching as McDonald shot Liberty. On the basis of the hearsay rule, Hardin was barred from telling the jury that on the night of the shooting McDonald had confessed to him. Despite defense counsel's vehement objection, Hardin was cross-examined about his connection to the Deacons for Defense, and from his evidence it could be gleaned that he, McDonald and Chambers had all been armed on the day of the shooting.

The accused next called Gable McDonald. Chambers's lawyers seemed to have had two primary objectives in doing so; first, to establish a foundation for the introduction of his November 10, 1969, written confession and, second, to provide the court with evidence corroborative of that confession. Once a foundation was established the written confession was offered. The State made no objection, and the document was provided to the jury. Among the corroborative proof adduced was the fact that McDonald owned a .22 caliber pistol (the same caliber as the murder weapon) that went missing shortly after the shooting.

When McDonald was turned over to the prosecution for cross-examination the State's lawyers wasted little time in returning to one of their favorite themes—the involvement of the Deacons for Defense in the case. McDonald was asked how he knew Natchez gas station owner, James Stokes. He replied that Stokes "was over the Deacons for Defense." The prosecution underscored this association twice more and the defense, with some apparent alarm, objected. Counsel's objection was overruled and the witness was then led to admit he was "a member of the Deacons for Defense," that James Stokes "was over [the] organization," that Stokes was "black" and that as "the head of the Deacons he had sent for [McDonald]." Again the defendant objected and again the Court overruled the objection.

The prosecution then moved on to have McDonald explain how Stokes had ordered him to come to Natchez (Stokes's home), had cajoled the witness into making a statement through promises of money and safety, had schooled the illiterate witness in precisely what to say, had called the defendants' lawyers and had looked on as McDonald made his confession. The prosecution had McDonald conclude this second segment of his cross-examination by describing how the witness's father had come to visit him while he was in jail awaiting the December 9, 1969, preliminary hearing and had hired a lawyer to represent him at that hearing. All of this was suggestive of the theory that the unschooled McDonald had been taken advantage of by the unscrupulous Stokes. With that part of the story completed the prosecution had McDonald deny that he shot Liberty. Chambers's lawyers now asked the court to allow them to treat McDonald as an adverse witness and cross-examine him. The court denied the request, leaving McDonald's disavowal of his confession as his last word.

The defense next called Berkley Turner. McDonald had testified at his preliminary hearing that he had been with Turner in Gladys' Café when the shooting took place on the streets of Woodville. Turner denied McDonald's alibi claim and went on to describe his trip to the hospital in Centreville with James Williams, McDonald and the wounded Chambers. He was, however, prevented by the prosecution's objection (apparently on hearsay grounds) from describing the incriminating remarks made by McDonald during that trip and sometime later. The next two witnesses repeated the now familiar defense story. The first, Thomas Russ, said he was at the shooting scene, saw Chambers and knew that the accused had not shot Officer Liberty. The second, Albert Carter, testified that McDonald was his neighbor and that the two had several conversations about the shooting. When Carter was asked to recount those conversations the prosecution objected "because it's an attempt on their part to impeach their own witness, Gable McDonald." The Court sustained the objection. The final witness for the defense was William Vaughn. He was Officer Liberty's first cousin and an employee at Gladys' Café. He testified that at the time of the shooting McDonald was not in the café but soon afterwards appeared at its back door with a pistol in his hand. Chambers did not testify in his own behalf.[5]

The jury convicted Leon Chambers of murder and fixed his punishment at life in the state penitentiary. The case was appealed to the Mississippi supreme court which affirmed the conviction with one judge dissenting. The majority's *per curiam* opinion began by canvassing at length the evidence presented at trial. The court focused its greatest attention on the proof that suggested McDonald had been persuaded to make a false confession due to the blandishments of James Stokes, implying that the court credited the prosecution's claim that the confession was a fabrication. The reviewing court then turned to the trial judge's exclusion of the hearsay material offered by several witnesses who wished to testify that McDonald had told them he had shot Liberty. The majority began its hearsay analysis by noting that the trial judge had acted more liberally than authorized under existing Mississippi precedent by allowing the admission of McDonald's sworn statement of November 10, 1969.[6] It then held that exclusion of the oral confessions

---

[5] Peter Westen, Chambers's counsel before the United States Supreme Court, said in a telephone interview that Chambers's injuries were extensive, and "I think that is why he didn't testify at trial. He was still in bad shape." Telephone Interview by Sherry Barrett–Mignon with Peter Westen, Appellate Counsel for Leon Chambers (August 26, 2004).

[6] This ascription of liberality may be erroneous. The prosecution never objected to the written confession, and it is likely that this was the reason for its admission. Something of

was appropriate under Mississippi's hearsay rule. It separately noted that McDonald's testimony "was not adverse" to Chambers and that, therefore, prior confessions might also be barred as improper efforts by Chambers to impeach his own witness with what might be considered inconsistent statements.[7] The court concluded that "McDonald's connection to the case was fully and carefully explored." The case was nothing more than one about "conflicting testimony." The jurors, as triers of fact, had ample information, had weighed it and had chosen to believe the State's witnesses.

In dissent Justice Rodgers did not concern himself with factual matters but rather with the question of the propriety of recognizing a "declaration against penal interest" exception to the hearsay rule. In a brief but scholarly opinion he traced the roots of the denial of such an exception to *The Sussex Peerage* case[8] and the opinion of the United States Supreme Court in *Donnelly v. United States*.[9] He noted that the modern trend was toward accepting such an exception. In the *Chambers* case he thought that once the written McDonald confession had been introduced and corroborated the case should have been opened to a full exploration of the other confessions, and that failure to do so was reversible error.

### Hot Times in Washington

Washington too was hot during the years when the *Chambers* case was making its way through the courts. In 1968, Richard Nixon was elected President. During the months before his victory, Republicans in the Senate resolved to try to block President Lyndon Johnson's attempt to promote Associate Justice Abe Fortas to Chief Justice to replace the retiring Earl Warren. When a scandal involving Fortas and a financier named Wolfson was uncovered, the Senate, for the first time in 40 years, refused to ratify a presidential Supreme Court nomination. Not only did Fortas fail to win the post of Chief Justice, he felt compelled because of various adverse disclosures to resign from the Court. That meant that there were two Supreme Court seats for Nixon to fill upon his inauguration.

Nixon nominated District of Columbia Circuit Judge Warren Burger to become Chief Justice—a choice that generated little effective opposi-

---

the sort was suggested in Mississippi's oral argument before the United States Supreme Court.

[7] Chambers v. State, 252 So.2d 217, 220 (1971). The remaining quoted material in this paragraph, as well as the next, is drawn from the Mississippi Supreme Court decision.

[8] 8 Eng. Rep. 1034 (H.L. 1844).

[9] 228 U.S. 243 (1913).

tion. He then sought, in light of his electoral success in the South, to fill the second open Supreme Court seat with a Southerner of conservative persuasion. His first choice was the distinguished Fourth Circuit judge, Clement Hainsworth. Senate Democrats angered by the attack on Fortas, went after Hainsworth with a vengeance. In what looked like tit for tat, they attacked Hainsworth's ethics on the basis of his having failed to recuse himself in a number of cases concerning companies whose stock he owned. They also challenged his apparently illiberal decisions regarding labor unions and his seeming quiescence in the face of segregation in his native South Carolina. On November 21, 1969, the Senate voted to reject Hainsworth's nomination. Frustrated but undeterred, Nixon tried once more to appoint a Southerner, nominating Florida appellate court judge G. Harrold Carswell. The President's choice was an undistinguished jurist of dubious intellectual ability. He too was rejected by the Senate. Thwarted and smarting, Nixon turned to Chief Justice Burger who suggested his long-time Minnesota friend and federal appeals court judge, Harry Blackmun. This nomination succeeded, but a precedent of partisan hostility and distrust, which would, eventually, scuttle the Bork nomination and lead to the battles around Clarence Thomas, had been established.

In short order Nixon had two more Supreme Court vacancies to fill, as both Hugo Black and John Marshall Harlan retired before the beginning of the Supreme Court's 1971 term. Nixon, still anxious to make his Southern appointment sounded out American Bar Association (ABA) leader and nationally prominent Richmond, Virginia, attorney Lewis Powell, Jr. In fact, Powell had been on Nixon's short list two years earlier but had declined to be considered. This time the President was unwilling to take "no" for an answer. Nixon contacted Powell and insisted that it was his "duty" to agree to the nomination. Powell reluctantly did so, although the day before the President planned to announce the choice Powell had such doubts that he, albeit unsuccessfully, attempted to withdraw.

What underlay Powell's reticence is not easy to determine. He was 64 when nominated—an advanced age to be joining the Supreme Court. He had never served as a judge and would have to master a new craft. Perhaps most worrisome, it appeared likely that during the confirmation process he would be confronted with probing questions about his attitude toward and efforts to overcome segregation. He was vulnerable on that issue for a number of reasons. He was the leading partner of a large all-white Richmond law firm. He was a member of a number of segregated country clubs. Most significantly, he had been the chair of the Richmond School Board from 1952 to 1960, the era when *Brown v.*

*Board of Education*[10] became the law of the land. To say that Richmond's integration efforts were modest during this period is an understatement. Of the 23,000 black school children in Richmond in the fall of 1960 only two attended schools with white pupils. This could not be attributed to Powell's leadership because of pervasive state involvement in pupil assignment. Yet, Powell had done virtually nothing to enforce the law of the land.

In 1960 Powell was appointed to the Virginia Board of Education. There, again, the public record was devoid of any evidence demonstrating the nominee's commitment to integration. In fact, he and his Board of Education colleagues went beyond existing Virginia law to assure white parents of funds to help them pay for private schooling in Prince Edwards County, where public schools had been shut down as a means of avoiding integration. Powell was also, in 1968, author of an amicus brief in *Swann v. Charlotte-Mecklenburg Board of Education*[11] in which he and his law firm colleagues sharply attacked busing for the purpose of achieving integration.

Powell's confirmation hearing was, however, far less contentious than might have been expected given this history. Powell had been nominated at the same time as William Rehnquist. The latter drew most of the liberal fire in the Senate. Moreover, those troubled by Southern attitudes regarding integration had spent considerable energy and political capital in the Hainsworth and Carswell battles. Powell was a genuinely distinguished lawyer and bar leader. He handled the hearing process masterfully. Yet, the proceedings may have left their mark. As John Jefferies, Jr., Powell's authorized biographer observed:

> Powell had replaced Hugo Black as the Court's only southerner. His role in the (non) desegregation of the Richmond schools had been picked to pieces in his confirmation. Anything he said on the subject would be read with suspicion.[12]

Powell himself reached the same conclusion, declaring in a 1972 memo about a busing case that had come before the Court that "many will view an expression from me as reflecting a southern bias, if not southern racism."[13]

### Chambers Moves North

As Lewis Powell was making his way to the Supreme Court so was the *Chambers* case. Local counsel had taken the case as far as they felt

---

[10] 347 U.S. 483 (1954).

[11] 402 U.S. 1 (1971).

[12] John C. Jefferies, Jr., JUSTICE LEWIS F. POWELL, JR. (Macmillan 1994), at 292.

[13] *Id.* at 294.

they could.[14] They contacted the Lawyers Committee for Civil Rights Under Law in Washington, D.C., and asked if counsel could be found to pursue an appeal to the Supreme Court. As was its practice, the Lawyers Committee sent the case file out for evaluation. A lawyer at Williams and Connolly, a preeminent Washington law firm, reviewed the file and concluded that it presented no cognizable federal questions and, hence, that there were no grounds to appeal to the Supreme Court. Yet, there was something about the palpable unfairness of Chambers's trial and intimations that the defendant might not be guilty that bothered the Lawyers Committee staff. They sent the case out for a second opinion. This time the file went to Peter Westen, a talented young lawyer working at the Washington office of Paul, Weiss, Rifkind, Wharton and Garrison. Westen recognized the difficulty of framing a federal claim but felt that Mississippi's evidence rules had produced a serious injustice. Although there was no overt misconduct by state officials, an arguably innocent man had been convicted. Westen told the Lawyers Committee that a Sixth Amendment claim might be framed. The case was sent to volunteer attorneys at the Paul, Weiss office in New York City. But Westen could not stop thinking about Chambers. He requested an opportunity to handle the matter, and was given the case.

Westen had few illusions about the likelihood of the Supreme Court granting certiorari simply to right an apparent injustice, especially when the case involved the murder of a policeman. He did, however, think that pressing a long-shot appeal might serve Chambers's legal interests. Westen hoped that the denial of certioriari might be accompanied by a dissent from one or more of the more liberal justices. This, in turn, might help lend credibility to claims that Chambers might advance as part of a habeas corpus collateral challenge to his conviction.

At this point Westen made a fateful and canny decision. Although it was virtually unheard of, Westen made an application to the Supreme Court that his convicted and imprisoned client be admitted to bail.[15] He did so because he had become aware of favorable information about Chambers that was not incorporated in the record. This included the facts that Chambers was a home-owning family man, had a wife and nine children, had served for a time on the Woodville police force, was a deacon in his local Baptist church, had no prior criminal record and was a veteran. This material could be provided to the Court through affida-

---

[14] The description contained in this section is drawn in large measure from the telephone interview with Peter Westen *supra* note 5.

[15] Diligent research has yielded only three cases up to 1972 in which the Supreme Court considered bail. These cases all recognized the power of the Court to grant bail but none actually ordered it. *See* Carbo v. United States, 82 S.Ct. 662, 7 L.Ed.2d 769 (1962); Ward v. United States, 76 S.Ct. 1063, 1 L.Ed.2d 25 (1956); McKane v. Durston, 153 U.S. 684 (1894).

vits attached to the application for bail, though none of it was relevant to any issue in the case.

Westen contacted the Mississippi Attorney General's office and informed them of his intention to file a bail application. The novelty of the idea and the long odds against its success appeared to convince Mississippi's lawyers not to file any papers regarding the motion. Instead, they authorized Westen to note the state's opposition to the application in his papers. Only one step remained for Chambers's case to be presented for Supreme Court consideration. Since Westen was not a member of the Supreme Court bar, an attorney who was admitted to practice before the Court would have to be found to sign the moving papers. Ramsey Clark, son of a retired Supreme Court Justice, and erstwhile Attorney General in Lyndon Johnson's administration agreed to join Westen on the case. Although Clark was later to veer into radical politics, at this moment he lent substantial credibility to the filing.

## The New Justice Confronts an Old Style Southern Verdict

Lewis Powell, Jr., was sworn in as a Justice of the Supreme Court on January 7, 1972. Awaiting him on his arrival were a number of difficult cases. His very first day on the job the Justices held their usual weekly conference. At that conference they considered, among other questions, whether to grant certiorari in *Keys v. School District No. 1*, a case from Denver raising questions about the propriety of using the busing remedy outside the South. Powell's opposition to certiorari notwithstanding, the Court accepted the case. Powell thus knew that he would, in his first year on the Court, have to confront busing—a remedy he abhorred and would oppose, although he knew this would invite critics to attack him as a racist. Shortly thereafter, on January 31, 1972, Chambers's application for bail arrived and attached to it his petition for certiorari (filed on December 23, 1971).

Upon joining the Court, Powell had been designated Circuit Justice for the Fifth Circuit (including Mississippi as well as a number of other states). In that capacity Powell was responsible for the review of a wide range of applications for interim relief in cases that might be heard by the Supreme Court. Among the matters he was to consider were bail applications. It was for this reason that Powell received the *Chambers* materials. Powell scrutinized the papers and then did something extraordinary—he granted the bail application. The virtually unprecedented decision stunned Mississippi. Moving with an alacrity it had theretofore not displayed, the State within ten days of the February 1 order filed an application for reconsideration. Mississippi's Attorney General declared Chambers's case "frivolous" and claimed that his "return to the commu-

nity will create a dangerous situation to citizens of that community."[16]
The State submitted affidavits from the Wilkinson County Sheriff and
the Woodville Chief of Police, among others, asserting that Chambers
would create an "explosive situation in the community" and a risk of
"bloodshed." Powell was not swayed. On February 14, 1972, he wrote an
opinion responding to Mississippi's Application for Reconsideration. He
criticized the State's initial unresponsiveness and its subsequent reliance
on "conclusory" claims unsupported by "specific facts." He set forth the
information Westen had provided which demonstrated Chambers's exemplary prior history. Perhaps most ominously for the State, Powell
noted that Chambers's petition for certiorari presented "two non-frivolous constitutional questions."

The new Justice had done something remarkable in his first month
on the bench. He had also placed his colleagues in a position where they
would either have to grant certiorari or denigrate the new man's written
judgment concerning the "non-frivolity" of the constitutional questions
raised. The *Chambers* case had been transformed from one of hundreds
of criminal case filings asserting tenuous constitutional claims to a case
that the new Justice had signaled deserved the most careful scrutiny.

Peter Westen believes that the granting of bail is, in all likelihood,
best understood as the action of a new and inexperienced judge and that
by placing his prestige on the line, Powell generated enormous pressure
on his colleagues to back him up. Westen thinks Powell's decision was
most likely a newcomer's reaction to sympathetic background information, a well framed argument about unfairness and the endorsement of a
former Attorney General (Ramsey Clark). Mississippi, according to Westen, overreacted and thus provoked Powell into writing the brief opinion
in which he declared Chambers's claims to be "non-frivolous." Westen's
analysis makes sense. Powell was new to his job. He had not practiced
criminal law. The bail application was one of the first things he handled.
His ruling may have been little more than an unpremeditated from-the-
heart reaction. Yet there are grounds to suspect that more than inexperi-
ence or gut reaction was involved.

Although it was not much emphasized in his confirmation hearings,
Lewis Powell had a deep and genuine sensitivity to questions of institutional justice. The idea that a man accused of murder might be barred
from fully exploring the confessions of another may have offended him.
Although Powell had made his share of law-and-order speeches, he had
also, as President of the ABA, shown himself to be deeply concerned
about securing a genuinely fair day in court for all Americans. He had

---

[16] Application for Reconsideration of Order Admitting Petitioner to Bail, Index at 164,
*Chambers* (No. 71–5908) (Opinion of Powell, J.). The remaining quoted material in this
paragraph is drawn from the same source.

worked tirelessly to ensure the success of the federal government's Legal
Services Corporation (which provided legal services to the poor) when
many within the bar wanted it scuttled. In 1968 he was the recipient of
the Federal Office of Economic Opportunity Award for Contributions to
the National Legal Services Program. He displayed his concern for fair
representation in criminal cases by joining the National Legal Aid and
Defenders Association and by frequently asserting the importance of
guaranteeing all criminal defendants the right to counsel. All of this
suggests that Powell was strongly inclined to seek to level the playing
field when confronted with an unbalanced contest.

J. Harvie Wilkinson, III, was one of Powell's clerks in his first year
on the bench. Wilkinson became a keen admirer of the Justice and wrote
a book about his time with Powell entitled, Serving Justice. The title
neatly summarizes Wilkinson's assessment of Powell's approach in his
early years on the Court. One of the first topics Wilkinson considered in
his book was the difficulty he experienced in remaining suitably sensitive
to the claims presented in the flood of petitions filed in the Supreme
Court by criminal defendants. Having made that admission, Wilkinson
immediately turned to the "remarkable" case of Leon Chambers and the
important contribution it made to the pursuit of justice. Although he did
not discuss why Powell granted bail or eventually wrote the Chambers
opinion reversing the decision of the Mississippi Supreme Court, he did
say:

> There are many Leon Chamberses ... who come before the Su-
> preme Court. The subjects of its cases seem to be so often society's
> unfortunates seeking a better shake. Many of Justice Powell's early
> opinions involved such persons....[17]

Powell's sensitivity to fair play is strongly suggested here. Cases that
patently deprived poor citizens of a fair "shake" were likely, Wilkinson
suggests, to catch the Justice's attention and garner his sympathy.

Powell's sensitivity to questions of fairness was augmented by the
Justice's particular attentiveness to the facts of each case. Powell was a
practitioner who had tried cases. He had the trial lawyer's feel for
factual nuance. Both his clerk, Harvie Wilkinson, and his colleague,
Justice Sandra Day O'Connor, were moved to remark on this aspect of
Powell's approach to judging. Wilkinson said, "As a former practitioner
and litigator, he was conscious of the importance of facts; he relished the
facts; he placed stock in them."[18] In the Chambers case the facts and
their implications leave one in doubt about the fairness of the trial and

---

[17] J. Harvie Wilkinson, III, Serving Justice 23 (Charterhouse 1974), at 27.

[18] J. Harvie Wilkinson, III, The Powellian Virtues in a Polarized Age, 49 Wash. & Lee L.
Rev. 271, 272 (1992).

verdict. Why would an innocent McDonald confess half a dozen times shortly after the shooting? Why did the prosecution keep mentioning the Deacons for Defense? If the policemen were so sure that Chambers was a pistol-wielding murderer, why didn't at least one of them rush to see if he was dead? What was the jury to make of a swearing contest when some of the best evidence for one side was kept from them? These and similar questions leap from the pages of the trial transcript. They may not, by themselves, create a constitutional question but they do give the *Chambers* case a peculiar smell.

According to O'Connor, Powell was not only sensitive to facts but predisposed to follow their trail to the issues of fairness they suggested. In her *Harvard Law Review* tribute to Powell, O'Connor said:

> At conference discussions, he would often focus on the equities of the particular case, for the parties and the problems they presented were very much alive to him. With his deep sensitivity to the real people whose hardships or injuries sometimes recede from view in appellate litigation, Justice Powell always strived to reach a fair result in each and every case.[19]

It was not the grand claim that captured Lewis Powell's attention but the factual bits and pieces that spelled fairness or oppression. Again, *Chambers's* troubling facts might have drawn in such a man.

While all this by itself may be enough to explain Powell's reaction, there is one more piece of the puzzle to consider—the racial overtones of the case. Powell had just come through a confirmation process in which his sympathy toward African–Americans was repeatedly questioned. His record as chair of the Richmond School Board was by any objective measure troubling. His firm was even whiter than the schools he oversaw, and his country clubs were segregated. From his first day on the Court it was clear he was going to be drawn into the busing controversy in a way that would furnish critics with fresh reasons to accuse him of racist inclinations. Then the *Chambers* case came across his desk. It was a case in which a hard-working, seemingly honorable black man had inexplicably become involved in the murder of a black police officer. The case took place in a state bedeviled by racial strife at a moment when some of its citizens were violently trying to preserve its segregationist ways. As President of the ABA, Powell had condemned the "small and defiant minority in the South ... that still uses violence and intimidation to frustrate the legal rights of Negro citizens."[20]

---

[19] Sandra Day O'Connor, *A Tribute to Lewis F. Powell, Jr.* 101 HARV. L. REV. 395, 395–96 (1987).

[20] Quoted in *Jefferies, supra* note 12, at 211.

All the witnesses against Chambers were white police officers. Most of those who spoke in his favor were black men who had been linked to the Deacons for Defense or the NAACP. Many had gone about armed during that hot summer night in a Mississippi town where they could not vote, have their children attend integrated schools or even enjoy a movie. Powell had lived virtually all of his life in the South. He could decipher the race-based message encoded in these facts. The *Chambers* case may have offered the Justice a chance to express his conviction that Southern blacks deserved a fair "shake." The case may have offered an irresistible opportunity to make such a statement at just the moment Powell felt it was needed. Granting bail and suggesting that substantial constitutional questions existed may not have been the naïve decisions of a new judge but the reaction of a man exquisitely sensitive to questions of fairness and to signals of racial oppression, who had recently been empowered and energized to do something about them.

## Argument and Decision

The Supreme Court granted certiorari in the *Chambers* case on March 20, 1972. Chambers's written argument to the Court could be quite simply summarized:

> Chambers was denied a fair trial in violation of the Sixth and Fourteenth Amendments. The Mississippi hearsay rule barred him from offering the exculpatory testimony of witnesses in his favor. The party witness rule barred him from confronting the witnesses against him. They effectively prevented him from putting on a defense.[21]

The heart of the matter was that the combined effect of Mississippi's rules prevented Chambers from exculpating himself with critical confession testimony and thereby deprived him of his constitutional rights. The Court had previously held in *Brady v. Maryland*[22] that the state was required to inform the defendant of the existence of a confession by another. The *Chambers* case presented the logical next step—the opportunity, under conditions that ensured reliability, to use that confession at trial. The defendant conceded that the due process right to offer such evidence was not unlimited but argued that the state needed a powerful justification to bar such important exculpatory evidence. Moreover, Chambers's counsel argued that, pursuant to decisions like *Washington v. Texas*,[23] the defendant had a right under the compulsory process

---

[21] Brief for the Petitioner at 12, *Chambers* (No. 71–5908).

[22] 373 U.S. 83 (1963).

[23] 388 U.S. 14 (1967).

clause of the Sixth Amendment to obtain witnesses in his favor and to offer their testimony concerning the confessions of another.

However, the 1913 decision of the Supreme Court in *Donnelly v. United States*[24] posed a significant challenge to the defendant's position. In that case the Court had decided that, in federal trials, statements against penal interest, including those exculpating a criminal defendant on trial for the same crime, could be excluded as hearsay. It had stood for 60 years and allowed just the sort of evidentiary ruling Chambers claimed was unconstitutional. The way around this problem was far from clear. If the Court held that the Constitution required unfettered admission of exculpatory evidence then not only *Donnelly* and the hearsay rule but all the rules of evidence could be overthrown whenever a defendant sought to introduce exculpatory evidence. This was a radical notion and not one likely to appeal to the Supreme Court. The key for Chambers lay in arguing that the particular combination of restrictions imposed by Mississippi posed a unique and irrational hardship.

While focusing the bulk of his brief on the due process and compulsory process questions, Chambers devoted some attention to the injustice caused by Mississippi's "voucher" rule. That rule deprived Chambers of the opportunity to impeach McDonald simply because he had been the one who called McDonald to the stand. Chambers argued that the voucher rule was antiquated and absurd in criminal cases where the defendant had little choice about who he would need to call to testify. The voucher rule blocked Chambers from impeaching McDonald with his prior confessions—now not being used to prove McDonald's guilt but his lack of trustworthiness as a maker of inconsistent statements. This, according to Chambers, fell afoul of the Sixth Amendment confrontation clause.

Mississippi's submission to the Supreme Court was only 13 pages long (about one-third the length of Chambers's brief). Its argument was quite simple. *Donnelly* was still good law and almost identical to Mississippi's hearsay rule. Refusal to recognize a penal statement against interest exception to the hearsay rule had the entirely legitimate objective of seeking to thwart trickery and deceit by defendants and confederates who might conspire to fabricate hearsay evidence conducive to the acquittal of guilty individuals. To suggest that these well settled rules somehow infringed on constitutional rights was to fly in the face of 60 years of precedent. As to the impeachment question, Mississippi made the simplistic and mechanical argument that because McDonald's recantation did not declare Chambers's guilt, McDonald was not a witness "against" Chambers, so the Sixth Amendment right of confrontation did not apply. Mississippi did not engage the *Brady* point or the claim that

---

[24] 228 U.S. 243 (1913).

the combination of its rules created a special hardship. Instead the State insisted that the jury had been fairly apprised of the issues surrounding McDonald by the detailing of his confession and subsequent recantation.

Oral argument was heard on November 15, 1972. Peter Westen, speaking on Chambers's behalf, began by highlighting the facts of the case. His opening line captures the thrust of his presentation:

> The petitioner in this case, Leon Chambers, was convicted of a murder which another man was seen committing, and to which that other man spontaneously and repeatedly confessed within hours of the shooting.[25]

Westen told the Court that the case arose out of a "racial disturbance" and that the evidence against Chambers was "practically non-existent." The Justices followed Westen's lead asking friendly questions about the "other man" (McDonald). The most difficult trial testimony facing Chambers was Officer Geter's claim to have seen the accused shoot Liberty. Westen attacked it vigorously, belittling Geter's claim and emphasizing evidence that this alleged eyewitness was seen the next day "asking members of the black community if they knew who shot Liberty."

When Westen shifted his focus to the constitutional questions he led with his briefing point about *Brady* and Mississippi's exclusion of what that case had designated as critical exculpatory material. Though the Justices remained friendly, one wondered if Westen's argument wasn't a direct attack on the hearsay exclusion declared by *Donnelly*. Westen was ready for the question. He argued that *Chambers* was distinguishable from *Donnelly*. In *Chambers* the hearsay witness was alive and testifying at the trial,[26] there was not one but a series of spontaneous confessions to different witnesses and there was a great deal of corroborative evidence. These differences greatly enhanced the reliability of the material offered in Chambers's case and invited a ruling that might confine the decision to its peculiar circumstances rather than necessitating a sweeping overhaul of *Donnelly*.[27] Justice Powell jumped at the idea of focusing on special circumstances, asking:

---

[25] Oral Argument of Peter Westen, Esq., On Behalf of the Petitioner at 3, *Chambers* (Nov. 15, 1972) (No. 71–5908). The remaining quoted material in this paragraph is drawn from pages 3–6 of the same source.

[26] It is ironic that under FED. R. EVID. 804, statements against penal interest can only be introduced if the out-of-court declarant is "unavailable" as defined in FED. R. EVID. 804(a).

[27] The *Donnelly* doctrine was about to be undone in federal courts by the proposed Federal Rules of Evidence, which included recognition of a hearsay exception for statements against penal interest in FED. R. EVID. 804. This, however, did nothing to change

> But your theory, as I understand it, is that in effect you look at
> the totality of the circumstances, to see whether or not the
> evidence could be admitted, it was inherently reliable?[28]

Westen was not willing to concede quite that much, stressing instead a
theory of the presumptive right of a defendant to offer exculpatory
evidence and the obligation of the state to overcome that presumption.
Justice Powell's question seemed to signal that certain members of the
court were groping for a solution that could free Chambers without
upsetting a vast body of criminal evidence law.

Timmie Hancock, the Special Assistant Attorney General who argued on behalf of the State of Mississippi, faced a good deal more
vigorous questioning than his opponent. Chief Justice Burger started
things off by posing a hypothetical for Hancock:

> What would be the situation under *Brady*, if all three of these
> witnesses had gone to the prosecutor or the police and told them
> of this confession? And let's add that McDonald himself went to
> the police and told them what he told the others.
>
> And the prosecution never disclosed that to anybody, and it
> was never discovered until after a conviction. What would be
> the situation in this case under *Brady*, and subsequent cases?[29]

Hancock had no choice but to admit the prosecution's duty to inform the
defendant of the favorable evidence. From there it was but a short step
to recognizing the serious nature of the impediment Mississippi had
erected to Chambers's use of potentially critical exculpatory evidence.
Hancock fared little better when the questioning shifted to the facts. He
was briskly challenged about why the authorities had not arrested
Chambers "promptly," had not arraigned him for a year, and had, in
short order, freed him on bail. All this suggested that the State had little
confidence in its own accusations.

In what appeared to be an attempt to suggest that due process had
been served, Hancock argued that the decision below was sound because
Chambers had been permitted to call a number of witnesses to present
his theory of the case and to introduce the written confession. One of the
Justices, however, forced Hancock to admit that, had Mississippi's rules
been rigorously enforced, even the written confession would have been

---

state evidence rules, like Mississippi's, that relied on the same approach as *Donnelly*, and
even under the federal rule the declarant, unlike McDonald, had to be unavailable.

[28] Oral Argument of Peter Westen, Esq., On Behalf of the Petitioner at 20, *Chambers*
(Nov. 15, 1972) (No. 71–5908).

[29] Oral Argument of Timmie Hancock, Esq., On Behalf of the Respondent at 25,
*Chambers* (Nov. 15, 1972). The remaining quoted material in this paragraph, as well as the
next two, is drawn from pages 25–38 of the same source.

barred. Pressing further, a member of the Court sought to get Hancock to concede that the oral confessions might have been even more reliable than the written one. Hancock resisted, no doubt recognizing a challenge to Mississippi's central claim that oral hearsay confessions by individuals other than the accused are inherently unreliable. The Justices bore in, one asking:

> But unless he claimed, unless McDonald claimed that these other three people to whom he made the oral declarations had also promised him money, would they not [be] more cogent, more reliable than the one that he said was given for a promise of money?

Hancock was in a difficult spot. One way out would have been to claim that a conspiracy, perhaps by the Deacons for Defense who had been repeatedly referred to at trial, tainted all the reported confessions. Apparently, such a provocative and speculative reference was off limits, at least in the Supreme Court.

The Court moved on to the question of Mississippi's having denied Chambers an opportunity to interrogate McDonald. Hancock argued that Chambers had been free to question McDonald but simply had failed to do so. The Justices would not accept this blithe assertion. Under close questioning, Hancock was forced to admit that Chambers would not have been permitted to cross-examine and that the defendant would have been "bound by the answer[s]" given by the witness he had called to the stand. Sensing the Court's resistance, Hancock sought to finish as strongly as possible by re-emphasizing the point that the jury had been fully apprised of Chambers's claims about McDonald. He now added an argument with a hint of concession in it: "But, in any event, we would consider that if there were error, it was a harmless error."

On February 21, 1973, the Supreme Court announced its decision in the *Chambers* case. By a vote of 7 to 2 the Court reversed the Mississippi Supreme Court's decision. Justice Powell delivered the opinion of the Court. Powell began by reciting the now familiar story of attempted arrest, melee, gunfire and death. Powell signaled his skepticism of the State's case throughout this early part of the opinion. Powell next turned to Gable McDonald, concentrating attention on McDonald's suspicious behavior and multiple confessions. Rejecting the State's argument that the jury had gotten a clear picture of the defendant's claim, Powell concluded:

> In sum, then, this was Chambers's predicament. As a consequence of the combination of Mississippi's "party witness" or "voucher" rule and its hearsay rule, he was unable either to cross-examine McDonald or to present witnesses in his behalf who would have discredited McDonald's repudiation and demon-

strated his complicity ... Chambers' defense was far less persuasive than it might have been had he been given an opportunity to subject McDonald's statements to cross-examination or
had the other confessions been admitted.[30]

Now Powell turned to the constitutional question. He began by
affirming the due process right of the accused to defend himself against
the state's charges. That right had two salient characteristics, the ability
both to cross-examine or confront witnesses against him and to offer
testimony on his own behalf. Chambers's rights had been infringed in
both regards. Powell found that the defendant had been denied a chance
"to subject McDonald's damning repudiation and alibi to cross-examination." Although the right to cross-examine is not absolute, it was
thwarted in Chambers's case not by some important state interest but by
the antiquated and outmoded voucher doctrine. Moreover, Mississippi
had not even seen fit in its Supreme Court submission to "defend the
rule or explain its underlying rationale," seeking instead to sidestep the
issue by claiming McDonald was not "adverse" to Chambers and therefore, confrontation concerns did not come into play. Powell would have
none of it, declaring, "The 'voucher' rule, as applied in this case, plainly
interfered with Chambers' right to defend against the State's charges."

Pursuing a cautious line, Powell did not choose to reverse on this
ground alone but emphasized its "conjunction with the trial court's
refusal to permit [Chambers] to call other witnesses." Powell noted that
the hearsay rule, which had created the testimonial barrier in Chambers's case, served an important function by excluding untrustworthy
evidence. He also noted that most states, in 1972, were still wedded to
the exclusion of the sort of statement against penal interest barred in
*Donnelly.* While not challenging that exclusion in all contexts, Powell
found that in the *Chambers* case the defendant's right to due process
had been violated when a series of spontaneous, independent and incriminating statements were excluded despite the presence in court of the
man who had made them. All these factors when combined created
"persuasive assurances of trustworthiness" that, under the authority of
the due process clause, required the negation of the hearsay bar because
"the hearsay rule may not be applied mechanistically to defeat the ends
of justice." Powell sought to cabin this potentially sweeping due process
principle by limiting it to the facts of Chambers's case and denying that
the Court was establishing any "new principles of constitutional law."

After the Supreme Court's ruling, the State of Mississippi elected
not to retry Leon Chambers.

---

[30] Chambers v. Mississippi, 410 U.S. at 294.

## *Chambers* as Precedent

Powell's effort to circumscribe the principle he announced in *Chambers* was indicative of the approach he would employ throughout his 15 years as a member of the Supreme Court. It was a cautious approach which sought to eschew grand pronouncements in favor of fact-specific decisions. Speaking about the "Powellian Virtues," J. Harvie Wilkinson, III, in a 1992 piece noted the Justice's strong inclination to treat "legal principles not as hard and fast rules but rather, as presumptions that could be rebutted in an appropriate case."[31] This description fits Powell's approach in *Chambers* almost perfectly.

Early on it appeared that Powell's circumscribed approach might win out and leave *Chambers* as little more than a fact-bound oddity. Writing about ten years after the decision, one scholar concluded that lower court reaction to *Chambers* was "ambivalent" and "clearly mixed."[32] The Supreme Court did not return to the *Chambers* principle in any serious way until 1987. At that point it struck down Arkansas's ban on the use of hypnotically-enhanced testimony because it impeded the defendant before the Court from providing, through her own testimony, material crucial to her defense.[33] Since the start of the 1990s, a growing number of analysts have viewed *Chambers* as a seminal precedent justifying, in appropriate cases, the overriding of "state restrictions on the presentation of witnesses" and impediments to the offering of exculpatory evidence.

*Chambers* has had its critics as well as fans. Peter Westen, counsel for Chambers in the Supreme Court, joined the ranks of legal academics not long after the case and wrote a series of outstanding articles about the issues addressed in the decision.[34] He suggested that both his and the Court's analysis were seriously flawed with respect to the identification of the rights involved and that the true constitutional locus of the case was not due process or confrontation but compulsory process—the Sixth Amendment right to call witnesses. Other scholars have viewed *Chambers* as a narrowing of the right to present a defense. They argue that it lends too much credence to the rules of evidence and overemphasizes the particular and peculiar facts of the case.

---

[31] Wilkinson, *supra* note 20, at 273.

[32] Steven G. Churchwell, *The Constitutional Right to Present Evidence: Progeny of Chambers v. Mississippi,* 19 Crim. L. Bull. 131, 137–38 (1983).

[33] Rock v. Arkansas, 483 U.S. 44, 62 (1987).

[34] *See* Peter Westen, *The Compulsory Process Clause,* 73 Mich. L. Rev. 71 (1974); Peter Westen, *Compulsory Process II,* 74 Mich. L. Rev. 191 (1975); Peter Western, *Confrontation and Compulsory Process: A Unified Theory for Criminal Cases,* 91 Harv. L. Rev. 567 (1978) [hereinafter *A Unified Theory*].

Yet the principles that Powell articulated in *Chambers* have not been easily closeted. According to databases of federal and state cases, Chambers has been cited more than 2,700 times since 1973.[35] Of these

---

[35] In order to arrive at aggregate statistics regarding *Chambers's* reception as precedent it was first necessary to identify subsequent rulings (majority decisions) referring to the case. West Publishing's online database stores, in electronic form, all cases published in the *Westlaw* reports. Within each case citation is a link allowing the user to access a listing of all cases that discuss the original decision. This listing distinguishes between rulings and dissents. Making use of this link and removing dissents yields an enumeration of all rulings (majority decisions) making reference to the original case. There were 2647 rulings referring to *Chambers*.

West maintains a staff of lawyers whose responsibility it is to read subsequent decisions and identify within them references to points set forth in the headnotes of original decisions like the *Chambers* case. Each subsequent case is then reported with a notation of the West staff attorney's assessment of what headnote points have been utilized as well as whether the use was positive (following the headnote point) or negative (declining to follow or distinguishing the headnote point).

This combination of information made it possible to analyze percentages and trends in the use of *Chambers's* headnote principles in the aggregated list of subsequent cases. The cases and attendant information were inputted into a Microsoft Excel spreadsheet for analysis. References to various headnote principles expressed as a percentage of the total number of cases as well as percentages of positive and negative uses could then be calculated. What follows is a partial listing of findings (those that produced double-digit percentages) regarding positive and negative uses of various headnote propositions. (The ever-expanding universe of cases require that it be noted that this analysis is only current through August 1, 2005):

(1) Headnote 3: "Rights to confront and cross-examine witnesses and to call witnesses in one's own behalf are essential to due process." Cited positively: 451 cases (17.0% of all cases). Cited negatively: 1 case (0.1% of all cases).

(2) Headnote 5: "Right to confront and to cross-examine is not absolute and may in appropriate cases bow to accommodate other legitimate interests in the criminal trial process, but its denial or significant diminution calls into question the ultimate integrity of the fact-finding process and requires that the competing interest be closely examined." Cited positively: 504 cases: (19.0% of all cases). Cited negatively: 11 cases (0.4% of all cases).

(3) Headnote 6: "Testimony of third person who had made, but later repudiated, a written confession to the murder with which defendant was charged was seriously "adverse" to defendant for purposes of his right to confront and cross-examine those giving damaging testimony against him, despite contention that third person did not "point the finger" at defendant, where, in the circumstances of the case, third person's retraction inculpated defendant to the same extent that it exculpated the third person, and thus, when defendant called such person as witness upon failure of state to do so, application of Mississippi's common-law "voucher" rule to preclude cross-examination by defendant, together with corollary requirement that party calling the witness is bound by anything he might say, interfered with defendant's right to defend against the state's accusations." Cited positively: 306 cases (11.6% of all cases). Cited negatively: 52 cases (2.0% of all cases).

(4) Headnote 8: "In the exercise of his right to present witnesses in his own defense, the accused, like the State, must comply with established rules of procedure and evidence designed to assure both fairness and reliability in the ascertainment of

citations more than 2,600 employ the doctrines set forth in the case in their ruling. Roughly speaking, there have been three points that are stressed. First, the case is viewed as standing for the proposition that the rules of evidence and procedure cannot be mechanistically applied to defeat the ends of justice (the thrust of approximately 29 percent of the cases). Second, the case is seen as urging that evidence bearing substantial indicia of reliability should be admitted even if it violates an established rule of evidence (the point in about 20 percent of the cases).

---

guilt or innocence." Cited positively: 539 cases (20.4% of all cases). Cited negatively: 25 cases (0.5% of all cases).

(5) Headnote 9: "Where third person, on separate occasions shortly after murder, made spontaneous confessions to three close acquaintances, where such confessions were corroborated by other evidence in the case, where such confessions were unquestionably against interest, and where such person was present in the courtroom at defendant's trial for the same murder and was under oath and subject to cross-examination, constitutional rights directly affecting the ascertainment of guilt were implicated, and the hearsay rule, as applied in Mississippi which does not recognize admission against penal interest exception, could not be applied mechanistically to defeat the ends of justice by preventing defendant from introducing the testimony of the three persons to whom the confessions had been made." Cited positively: 768 cases (29.0% of all cases). Cited negatively: 109 cases (4.1% of all cases).

(6) Headnote 10: "Where third person on separate occasions orally confessed murder with which defendant was charged to three different friends, under circumstances which bore substantial assurances of trustworthiness, and where such person made, but later repudiated, a written confession, exclusion of the testimony of the persons to whom the oral confessions were made, under hearsay rule, coupled with State's refusal to permit defendant to cross-examine the third person under Mississippi's common-law "voucher" rule after defendant called such third person as witness when the State failed to do so, deprived defendant of a fair trial in violation of the due process clause of the Fourteenth Amendment." Cited positively: 534 cases (20.2% of all cases). Cited negatively: 93 cases (3.5% of all cases).

The West data also include notation of the court making the decision. Those data were as follows:

(1) United States Supreme Court. Positive decisions: 18 (0.7% of all cases). Negative decisions: 2 (0.1% of all cases).

(2) Federal Appellate Courts. Positive decisions: 451 (17.0% of all cases). Negative decisions: 31 (1.2% of all cases).

(3) Federal District Courts. Positive decisions: 422 (15.9% of all cases). Negative decisions: 12 cases (0.5% of all cases).

(4) State Supreme (Highest) Courts. Positive decisions: 649 cases (24.5% of all cases). Negative decisions: 48 cases (1.8% of all cases).

(5) State Appellate Courts. Positive decisions: 830 cases (31.4% of all cases). Negative decisions: 46 cases (1.72% of all cases).

(6) State Trial Courts. Positive decisions: 45 cases (1.7% of all cases). Negative decisions: 1 case (0.1% of all cases).

(7) Miscellaneous. Positive decisions: 66 cases (2.5% of all cases). Negative decisions: 1 case (0.1% of all cases).

And third, it has been used to support the proposition that defendants have a due process right to offer a robust defense (the contention in more than 17 percent of the cases). Appellate courts have made frequent reference to *Chambers*. State supreme courts are responsible for about a quarter of all the citations and intermediate appellate courts in both the federal and state systems are responsible for about 48 percent of the references.

*Chambers* has created a powerful, if ill-defined, constitutional principle. Its reliance on the Due Process Clause of the Fourteenth Amendment to address an apparent unfairness worked by a well-established evidence rule opens the way to review of the rule-based exclusion of almost any sort of proof important to a criminal defendant's case. It has, as already noted, been used to overturn a ban on the introduction of hypnotically enhanced testimony despite the acknowledged risk that hypnosis may render evidence unreliable.[36] It has also been used to overturn a court's refusal to allow any access to potentially important information in child protective agency files. This despite their being designated as privileged pursuant to the state's legitimate desire to promote more effective investigations of cases of alleged or suspected child abuse.[37] At their core, *Chambers* and its progeny seem to be grounded in Compulsory Process Clause notions about providing each criminal defendant a fair opportunity to assemble evidence and present witnesses in his or her defense. These cases have, however, steered clear of the potentially sweeping implications of compulsory process—a basis for decision that might be held to invalidate denial of access to or exclusion from evidence of all forms of exculpatory material. Instead the Court has emphasized the Due Process question of fairness in each particular case. While such a vague rule raises questions about supervision and predictability, it emphatically signals that a criminal trial is not a game and that prosecutors must, sometimes, decline to exercise exclusionary rules in deference to a full and fair airing of all the important evidence.

*Chambers* deserves to be viewed as a seminal decision in the borderland between the Constitution and evidence law. In it Justice Powell struggled to do justice in a case where established evidence rules appeared to help perpetrate a wrong—one that may have been motivated by racist attitudes. Though Justice Powell sought only the most modest change in constitutional principle, his recognition of due process rights to defend, confront and compel has provided an important means of protecting the integrity of the criminal trial process.

---

[36] Rock v. Arkansas, 483 U.S. at 61.

[37] Pennsylvania v. Ritchie, 480 U.S. 39 (1987).

## Afterward

*Chambers* was not the last time Justice Powell chose to take on a well-established rule in the name of fairness. He did so in 1986 when he authored the seminal decision in *Batson v. Kentucky*.[38] In *Batson,* as in *Chambers*, the challenge was to a long-standing fixture of trial practice (this one allowing unfettered use of peremptory challenges). Again, there were concerns about racial discrimination.[39] Again, Powell crafted a careful, fact-based opinion. And again, as in *Chambers*, Powell's insistence on moving beyond established rules loosed a principle with broad sweep and abiding concern for protecting the fairness of the trial process. Despite criticism, *Batson*, like *Chambers*, has become a fixture of our trials. It too forms part of the legacy of "fair shake" jurisprudence left to us by Lewis Powell—a legacy warranting our gratitude.

---

[38] 476 U.S. 79 (1986).

[39] As Justice Powell put it: "The prosecutor used his peremptory challenges to strike all four black persons on the venire, and a jury comprised only of white persons was selected." Batson v. Kentucky, 476 U.S. at 83.

*

# ABOUT THE AUTHORS

KENNETH BROUN is Henry Brandeis Professor of Law at the University of North Carolina Law School where he has taught since 1968. He served as Dean of the school from 1979 to 1987. He was in the private practice of law for seven years. Broun was Director of the National Institute for Trial Advocacy (NITA) from 1976 to 1979 and has been a member of NITA's Board of Trustees since 1979. He served on the Advisory Committee on the Federal Rules of Evidence from 1994 to 2000 and presently acts as a special consultant to that committee on a project concerning evidentiary privileges. Since 1986, he has made more than twenty trips to South Africa to conduct programs in trial advocacy training for the Black Lawyers Association of South Africa and is also the author of *Black Lawyers, White Courts*, published in 2000, about the black lawyers of South Africa. He is the author or co-author of several books and articles on evidence and trial advocacy. He is general editor of the *McCormick on Evidence* hornbook.

GEORGE FISHER is Judge John Crown Professor of Law at Stanford University and a former Massachusetts prosecutor. He is the author of *Evidence* (Foundation Press 2002) and of various works on the history of the criminal process.

RICHARD D. FRIEDMAN is the Ralph W. Aigler Professor of Law at the University of Michigan Law School. He is General Editor of *The New Wigmore: A Treatise on Evidence* and the author of a coursebook, *The Elements of Evidence* (3d ed. 2004), as well as many articles on evidence and other legal topics. He is a graduate of Harvard College and Harvard Law School, and earned a D.Phil. from Oxford University. He began his teaching career at the Benjamin N. Cardozo School of Law.

PAUL C. GIANNELLI is the Albert J. Weatherhead III & Richard W. Weatherhead Professor of Law at Case Western Reserve University. He received his J.D. degree from the University of Virginia, where he served as Articles Editor of the Virginia Law Review. His other degrees include a LL.M. from the University of Virginia and a M.S. in Forensic Science from George Washington University. Professor Giannelli has written in the field of evidence and criminal procedure, especially on the topic of scientific evidence. He has authored or co-authored nine books and has published articles in the Columbia, Virginia, Cornell, Vanderbilt, Wisconsin, Ohio State and Hastings law reviews, among others, as well as in the Journal of Criminal Law & Criminology, Criminal Law Bulletin, and the American Criminal Law Review. In addition, his work has appeared in interdisciplinary journals, such as Issues in Science and Technology

(National Academies), International Journal of Clinical & Experimental Hypnosis, the New Biologist, Profiles in DNA, the Journal of Legal Medicine, and the Journal of Forensic Science. He currently serves as Reporter for the American Bar Association Criminal Justice Standards on DNA Evidence and is co-chair of the ABA Ad Hoc Committee on Innocence.

ED IMWINKELRIED is the Edward L. Barrett, Jr. Professor of Law at the University of California, Davis. He is the author or coauthor of over 80 law review articles. His writings include six multi-volume evidence treatises as well as several other texts. One treatise, *Uncharged Misconduct Evidence* (rev.ed. 1999), is devoted to the topic of the admissibility of evidence under Federal Rule of Evidence 404(b).

STEPHAN LANDSMAN holds the Robert A. Clifford Chair in Tort Law and Social Policy at DePaul University College of Law. He is a nationally recognized expert on the jury system and served as Reporter to the American Bar Association (ABA) American Jury Project which has rewritten the bar's Principles for Juries and Jury Trials. He is the author of numerous books and articles, both historical and empirical, about the jury as well as pieces on a range of other topics including the adversary system, punitive damages, human rights and the rules of evidence. He is also the author of *Crimes of the Holocaust:The Law Confronts Hard Cases*, a book recently published by the University of Pennsylvania Press. His historical work on the hearsay rule was recently cited in *Crawford v. Washington*. Professor Landsman attended Kenyon College and Harvard Law School.

RICHARD LEMPERT is the Eric Stein Distinguished University Professor of Law and Sociology at the University of Michigan. He is coauthor of *A Modern Approach to Evidence* and of *An Invitation to Law and Social Science,* and he has written numerous articles on the law of evidence and the sociology of law, with special attention to the jury system, the death penalty, dispute processing, DNA evidence, and, most recently, affirmative action. He is an elected member of the of the American Academy of Arts and Sciences and secretary of Section K of the American Association for the Advancement of Science. From June 2002 through May 2006 he served as Division Director for the Social and Economic Sciences at the National Science Foundation.

JENNIFER L. MNOOKIN is a professor at the UCLA School of Law. She received an A.B. from Harvard College, a J.D. from Yale Law School, and a Ph.D. in the History and Social Study of Science and Technology from M.I.T. She teaches evidence, torts, and a variety of seminars. Mnookin's scholarship focuses on expert evidence, evidence theory, and the intersections between law, science and culture. She has published articles on fingerprint evidence, photographic evidence, handwriting identification expertise, and documentary films and the law, among other topics, and she is a co-author of the treatise *The New Wigmore: Expert Evidence* (with Kaye and Bernstein, 2004). She is currently writing a book about the intertwined histories of visual and expert evidence in the American courtroom in the 19th and 20th centuries, from the advent of photography to the rise of DNA. Mnookin has chaired the AALS Section on Evidence and served as a member of the section's executive committee. She has been on the faculty at the University of Virginia Law School and been a visiting professor at Harvard Law School.

CHRISTOPHER MUELLER is the Henry S. Lindsley Professor of Procedure and Trial Advocacy at the University of Colorado Law School, where he has taught since 1985. Professor Mueller writes extensively in the area of Evidence law. His books, written with his friend and collaborator Laird C. Kirkpatrick, include *Evidence Under the Rules* (Little, Brown, 5th ed. 2005), *Evidence* (Aspen Law and Business, 3d ed 2003), and an Evidence Outline (West Black Letter Series 2005). He is the author of a 5–volume treatise, *Federal Evidence* (Lawyers Co-Operative Publishing Company, 2d ed. 1995) that is currently in process of revision. In addition, Mueller has written numerous journal articles on various aspects of evidence law, presented on evidence law to judges and practitioners, and has taught courses for judges at the National Judicial College in Nevada. Mueller teaches, in addition to evidence, civil procedure and complex civil litigation. He serves on the Colorado Civil Rules Committee and the Colorado Evidence Rules Committee, and is a member of the American Law Institute. Mueller is a graduate of Haverford College and holds a law degree from the University of California at Berkeley (Boalt Hall). He has also taught at the University of Wyoming, Emory University, and University of Illinois law schools.

DALE A. NANCE is Professor of Law at Case Western Reserve University. Professor Nance has taught basic and advanced courses in the area of evidence law for over twenty years. During that time, he has authored numerous articles—doctrinal, theoretical, and empirical—about issues in evidence law, and he is one of several scholars working on *The New Wigmore*, the successor to the famous evidence treatise by John Henry Wigmore. Professor Nance also teaches and writes about general jurisprudence and legal theory. Before joining the faculty at Case Law School, he taught at Illinois Institute of Technology's Chicago–Kent College of Law, where he was named a Norman and Edna Freehling Scholar and was Associate Dean for Program Development. He has also taught at Northern Illinois University, the University of Colorado, the University of San Diego, and Cornell University. He holds degrees from Rice University, Stanford University, and the University of California, Berkeley. Before entering teaching, he did civil litigation work for private law firms in California.

PAUL ROTHSTEIN is Professor of Law at Georgetown University Law Center, specializing in evidence, torts, and other subjects related to civil and criminal litigation and the judicial process from the Supreme Court on down. A former Washington, D.C. practitioner, Oxford University Fulbright Scholar, and law review editor-in-chief, his publications as author or co-author (with Myrna Raeder, David Crump, and/or Susan Crump) include the books *Evidence: Cases, Materials & Problems* (Lexis–Nexis, 2d ed. 1998, 3d Ed. forthcoming May, 2006), *Evidence in a Nutshell* (Thomson–West, 4th Ed. 2003, 5th ed. forthcoming 2007), *Federal Testimonial Privileges* (Thomson–West, 2d Ed. 2006), *Federal Rules of Evidence* (Thomson–West, 3d Ed. 2006), and numerous articles. He has been special counsel or consultant on matters of Evidence, including the Federal Rules of Evidence, and related topics, to numerous groups, firms, states and agencies, including: both Houses of Congress, the Nat'l Conf. of Comm'rs on Uniform State Laws, the Nat'l Academy of Sciences, the Fed. Judicial Cntr., Rand, AEI–Brookings, the United States Department of Justice and the governments of Canada, the Philippines and states emerging from the former Soviet Union. He chaired the Ass'n of Amer. Law Schools Evidence Section and an American Bar Association committee monitoring developments under the Federal and Uniform Rules of Evidence that suggested changes to the Rules, a number of which have been made. His series of national conferences on the Federal Rules of Evidence just before they came out, and his accompanying book, the first on the Federal Rules of Evidence, are credited with introducing the bench, bar, and much of academia to what they would be facing under the new Rules.

CHRISTOPHER SLOBOGIN holds the Stephen C. O'Connell chair at the University of Florida Fredric G. Levin College of Law. He is a graduate of Princeton University and the University of Virginia Law School. His writings on criminal procedure and evidence issues include two textbooks and numerous articles. His book *Proving the Unprovable: The Role of Law, Science and Speculation in Assessing Culpability and Dangerousness*, will soon be published by Oxford University Press.

ELEANOR SWIFT is Professor of Law at the School of Law (Boalt Hall) at the University of California at Berkeley. She is a graduate of Radcliffe College and Yale Law School. Following law school she clerked for Judge M. Joseph Blumenfeld of the U.S. District Court for the District of Connecticut and for Chief Judge David L. Bazelon of the U.S. Court of Appeals for the District of Columbia. She practiced law with Vinson & Elkins in Houston, Texas for five years prior to joining the faculty at Boalt Hall. She is a co-author of a casebook *Evidence: Text, Problems and Cases* (Aspen Law & Business, 4th ed. 2006) (with Ronald J. Allen, Richard D. Kuhns and David S. Schwartz) and has recently become an author of three Chapters in the Sixth Edition of *McCormick on Evidence*.